SO-BFE-855

A Civil Economy

Evolving Values for a Capitalist World

In most of the world today, the issue is not whether or how to embrace capitalism, but how to make the best of it. The currently dominant capitalist values include competitive individualism, instrumental rationality, and material success. The series will explore questions such as: Will these values suffice as a basis for social organizations that can meet human and environmental needs in the twenty-first century? What would it mean for capitalist systems to evolve toward an emphasis on other values, such as cooperation, altruism, responsibility, and concern for the future?

Titles in the series:

Neva R. Goodwin, Editor. *As if the Future Mattered: Translating Social and Economic Theory into Human Behavior*

Severyn T. Bruyn. *A Civil Economy: Transforming the Market in the Twenty-First Century*

A CIVIL ECONOMY
Transforming the Market in the Twenty-First Century

Severyn T. Bruyn

Ann Arbor

THE UNIVERSITY OF MICHIGAN PRESS

HB
501
.B8453
2000

2003   2002   2001   2000   4   3   2   1

*A CIP catalog record for this book is available from
the British Library.*

Library of Congress Cataloging-in-Publication Data

Bruyn, Severyn Ten Haut, 1927–
    A civil economy : transforming the market in the twenty-first
century / Severyn T. Bruyn.
        p.   cm. — (Evolving values for a capitalist world)
    Includes bibliographical references and index.
    ISBN 0-472-09706-7 (cloth : alk. paper)
    ISBN 0-472-06706-0 (pbk. : alk. paper)
        1. Capitalism—Social aspects. 2. Economics—Moral and ethical aspects.
3. Democracy—Economic aspects. 4. International trade—Political aspects.
5. International business enterprises—Political aspects. 6. Evolutionary
economics. 7. Civil society. 8. Twenty-first century.   I. Title. II. Series.

HB501 .B8453 2000
338.9—dc21   99-046137

Contents

Foreword

David Rockefeller

In January 1995 I spoke in Mexico City before the first plenary meeting of CIVICUS, the pioneering alliance that seeks to nurture and sustain global society. It was a heady and optimistic moment for individuals in the nonprofit and nongovernmental world. Capitalism had vanquished communism, democracy had triumphed over autocracy, in essence, Tocqueville had defeated Marx. Of course, massive problems remained—poverty, disease, illiteracy, powerlessness—and we were all deeply aware of them. But most people believed that these ancient afflictions would be eliminated once we readjusted the relationships among government, the private sector, and civil society and unleashed their latent power to transform.

This process of readjustment and re-engineering has proven to be a great deal more complicated than we imagined. Nothing has been automatic or natural. The globalization of the world economy, for instance, has not only generated vast amounts of new wealth while transforming traditional social relationships in many parts of the world, it has also exacerbated environmental degradation and weakened systems of governance.

How do we come to grips with these new challenges? If the devil is in the details, then Professor Severyn Bruyn has provided ample evidence of the care and thought that will be required if we are to create an economic structure that is equitable and accountable to everyone. As Professor Bruyn himself notes, "Social problems need to be solved in the economy where they originate, not solved only by adding more laws and agencies to government. Democratic governments exist to support a self-regulating market as well as to promote public safety, national defense, and the general welfare. A democratic government can help people govern themselves with greater freedom, civic responsibility, and accountability. The organized economy is not simply a private system of markets; it is part of a public domain designed for the common good."

For me the most interesting portions of the book started in chapters five and six. Readers who, like myself, are in business or some other part of society outside of academia may find that the best way to approach this important but complex material is to begin by jumping into the middle of the book. Not everyone will agree with all of Professor Bruyn's analyses, interpretations, or prescriptions; I do not. But the book deserves a careful reading by a broad audience because of the role that civil society must play in the future if we are to avoid the tragic mistakes of the past. This book points toward an ideal in which both government and business exist to serve the people—rather than the other way around.

Series Foreword

The University of Michigan Press is pleased to offer *A Civil Economy: Transforming the Market in the Twenty-First Century* as the second volume in its series Evolving Values for a Capitalist World. The series, edited by Neva R. Goodwin, Co-director of the Global Development and Environment Institute at Tufts University, is based on the following beliefs. Capitalism is the socioeconomic system that will prevail for the foreseeable future, not only because it appears to be an irresistible force, but also because there is no known system that works better. At the same time, capitalism is not a single, monolithic system but is rather a concept on which a number of variants are possible. There may well be better variants than any now prevailing; there is good reason to investigate how we might move toward such improvements.

The basic assumption of the series is that the ultimate source of change in any human system is the set of values that dominate the system's culture. These values are beliefs about what matters, what "good" means, what makes life worth living. They are, critically, shared values; they have much to do with self-respect, which partially reflects the respect accorded by others. Evolving Values for a Capitalist World examines the interplay between economics and values, taking a hard-headed look at shifts in values or in emphasis that could provide the foundation for improvements in the world's dominant socioeconomic systems.

The first volume in the series is *As if The Future Mattered: Translating Social and Economic Theory into Human Behavior,* edited by Neva R. Goodwin and including articles by a number of broad-thinking sociologists, economists, and other scholars and activists such as Michael Porter, Robert McNamara, and Alisa Gravitz. It is based on the premise that the longer the time horizon of each actor in an economy, the more likelihood there is of a convergence of interest among different groups and individuals. Convergence of interests is an essential theme for a market society, which operates on Adam Smith's principle that socially desirable outcomes can be achieved while everyone rationally pursues his or her own self-interest.

The second volume, *A Civil Economy: Transforming the Market in the Twenty-First Century*, pushes Smith's principle in some very interesting ways.

On the one hand, its author is optimistic regarding the ability of private, for-profit institutions to regulate themselves in a manner that is cooperative, rational for a particular industry, and often (though not always) good for the larger society. This optimism is based on a wealth of illustrations of businesses that have already acted in just such a manner. On the other hand, however, Dr. Bruyn strongly emphasizes that the legal/institutional/ethical context makes a great difference in whether and how business self-regulation will actually occur. The author stresses the regulatory environment and the forms that enterprises are encouraged to take as crucial to outcomes that, at best, will include worker empowerment as well as identification of a firm's interests with the health of its surrounding community and the natural environment.

Also in press, due for release by the University of Michigan Press in spring 2000, is the third volume in the series, *Rethinking Sustainability: Power, Knowledge, and Institutions,* edited by Jonathan Harris. Development—the dynamic form of capitalism—is commonly understood to harness market systems to deliver material progress, with the goals of reducing poverty and improving the general quality of life. Through lively examples from many parts of the world, the essays assembled in *Rethinking Sustainability* probe the ways in which development depends on webs of relationships, structured according to how power and knowledge are allocated and used in different institutional contexts. They illuminate the critical, too-little-understood socioeconomic and politicl requirements for sustaining progress.

Preface

People are talking about the idea of civil society but do not see its relationship to the market economy. Is there such a thing—could there be such a thing—as a civil economy? The purpose of this book is to explore that relationship, to examine the civil underpinnings of capitalism. We will investigate the way a civil economy develops, embedded as it is within civil society.

Over the centuries, philosophers have debated the idea of civil society. The idea was gradually defined with two basic components: *a democratic government* and *a market economy*. Civil-society advocates today, however, are making revisions of this idea, refining it, believing that today's government should create conditions for people to solve their own problems. They argue that power should be sited at the lowest level of organizational authority that is consistent with effective governance. In other words, they propose that governments should be decentralized, reduced in scope and power. Civil-society advocates believe in a mix of cooperation and competition that combines for the common good.

Yet most of them think that civil society has nothing to do with capitalism. Hence, the definition of civil society in relation to the economy remains a mystery. The popular idea of civil society does not carry a view of the economy as "developing." Many theorists assume that capitalism will always remain the same, forgetting that societies have changed over the centuries in fundamental ways. This book will suggest that a basic change in the market system is taking place with the development of a global economy.

The idea of civil economy points the way. It presumes that people can solve social problems within the market itself. Already competing firms—in both the business and nonprofit sectors—show the potential to set standards for justice and welfare in a system of free markets.

The problem that is addressed by the idea of civil society, and by the more focused concept of civil economy in this book, is that a capitalist market keeps producing social problems that then require more government. When businesses lay off workers, the government pays the bill, solving problems of the unemployed through expensive welfare systems and job-training programs. When corporations exploit labor, the government creates labor departments and labor legislation. When business produces hazards in the workplace, the government sets rules for safety and health on the job. When business harms or lies to customers, the government establishes consumer agencies and legislation to regulate product safety, truth in lending, and precise labels on product ingredients, as well as hundreds of other regulations to protect buyers. When big business destroys its weaker competitors by underpricing and making monopolistic mergers, governments create agencies and laws to establish fair competition. When markets widen the gap between the rich and poor, governments raise wage standards nationwide and establish a progressive tax system. When business destroys the environment, governments create environmental protection agencies to stop the devastation. And on and on, ad infinitum.

Thus, the market economy can be self-destructive, nullifying a basic freedom to manage its own affairs. It fails to be adequately self-regulating. Government expands its power to monitor and intervene in the name of justice and welfare. Market freedom erodes, and governments grow into bureaucracies.

The need for developing a civil economy is made more urgent by the globalization of markets. Global markets are expanding rapidly without regulatory agencies to monitor and regulate them. Business analysts and international scholars argue that an unregulated global market threatens democratic governments around the world. Global corporations are seen to widen the gap between the rich and poor, destroy the environment, support authoritarian regimes, and endanger the existence of civil societies. The global financial crisis is an example of the destructive potential of capitalist markets as well as their social interdependence. The collapse of a market in one region of the world can seriously affect the well-being of nations in other world regions.

The economy is popularly conceived to be the business sector, but we see it as reaching throughout the entire society. This includes business, government, and the "Third Sector"—the latter referring to various nonprofits, nongovernmental organizations, voluntary associations, and grassroots organizations. All three sectors (business, government, and Third Sector) are distinct and yet interdependent in the economy. Our attention will focus on the business sector because of its overall impact on society. It has a vast destructive and creative power that strongly affects the other two sectors. We will argue that its creative power is realized through a civil development in relation to the other sectors.

Capitalism is creative because it is innovative; it adjusts itself to different cultures and adapts to civic concerns. The market system as we know it today has brought enormous benefits to society, including efficiency, innovative drive, and the harnessing of skills in training and employment. In theory, these benefits should spread around the world as democracy begins to thrive in more and more countries. However, the market system that we call "capitalism" is also destructive, because it produces serious problems that, in turn, cause bigger government.

The market economy, as we define it, is a system of exchange that is partially self-regulating. There is still a long way to go before this ideal of self-regulation is fully understood. To increase the power of self-regulation, people in the market must show more signs of being socially accountable, symbiotic, and self-reliant, while remaining productive, competitive, and profitable. As the links are made between such different values, the market becomes more civil and contributes to the development of society.

We will examine the way in which contrasting values, such civil freedom *and* justice, develop in the market. Many values that seem contrary, such as individuality *and* community, can be advanced together by reinventing systems of exchange. This simultaneous development of conflicting values is accomplished by the synergistic work of leaders in our three sectors. As this integration of different values takes place, competitors become participants in the development of civil society.

To put this another way, "free markets," as we now know them, push governments to become giant bureaucracies. New laws and government agencies are constantly created to monitor and control the economy. Government regulations will continue to be made as long as rules of fair play are not created by competitors themselves. Competitors need codes of conduct and more transparency in their systems of exchange. The public needs accurate information to make the right decisions. A more self-regulating economy requires goals to develop stakeholder relations, answerability, and transparency as well as productivity, efficiency, and profitability.

In sum, a self-regulating economy is developed as people learn how to resolve differences in the context of their competition. Our outlook is that government regulation cannot work by itself, and self-regulation cannot work by itself. Free markets are possible only when these two types of regulation are in balance and are able to supplement one another. To sustain a healthy private sector, strong competition must be held in check by strong cooperation for the common good. We will discuss how competitors establish codes of conduct and appoint professional arbiters. Civil development requires a lot of negotiation among competitors who must work together to synthesize their differences. Private interests should be pursued with more understanding of the intricate relation between the individual and the common good. When that understanding is put into practice, we see the formation of a civil economy.

Plan of the Book

Part 1 examines the evolution of a self-regulating civil economy. Chapter 1 begins with the classic concept of civil society, recalling the work of Adam Smith, who first spoke about a self-regulating economy in concert with a moral life. We show how the principles of that "moral economy" are invoked in the relationship between business and the Third Sector. In chapter 2, we describe systems of accountability in the market economy and evaluate their effectiveness at different levels of governance. In chapter 3 we discuss how popular movements generate cooperative markets and suggest how their principles integrate with the frontier of business management. In sum, these three chapters tell us how the economy is evolving as a civil system of exchange and thus, given the right conditions, could become more able to sustain the values of a free society.

Part 2 explores how a civil economy is developed by careful planning. In chapter 4, we explain how conventional privatization has many advantages but the disadvantages outweigh them, requiring an alternative we call "civil privatization." We explain how capitalist privatization produces serious problems around the world, creating the imperative for civil development. In chapter 5, we give specific examples of how that civil privatization is practiced, transforming government facilities and services into civil markets. In chapter 6, we explore how business consultants, executives, public officials, and corporate lawyers can structure markets to work in the public interest. The message of Part 2 is that civil development in a capitalist society requires planning a self-governing economy. This entails developing freedom, justice, productivity, profitability, and cooperation in the context of market competition.

Part 3 investigates the problems and the destructive impact of business global markets, and then explores the civil alternatives. In chapter 7, we inquire into worldwide patterns of corporate exploitation, environmental damage, and systems of dominance—all requiring civil solutions. In chapter 8, we define the concept of "civil market" as a prototype to follow in formulating global policies. We illustrate how the use of this prototype helps people resolve market problems, and we propose global workshops on combining corporate accountability with profitability. The workshops are designed to speed the construction of competitive markets, which should reduce social and financial costs in global systems of exchange.

In summary, the market economy is undergoing a major change at this turn of the century. If one looks at the change carefully, it becomes apparent that a financial crisis is rooted in the social and political organization of markets. The current forms of economic analysis no longer work. The market system is in a process of social reinvention. We propose that a more civil economy will be high on the agenda for people in the twenty-first century.

Acknowledgments

The framework for this book has been forming in my mind for many decades. I have spent time in corporate research as well as consulting with firms for over 30 years, but this particular book was inspired by the Boston Coalition for a Strong United Nations. This coalition is a group of over 90 nongovernmental organizations that have been holding conferences at the Kennedy Library on local-to-global issues.

The idea for the book began when this coalition organized a Task Force on International Business and then a regional conference on globalization. That conference included former Massachusetts governor Endicott Peabody, former secretary of state Elliot Richardson, economic analyst Hazel Henderson, and dozens of other political leaders and scientists. The task force, of which I was co-chair, made proposals to treat the growing problems of civil justice and fairness in global markets. The proposals were accepted unanimously by the plenary session of 800 people.

Our international task force then received an invitation to talk with leaders in the business sector and nongovernmental organizations (NGOs) at the United Nations in New York City. Members of both business and NGO sectors praised the direction of our work, and we were invited to talk with the UN assistant secretary general at that time, Rosario Green. She encouraged us to continue this endeavor and to stay in touch with her office on our progress.

My special thanks to members of that task force, including Virginia Mary Swain, Joseph Barratta, Darwin Gillett, Tom Hansen, and Steven Hall. Helpful commentators on the book manuscript include graduate students Sharon Brassey-Brierley, David Satterthwaite, Alfredo DaCunha, and Phyllis Greenwood, as well as distinguished retired professors Elise Boulding and John Buell. My loving wife, Louise, was vital as a reviewer of the work. She is my dearly beloved, who has taught me so much.

I also benefited from discussing this subject in sessions of the American Sociological Association, the Committee on Ethics of the Boston Theological Institute, and a committee of activists organized by Professor Charles Derber. Finally, I am especially indebted to Professor Neva Goodwin at Tufts University for her long and hard editorial work on the manuscript. None of these people can assume responsibility for my mistakes.

I | An Evolving Economy

1 The Moral Economy

Every monopoly and all exclusive privileges are granted at the expense of the public, which ought to receive a fair equivalent.

—Andrew Jackson, veto of the bill to renew the charter of the Bank of the United States, 1832

The public be damned! I'm working for my stockholders.

—William H. Vanderbilt, comment to a news reporter, October 2, 1882

Private enterprise is ceasing to be free enterprise.

—Franklin D. Roosevelt, to Congress, proposing investigation of monopolies, 1938

The idea of civil society began with philosophers centuries ago, but today this classic idea is interpreted in a fresh fashion around the world. Advocates of civil society in fallen communist countries revived the idea out of the ashes of communism. They wanted to build an alternative to communism and capitalism, believing that "civil society" could signal an advanced phase of freedom, democracy, and justice. For them, a new definition of civil society required a different way of thinking about the economy. The economy needed to function justly and fairly apart from the state. New interpretations of civil society then began to catch fire in many countries. Across a wide political spectrum, national leaders showed an interest in civil society, but they had no agreement on its meaning. Worse, most advocates had no thought that the idea connected with a market system, no view of the economy as undergoing "development." Some theorists still argue that there is no connection between the principles of civil society and capitalism.[1]

Our argument in this chapter is that the development of civil society is connected to capitalism and represents a major change in the formation of markets. The crucible of change, the severe test of development, takes place between the connected fields of business and the Third Sector. The Third Sector—composed of nonprofit organizations and grassroots movements—stands in tension with the business sector. This tension is the location for major changes taking place in the constitution of the marketplace. We will discuss the birth, death, and resurrection of civil society with a capitalist economy that is being reinvented today in the new connection—and the difference—between business and the Third Sector.

The Birth and Death of Civil Society

In the eighteenth century, Scottish philosophers David Hume and Adam Smith saw the new European class of bourgeoisie rising as a "civil society." They saw the world of commerce and business as an alternative to feudal rule, a path toward freedom and progress where competition could be combined with a sense of mutual relations in the market. It was a realm of personal autonomy, in which people were free to develop their own moral accounting. People were more responsible for their own lives and actions. This enterprise system required a moral energy much more advanced than feudalism. The new commercial order of the eighteenth century was creating a space in which individuals could become free from monarchal rule and organize their own systems of exchange.[2]

Adam Smith's *Theory of Moral Sentiments* argued that the moral basis of enterprise was found in "mutual sympathy." Smith was not precise with his meaning, but he said that something like mutual sympathy (or compassion) was buried in the development of human nature. It was evoked quietly, silently, through the social experience of people in society. People lived in a social relationship, participating with others, sensing from that experience that individual judgments become part of a moral life. Although most people did not see that hidden sympathy, it elicited a sense of justice in them. Justice developed through human interactions and the self-reflection of individuals in a social context. (See the appendix.)

Smith's later work *The Wealth of Nations* (1776) was based on an implicit assumption that self-interest combined with this principle of "mutual identity" and was present in this market of small enterprises. Civil society was grounded in both self-interest and mutual sympathy, joined together as the driving force behind "all the toil and bustle of the world." A moral economy, based on a sense of mutual self-interest, was at the heart of the competitive market, at which point an "invisible hand" produced a self-regulating economy.

Now we come to an idea that, to some, may seem surprising. Adam Smith did not accept corporations as having a proper role in the market; in fact, he warned against the selfish power of corporations. Yet a corporate society began to evolve in the following century. Governments were transforming into democracies in the nineteenth century, but a corporate economy was developing more characteristically around a feudal model—people spoke of the "lords and barons of industry." A strong public reaction developed against railroad price gouging and the gigantic fortunes made by "moguls" in the late nineteenth century, such as Andrew Carnegie and John D. Rockefeller.[3]

Competitive markets now seemed to attach a monetary value to everything. This caused critics to argue that the commercial system was destructive to "morality." There was a concern that corporations had become more powerful than governments. Marx had published his damning analysis of bourgeois consciousness and claimed that the two greatest achievements of the modern period—the market and the state—were not adequate to represent civil society. Neither the market system nor the state was organized to realize the value of the individual and the humanity of people.

With the rise of corporations, governments grew in size to protect the public from monopolies and exploitation. Governments set standards against unfair competition and solved other market problems. A whole range of agencies and laws was formulated to monitor and control business conduct. Indeed, governments became bureaucracies in their attempt to create and inject norms of justice, fairness, and morality into commercial competition.[4]

These government agencies and laws were formulated to monitor and control the market in order to achieve higher levels of justice and morality. Governments became bureaucracies in their attempt to introduce a moral order into a market that had developed cruel competition. This policy of government regulation continues today.[5]

The Scottish philosophers never expected commerce to be divorced from civil society and never anticipated that markets would function without ties to a moral life. The market had been conceived as flourishing in a moral order defined by qualities of trust and solidarity. Political scientists today applaud these qualities of trust, calling them "social capital" when they are visible in the market. However, the very emergence of the term *social capital* suggests that trust is no longer assumed in the marketplace.[6]

The Death of Civil Society: The Battle for Corporate Dominance

The growth of corporations in the early nineteenth century was seen not only as a threat to democracy and private freedoms but also as a threat to the proper working of the market. To counter this threat, politicians wrote moral principles into state charters for corporations to assure that they would function in the public interest.

Early corporate charters regulated business, establishing strong sanctions against "venal" (mercenary, corrupt) corporate conduct. Because of widespread public opposition to corporations, early legislators granted very few corporate charters and then only after long debate. Legislators denied a charter to would-be incorporates when communities opposed their prospective business project. As the Supreme Court reasoned in 1809: "If the applicant's object is merely private or selfish; if it is detrimental to, or not promotive of, the public good, they have no adequate claim upon the legislature for the privileges."[7]

In order to promote the public good, states limited corporate charters to a set number of years, such as 40 years for manufacturing charters in Maryland, 20 years in Pennsylvania. Corporations were limited in capitalization, debts, landholdings, and sometimes profits. The power of large shareholders was limited by scaled voting, so that large and small investors had equal voting rights. Interlocking directorates were outlawed.

Until the Civil War, most states enacted laws holding corporate investors and officials liable for the abuse of their charters. New Hampshire governor Henry Hubbard argued for the principle of liability in 1842:

> There is no good reason against this principle. In transactions which occur between man and man there exists a direct responsibility—and when capital is concentrated . . . beyond the means of single individuals, the liability is continued.[8]

The penalty for abuse of the charter at that time was not a fine but revocation of the charter and dissolution of the corporation. Citizens believed it was society's inalienable right to abolish an "evil." Revocation clauses were written into Pennsylvania charters as early as 1784, into insurance charters in 1809, and into banking charters in 1814. New York State's 1828 corporation law specified that every charter was subject to alteration or repeal. The law gave the state authority to secure a temporary injunction to prevent corporations from resisting while legal action to dissolve them was under way. Pennsylvanians adopted a constitutional amendment in 1857 instructing legislators to "alter, revoke or annul any charter of a corporation hereafter conferred . . . whenever in their opinion it may be injurious to citizens of the community."[9]

Fewer than 20 years later, by 1875, states began to compete for corporate charters and the economic advantages they brought. Charters were "liberalized." Delaware and New Jersey became the winners in a competition to charter corporations with the fewest moral inhibitors. The ideal of freedom in the market won over the ideal of justice and morality in this interstate battle to get corporate charters. The only remaining avenue for exercise of moral influence was through government regulatory agencies.[10]

In 1886, the Supreme Court ruled (in *Santa Clara County v. Southern Pacific Railroad*) that a private corporation is a natural person under the U.S. Constitution. Thus corporations were given the full rights enjoyed by individual citizens while being exempted from many responsibilities and liabilities of citizenship. Corporations today claim that they have the same right as any individual to influence the government in their own interest. This decision has come under debate in the U.S. Congress especially around campaign finance laws. Dissenters argue that the Court decision places each citizen in unfair competition with mammoth corporations, which have financial resources and communication systems far exceeding the power of the individual person. The corporation's centralized power, combined with its legal status as an individual imbued with individual rights such as freedom of speech, was the (near) fatal blow to competitive markets based on Smith's notion of trust between individuals in the marketplace.[11]

Civil society lost its appeal. Marx's *Communist Manifesto* was much more appealing. Communism now eclipsed the idea of civil society. Revolutionary leaders sought to destroy capitalism. The idea of civil society would not be taken up again until after the collapse of the Soviet Union and communist states in Eastern Europe.[12]

The Resurrection of Civil Society

Leaders in postcommunist nations began the resurrection of civil society; they called for a moral restoration of the whole economy by organizing a different system of sharing power. For them, civil society meant minimum government control and the development of civil associations wherein they governed themselves, autonomous from the state. Advocates defined civil society as a social matrix of voluntary groups and self-governing associations.[13]

In capitalist societies, other analysts identified civil society with the Third Sector, distinguishing it from government and business. The Third Sector included nongovernmental organizations, people's movements, citizens' groups, consumer associations, religious institutions, women's organizations, indigenous people's associations, civic groups, leagues, alliances, and confederations. Lester Salamon and Helmut Anheir were among those who viewed "civil society" as not including business or government.

> [Civil society is] . . . the plethora of private, nonprofit, and non-governmental organizations that have emerged in recent decades in virtually every corner of the world to provide vehicles through which citizens can exercise individual initiative in the private pursuit of public purposes. If representative government was the great social invention of the eighteenth century, and bureaucracy—both public and private—of the nineteenth, it is organized, private, voluntary activity, the proliferation of civil society organizations, that may turn out, despite earlier origins, to represent the great social innovation of the twentieth century.[14]

Not everyone defined civil society as the "Third Sector." Conservative analysts saw it as composed of a democratic government with a voluntary sector that included business as well as nonprofits. Philosophers saw civil society as a "public sphere" (not government) emerging within the "private sphere" of society. Cultural theorists saw it as the resolution of tensions between opposing principles in modernity (e.g., individual vs. community, public vs. private) leading toward a postmodern society.[15]

For many advocates, civil society is visualized today as a decentralized, voluntary, self-regulating system of civil associations based on a democratic and moral order. Salamon and Anheir described it as the great social innovation of the twentieth century, but they were puzzled by how it connected with the business sector. Civil-society analysts in this line of thought wondered how business could be a moral order. How could civil-society associations fit the reality of a competitive corporate economy?

Capitalism arose in the nineteenth century with no outline of a moral code. The critical question today has become: Will the Third Sector fall prey to the same forces that led to the downfall of Smith's civil society? To answer this question, we need to look at history again but in a different light.

The History of Mutual Self-Governance:
The Cradle of Civil Society

We explore the answer to this question by returning to Adam Smith, who assumed that a moral basis for free enterprise was found in "mutual relations." Along with self-interest, this mutuality was a driving force behind the web of activity called the market. Civil society was rooted in shared values, a mix of individual pursuits that also held a common concern for one another. This creative mix of self-interest and mutuality made the market system self-regulating. Let us look at history again but from this perspective.[16]

As moral standards seemed to decline with the rise of big corporations in a competitive market, a cooperative, mutually oriented activity quietly developed among associations of competitors. Less notable, but very significant, competitors developed civil associations that were mutually governed in all fields of exchange, in business, religion, education, science, and the professions. Nonprofit associations were created by the cooperative action of competitors in the same field of interest so that they could protect themselves from the self-destructive forces of competition and at the same time advance their shared goals.

Competitors in the silk industry, for example, established a system of civil, nongovernmental arbitration in 1898. They recognized that government courts could not settle the differences between seller and buyer because of the expense and delay involved, the bad feeling engendered, and the ignorance of the courts and lawyers of the technical points in their market area.

The paint and varnish industry established its own rules against "unfair competition in rebates" in the same year that the Federal Trade Commission was established (1914). The industry association also created a tribunal to punish offenders. Likewise, in the shoe and leather industries, a Joint Council of Arbitration was formed in 1920 by associations of manufacturers, wholesalers, retailers, and tanners. Disputes were referred to that council. The rules of procedures stated that the arbitrators "shall be guided by principles of equity and fairness."

Other business and service sectors did the same. Business leaders in trade associations—stockbrokers, realtors, retailers, and others in innumerable services and industries—devised codes of ethics for governing their competition and organized tribunals to judge and penalize offenders who broke their rules. These cooperative actions in business were a quiet part of civil development in the private sector.

Nonprofit trade associations established product standards in manufacturing, such as a uniform size for screws, shoes, lightbulbs, and a thousand more items. They also established product standards, as well as safety standards for employees. Business and professional associations organized private tribunals for the self-enforcement of ethical codes. There is no government agency organized to provide uniformity for thousands of products because this private civil system of product standardization arose out of the needs of the market itself, from the compulsions of competitors and consumers wanting those standards.

Many associations, like the American Society of Newspaper Editors, the National Association of Broadcasters, the National Association of Realtors, the National Association of Security Dealers, and others, developed self-regulatory practices. The detailed story of how the market came to socially govern itself—from factories to wholesale firms to retail stores and service outlets—cannot be told here, but our point is that moral standards and self-monitoring mechanisms in the market were part of this history. The practice of self-regulation became, in some measure, a substitute for government controls.

In this history of self-development people were quietly constructing what Adam Smith admired, that combination of self-interest and mutual concern, the bare bones of a moral order in commerce. Capitalist development as we often view it involved struggle, violence, and greed. This is true. There were more pain and suffering than our gentle philosophers from Scotland anticipated; yet still, mutuality, like an invisible hand, worked silently through each conflict in which people were led to solve their own problems. In each cooperative settlement, the common concerns of antagonists revealed a measure of civil development. People made moral choices and created a sense of community that was needed to conduct business. Mutual sympathy and common identity, along with self-interest, were central to maintaining markets that could be self-regulating. U.S. courts have supported these cooperative arrangements in the private sector wherever they saw them operating in the public interest.[17]

As we have seen, civil markets originate in the associations of competitors who collaborate for a common purpose and have a sense of mutuality, a degree of equity and democracy. The common purpose is, first, to avoid their own self-destruction in fierce competition. When businesses thus come together to protect themselves, they also set standards in the public interest.

Codes of conduct do not work as well when all the affected parties do not participate in the agreement. In such cases, business associations must settle their conflicts in court with outsiders. The motion picture industry, for example, adopted a code for rating films unsuitable for children. This code was held by courts to be "in the public interest" and not per se a violation of the Sherman Antitrust Act.

As another example, the National Association of Broadcasters (NAB) refused to run cigarette advertisements on the ground that they did not conform to the NAB's ethical codes of conduct. American Brands sued the NAB, charging that the three major television networks had violated the Sherman Antitrust Act by refusing to run its ads. The courts, however, denied American Brands an injunction on the basis that there "is a substantial, if not compelling, public interest in having a meaningful, full, specific and adequate disclosure of the relevant facts in cigarette advertising." They said that to prevent the NAB from implementing their code of ethics would be "contrary to the public interest."[18]

We want to follow this quiet evolution of the civil economy and include the Third Sector as part of the whole voluntary sector outside government. For some civil-society scholars, the Third Sector indicates today's quest for a moral economy envisioned by the Scottish philosophers and lost in the growth of competitive big business.

The Third Sector

The Third Sector is still being conceived, researched, and operationally defined. The Department of Commerce's national income accounts originated the concept of a "sectored economy" after World War II; the terms *nonprofit, third,* and *independent sector* entered scholarly usage in the 1970s, linked to an effort to defend philanthropy from government regulation. The literature involved prescriptions about management, funding, regulation, and responsibilities of nonprofits, positing a tax-exempt status under the federal tax code. In the United Nations, certain trade associations, like the International Chamber of Commerce, are considered nongovernmental organizations in effect identified with the Third Sector.

Nonprofit corporations in the Third Sector serve broad social-cultural interests and therefore can be tax deductible. Under the Internal Revenue Code, over 20 categories of organizations are exempt from federal income tax, but most organizations eligible to receive tax deductions fall into one category of the code: Section 501 (c) (3). One-third of nonprofits in this category are charities and foundations while the rest are universities, hospitals, fraternal organizations, day-care centers, and the like. To qualify under this section, an organization must operate technically for charitable, religious, scientific, literary, or educational purposes. Two narrower aims are also specified: testing for public safety and prevention of cruelty to children or animals. The code specifies further that no "substantial" part of an organization's activities may be devoted to influencing legislation and that the organization may not participate in political campaigns.[19]

Nonprofits have no shareholders and are not owned by anyone, except abstractly by the public. They are governed by a board, which has control over expenditure of revenue to advance public purposes. But upon dissolution, a nonprofit cannot distribute its assets to individuals; rather, the proceeds must go to other nonprofits. Efforts have been made to define public interest, but the law has been kept relatively fluid in order to permit new public needs to be perceived.[20]

We propose that civil development in the market economy is seeded when competitors come together in mutual-interest associations and then keep building them across services and industries that are in competition. In chapters 2 and 3, this silent development of civil associations has been active across the whole economy, resulting in systems of social governance in different parts of the world.

The Evolution of Civil Economy:
Inter-sector Dynamics

The history of mutual relations in both business and the Third Sector has been a nurturing place for civil society—accomplished in the principled tradition of those Scottish philosophers. Civil associations have been a latent force in the competitive system, evolving, unpublicized, as a part of a matrix of associations in the economy.

Civil action takes place not only in business but also in such fields as religion, law, medicine, architecture, and education. Professionals—physicians, social workers, engineers, nurses, lawyers, and artists—have organized codes of ethics and set up tribunals to referee, monitor, and judge what to do in cases where members broke the rules. These tribunals have not always arbitrated and judged in exemplary fashion, but people have learned in the midst of practice.

Churches, youth organizations, hospitals, colleges, and universities have competed for space and power and at the same time cooperated to settle their differences through civil associations. Colleges and universities created accrediting associations to evaluate and judge standards of excellence in education. Churches created community councils to handle their internal civil affairs. Medical associations set forth their own ethical code and tribunals to handle conflicts. This social order was not perfect, but advocates of civil society say that—given the complexity and extent of this matrix of associations—it was better than one imposed by government.

The point is that the quiet creation of social standards and self-enforcement in these associations helped civilize relationships among people who were often in competition or conflict with one another. It created a relatively civil order within an otherwise unfettered system of exchange. Competitors in both business and the Third Sector were learning how to build a civil (nongovernmental) economy within a capitalist society. Again, these self-governing and civiclike associations were based in principle on mutual governance. None of these systems of mutual governance could be called exactly "moral" within the framework of society, but they could be called "civil." These associations were civil forms of self-regulation. And when associations accomplished this task of self-governance effectively, the state did not need to regulate them in that social activity.[21]

For the remainder of this chapter, we will examine the dynamic interplay between business and the Third Sector. We will consider how government can help associations to solve their own problems and ponder how this new relationship yields answers to the development of a civil economy. We will see that an important change in the market economy is taking place through the interplay between sectors. The process of development in the future will not be easy. Certainly conflicts will occur but with more awareness about how the forces of competition and cooperation work in a democratic society.

The Study of Inter-Sector Relations

1. Conflict Resolution

Trade unions and business and professional associations are only relatively civil in competition, not always polite or fair to one another, but all the same, they provide a common ground to settle problems. These associations are part of the nonprofit sector where human conflicts arise and are settled outside government. These conflicts are settled in ways that people soon assume are normal because they are institutionalized—as though civilization advances by extending the number of operations that can be performed without conflict, without even thinking about what has been done.

In some European countries today, final arbitration between management and labor is determined privately by prior agreement. Compulsory arbitration boards have been established with half their members appointed by trade associations and half by trade unions. One member is chosen jointly to break a tie vote. Today the terrible labor-management violence that preceded such boards is almost forgotten. "Conflict resolution" mechanisms have become an institutional part of labor-management relations.

Much of what has become civil in the economy has been forged out of conflict where reasonable people sat down and worked out solutions. For example, many years ago great conflicts took place on the grading of lumber among competitors, consumers, and builders. Finally, business competitors formed a common grading system to settle their differences. One case is noteworthy for our purposes. Members of the Southern Pine Lumber Association began to grade lumber for the common good, but also, paradoxically, they began to function like a monopoly by virtue of an activity performed for the common good. Grading lumber is a fine self-regulatory activity that operates in the public interest, but in this case, the association acted like a monopoly because it had proprietary rights over grading.

The building and construction industry wanted the grading done, the real estate associations wanted it done, and consumers wanted it done, but anyone in the lumber business had to join the trade association to get lumber graded. Indeed, one could not survive in the market without "grading rights" that went with membership.

One day, a lumber firm that was not a member of the Southern Pine Lumber Association complained in court that it needed the grading of the association to sell its lumber but it did not want to pay the fees to join the organization. The association held fast to its requirement for membership, but the court did not agree. The association was subsequently ordered by the court to set up a "separate and autonomous bureau" to grade lumber for every firm in the industry—regardless of membership. Nonmember firms should get their lumber graded without having to join the association.

Thus, the new autonomous "grading bureau" was established and maintained by uniformly assessing charges against all "subscribers." The court found the collaborative grading of lumber to be in the public interest but corrected its monopolistic practice.[22]

In effect, the "autonomous bureau" became part of the public sector, not the government sector. It was equivalent to a government agency, but competitors were governing themselves. The industry has continued to operate quite well with institutionalized grading in the private sector.

We should add that other business associations monitored this lumber-grading activity. The construction industry, as a major customer of the lumber industry, kept an eye on the adequacy of grading. Other associations in the field of housing and real estate were vigilant to see that these standards were maintained. Related trade associations wanted to be assured of lumber quality. And members of the lumber industry wanted to avoid liability suits as well as to keep faith with their customers and their affiliated associations.

Trade and professional associations are confederations. Power and authority are decentralized, as opposed to the setup in federations. Federations centralize democratic power toward the top of the organization. The issue in the civil development of markets is how to cultivate more authority and responsibility among people working at the lowest levels of organization. In the midst of open conflict and competition, there is often a shared reflection and common interest, not exactly Smith's mutual sympathy but also not far from his idea.

To put this another way, competing actors in the same field of interest settle their differences through associations that work toward their common good. The principle of mutuality combines with self-interest in the private sector. In still other terms, *competition* is made possible through *cooperation.* The basis for a self-regulating economy is accomplished through negotiation between competing powers, through civil associations. The mystery in Adam Smith's theory of a self-regulating market could be explained in part through this social relationship.[23]

2. Countervailing Powers

John Kenneth Galbraith popularized the notion of "countervailing powers" in the market economy.[24] Countervailing powers in transportation, for example, include the airline, the automobile, and the railroad industries. The competition between these different modes of transportation helped to avoid corporate monopolies and reduced the need for government regulations. But now *nonprofits* should be considered part of this system of countervailing power. The question is how a balance of power between these sectors can work in the public interest.

For competing civil associations to work in the public interest, there needs to be a balance of power. Nonprofit insurance associations, for example, have established a research institute to monitor the safety of automobiles. This practice is in the interest of the insurance industry, but it is also operating for the common good. Insurance companies want to reduce traffic injuries to save money and cut costs.

The research institute on auto safety is a civil practice among countervailing powers. Nonprofit associations that lead to the common good tie the auto industry and the insurance industry together. They are quietly, perhaps unintentionally, balancing the values of *health* and *safety* against the values of *productivity* and *efficiency* in this area of the economy. Insurance executives are interested for selfish reasons in public accountability. Hence, the pursuit of self-interest at the level of whole industries can result, without fanfare, in partial self-regulation.

In other fields, the action between sectors is more dramatic. In the environmental movement, a *hot* (but nonviolent) war exists between some grassroots organizations (GROs), like the Native Forest Network, whose members have chained themselves to trees and logging equipment, and the lumber industry. At the same time, some big environmental organizations are in a *cold* (negotiating) war with business, as in the case of the Northern Forest Alliance. This forest alliance emphasizes sustainable logging, yet it is able to compromise and enter special coalitions with business.

These cases tell us that certain combinations of business and nonprofit associations—working at cross-purposes—can work toward the public interest. The activities of two actors in the same field with entirely different values and competitive interests can result in a larger good. Civil markets are systems of exchange in which competing actors mutually agree to common standards and codes of conduct and demonstrate that they are capable of enforcing them. Such markets develop through associations that set codes of conduct, establish monitors and tribunal systems, and issue penalties for members who break their rules and contracts.

3. Inter-sector Competition

When profits and nonprofits compete with each other, they activate moral energies and often create innovative solutions to persistent problems. At the same time, if they do not cooperate in the midst of their competition, adjusting their differences together, they produce social problems. The following case illustrates such a problem between the profit and nonprofit sectors.

In 1969 Marjorie Webster Junior College, a two-year proprietary (for-profit) institution in Washington, D.C., filed an antitrust action against the Middle States Association of Colleges and Secondary Schools (MSA). It had been excluded from the association for being proprietary. MSA was one of six regional accrediting associations in the United States. MSA's members included 246 nonprofit institutions of higher education, including 106 public ones. Proprietary (for-profit) institutions were not eligible for accreditation or membership in the association. The lack of accreditation for Marjorie Webster was damaging to the college. The relief sought was a decree declaring the exclusion of proprietary institutions to be illegal and an order that the plaintiff's application for accreditation be accepted. The trial court upheld the claim of the college, but in the federal court of appeals the decision was reversed, and the U.S. Supreme Court declined to review the decision in 1970.[25]

The conflict between profit and nonprofit values has been healthy and good for society, but there are legal issues to be resolved. They are part of this inter-sector dynamic of changing markets in a free society. In this case, the challenge in the field of education is to negotiate public standards between the sectors of government, business, and the Third Sector.

In the Marjorie Webster case, nonprofit associations and businesses cannot cooperate and adjust their differences; hence, some new form of co-operation is needed to settle their differences. This will be discussed in Part 2, where we examine the rise of charter schools. Charter schools are forc-ing settlements between religious and public standards of education.

4. Autonomy and Interdependence

The self-regulation of firms based on mutuality is very complex from a so-ciological perspective. Some of that complexity can be seen in the work of sociologist Diane Vaughan, who studied the regulation of safety at the Na-tional Aeronautics and Space Administration (NASA). She focused on NASA's failure to identify flaws in the management procedures and tech-nical design that preceded the *Challenger* tragedy. The tragic loss of this space shuttle on January 28, 1986, sent the nation into mourning. Her analysis of "the processes of discovery, monitoring, investigation, and sanc-tioning" in the Space Shuttle Program indicates that "regulatory effective-ness was inhibited by both the 'autonomy and interdependence' of NASA and its regulators." She sees her findings applicable to all intra- and in-terorganizational relations.

> Many organizations are self-regulating, initiating special subunits to discover, monitor, investigate, and sanction in order to control deviant events. . . . By using autonomy and interdependence to explore social control relations intra- and interorganizationally and by varying the types of organizations studied, we may (1) learn more about how the struc-tured relations of organization affect social control, (2) specify these two concepts more fully, and (3) move toward more broadly based theory on the social control of organizations.[26]

The conditions under which "autonomy" and "interdependence" among mutually managed organizations work best—and the way in which self-regulation becomes most effective—are not yet wholly specified. In this case, Vaughan found that this type of self-regulation was insufficient. Chief executive officers (CEOs), professionals, and government "regulators" be-came too invested in the success of their project to make adequate deci-sions. Professional engineers and scientists, who have their own expertise and peer groups and have their own associations watching them, became too personally involved in the success of this venture. The Aerospace Safety Advisory Panel had representatives from all sectors—government, business, and professionals—but relied too much on business firms to gather and interpret information. In this case, the dependency undermined the effectiveness of the varied units of the project. What went wrong at NASA, Vaughan says, can be generalized to all monitoring/enforcement relationships. Her findings are detailed, but we refer to a few regulatory issues here.

First, the *definition of a problem* for the "regulator" in this NASA case was influenced by the "regulated," who became the "informant." The regulator's informational dependency on the regulated produced friendly relationships. This made regulators too vulnerable to being influenced by the regulated. Regulators took the "point of view" of the regulated because they developed high regard for them, compromising their ability to identify and report violations. In this case, Adam Smith's "sympathy" appears at first to be a negative factor, but on second thought, there was no serious competition, no strong and impartial outsider to make the process work right. The government was the main overseer, but supervising itself was not enough. And professionals had too strong an interest in making the project a success for their own reasons.

Second, the *technical language* of science and engineering in separate units made it difficult for regulators to understand what was really happening. The regulators could not comprehend the complex terminology.

Third, this situation became ripe for *intentional distortion by "the regulated"* through the use of elaborate computer technology. Informational dependencies prevented regulators from detecting falsification by the regulated organization.[27]

The regulators and the regulated need to be separate, independent, and equally competent. Nonprofit scientific and engineering associations, rather than individuals, can sometimes be better watchdogs because of their collective responsibility. They are more likely to share the facts and search for the truth as a public responsibility.

The criteria for selecting good monitors must be judged in each case. For example, both the Sierra Club and lumber associations seem to manage to achieve such proper distance. The Consumer Federations of America and Common Cause have certain competencies in their specific areas of conflict with business, but the relationship between them and business is also growing complex, more subtle, more interfigured in some respects.

For example, big corporations that exploited the environment are now contributing significantly to foundations to prevent environmental exploitation. The Sierra Club solicits large individual donations from the rich, some of whom made their wealth exploiting the environment; 15 percent of the club's $52.6 million income is drawn from wealthy donors. This donation relationship can build closeness and familiarity, but the public needs more. As we saw in the NASA case, the public also needs distance and objectivity. This requires subtle balance and integration.

The purposes of business philanthropy and the purposes of nonprofit organizations have boundaries. The line between too close and too intimate, as opposed to too distant and too critical, is a special frontier of learning between sectors, a place where different sector relationships are maturing. Leaders are finding it possible to be friendly, objective, critical, sympathetic, and impartial, for the mutual well-being of everyone. New attitudes help define a self-regulatory economy that works for the common good.

The nonprofit Nature Conservancy (purchasing and preserving unspoiled land) in 1996 collected more than $1 million each from General Motors, Dow Chemical, and power-plant developer EnRon Corporation. All these business corporations have opposed the environmental movement at some point. Now they are in a collaborative relationship with environmentalists with complex motives, probably good, bad, indifferent, and mixed in all sorts of ways, but overall, the new relationship is testing a new frontier of civil development in the economy.[28]

A civil market is created in the synthesis (or balance or symmetry) between opposite conditions. In the NASA case involving business, professionals, and government, the synthesis had to be made between *distance* and *closeness*. In other cases, it requires symmetry between *cooperation* and *competition*.

5. Inter-sector Governance

Self-regulating systems have grown up stumbling, like an infant learning to walk, trying to form its first sentences, then learning new skills during puberty and adolescence and finally coming into maturity in a way that brings more freedom. But that freedom depends on learning social skills and developing a sense of responsibility. So too, the market system gropes its way toward greater responsibility and maturity.

The Federal Trade Commission (FTC) handles deceptive or unfair advertising in the United States, but the business of advertising is becoming self-regulated. Business scholar J. J. Boddewyn has identified the strengths and weaknesses of advertising self-regulation in the context of six tasks that must be performed. These tasks are (1) developing standards, (2) making standards widely known and accepted, (3) advising advertisers beforehand about gray areas, (4) monitoring compliance with the norms, (5) handling complaints from consumers and competitors, and (6) ruling on business behavior in violation of the standards, including publicity about wrongdoings and wrongdoers.[29]

According to Boddewyn, market self-regulation can take various forms. First, and most autonomous, there is *self-discipline,* where the firm controls its own advertising. Second, there is *pure self-regulation,* where the industry (the peer-group competitors) controls advertising. Third, there is *co-opted self-regulation,* whereby the industry, of its own volition, asks for help from nonindustry people—for example, a government department or a consumer association. Fourth, there is *mandated self-regulation* (a seeming contradiction of terms), where the industry is ordered by the government to develop, use, and enforce norms, whether alone or in concert with other bodies.[30]

The third type of self-regulation, where business asks for help from outside, can involve nonprofits in the Third Sector. This means a "profit-nonprofit" collaboration to sustain accountability. In the Netherlands, we might add, pharmaceutical advertising is self-governing by code agreements composed by representatives of the medical association, normally considered part of the Third Sector, as well as by associations of manufacturers, importers, advertising firms, publishers of periodicals, and newspapers.

The fourth type, the idea that government can mandate (or encourage) market self-regulation, suggests that public policies could bring together vastly different interests, such as the Sierra Club and the lumber industry, in planning a program for environmental protection. The creation of civil markets requires the right combination of contrary powers and principles represented in joint ventures between business and the Third Sector. A self-regulating civil economy requires this matrix of associations that have both conflicting and common interests.

6. Crossing Sectors

Important differences exist between business firms and the Third Sector. Each sector has its own purpose and values. The business sector emphasizes *financial* and *economic* values while the nonprofit sector emphasizes *social* and *cultural* values. The question is whether an institution can change its status from one sector to another and maintain that important difference. This tension of differences can lead the economy to operate in the public interest.

Some environmental groups (Third Sector) are crossing sectors and going into business. They want to make money to do a better job at fulfilling their social values. These nonprofits want to keep environmental goals and become financially self-reliant, not depending so much on outside charity and gifts. But crossing from one sector to another can be progressive or regressive. It depends on how one does it.

"Going into business" is a nonprofit strategy today. Most of the environmentalists' $4 billion in annual revenue comes from membership dues, T-shirt sales, and entry fees at sanctuaries, but that source of income may be changing. By the year 2002, the Conservation Law Foundation hopes to raise one-third of its budget from its own nonprofit business ventures, such as hiring out its lawyers as consultants to help communities control traffic. The aim is to reduce their 80 percent dependency on charity by making a healthy income through fees created by their own expert consulting.

Crossing sectors is progressive when an enterprise integrates these conflicting values and transcends their differences so that it is operating profitably for the common good. Then it is a civic enterprise. On the other hand, sector crossing is regressive if the new business seeks to do good and goes bankrupt. Or, it is regressive if a nonprofit becomes a business obsessed with moneymaking, losing its original purpose.

There is now a thin legal line dividing the profit and nonprofit sectors. We argue that this line cannot be crossed easily without careful planning. The two sectors are so close already that in some cases it is hard to tell the difference. Nonprofit (e.g., religious, philanthropic, charitable, educational) corporations can sometimes act like businesses when they compete fiercely against one another and offer big salaries to their executives. As we will see in Part 2, private universities, churches, and hospitals battle for "customers" like businesses do. The professions of medicine, law, and dentistry can function like monopolies, curbing price competition in the name of professional conduct or inhibiting innovation by their members. Nonprofits can become monopolies.[31]

These nonprofits are now big business. The Environmental Defense Fund, headquartered in New York City, works collaboratively with business to protect the environment. It had a 1996 income of $23.4 million. Greenpeace USA, headquartered in Washington, D.C., is a confrontational group known for nonviolent protests; it had a 1996 income of $22.9 million. The Natural Resources Defense Council, headquartered in Washington, D.C., pushes for energy deregulation; it had a 1996 income of $27.9 million. The Nature Conservancy, headquartered in Arlington, Virginia, is a low-key conservation group; it had a 1996 income of $133 million. The significance of size and influence goes on with like-minded associations—with the Clean Air Task Force, the Public Interest Research Group, the World Wildlife

Fund, Alternatives for Community and Environment, the Conservation Law Foundation, and more.

Such nonprofits are doing vital work in the public interest, but they are no longer small grassroots groups. In some cases, they match the power of big business. The relationship between the profit and nonprofit sectors is quite various and changing: close, distant, cooperative, competitive, and confrontational.

Environmental nonprofit corporations today have become a significant part of the marketplace. They show the potential for (1) becoming absorbed completely into the business environment and losing their original purpose, (2) creating civic-oriented businesses, (3) forming inter-sector partnerships for the common good, and (4) maintaining a very confrontational relationship with business as a countervailing power. So far, this nonprofit field of action has worked effectively on an enormous problem of environmental protection. The connection between countervailing powers needs supporting public policies. With the right policies, the two sectors together can complement (and reduce) the work of the Environmental Protection Agency.

Finally, moral sentiments are a driving force in both sectors. The nonprofit Boston Museum of Fine Arts must decide whether to return "antiquities" that the Guatemalan government—and prominent archaeologists—have said were "looted" from Mayan grave sites and illegally exported two decades ago. At the same time, the profit-oriented Dow Corning Corporation faces a court decision to pay $3.2 billion to settle claims of some 170,000 women who say their silicone breast implants made them sick. This new market system strains to find a moral order.

7. Inter-sector Power

We noted that the main goals in business are economic and financial while the main goals in the nonprofit sector are social and cultural. Now we contend that each sector has something to teach the other. The issue is how the integration of these different goals may create a more civil economy. One way in which this happens is through intersector monitoring between business and nonprofits. This work has already begun.

Under certain conditions, the monitoring and regulating influence of nonprofits is more powerful than that of government. Nonprofits become like another aspect of Smith's invisible hand. When a social concern for others in the nonprofit sector acquires a collective power equal to that of business, it works for the common good. Nonprofit associations exercise their power by exposing corporate misdeeds through the mass media, "going public," so to speak, pressuring conscientious executives to stop what may be a disastrous action. Here is one example on public health and safety.

Thirty-seven environmental, medical, religious, and consumer groups asked U.S. oil refiners not to use Ethyl Corporation's new manganese-based gasoline additive MMT, marketed to refiners under the trade name HiTEC 3000. The toxic effects on humans of high levels of airborne manganese, which include severe and progressive brain degeneration, are well documented, but little is known about low-dose exposure, chronic toxicity, or age-related susceptibility. The Environmental Protection Agency sought to stop the use of MMT, but the courts decided the government lacked authority to halt its sale until the product went on the market. And then it could be too late. The nonprofit groups protesting its use without testing included the American Psychological Association, Center for Auto Safety, League of Conservation Voters, National Wildlife Federation, Natural Resources Defense Council, Parkinson's Action Network, the Environmental Defense Fund, and the Society for Developmental and Behavioral Pediatrics. These national associations had a significant effect in stopping the use of MMT before careful studies were made.[32]

In this example, the nonprofit sector was engaged in a civil action. Each sector had to calculate the probabilities of danger in its own way, but the nonprofit sector fought for a stronger emphasis on safety in the public interest. Nonprofits can make the issues of safety, health, justice, and morality a more vital part of the capitalist economy.

This tension between the nonprofit and for-profit sectors shows a potential for creating resolutions for the common good, generating a more civil economy. A civil economy requires an increase in moral energy and more "transparency." Transparency means sharing more market information with the public. We shall note more about this need for transparency in profit and nonprofit sectors in chapter 6 on civil associations.

The Third Sector and the government sector have learned a lot from the business sector. They have held consultations and conferences with business leaders on issues of management efficiency. David Osborne and Ted Gaebler discuss these matters in more detail, but they also suggest, importantly, that governments are in a position to restructure markets "to fulfill a public purpose."[33]

We will have more to say about restructuring markets in Part 2, but here we point to the influence each sector already has on the other. Business leaders with a social concern develop their own mutual support. Business for Social Responsibility (BSR) was created in 1992 to develop, support, advocate, and disseminate business strategies and practices that aim for higher performance in both financial and moral accountability. BSR has a diverse membership of large, medium, and small companies in manufacturing, retailing, and service from across the United States. The members are joined in a nonprofit corporation. The two sectors may be blending principles of efficiency with social (moral) principles.[34]

The nonprofit sector is catching the public eye because of its influence in the economy. In a study of nonprofits in the greater Boston area, Robert Hollister, dean of the Tufts Graduate School of Arts and Sciences, concluded that the nonprofit sector is a "growing rival" to government and the business sector. It is a social leader, a deliverer of services, an "economic force," and a major employer in the region, stimulating business activity. There are some 3,700 nonprofit organizations headquartered in Greater Boston that pour $19 billion into the economy, ranging from Harvard University to groups such as City Year and the Conservation Law Foundation.[35]

The nonprofit sector seems destined to become a major player in the marketplace along with business in the next century. The mystery of how Smith's invisible hand plays a role in producing a self-regulated economy becomes clear when viewed in this long-range history. The basis for a market economy to operate successfully in a civil society is found through mutual (self-) interest. The pieces of the puzzle for building a civil economy are coming together.

8. Inter-sector Ownership

There are significant "interdependencies"—as well as autonomous and strong differences—between these two sectors of the economy. The endowments of nonprofit corporations like universities, churches, pension funds, family estates, and charitable foundations are heavily invested in a large portion of the business sector. By virtue of this stock ownership in business, many executors of nonprofit funds exert pressure on firms to correct malpractice and pursue ethical conduct in the market.

"Social investment" began within Third Sector (nonprofit) corporations, like churches, foundations, and universities. When this growing ethical concern indicated that this type of capital allocation could be profitable, new entrepreneurs turned the idea into a business. The capital allocation of ethical funds now amounts to about a trillion dollars nationwide, all directed toward creating a moral ground for doing business.

The Council of Institutional Investors, composed of pension fund managers (states, unions, and nonprofits) across the nation, regularly reviews the social-economic performance of business. These executors of pension funds have been concerned about "greenmail" (payoffs to corporate raiders), "golden parachutes" (payoffs to CEOs), and "excessive salary ratios." They consider these practices not in the interest of their beneficiaries. Managers of state and private pension funds monitor the conduct of business in the interest of employees, which includes a wide public. They want to maximize financial returns to them as beneficiaries, and they find that ethical practices can optimize those returns.

Social investors are indexing standards for allocating capital in the interest of beneficiaries and the public. Their social screens select ethical issues around environmental protection, job safety, quality of working life, public health, and consumer product safety. Their action reduces the need for government agencies to enforce principles of morality, justice, fairness, and public welfare. Today businesses themselves (banks and mutual funds) are using social screens because there is a large market for ethical investment.[36]

There is a reality to face here. Social investors intend to be ethical, but they are not perfect moral agents. Making good investment decisions is complex. The enhancement of both social and economic returns requires wisdom. The following example of a social-investment decision exemplifies the complexity.

When the Wisconsin state pension fund wanted to oppose the $742.8 million "forced greenmail payment" by General Motors (GM) to Ross Perot on ethical grounds, it was stopped by the governor, who was trying to get General Motors to build some plants in his state.[37]

Social investment decisions are not all formulated on pure and universal principles. The Wisconsin governor in this case did not permit his state pension-fund managers to protest General Motors' "payoff" (greenmail) to Ross Perot for his own ethical reasons. GM's payoff would have got rid of Perot's influence over the GM board, but the governor wanted GM jobs brought into his state. The stockholder protest would have acted negatively on GM's decision to create employment in Wisconsin. For the governor, it was an important public policy to help the jobless. The pension board, on the other hand, protested the payoff because it was not maximizing returns on the investment they made on behalf of their beneficiaries. Greenmail can be positive in eliminating certain corporate takeovers, but pension managers saw this one as a "payoff," an unwise and unproductive decision.

As a second example, several police pension funds were used as proxies in Time Warner to protest the ethics of the Ice-T "Cop Killer" record.

(Time Warner was a parent company of Ice-T's record label.) This case is also complex on moral grounds, having to do with free speech in making records and in composing songs. It is also an issue of how decisions are made by managers of police pension funds without consulting all of their constituencies. But without exploring such issues in detail, our point is that a new force is entering the market to settle moral issues "head-on" by owner representatives. The process of combining moral judgments with financial judgments is complex, but it is part of civil action within this inter-sectored economy.

9. Nonprofits Creating For-Profits

Strong evidence exists that a trend for turning profits into use for the common good is a civil frontier, a new opportunity to combine the contrary intentions of these two sectors of the economy. Nonprofit corporations now create for-profit subsidiaries to earn income so as to "do good" better, more effectively and reliably.

The Local Initiatives Support Corporation (LISC) mobilizes civic partnerships to help local people rebuild deteriorated neighborhoods. Established by the Ford Foundation and six business corporations in 1979, LISC is the nation's largest nonprofit community development support organization. It has 37 local programs working in over 100 cities and urban counties across the country. Through strong relationships with over 1,600 corporations, foundations, and public agencies, LISC has raised over $2.2 billion to support grassroots community revitalization in partnership with business. LISC is a nonprofit channel to help grassroots organizations become profitable.[38]

In this process, we see nonprofits taking direct control over their own for-profit business. We have to think for a moment about what this means. Nonprofit corporations (like museums, churches, universities, and community development corporations [CDCs]) are organizing business subsidiaries. These business subsidiaries then provide a direct income for the nonprofit sector to advance its cultural, educational, and community work. In other words, a business subsidiary in this case is monitored and guided by the purposes of its parent "nonprofit" firm. The noneconomic purposes (religious, educational, scientific) of the nonprofit firm are now in charge— governing business. The conduct of the business firm is defined by what the nonprofit firms deem to be "good," not just profitable. If this relationship continues, it could make the market system turn around in a most unusual way; perhaps a civil venture in transforming the marketplace.

What does this change in inter-sector relationships mean? The business sector has been dominant, and the nonprofit sector has been sub-dominant. Business and nonprofit sectors are legally different, but such cases of collaboration could lead economists to think about capitalism as though it were in a major transition, moving into a different stage of history. Optimists would call this a historic time, a period for social development in the formation of markets. At best, however, any broadscale positive change, any transformation of the market system, is more akin to a slow process of evolution.[39]

This mix of inter-sectored relationships shows problems as well as promise. We are experiencing a critical transition that ranges from friendly transactions to outright warfare. While the current situation is hard to evaluate, advocates from both sectors argue that civic inventions show great promise.

10. Civic Inventions

The collaboration of the three powers—government, business, and the Third Sector—shows how the different sectors can become allies by their own design. Advocates argue—and we agree—that civil development begins at best "inside markets." Government policies can encourage partnerships and private systems of accountability, but only the people in a particular market are capable of producing them. Antagonists who nonetheless join to create the basis for social self-regulation invent a more civil economy.

In the following list we see cases that illustrate how business, government, and nonprofits are producing partnerships, how people in different sectors are in mutual systems of governance, and how sometimes all three sectors work to create an order of civil markets.

Civic Inventions: Examples

Civil Partnerships: Government, Business, Third Sector

1. The Connecticut Community Economic Development Program is jointly controlled by *representatives of low-income communities, private business investors,* and *government.* This program provides funding and technical assistance for private, public, and cooperative enterprises in disadvantaged communities. Its goals include the creation of jobs and the development of skills, particularly for the unemployed; community participation in decision making; the creation of self-sustaining firms; improving the environment; promoting affirmative action, equal employment opportunities, and minority-owned businesses; and coordination with environmental and economic planning.

2. The Industrial Areas Foundation in San Antonio, Dallas, and Fort Worth, Texas, developed a new job-training initiative called Project

QUEST. It mobilized *religious congregations* across racial and ethnic lines and incorporated volunteer mentoring strategies resulting in some 16,000 hours of volunteer mentoring. The project built partnerships with *local banks* and *industry,* as well as with *government agencies,* creating well-paying jobs for low-income communities. The partnerships created an inter-sectored market in the public interest.

3. The civic environmental group Save the Bay in Providence, Rhode Island, initiated citizen monitoring of water quality, environmental education in schools, and workplace education to reduce toxins. It not only mobilized thousands of new volunteers but developed new public relationships among *environmentalists, schools, businesses, civic associations, boating and fishing clubs,* and *state and federal agencies.* These relationships embody new forms of social capital that cultivate financial capital for the common good. This association is informed and monitored by the nonprofit sector. Thus, it becomes a publicly oriented sector of the private economy.[40]

Civil Banking.

1. The South Shore Bank in Chicago, Illinois, used its resources in *the nonprofit and profit sector* to rebuild a low-income African American neighborhood, which was refused credit by other area banks. By providing residential mortgages and small business loans and organizing initiatives in commercial development and housing rehabilitation, South Shore redeveloped the neighborhood's infrastructure and services, a unique combination of profits and nonprofits working together. Some conventional banks collect deposits in disadvantaged and middle-class communities and channel the money into speculative and exploitative investments, but "civic bankers" use deposits to improve underdeveloped communities while making a profit.

2. Dozens of *citizen coalitions in U.S. cities* have followed the Mondragon model of the *Caja Laboral* in the Basque region of Spain, which is governed by the firms it generates. People have organized a Federation of Industrial Retention and Renewal (FIRR) association, mobilizing community support to aid employee buyouts and to start co-ops and innovative banks. In a different case, the ICA Group in Boston, Massachusetts, has taken the Mondragon system as a model for funding self-managed (co-op) business systems.

Civil Legislation

1. The federal government created legislation for the employee stock ownership plan (ESOP), offering incentives for companies to provide stock to their employees. By the mid-1980s, over 10,000 firms, with more than 11 million workers, had ESOPs or their equivalent. Although the legislation is imperfect and needs basic revisions, it nevertheless pro-

duces a ground for establishing a better system of corporate accountability to workers. Civil legislation occurs when its purpose is to implement the foundation for a self-accountable economy.

2. In the Ninetieth Congress, both Republican and Democratic senators joined in sponsoring a bill called the Community Self-Determination Act, designed to initiate community corporations, that is, local *democratic corporations,* across the country. Begun in 1967, today these corporations exist throughout the United States.

Civil Investment

1. The Interfaith Center for Corporate Responsibility, the Council on Economic Priorities, and other nonprofits encourage shareholder resolutions in the public interest. Social investment has brought a conscience into capital markets. The practice can have some shortcomings, but it is part of a process of "inventing" a more civil economy.

2. Calvert Social Investment Fund, E. L. Putnam, U.S. Trust Company of Boston, Drexel, Burnham Lambert, Travelers Corporation, Working Assets Money Fund, Franklin Research, and other profit-oriented firms have developed social screens to monitor industrial practices from a social-ethical perspective, setting standards for allocating capital for the common good. These cases are not all perfect in their judgments, but they plant the seeds for a civil-society economy. There is a synergy in *profits* and *nonprofits* working together here. Banks and investment firms apply ethical criteria to the allocation of capital, and nonprofits help them make decisions with social screens. The nonprofits study socially responsible companies and offer facts on performance.[41]

People in the cases just cited have created models for building a civil system of exchange. Social accountability is based on the assumption that *people affected by a problem are included in the solution.*

These social inventions in the marketplace—creative partnerships, civil legislation, community banking, and social investments—are not a panacea, a solution to all the moral problems in a market economy, but they represent a step toward civil-society formation. They constitute tiny moves toward connecting self-interest with systems of mutual governance that operate for the common good.

11. Stakeholder Participation

The "common good" cannot be defined in a permanent way—its meaning is developing every day—but one practical way to define it is through stakeholder participation. Stakeholders are people who are affected by corporations and who can exercise an influence over them. People who have a stake in an enterprise make a claim, assert a right, believe that something is due them, or help the firm make money in their own interest. "Stakeholdership" in business is inter-sectored, including grassroots groups, communities, institutions, and national governments. Any group affected by business is a stakeholder.

In business management, primary stakeholders are those who have an official relationship to a firm, like owners, stockholders, and employees. Secondary stakeholders are all others, like customers, suppliers, creditors, nonprofits, governments, and communities. But this difference, easy to describe conceptually, becomes blurred in reality. For example, secondary stakeholders can wield more power in some cases than primary stakeholders, making them prime power players.[42]

Management theorists recommend that corporations "map" their stakeholders when formulating their policies. The map helps them develop strategies that are ethically based and "cost effective." It helps a firm avoid court costs resulting from stakeholder actions. The following two stories of corporate misconduct illustrate why such a map is used today. The moral dimension of the economy becomes "real" when serious damages take place.

Nestlé Company

Nestlé invoked moral outrage from the public in 1974, when it became known that it was selling infant formula in the Third World using intense promotional techniques. Observers of this practice alleged that the infant formula could be misused, leading to malnutrition, diarrhea, and death. Nestlé's aggressive marketing tactics encouraged women to choose bottle feeding, resulting in a decline in breast feeding, which is safer and more healthful. Poor sanitation, impure water, and the inability to read and follow directions did result in disease and malnutrition. Stakeholders in many sectors of society participated in protests against Nestlé's actions.[43]

In 1984, after spending tens of millions of dollars resisting the boycott, Nestlé finally reached an accord with the protesters. This civic movement achieved a great success although the follow-up was not perfect. In retrospect, besides employees, UN agencies, and customers, Nestlé's map would include the U.S. government, governments and populations in less-developed countries (LDCs), retail trades and distributors in host countries, the International Nestlé Boycott Committee, the Interfaith Center on Corporate Responsibility, the National Council of Churches of Christ, International Baby Food Action Network, Infant Formula Action Coali-

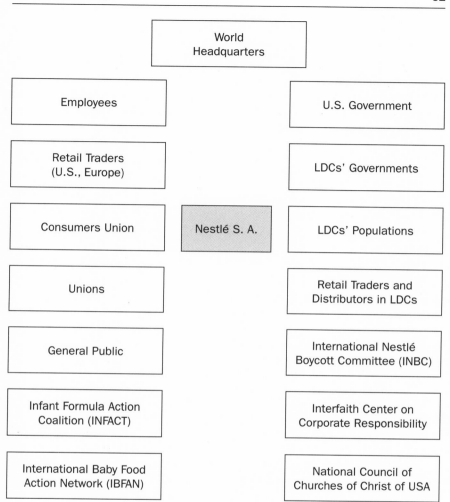

Fig. 1. Stakeholder map of Nestlé S. A. during the infant formula controversy. (Adapted from Archie B. Carroll, *Business & Society* [Cincinnati: South-Western College Publishing, 1996], 84, 85.)

tion, the general public, unions, Consumers Union, and retail trades in the United States and Europe (fig. 1).

Hooker Chemical Company

Hooker Chemical Company, later a subsidiary of Occidental Petroleum Company, built a canal in the southeast corner of the city of Niagra Falls,

New York, originally to be used for transmitting hydroelectric power to businesses in the city; in the 1940s, it became a toxic waste dump for chemical companies. The contaminated land was purchased by the local school board, and a tract of homes was built around it. Residents began to discover they had serious health problems, such as liver damage, miscarriages, birth defects, and other ills. The "stakeholder map" of Hooker Chemical then became apparent to executives. It included trade associations, the media, tourists, unions, employees, insurance companies, residents, customers, political groups, the financial community, competitors, suppliers, and more.[44]

In figure 1, we see how management analysts view the characteristics of stakeholders in the Nestlé case. This is a graphic picture of human interdependence, groups of people affected by corporate behavior. Today corporations are beginning to "factor in" moral costs in relation to financial costs. This practice is called "internalizing externalities" and is becoming common today. It is an effort to integrate corporate self-interest with the public welfare. Neva Goodwin, an economist at Tufts University, says:

> If there is a single problem which can be described as the most urgent for all market economies of the future, it is this: to discover how far it is possible to go in "internalizing the externalities"—*to insert into the cost and profit accounting of individual or institutional actors the costs and benefits to society or to other individuals which result from their actions.*[45]

Economists and sociologists should study this cost-benefit strategy. In chapter 6, we will discuss how the "internalization of costs" becomes most effective through civil associations of competitors. It can be more effectively practiced when individual competitors agree to standards that are set in their own associations—where mutual self-accountability overcomes the destructive aspects of competition and advances returns for all stakeholders.

Summary and Conclusion

We noted how the Scottish philosophers saw the new European class of bourgeoisie as a "civil society" emerging to protect individuals against feudal rule, a path leading toward greater freedom and progress. The new commercial order in the eighteenth century strengthened individual freedom and carved a new place for people to depart from monarchal rule and organize their own enterprises. The idea of "civil society" was a realm of personal autonomy where entrepreneurs were free to develop their own moral accounting.

Though Adam Smith warned against the development of corporations, they became a significant part of the market in the nineteenth century. In turn, governments grew in size to solve problems business competition produced. Yet, at the same time, competitors came together to create their own rules of fairness and justice, rules that operated for their common good. We suggested that in some cases this cooperation reduces the need for government controls. Competitors have begun to standardize products, create uniform accounting procedures, and establish codes of conduct in ways that go unnoticed by the public. This type of civil action is like an invisible hand, improving self-regulation.[46]

Our conclusion is that, under the right conditions, inter-sectored competition—combined with prudent cooperation—should reduce the need for government regulations. The potential for a more civil order of markets can be seen in the creative interplay of these sectors. Civil markets are composed of antagonists who are willing to collaborate and establish standards for themselves and for other stakeholders.

To understand the development of a market economy in civil society, we need to study the changing relationship between business and the nonprofit sector. Categories to study that we have described in this chapter are: (1) *Conflict Resolution*—the mechanisms by which business competitors set public standards (e.g., codes of conduct/product grading) and resolve differences (e.g., private tribunals/arbiters) through nonprofits; (2) *Countervailing Powers*—the way in which nonprofits monitor business performance (e.g., insurance associations monitoring public safety); (3) *Inter-sector Competition*—the manner in which business moves competitively into the nonprofit zone, as in "for-profit schools" (e.g., Webster Junior College) versus nonprofit accrediting associations (e.g., MSA); (4) *Autonomy and Interdependence*—the way private and public (nonprofit) managers become effective partners (e.g., the Challenger disaster); (5) *Inter-sector Governance*—the way in which professional associations (e.g., medical) assess the performance of profit firms (e.g, pharmaceutical advertising); (6) *Crossing Sectors*—the practice of nonprofits rechartering themselves as a business (e.g., environmental groups, universities, and hospitals); (7) *Inter-sector Power*—the nonprofits' pressure on business to operate in public interest (e.g., thirty-seven nonprofits persuading the petroleum industry to stop using toxic chemicals); (8) *Inter-sector Ownership*—the practice of nonprofit organizations (churches, universities, and pension funds) voting their corporate stock according to ethical principles; (9) *Nonprofits Creat-*

ing For-Profits—the practice of nonprofits (e.g., museums and universities) integrating business subsidiaries into their organization; (10) *Civil Inventions*—the way in which business-and-nonprofit organizations collaborate for the public good (e.g., civic banking, civic partnerships, etc.); (11) *Stakeholder Participation*—the degree to which private corporations include stakeholders in their policy decisions in light of costly lawsuits (e.g., Dow Chemical in Bhopal, India).

In brief, how does civil development take place in a market economy?

Research is needed on the changing character of business and nonprofit organizations. Case studies of the dynamics between these sectors could result in a thousand stories of conflict and confluence, conversion and conspiracy. Will excesses in the business sector (monopoly, exploitation, and dominance) require more government legislation and agency control over the market? Or, could market structures be created for the common good? Will the battle between (social) nonprofit versus (economic) business grow stronger, fiercer, and deeper? Or, will legal boundaries erode between the profit and nonprofit sectors? Will one side win over the other? Or, will profit and nonprofit goals be synthesized to create a civil market? Studies of the ongoing reformation of these sectors should provide a sociological perspective on the decline and/or development of civil society.

The creative interplay of forces in different sectors could represent a path toward greater progress, justice, mutuality, and freedom. Yet, there is a struggle ahead in this cyclical, unpredictable economy. Some people today are fighting to survive in the midst of poverty. The rich are getting richer, and people overseas are still exploited by unruly markets. There is a lot of room for civil action and research.

We see in the next chapter how self-regulation, productivity, and profitability coevolve through systems of accountability. These systems are being constructed on mutual self-interest, resulting in a better basis for making capital work for the common good. Our cases will suggest a halting, experimental movement toward civil association, a change that might be called "civicization," if that word were not so clumsy. We will examine the planned and unplanned growth of a private economy that could move toward being more transparent and public oriented. Although no one knows for sure what is ahead, we need to look more carefully at how self-regulation is constructed outside the state, where social and financial principles optimize each other in a civil economy.

2 Systems of Accountability

All great and honorable actions are accompanied with great difficulties.

—William Bradford, *History of Plymouth Plantation,* written 1630–51

Sympathy, though its meaning was perhaps originally the same [e.g., as compassion] may now, however, without much impropriety, be made use of to denote our fellow-feeling with any passion whatever.

—Adam Smith, *The Theory of Moral Sentiments* (1759)

In the preface and in chapter 1, we asked how a market economy could be related to the idea of civil society and a moral order. We noted that Adam Smith conceived the market to be a self-regulating system operating for the common good, but in the succeeding generation the organization of corporations went against much of what he had imagined as a civil economy. Now in this chapter we will show that the social idea in Smith's moral economy has its place today. Civil accountability can be developed in the economy.

The idea of a "free market" system is misleading. *Civil freedom* in the economy cannot develop without *civil order.* It is impossible to have freedom without order; civil liberty cannot exist without rules of conduct. In a free market, we propose, a civil order develops through systems of accountability.

Systems of accountability have been developing for over a century, but they often go unnoticed. They keep the market relatively stable and free, working like Smith's invisible hand. These systems are composed of rules that enable some freedom in associations and markets, requiring less government intervention. In other words, rules of accountability must exist within organizations and markets to have some freedom and justice without government regulations. To put this another way, market freedom requires accountability, which then provides some degree of justice inside markets.

We ask, first, what concepts define accountability in civil development? Second, how do people solve problems through systems of accountability? Finally, how are current systems of accountability flawed or imperfect?

Basic Concepts: Theoretical Orientation

The definition of concepts is tedious, and we make this task brief for the reader, but we must have consistency in understanding special terms. We start with the idea that a *common good* is relative to a market organization in which participants are socially interdependent. Nonetheless, every one must see this interdependence in order to establish systems of social accountability. Accountability is connected to a concept of a common good because everyone is interdependent within it. People who are interdependent in an organization define what is the common good for them. In other words, the common good carries special meanings at different levels of governance: the local community, the enterprise, the industry, the society, the nations hosting global corporations, and the globe itself. In all these cases, we see stakeholders are defining what is good for them as an association.

In this process of self-definition, people show some degree of *social governance*. Social governance is a basic concept explaining the human nature of all these interdependent levels of organization. *Self-governance* is a term within the former term that refers to people in organizations with some autonomy. Every market organization has some allowable measure of self-direction and independence within its interdependency. *Command governance* refers to systems based on a hierarchy of power and authority; that is, people work in superordinate and subordinate offices, or higher/lower systems of authority. *Mutual governance* refers to the degree to which an organization allows for equity in the reciprocal action of its members. The task in establishing accountability requires some degree of equity and coresponsibility for stakeholders at some level of organization.

Social responsibility refers to the conscientious efforts of people in markets to take into account those who might be adversely affected by corporate policies. *Social accountability* refers to formal structures that *require* people to act responsibly toward one another on the basis of established norms. Systems of accountability give assurance that certain business actions are answerable to those affected by them in the marketplace. To put this another way, parties in a system of exchange are *obligated* to act with norms of fairness and justice on the basis of some degree of consent.

The market is based on patterns of *social* and *economic* exchange. Every economic action invokes a certain type of social action. Social accountability is important to stakeholders (people affected by a firm) who feel they have been injured or that rights have been breached. Stakeholders may seek to redress injuries and act to influence corporate decisions. Some of the structures for corporate accountability include electoral methods of governance, judiciaries for resolving problems, and participatory methods for making market decisions.

The term *accountability* is explored in this chapter by using government as a metaphor. I describe cases that reveal legislative, electoral, and judicial features within the governance of organizations. Using this metaphor, we examine systems of accountability as if a government was developing inside private markets. The "legislative" features can be seen in the way stakeholders influence rule making or control corporate policy. The "electoral features" are in the way stakeholders (not just stockholders) participate in voting or in the way firms collectively govern their trade associations. The "judicial features" exist at different levels of governance, from private tribunals operating at the workplace to judicial systems working in global trade associations.[1]

Accountability systems are always changing and evolving, showing promise of building toward a more civil economy. These systems are experiments in the construction of a more civil marketplace, but they are still flawed in certain ways.[2]

Experimental Models: Local-to-Global Systems of Accountability

This section will present a series of cases as models of different systems of accountability that have been evolving for stakeholders, specifically in these cases: (1) employees; (2) the local community; (3) society; and (4) people in host societies or cultures foreign to a firm's dominant ownership. In the following examples, people are inventing civil solutions to market problems within societies around the world.

1. Accountability to Employees: Self-Governing Corporations

Two major changes in corporate labor relations have taken place in the last 50 years that are relevant for our purposes. The first change is toward greater *employee participation* in management through the establishment of suggestion boxes, autonomous work groups, quality circles, labor-management committees, worker councils, codetermination, employee tribunals, and disclosure agreements. The second change is toward a greater degree of *employee ownership.* In the United States today, over 11,000 firms now have varying percentages of employee ownership.[3]

These two types of changes have involved many adjustments in each firm. Experiments in employee participation and ownership are evolving at different levels of management and with different results. A multitude of variables is involved in evaluating what produces success rather than failure, but in spite of many failures, some analysts nonetheless conclude that there has been a positive trend, an increasing degree of employee participation and ownership over the long haul.[4]

The firms that evidence both trends (participation and ownership) are relatively "self-managed" or "self-governing" or "socially managed" firms. If these two accountability trends (comanagement and co-ownership) continue to evolve, it can be argued theoretically that they will move toward a point of convergence where the internal system of the corporation maximizes *self-accountability.* Yet, this is only a theoretical idea. Other factors must be constantly balanced in this development, such as managing efficiency, corporate expansion, competitive pressures of the market, and so on. But self-management theorists argue that when firms have fully optimized self-accountability, employees will not need a U.S. Department of Labor or labor laws to protect them. These firms will contribute toward the making of a self-governing civil economy.[5]

Empirical evidence shows that firms with a high degree of self-management help save jobs, maintain local flows of capital, and promote community development. They foster high levels of productivity and efficiency, reduce absenteeism and labor turnover, curb tardiness and malingering among employees, reduce pilferage inside the firm, reduce corporate bureaucracy, eliminate the need for middle-range supervisors, and, finally, provide a sense of purpose and meaningfulness for employees in their work. Ultimately, self-management pays off for everyone because the government does not have to create agencies and laws to protect workers from abuses.[6]

Margaret Blair, an economist in the Brookings Institution in the United States, argues for employee ownership of corporations. Corporations should be regarded not just as "bundles of physical assets that belong to shareholders" but rather as institutional arrangements for governing the relationship among all of the parties that contribute "firm-specific assets." This includes not only shareholders but also long-term employees who develop skills of value to the corporation, as well as suppliers, customers, or others who make special investments.[7]

Indeed, in a variety of countries, corporations are becoming more and more self-managed, showing considerable diversity in their types of accountability. Of three prototypes often cited by management consultants, one is Asian, one European, and one Spanish.

Model 1. A Special Pattern of Mutual Relations: The Case of Japan

For major Japanese corporations, groups hold the bulk of corporate stock "mutually." Robert Ozaki uses the term *mutuality* to describe systems of ownership and labor relations. He describes the bulk of stocks as held institutionally rather than individually. Firms practice mutual stockholding when Company A holds shares of Company B's stock and Company C's, B owns shares of A's and C's, and so on. Hence, the competitive intercorporate market is more collectively organized than in the United States. This makes firms accountable to one another. Intercorporate ownership requires collaboration, and this integrates the moral-economic decisions of firms who work together. This method discourages outside takeovers because of the "power balance" in mutual ownership. This balance is achieved by the practice of cooperation among "enterprise groups." Certain firms in the same trade area sometimes work together to advance their common interest and can aid each other in times of crisis. However, management still has control over the administrative direction of each firm.[8]

The Japanese model also involves a different internal organization than is typical of U.S. firms. The after-tax salary of the president is about six times as large as the lowest starting salary of a new worker, as opposed to more than 200 times in the United States. There are internal unions, which work with management on a greater trust basis than is the case with U.S. unions. Accountability becomes manifest as management shares proprietary information with unions, offers guaranteed lifetime employment, and talks over company research and development (R&D) policies and their potential impact on employees. This type of collaboration results in a union contract that is "general" (flexible) and "implicit" (trustful) as opposed to U.S. labor contracts, which are "specific" (inflexible) and "explicit" (distrustful). The subculture of the firm emphasizes cooperation and mutual trust. In Japan, a pension reserve is maintained as part of the firm's own assets, in contrast to the United States, where employer/employee contributions to retirement benefits are in diversified portfolios external to the firm.

Model 2. Codetermination: The Case of Germany and Scandinavia

In the 1970s, West German and Scandinavian countries adopted a system of codetermination between labor and management on top boards. West Germany's 1976 law required that a board of supervisors be appointed whose membership represented stockholders and labor equally (50 percent each). The task of the supervisors was to oversee a broad range of company affairs, from the performance of senior managers to personnel policy and the financial condition of the firm. The supervisors were empowered to dismiss all executives except the president of the company; the board of directors was obliged to comply with supervisors' decisions. In case of a deadlock in decisions, the chair of the board of supervisors, who represented the stockholder-owners, would cast the tie-breaking vote. In this way, although the ultimate control of the board was preserved as "capitalist," the new organization changed the orientation of the firm in a social direction. Labor representatives were now in a position to learn inside information and felt responsible for working together for the common good of the firm. A new system of mutual accountability was created.

The design of codetermination systems in Sweden and Norway varies from that of Germany, but all of these forms differ from the systems in U.S. firms in terms of a legal representation of workers on the corporate board. U.S. firms generally have no elected worker councils or legal systems that require adjudication of disputes and monitorable safety and health standards in the workplace.

Model 3. Worker Cooperative: The Case of Mondragon in Spain

For some corporate observers, the system of cooperatives around the village of Mondragon in the Basque region of Spain is an example of a fully self-governed system. In terms of design and economic success, it represents the most serious model for the development of self-management.

The corporate board is elected by an annual meeting of all employees. Employees own and manage their own firms on the basis of one vote per person, and social councils operate at levels of middle management. A system of internal capital accounts operates in each firm: each worker's share of the net annual product is credited to his or her account. Ten percent of the profits is allocated for community development, 30 percent to internal development of the firm, and 60 percent to the employee accounts, which accumulate with interest until the time of retirement.

By adopting the capital accounts system described, Mondragon avoids a common failing that has plagued U.S. and Canadian cooperatives, which award yearly shares of the whole profit to each worker. While it might be in the interest of any single worker to receive a yearly share of the whole profit, it is not in the long-term interest of the whole firm. If the whole profit is divided among the member workers, then any necessary financing for expansion must come from external sources. The Mondragon system avoids putting the firm at the mercy of banks and other lenders.

The Mondragon system has over 26,000 workers and more than 150 cooperative businesses, ranging from heavy industry to department stores, with $3.1 billion in 1993 sales, a bank with billions of dollars in assets, a research center, a social insurance and health system, and housing and educational institutions from preschool to postgraduate technical education. Co-ops are basic units of democratic decision making. The Co-op Congress decides broad policy questions: its decisions must generally be voted upon by each co-op. For example, the Congress may decide to change the salary ratio (differential from lowest to highest paid cooperator), but implementation depends on a further vote by each co-op.

In sum, Mondragon is a system of social self-governance that democratically operates programs such as schools, welfare, and insurance in a social sector. It stands relatively autonomous from government as a "social sector," developing its own mode of civil society.[9]

The Flaws in Self-Governed Firms

The modes of accountability to employees described previously have shown themselves generally productive and profitable, but they all have problems.

Civil rights are an issue in all three cases. Women and minorities in all these examples have had limited participation at top levels of the corporation. In Mondragon, male paternalism persisted for years even with the fully democratic system of management.[10]

Another problem in all three cases is that labor conflict arose when firms grew large, even when workers elected the corporate board. Subsequently, many self-management consultants have recommended decentralizing big firms into smaller companies—even if they are democratically organized.

The Mondragon system had difficulty with "bigness" in a firm called Ulgor. Unwieldy, with 2,000 employees, the firm made the decision to decentralize into a federation of smaller firms. Each major division of Ulgor became a company with its own board of directors. Each board then appointed directors to the larger federation board, which coordinated their activities. The federation board, however, was given authority over specific management areas outside labor issues, like overseas marketing and accounting procedures. Each smaller company maintained complete authority over its own employees (hiring and firing) and work process.

After 40 years of success, some observers have reported that the Mondragon system shows signs of regressing. Management organized an overall corporation (called Mondragon Cooperative Corporation [MCC]) to increase the system's capacity to compete in the world market, but observers are suspicious of it. This corporation is democratically organized but is reportedly top heavy, suggesting a tendency toward bureaucratization. Furthermore, MCC has started new firms overseas, which, unlike its original firms, are not owned or operated by their employees. Also, Mondragon's famous Caja Laboral Popular Bank has begun investing capital in non-co-op firms through stock market sales. Finally, some of the co-ops have hired temporary workers who are not member-owners.[11]

The problem of corporate "bigness" is also apparent in Germany. The German system of big companies (some over 40,000 employees) had to create tiers of "worker councils" (not just one company council) at local and regional levels. Local councils then elected higher councils between regions in a system of self-governance. Very large corporations also had to develop ombudsmen at the floor level. The point is that to have effective systems of accountability, the skills of self-management must develop from bottom to top levels of the hierarchy. In German companies, employee representation goes all the way to the corporate board.[12]

The systems of accountability to employees differ markedly in each nation because of the societal context, but they are also assessed differently by professionals. Joel Rogers raises questions about the power of works councils to equalize wages in the German model. He compares this model to the setups in the United States and emphasizes the key difference in the role of labor unions and trade associations; the movement toward greater equity in wages and employee authority in the United States will take a different turn in the future from that of Germany.[13]

England's large John Lewis Partnership, a democratic firm of 25,000 employees, maintains a set of newspapers to help workers have a "public voice." These newspapers are part of the employees' "public domain." John Lewis allows any employee to complain (anonymously) about a department policy or floor rule. The appropriate supervisor must respond to the question in the same company newspaper. This helps to keep the corporate hierarchy accountable to the needs of employees at the bottom.

The Japanese model is significant because it expresses social responsibility within the firm, but critics point out how this model also expresses powerful pressures to conform, so that individuality can suffer. Understanding Japanese patterns of social responsibility is valuable in looking at quality circles, equitable pay, information sharing, permanent jobs, the avoidance of outside takeovers, and systems of accountability in union contracts. But the Japanese model of a "corporate community" still operates in an oversocialized hierarchy, without full judicial recourse for offended individual employees. The system lacks labor representation on top governing boards and suffers from patterns of paternalism and sexism, and inhibitions against whistle-blowing. When the sense of solidarity breaks down in a Japanese firm, there are no formal judiciary to hear complaints of disaffected employees and no voting rights for employees on the board of directors.

Every corporate system is interdependent with the conditions of the general economy. The rapid expansion of Japan's economy from the late 1950s through the 1960s was powered by a vigorous investment of private industry in new plants and equipment. There was a high level of saving of Japanese households, providing banks and other financial institutions with ample funds for heavy investment in the private sector, as well as the introduction of new technology. Now, because of a slowdown in the larger economy, Japanese firms have difficulty in maintaining their no-layoff policies. An overvalued currency, deflationary pressures, and a wobbling financial system suggest that Japan may need to rethink its economic system in relation to global markets.

The Mondragon system is more decentralized and local. Yet it offers these same liberal structures, that is, shared information, permanent jobs, and equitable salaries, and guarantees accountability for employees from the bottom to the top of the corporate hierarchy. Mondragon has had no job layoffs. When a company is in financial trouble or an employee wants to change jobs with good reason, a system of retraining is set up so that he or she can be transferred to another firm. As the Mondragon system moves into world markets like Japan, however, it may suffer some of the same rewards and penalties that come with business cycles at the global level.

These three models show the difference between social "responsibility" and "accountability" in management systems. The Japanese manifest a powerful sense of social responsibility for employees within the firm but have limited formal accountability to workers. The German model, on the other hand, has steps to assure formal accountability to workers by elections, due process, and easier recourse to the courts but has less powerful norms for social-personal responsibility than the Japanese. Mondragon combines both responsibility and accountability, though some researchers say that there are signs of alienation and backsliding as top management tries to expand into global markets.

The Flaws in ESOPs: The Need for
More Accountability

United Airlines is one of the largest U.S. employee-owned firms. Its employees acquired 55 percent of the company's stock in July 1994 in exchange for reduced wages and benefits and other concessions. United employees have majority voting rights as long as they continue to own at least 20 percent of the company's stock. They have increased job security and three out of 12 places on the board of directors, as well as veto power over major company decisions.[14]

In the United States, the number of employees who own stock in their companies grew from about 6.5 million in 1983 to approximately 14 million in 1995, with shares worth almost $300 million. In 1998 at least 18 million employees owned stock through employee stock option plans (ESOPs), but employee ownership/participation in the United States is still very experimental.

Joseph Blasi, a self-management consultant, argues that the current legislation on ESOPs blocks the social development of these firms. Blasi wants to see the following: (1) more equity given to employees who have the least savings and access to credit, (2) a substantial increase in the limit on the amount of stock distributable to an employee, and (3) stocks allocated on a more equitable basis than salary alone. He says that the practice of excluding workers from stock equity because of age should be eliminated and worker-owners should be able to protect their rights through their involvement in corporate governance, instead of depending upon the complex rules of government regulation that encourage court cases.[15]

In other words, internal corporate self-accountability is not established merely by the opportunity for workers to elect a board of directors. Systems of accountability are needed at every level of the firm. That is why the two trends, "employee ownership" and "employee participation," are both vital to the development of a fully self-accountable firm.

When I studied the effects of change in the German law of codetermination in 1977, I was impressed not simply by the legal problems of "constitutionality" that were invoked by electing workers to corporate boards but by the vast change in worker attitudes that took place. Union leaders told me how difficult it was for them to imagine working on behalf of the whole corporation, including "those executives," after all the years of fighting against them. It takes time for employees and executives to make the needed adjustment to corporate self-management.

Scholars of self-management state that the attributes of a "fully self-accountable firm" are as follows: (1) employee ownership with equitable voting rights for work groups and appropriate stakeholders on the board of directors; (2) high employee participation in decision making at key levels of internal management; (3) profit sharing among employees; (4) full information sharing; (5) an internal representative judiciary; (6) employee attitudes grounded on principles of respect, fairness, and democracy; (7) continuous training and educational programs; and (8) support from trade or professional associations.[16]

2. Accountability to Local Citizens:
The Self-Governed Community

There is a variety of "community-based organizations" (CBOs) designed to be accountable to citizens in localities within the United States.[17] Local citizens democratically organize all of those we describe subsequently. Many of them have manufacturing contracts with big businesses: Kodak, in Rochester, New York, for example, contracts with a local community development corporation in the African American community. During the last few decades, people in localities who feel oppressed by corporate business practices have spearheaded CBOs. Women, African Americans, and other minorities have established CBOs to maximize business accountability to the whole community.

All of the following CBOs have electoral systems that ground the conduct of the business in one person/one vote representation for local people. The CBOs offer local people a system of accountability even when their businesses link with global markets.[18]

Model 1. Community Development Corporations

Community development corporations (CDCs) began to be formed in the late 1960s and early 1970s in response to locally felt injustices of the business system. Prices for low-quality goods were higher in disadvantaged neighborhoods than in rich neighborhoods; small shops in low-income neighborhoods had to pay higher insurance costs than shops in rich neighborhoods; there was a high jobless rate: these plus a dozen other factors led to a revolt. In the late 1960s, African Americans rioted in cities across the land against the oppressive system, and their leaders called for the establishment of CDCs as an alternative to the reigning system.[19]

CDCs are designed to optimize profits in the interest of the whole community. Their boards of directors are accountable to the local citizens who elect them. Local people elect board members who hire a professional staff to manage the corporation. Since the 1970s, CDCs have created both housing and local businesses, including shopping centers, factories, and professional services. Their presence reduces the need for governments to intervene in the private market to protect local citizens from the failures of conventional firms to be accountable to local citizens.

Valerie Pope, an activist and former welfare mother in southern California, creates community jobs as executive director of the San Bernardino West Side Community Development Corporation. She arranged training for several hundred young workers for construction work and solar energy jobs during the rehabilitation of over 400 housing units. Through her incentive, another CDC established a light manufacturing facility making solar panels to be used in retrofitting housing, and her CDC members collaborated with the city on an innovative program for purchasing, rehabilitating, and reselling abandoned and deteriorated property.

Model 2. Community Land Trusts

Community land trusts (CLTs) are nonprofit corporations controlled by local citizens. Local citizens who own their land in common elect CLT boards of directors. They rent parcels of land to private businesses that, in turn, become represented on their local board. CLT boards are structured to balance the representation of "leaseholder members" with nonleaseholder residents.

The CLT is democratically run and has the effect of both honoring free enterprise and helping to support disadvantaged people. Low-income residents of Appalachia, for example, who belong to a CLT can collectively deal with a big business like Peabody Coal. If a company wants to do business in the locality, it must write a contract with the CLT. Peabody can have a representative on the CLT board to argue its case when contract problems arise. The board is there to set standards for the environment and see that fair rent is given to people in the local community.

The National Association of Community Development Loan funds can make loans to people who want to organize a CLT. From inner-city areas to small towns, today's housing crisis has spurred the development of CLTs. They become vehicles for providing home ownership opportunities for low-income people without racial/ethnic discrimination and at affordable prices.

Model 3. Community Development Finance Corporations

The community development finance corporation (CDFC) movement began as a protest against "redlining" by banks. Bank executives were drawing red lines on maps to demarcate low-income neighborhoods, which were home to minority residents thought to be high-risk customers. Banks would not lend money to the residents to fix up their houses or to develop businesses in their neighborhoods, thus contributing to neighborhood decline. Minorities protested through what they called a "green line" movement, and, with the aid of federal legislation, the customer-owned bank or community development finance corporation (a local bank with a board elected by its customers), was created.

CDFCs invest in local businesses and real estate projects in disadvantaged communities. They often invest in minority enterprises. For example, a Boston CDFC invested in BHM, an acronym for a local organization that began in 1987 to provide outpatient mental health programs and forensic residential services and a wide range of social services to Spanish-speaking residents of Roxbury and North Dorchester in Massachusetts. CDFCs also offer their members educational programs on issues of finance.

CDFCs now exist in low-income neighborhoods across the nation, but they constantly face pressures from a hostile business environment. Supportive legislation could advance their position in a civil economy.[20]

Other types of civic-oriented corporations are accountable to local citizens. For example, local customers have organized public utilities in some cities, and some government-run utilities have encouraged customers to buy stock in the company. The main electric utility serving the Cleveland area offered customers a chance to buy stock; in two months, 17,000 customers responded by buying 729,000 shares for $13.7 million. Such utilities are examples for incorporating a system of local accountability that—depending upon how it is organized—can work for the local common good.[21]

Community-based organizations (CBOs) are a basis for increasing the accountability of big firms to the poor and minorities. Those who argue that conventional business practices have created urban slums, crime, and family disintegration think that community corporations may alter this pattern. Contracts between big corporations and CBOs can foster local accountability even in global companies. (We discuss this issue further in Part 3 on global markets.)[22]

The Flaws in Community Corporations

Critics of community-based organizations assert that they are not as widely "participatory" as they claim. Most of the studies have been conducted on CDCs: for example, Ram Cnaan utilizes a typology with 10 criteria to determine whether CDCs are in fact democratic. In effect, the criteria are measures of accountability, including the degree to which elections are open and members are participating in and informed about activities. Cnaan finds that CDCs have special difficulties in (1) finding people willing to hold office, (2) maximizing community participation, (3) acquiring adequate communication systems, and (4) adequately using "due process" procedures in their judicial systems.[23]

Another problem with CDCs is that they focus more time on housing projects than on profit-making industries/services, thus barely surviving.

They also fail to diversify their contracts with big companies and hence become dependent upon their benevolence. But CDCs, like small business, operate in competition with big corporations, often needing public policies that support their work.[24]

In summary, community corporations are designed to represent the citizens in a locality, indeed, to work for the local common good, but they are not perfect. Problems involving adequate communication systems and active participation and community awareness, coupled with a poor record in retaining skilled leadership, have hampered some of these organizations. More training for effective managers is needed.

3. Accountability in Market Sectors: Self-Governed Associations

In the business world, as we noted in chapter 1, competing firms experiment with systems of mutual governance and accountability through trade associations. Associations often set standards to protect the environment, health, safety, and the civil rights of people and can work for the common good. Their efforts can reduce the need for government agencies, but trade alliances, federations, and networks of competitors vary in the degree to which they are able to work effectively.

In most cases, associations are steps in the direction of becoming accountable to the larger society, but they are not fully advanced in their accountability to all stakeholders. The following example in Japan illustrates this case.

Model 1. Enterprise Groups in Japan

Major Japanese companies affiliate in enterprise groups. A group might consist of a city bank, a trading company, and a manufacturing firm as the central core. Branching out from the core might be several manufacturing firms with different product lines related to a pyramid of smaller subcontracting firms, all of which maintain a contributing relationship to the core. There is no formal charter spelling out rights or obligations. Each enterprise group has a President's Club, whose members are the CEOs of all the firms; these people meet periodically and exchange information. The club is said to make no groupwide managerial decisions; its purpose is to reduce transaction costs and enhance joint productivity. Enterprise groups exist in all major industries even when their member firms are in competition with one another. Some business scholars say that these groups provide the dynamic behind Japan's success in the world market.

The point is that affiliated firms agree to offer mutual assistance in difficult times, as during a recession, or when a firm member begins to fail. Rescue for a failing firm may come from the affiliated firms in the form of credit or expertise. Nissan's 1990 takeover of Fuji Heavy Industries, maker of Subaru, is an example. A new president was appointed, a bank advanced credit, and production in the firm was reduced. There were no changes in stock and no purge of executives, as often happens in the United States with such failures. A measure of mutual interest and common purpose prevails in these groups.

This example reveals the value of mutual aid and planning for the companies in these enterprise groups who might otherwise be in trouble, but the organization does not extend its mode of accountability to other important stakeholders, such as subcontractors and customers. Similar alliances can be found in the United States, but they are only accountable to one another on an informal basis and only in a limited sense.

In model 2, we see a much broader system of accountability in which many associations of firms collaborate across the economy to set technical standards in the public interest as well as in their own interest.

Model 2. Trade Associations in the United States

The American National Standards Association (ANSA) developed historically as an association serving the public interest. It administrates and coordinates the U.S. voluntary standardization system. It also promotes the use of U.S. standards and encourages the adoption of global standards. It became a clearinghouse for the creation of technical standards in the public interest as well as in the interest of its members. ANSA does not develop standards itself but provides educational materials and recommended procedures for those who are interested in standardization. It is a federation of over 1,400 trade associations, technical societies, professional groups, and consumer organizations, with a membership of over 25,000 firms. Its member organizations developed more than 13,056 standards dealing with almost every facet of the economy. Trade associations have made it possible to manufacture a lightbulb in New York that will fit a socket in Los Angeles, for a size five shoe made in Boston to fit a wearer in New Orleans, and for a doctor's prescription issued in Pittsburgh to be filled safely in Denver.

For example, the National Electrical Code (NEC) has 20 Code-Making Panels who review and process changes to the code. The code changes every three years. A state, county, or municipality can adopt the code, and then it becomes law of that particular jurisdiction. Enforcement is exercised only by its government adoption, but the work is done through the collaboration of firms in the private sector and is extensive. For instance, Article 250 of the NEC discusses electrical grounding for the safety of personnel and property and lists provisions for planning and installation on circuit and system grounding, enclosure and raceway grounding, location of system grounding connections, and so on.

Trade associations also establish codes of ethics and standards for "fair competition." Most of these standards are directed to specific markets. We mentioned in the last chapter that when the Federal Trade Commission was established in 1914, paint and varnish manufacturers had already adopted an ironclad antirebate agreement as a condition of membership. Competitors agreed not to pay any gratuities, commissions, rebates, or loans to employees of business concerns to whom they sold their product and not to permit expense money for their sales personnel for anything other than legitimate expenses. The two associations set up their own Unfair Competition Bureau, which solved problems by investigating complaints and settling issues through private consultation with the parties involved. This cooperation among competitors was in their own interest. It voided the necessity for the FTC to spend time and money monitoring their activities. There are many types of accountability systems in trade associations that are taken for granted; they do not make headline news.[25]

Sweden has not needed a government agency like the Occupational Safety and Health Administration (OSHA) because problems in the workplace have been solved through society-wide cooperation between labor and management. Employer associations and unions have designed a self-monitoring system. Firms have saved money by working with unions to establish common safety and health standards; the standards have been enforced with equity and fairness under this arrangement, reducing the need for a government agency to exist with all its costs to the public.[26]

Association practices are vital to the creation of a civil economy because it is impossible for government agencies to monitor safety and health in the millions of firms competing across the country. The U.S. Occupational Safety and Health Act of 1970 was written to protect every worker by seeking to provide safe working conditions. However, the National Safety Council shows that thousands of workers are killed and millions are injured each year in job accidents. As corporate cost-cutting measures increase, the frequency of deaths and on-the-job accidents also increases.

Governments need the aid of accountability systems among trade associations.

Standard making is a widespread practice among trade, professional, and business associations. These are nongovernmental organizations and include the American Pet Association, American Association of Oral and Maxillofacial Surgeons, American Heart Association, American Automobile Association, North American Chronic Pain Association of Canada, American Lung Association, and the Association of Iron and Steel Engineers.

Model 3. Housing Councils

In the field of housing in Sweden, private landlords, cooperative housing, and municipal housing companies each have their own negotiating association for bargaining with tenants, who, in turn, are organized in the National Federation of Tenants' Associations. Private landlords usually belong to the Swedish Federation of Rental Property Owners, while municipal housing companies belong to the Swedish Association of Municipal Housing Companies. Negotiations between municipal housing authorities and local and regional branches of the National Federation of Tenants' Associations set the norm for annual rent increases. Regional rent courts, together with the national rent court, provide a system of institutionalized arbitration and sanction. These are bipartite bodies, with an equal number of members chosen from representatives of the landlords' and renters' organizations, who choose a "neutral" legal counsel to serve as chair. Thus housing in this nation is organized locally, regionally, and nationally.[27]

These cases show that associations can set standards for their professional or market arena and help active members to learn about them. In some cases, there is a monitoring practice. When an offending firm breaches an ethical code, it is subject to judiciary action within the framework of the association. Trade associations thus reduce the need for government agencies (e.g., OSHA, the Federal Trade Commission, the Antitrust Division in the Justice Department) to settle their problems by official regulatory action. Associations represent a mode of social self-governance that reduces the need for government to monitor the market of competing firms.[28]

The Flaws in Self-Governed Associations
Like trade unions, business associations can claim to operate democratically, but their conduct does not always coincide with their ideals. Trade as-

sociations develop judiciary and legislative systems, but they also show problems of internal dominance and oligarchy.

For example, when some competing firms in a trade group are wealthier, they can be overinfluential in decision making; or when associations charge high fees to increase operating income, they can prohibit less wealthy firms from joining. Judges in private tribunal systems can be friends of offenders, and an injustice can take place. Friendship with members of the organizational court violates constitutional principles; hence, federal courts have demanded systems of "due process" to insure that public justice is administered through these private associations.[29]

Although trade and professional associations can monitor their own members' behavior effectively, they do not do so well in settling problems with "outsiders." Physicians and lawyers settle conflicts among themselves, but they perform poorly in protecting patients and clients from the misconduct of their colleagues through their own tribunal systems. In such cases, a fair judicial system should include the outsiders. In this case, patients and clients, to be treated justly, should have representation on the private judiciary panels of the American Bar Association and the American Medical Association.

Similarly, producers cannot represent distributors and retailers. In these cases of producer vs. distributor-retailer, the latter group must also be represented in tribunal systems. Such intercorporate systems are becoming developed. For example, General Motors and the National Association of Automobile Dealers established a private court to settle conflicts that arise within their competitive/cooperative system of exchange. It operates to solve problems of the "producer vs. retailer."[30]

4. Accountability to People in Host Nations: Global Experiments

There are 2,600 U.S. multinational corporations with more than 19,000 subsidiaries and affiliates in 127 different countries. The average multinational has about 17 diversified operations in separate countries. Corporations are constantly searching for ways to increase their business effectiveness. They explore new production, marketing, or distribution strategies and new practices in their internal organization, labor relations, and management procedures.[31]

A foreign corporation assumes certain responsibilities in a host nation: it creates local jobs, offers training in management skills, and can supply capital for host societies, but critics have shown that such firms also exploit people, extract profits unfairly, and collude with government elites to dominate the host economy. Global firms in foreign lands need formal systems of accountability to the host stakeholders.

We treat the question of how to avoid exploitation by global firms in more detail in Part 3, but a few experimental models are offered here.

The point is that global firms in the big "core nations" can be socially accountable to the smaller less-developed "peripheral nations" and still make good profits. There are many ways for global firms to cultivate both accountability and profitability. These ways include sharing the ownership of subsidiaries in the host nation, employee stock option plans (ESOPs), and social contracts with community corporations. They all involve decentralizing company administration and cultivating local development. All of these models show promise but also have flaws.

The following three models illustrate how measures of equity (such as sharing ownership, power, and profits) are introduced into the subsidiary system of multinationals. The descriptions are brief, but details can be obtained in the referenced sources.

Model 1. Contracts with Community Corporations, Puerto Rico

When Kennecott and Amax Corporations were exploring the advantages of copper mining in Puerto Rico, local citizens fought against them because their exploratory excavations were damaging the environment. The Council of Churches in Puerto Rico asked university researchers to investigate the problem. The council asked: How can a multinational firm operate fairly in a host country without exploiting the environment? Council members said that a multinational firm would need to contract with the private sector through socially accountable systems, because the government, representing an elite group in Puerto Rican society, had previously colluded with foreign firms, supporting them with special kickbacks and political advantages.

The following alternative structure was devised in Puerto Rico.

Government	*Islandwide Cooperative* (A public nonprofit firm)	Foreign Global Firm
Public Review Board (University researchers)		Judicial Board (Professional arbiters)

Regional Community Development Corporation
Utuado CDC   Lares CDC   Other Village CDCs   Ponce Refinery CDC

The preceding diagram illustrates how a plan for an islandwide nonprofit cooperative ("public corporation") was designed and debated among people. In this scheme, all citizens on the island could pay $5.00 for membership, allowing them to vote for the board of directors. This islandwide "public corporation" would negotiate a contract with the global firm to develop a copper mining system. Such a contract would require the organization of community development corporations within each village near where the mining takes place. The global firm would have the right to mine copper for five years. During this time, CDCs would be organized, with the cooperation of the island government, the nonprofit corporation, and the municipalities. CDCs would gradually be given authority to oversee future development of copper mining on the island.

The profits from the mining operation would return to three parties: the local CDC, the public corporation, and the global firm. A fair and proportionate distribution of profits would be determined by negotiation with competing world copper companies. The "open world competition" (not bound only to U.S. firms) increases the bargaining power of the island's public corporation. The distribution of profits to the community corporation thus reverses the tendency for revenue from the global operations to be retained by the company and totalitarian governments. Global companies often fail to share financial benefits at the local level.

The model calls for a public review board composed of science faculty in the universities, whose task is to monitor the process of mining and its impact on air, sea, earth, and rivers in the region. This makes it harder for government to collude with multinational corporations (MNCs) to overlook local environmental damages. A judiciary board, composed of employees of the local firm and representatives of the village, receives complaints made by anyone who feels injured or unjustly treated. This system ensures openness, avoiding the secrecy that often attends global-firm activities, and allows citizens to blow the whistle on corporate misconduct. The bill for these self-accounting mechanisms is paid though a common trust fund generated by the revenues from the mining.[32]

There are other variations on this theme. A global firm can contract with a community land trust in a host nation and rent a portion of local land for its use, while local people, sometimes getting help from their government or civic-minded professionals, set standards and maintain control over environmental conditions. The host's community land trust and the outside company then share in the profits. A community corporation gives host people the right to control certain aspects of what is done by the global firm in their locality. Foreign investors, in turn, are given a right to participate on the board of the host's land trust, to be present and argue their case in a global-local contract, making certain that day-to-day decisions keep the corporate subsidiary profitable.

Model 2. Multinational Cooperatives, Canada

Multinational cooperative-networks do not operate like conventional corporations because they are organized to be democratic rather than operating through a strict hierarchy of command. They are proving to be fair and just, and they make profits at the same time. These types of cooperative global firms have been organized and studied in Canada, and while each differs in its organization, we can describe typical attributes of the board's relationship to its subsidiaries.

Global Board of Directors
(Composed of representatives from autonomous subsidiaries)

Contracts are written with each host-nation firm.

Autonomous Firm 1	Autonomous Firm 2	Autonomous Firm 3
(Worker owned)	(Community owned)	(Customer owned)

The model synthesizes the principles of democracy with profit making. First, the "subsidiary" firms in host nations may appoint representatives to the board of directors of the global firm. Second, the host firms can be employee owned, community owned, or customer owned; they contract with the global firm for production or retail purposes. Third, a cooperative multinational may itself be owned by its host constituencies who are employees or customers. Finally, special systems of accountability are developing whereby social audits are conducted along with financial audits.[33]

Model 3. International ESOPs, United States

In 1987, the headquarters of the Polaroid Corporation in the United States introduced a special employee-ownership plan in its U.K. subsidiary. The aim of the plan was to encourage all employees to build up a personal shareholding in the business and to participate in the company as part owners as well as employees.

In the Polaroid Equity Participation Plan, all employees with two or more years of service can participate. Each participant can purchase (U.S.) Polaroid Corporation shares through a trust created for this purpose. Employees can invest up to 2 percent of their yearly salary. The company matches the employee contributions on a one-share-for-one-share basis. Under current English rules for approved profit-sharing schemes, the purchased shares need to remain in the trust for at least two years. At the end of the two years, the employees can leave their purchased shares with the trustees until they leave the company, have them transferred into their name, or have them sold by the trustees. Dividends are distributed to all participating employees. About 80 percent of the employees are participating in the plan on a voluntary basis.[34]

A Century of Corporate Globalization

In 1917, Walter Weyl visualized a world organization of industry, suggesting the possibility of a common control of firms established among companies through the interchange of stock. Weyl was an early progressive leader in the United States who, along with Walter Lippman, later helped establish the journal the *New Republic.* Weyl believed that global economic cooperation would eventually create a situation in which the interest of each nation in the welfare of its neighbors would become so great as to "make international war as unthinkable as war of Pennsylvania against New York."[35]

In the 1970s, Barnet and Müller said:

> The men who run the global corporations are the first in history with organization, technology, money, and ideology to make a credible try at managing the world as an integrated unity. . . . The Napoleonic system, Hitler's Thousand Year Reich, the British Empire, and the Pax Americana left their traces, but none managed to create anything approaching a global organization for administering the planet that could last even a generation. The world, it seems, cannot be run by military occupation, though the dream persists.[36]

The managers of the world's corporate giants, they argued, proclaim their faith that where conquest has failed, business can succeed. The global corporation is the first institution in history dedicated to centralized planning on a world scale. These researchers are pessimistic about the future.

John Naisbett, a business analyst and forecaster, is optimistic about the future of global business. He argues "the bigger the system, the more efficient must be the parts." He sees *subsidiarity* as part of the future. Subsidiarity means that power is transferred, wherever it can be effective, to the lowest possible point in an organization. This is a principle espoused by civil-society theorists.

A good example of subsidiarity, Naisbett says, is IBM UK. The corporation is deconstructing into small companies to improve "nimbleness, speed and customer responsiveness," while retaining some of the advantages of size, like breadth of investment in research and development. In mid-1993, IBM's London headquarters announced that the U.K. sales operation was being divided into 30 separate businesses, each of which, on its own authority, could establish prices and costs and be totally responsible to its customers. Some businesses would have only 50 employees. Headquarters will exercise no control unless the business starts to fall apart. The IBM announcement said, "The creation of a business federation will give more ownership and accountability to business managers, enabling the company to return to profit more quickly." A press release by IBM in April 1999 announced that it had signed "the biggest ever" automated teller machine (ATM) partnership with the Co-operative Bank in the United Kingdom.[37]

Naisbett is not the only contemporary optimist on the future of global markets. George Gilder writes in the *Harvard Business Review,* "As new computer systems decentralize control and empower people all along the information chain, they dissolve conventions of ownership, design, manufacturing, executive style, and national identity." The Brooktree Company, he says, is a case in point. It is a global firm specializing in digital video information, owned by one-third of its 450 employees, half of whom are engineers. Gilder explains, "Brooktree is not a hierarchy but an information heterarchy with multiple centers of power and hundreds of on-line workstations around the globe. The company has no one factory of its own but links its process technology with any number of major chip fabs [fabricators] around the world. Its devices are made in Japan or the United States, packaged in Korea, and tested in San Diego."[38]

The Flaws in Global Enterprise Experiments

Not all observers of experiments in decentralizing global corporations are optimistic. Critics point to the exploitation of workers, dangerous products, and environmental damages produced by multinationals. Experimenting with international ESOPs, they say, is a bad practice. The ESOP's incentives and dividends for host employees will increase host support for a foreign firm—even when it is exploiting the environment. This step in foreign worker ownership does not normally mean that these workers vote for the corporate board but rather focuses worker incentives on getting money through dividends; host ownership will increase employee loyalty but will not serve as a monitor against worldwide malpractice.

ESOP researchers argue back. Employee-ownership firms in the United States, they say, have increased worker participation in management faster, when compared with conventional firms. (As more firms become worker owned, theoretically, greater levels of participatory management will rise; indeed, there is a positive statistical correlation between ownership and participation.) Participative management includes self-organizing employee teams, enhanced job responsibility, and other types of autonomous groups in which employees increase their self-initiative and degree of control in decision making. Therefore, even if an ESOP firm will require monitoring, it is a first step toward creating a self-accountable corporation.[39]

Critics of global corporations would likely agree that the model of the proposed decentralized system in Puerto Rico and the system of multinational cooperatives in Canada (models 1 and 2 discussed previously) show great promise for strong local checks against global corporate power, but there is much more observation needed in the coming decades. We review global problems and solutions again in Part 3.

Final Comment

Corporate employees, local communities, industries, and the society at large as well as people in host countries have cultivated the principle of mutual self-governance. At each level, we can see how old systems of command are transforming into systems of mutual accountability. The past systems in which a few people were in direct authority over many are changing. The business corporation is no longer the command system that it was in the early twentieth century. It has been modified by systems of accountability and self-management. Local communities are discovering that they can avoid the old political oligarchies and "company towns" by organizing democratic community corporations. Whole industries have organized to set standards of safety and health. People in host communities are increasingly given the option to participate in corporate governance through joint ownership in global subsidiaries or by contracts, franchises, or partnerships.

Such systems of accountability are emerging slowly and experimentally. People are "reconstructing corporations," so to speak, as these systems expand around the world. People are introducing principles of mutual interest and accountability into a capitalist market that continues to be organized on the principles of self-interest and profitability.[40]

Meanwhile, leaders in the United Nations are seeking a world economy that is reliable, profitable, civil, and accountable. A self-accountable economy neither exploits workers by lowering safety and health standards nor destroys the environment. The UN's Economic and Social Council, the Study of Transnational Corporations within the UN's UNCTAD, the Food and Agricultural Organization, the International Labour Organization, and other agencies concern themselves with the deleterious effects of global firms.

But today there are no world law or global agencies designed to monitor firms in the way government agencies do in the United States. The UN has no authority to regulate global stock exchanges or to monitor electronic banking at the global level, even when critics say these business systems jeopardize the stability of financial markets. As we shall see in chapter 8, UN leaders are seeking to create a legal basis for establishing a civil (accountable) economy operating as a "global commons."[41]

In the next chapter, we continue to discuss this principle of accountability developing through civic movements in which people fight to establish a more civil society. People in countries around the globe become a force for thinking about an economy that goes beyond standard capitalism and does not become fascism or state socialism. Local citizens are calling for a form of market economy that works in the interest of people as well as in the interest of business and government.

3 A Community-Oriented Economy

> The community is already in the process of dissolution where each man begins to eye his neighbor as an enemy.
>
> —Justice Learned Hand, speech to the Board of Regents, October 24, 1952

The loss of local self-determination in the face of the growing power of global markets is evident around the world, but civic leaders could reverse that trend. Local civic leaders and global corporate executives have an interest in creating social capital, that is, those kinds of cooperative relationships that result in efficiency and profitability. Local and global leaders both view cooperation as essential to their interests. New partnerships between local and global leaders could produce a more productive, humane, remunerative, safe, and energetic community life.

Our proposal is that civil partnerships happen when civic and executive leaders cooperate to maximize their separate interests. Civic leaders seek local development, and executives seek decentralized management for more effective global competition. Local leaders and global executives are both able to fulfill their objectives in a civil development of the marketplace. The purpose of this chapter is to show how the problem of declining local power in the face of increasing global power is solved.

First, we will examine the problem of declining communities as business corporations expand from local to national and rapidly into global markets.

Second, we will look at civic movements that represent a "bottom-up" force fighting against the negative impact of big firms and governments. Local people are in civic movements to gain power, to increase their authority in the midst of the centralizing trends of big business. We will survey models of new co-op businesses that result from civic movements and visualize their connection with recent business strategies.

Third, we will look at business strategies, that is, the "top-down" policies of CEOs who "de-center" the corporate line of authority. Some CEOs try to advance the strength of local management and to improve communities in ways that combine with greater returns for themselves.

Fourth, we will compare these two trends—civic (bottom up) and corporate (top down)—to see how they produce civil markets. Considering a possible mix of "civic cooperation" with strategies of "business decentralization," we will propose how local authority can develop in the midst of competitive markets. We suggest that local grassroots organizations could become more self-reliant and corporations could become more accountable at the global level. But this will require the right conditions and a meeting of different minds.

The Problem: Declining Community Life

Social scientists have argued that the overall strength and solidarity of local communities began to decline with the rise of capitalism and industrialization. Now, with the appearance of global markets at the end of the twentieth century, the solidarity of towns, villages, and city neighborhoods is even more threatened. The power of local self-determination erodes with expanding market forces. Conglomerate corporations centralize control in big cities in their effort to compete with one another. Small communities and city neighborhoods then have less control over their economy. There are fewer locally owned firms where resident owners are sympathetic to personal needs in the way Adam Smith thought was essential to a moral economy. Localities are increasingly served by subsidiaries and franchises controlled by absentee executives. For some social scientists, the deterioration of local communities appears to be an inevitable and unavoidable consequence of expanding markets.[1]

The problem is worsened when communities compete against one another to get corporations to locate in them. Hoping to create more jobs and capital, local officials agree not to tax (or regulate) business, consent to build roads to factories, and give municipal money to attract firms. Big corporations, with their greater agility to move globally, become more powerful and profitable while communities give away their assets. Absentee executives, out of touch with local needs and sustainability, transfer local offices, move retail outlets, and shut down factories on the basis of market demand on input availability and price. Absentee managers making decisions in distant cities often determine whether local economies can survive. When firms move out, communities lose taxes and jobs, and the churches and schools, which depend on the economic base, also suffer. In the process, there is an increase in crime, drugs, and violence in the streets.[2]

An overemphasis on community control can lead to its own problems of local oligopoly, class-based prejudice, discriminatory practices, loss of privacy, narrow self-interest, dogma, and resistance to change. When business expanded its markets to the national level, the creation of big cities seemed to be the answer—greater freedom, plurality, separateness, interracial and multicultural life, and an alternative to the problems of localism and provincialism. Yet, the growth of the metropolis has shown its own problems of anarchy, crime, impersonality, detachment, isolation, and oligarchies.[3]

We are talking about a balance in community life in which the worst of two extremes (local prejudice/dominance and metropolitan crime/anarchy) can be eliminated by respecting the virtues of closeness and distance, individuality and community. Iris Marion Young, professor at the Graduate School of Public and International Affairs, University of Pittsburgh, asks:

> Could Americans design local political institutions that correspond to regional economic interdependence at the same time that they encourage neighborhood-level participation, public discussion about regional problems in diverse local publics, and a sense of justice that people in the region owe one another?[4]

Development analysts see the Third Sector as a movement independent of government. The Third Sector grows from the inside out, like the big bang, from particles to atoms to molecules to cells, moving upward and outward, not from the outside in, and not so much by top-down decisions of big governments. This Third Sector is an inside-out, bottom-up development, which is happening around the world.

Civic movements are capable of overthrowing oppressive states and dictatorships. The destruction of communist states in Europe happened suddenly and dramatically through civic movements, including the Solidarity movement in Poland and the Velvet Revolution in Czechoslovakia. Historians argue that nongovernmental organizations (NGOs) were an effective force in toppling the authoritarian regimes in Eastern Europe and the Soviet Union, more than resistance groups steeped in political ideology and backed by paramilitary campaigns. Soviet historian Frederick Starr argues that the rapid growth of the Third-Sector activity placed enormous pressure on the already weakened Party apparatus. The effervescence of NGOs of all types was the single most distinctive aspect of the revolution of 1989.[5]

Civic movements were also part of the democratization of Argentina and Chile. These movements were forged from people below, citizens without power, toppling regimes that seemed to have absolute power.

These movements are best explained in the idea of civil society. Civil-society analysts are interested in how people can transfer power from big governments and big corporations to local organizations. This civil-society idea is represented in the assertion that civic authority is best located in a socially mediated market. Civic leaders want their localities to have self-sustaining and self-governing economies.[6]

Civil society is created through the action of people in local associations—political organizations, social clubs, nonprofit corporations, community development corporations, religious associations, and small businesses. In these civic movements people make decisions by personal agreement, consensus, and one person vote more than by command bureaucracy, or by the power of money, or by voting on the stock market. Civic movements are active around the world, building beyond conventional markets and states. Let us look at some of them.

Civic Movements around the World: Grassroots Development

The civic movements described in the following are part of a Third Sector emerging between business and government. NGOs are constructed in this global "movement." Civil society develops when people create cooperative associations that go beyond sheer competition and emphasize cooperation and self-reliance.

A "civic movement" took place in a suburb of Karachi, Pakistan, where the Orangi Pilot Project enlisted the voluntary help of 28,000 families to construct 430,000 feet of underground sewers and built more than 28,000 latrines for local residents. A civic movement happened in India, where the Self-Employed Women's Association, a trade union of low-income women in Ahmedabad, provided free legal services for women, child-care services, and training courses in carpentry, plumbing, bamboo work, and midwifery. In Nepal, grassroots NGOs, working with local populations, built dams at one-fourth the cost of comparable construction done by the government.

In Sri Lanka, the Sarvodaya Sharanadana movement lists 7,700 on its staff working in more than 8,000 villages, helping local populations mobilize resources and create self-sufficient communities. In Malyasia, the Consumers Association of Penang works with rural communities, helping them secure governmental assistance and protecting them from exploitative development schemes. In Senegal, the Committee to Fight for the End of Hunger has 20,000 members helping farmers promote food crops rather than exports. A civic movement is evident in the Philippines, where PAMALAKAYA, an NGO representing 50,000 fishers, lobbied to preserve communal fishponds and provides ongoing training and education for its members.[7]

There was a struggle of the Chiapas people in Mexico for greater local autonomy, economic fairness and equity, and political rights within their communities. Gustavo Esteva, a Mexican political analyst, calls the Chiapas rebellion the first revolution of the twenty-first century. Unlike earlier rebellions, in which local citizens called upon their fellow Mexicans to take up arms against the state, in this case citizens joined with one another to establish the liberation of local spaces from outside colonization.

Indigenous people are at the forefront of many civic movements. In Ecuador, for example, they have organized to reclaim their lands, protect the Eucadorean rain forests from foreign oil companies, and block a government agricultural modernization program that would drive them off their farms. In Peru, they have formed a 300,000-member alliance to initiate projects that combine environmental and indigenous land objectives. National Indian organizations from Peru, Bolivia, Ecuador, Brazil, and Colombia have formed an international alliance representing over a million people to press for Indian land rights.

The women of Kenya's Greenbelt movement have established a cooperative that created 1,500 nurseries and planted over 10 million trees. The fishers of Kerala State in India have organized cooperatives to protect their coastal fisheries' resources. Japanese women have organized their own (Seikatsu) cooperatives with suppliers to assure safe and healthful products and require that they treat workers and nature properly. In hundreds of communities in Canada, Argentina, Australia, New Zealand, and the United States, and elsewhere, people are creating their own community currencies with such names as LETs, green dollars, or time dollars. Local people want to free themselves from colonization by the global financial system, to revitalize their communities, and to build economic self-reliance.[8]

Observers of these co-ops and nongovernmental organizations call them "social markets." Indigenous people create a market of microenterprises, like cooperative taxis for public transport or intervillage food trading networks. These networks are shaped as much by personal exchange as by economic exchange. These social networks are growing. People in this Third Sector promote businesses to finance their own expansion, but they remain in charge; the nonprofit sector is sometimes in charge of the profit sector. Today there are more than 35,000 voluntary associations in "developing" nations.[9]

The same democratic associative trends can be seen in the economies of "developed" nations. England has more than 350,000 voluntary organizations; France has more than 43,000; Germany is "growing" a Third Sector at a faster rate than its business sector and its government sector. Between 1970 and 1987, the nonprofit sector grew by more than 5 percent: in the late 1980s there were more than 300,000 voluntary organizations in Germany. In Italy during the 1970s the voluntary sector was largely centered on the Catholic Church, but in the past two decades nonreligious volunteer associations and groups have been taking an important role in local communities. More than 15.4 percent of the adult population in Italy volunteers its time to activities in the Third Sector.

Today in Japan, the Third Sector has grown so dramatically that thousands of nonprofit organizations attend to the cultural, social, and economic needs of the populace. Some 23,000 charitable organizations *(koeki hojin)* operate in Japan. In addition, there are 12,000 social welfare organizations *(shakaifukushi hojin)* that administer day-care centers, services for the elderly, maternal and child health services, and women's protective services.[10]

In December 1993, representatives from dozens of countries announced the formation of an international association called Civicus. Civicus organizers had witnessed and participated in local movements advancing voluntary social development all over the world. The first executive director, Miklos Marschall, labeled the growth of NGOs as "civil society." The mission of Civicus was to help such movements "cultivate volunteerism and community service."[11]

The world's civic movements are too many to describe here, but they produce democratic structures, such as co-ops, community-oriented enterprises, confederations, and nonprofit firms in the Third Sector. This social economy is characterized more by "cooperation" than by competition; its interest is more often in people than high profits; and it looks more toward values of equity and human interdependence than toward dominance and hierarchies.[12]

Let us look in more detail at the business structures created by people in these civic movements before we examine how they link in principle with a corporate "top-down" management policy in big business. These civic movements produce businesses based on the principles of cooperation while current management debates the meaning of cooperation and cautiously moves in this direction.

The Result of Civic Movements: Models of Co-op Businesses and Markets

The cooperative movement began with the historic appearance of corporate capitalism in the 1840s, though some proponents claim earlier origins. Civic movements carry the ideals of that co-op movement, and they also show kinship with what we have called "transitional" capitalist enterprises, such as profit/nonprofit partnerships, employee-owned firms, social-investment firms, and community corporations. The question is whether the capitalist society is giving birth to a different order of markets in this cauldron of competitive change.

Cooperatives are based on Adam Smith's principle of mutual self-regulation, but they did not develop as a movement until after his death. They are businesses in which people join in a common cause to provide members with goods and services. They are owned and democratically controlled by their members. Surpluses generated by co-ops are allocated to members in proportion to their purchases or to the kind of work they do in them.[13]

The people who work in producer cooperatives are the owners, while the customers who select and buy their products and services own consumer cooperatives. Producer (worker) co-ops and consumer (customer) co-ops have developed successfully in countries around the world. In the United States, the co-op movement developed in a whole variety of fields, including banking, media, services, industry, and agriculture.[14]

Producer co-ops have had less development numerically in the United States than consumer co-ops, but employee stock ownership plan (ESOP) legislation—along with management strategies for employee participation in firms—is changing that picture. The two trends in U.S. corporations—employee participation and employee ownership—are continuing to grow at a steady pace. If this pace continues, the logical outcome should be a system of producer co-ops that looks like the outcome of that civic-oriented movement of workers in Mondragon, Spain (see chap. 2).

Civic movements have led toward the establishment of business cooperatives in firms and market sectors. In co-op model 1, we see the result of a civic movement in Japan, motivated in part by the concern of women who wanted local power.

Co-op Model 1. The Seikatsu Consumer Cooperative Club

The Seikatsu Consumer Cooperative Club was founded in Tokyo to allow families to buy pure milk at affordable prices. It is basically a "woman's movement." Beginning in 1965, this cooperative club evolved into an activist network so that by 1992 Seikatsu, with 225,000 families, had $700 million in total sales, which included 161 related worker collectives with 4,200 worker-owners. The club relies on a group structure based on the *Han*, an association of eight to 10 neighbors who facilitate local decision making. Its aim is to sustain a society of communities emphasizing cooperation. Seikatsu evolved from being a network of buying clubs with the work done by members to offering goods and services to the public. It began to organize worker co-ops, managed on a one person/one vote basis. Its members generated most capital for the co-ops.[15]

These kinds of civic movements have been happening around the world, but they do not get the press that focuses on big corporations and politics. Nonetheless, these movements are important to understand as growing seeds in the garden of global markets.

Atlantic Canadians started co-ops early in this century, and they have grown as a civic movement that is better prepared than other regions of the world to deal with global corporations. On the northwest coast of Cape Breton Island lies the small Acadian community of Cheticamp. Sandwiched between the sea and the highlands, Cheticamp looks like many other Maritime coastal towns, but there is a big difference; the town's 10 cooperatives form the economic backbone of the area. Residents report that they have "a deep-rooted sense of community and identity." The community may not be without problems, but Cheticamp stands a better chance than other localities to survive as a self-reliant community. They may be able to negotiate a civil solution to the "takeover" of their community by global corporations.

Canadians in this Atlantic region are concerned about

a few huge transnational corporations [coming to] dominate large parts of our economic, cultural and social environments. They achieve this control through vertical integration and diversification. Vertical integration means, in the grocery business, for example, that one large corporation controls the farms, food processing plants, wholesalers and grocery stores. Diversification means that a single transnational controls a wide range of enterprises, such as manufacturing, forestry products, banking, the media, real estate and entertainment. This may generate plenty of profit in the Maritimes for these corporations, but it flows outside to be invested elsewhere.[16]

Atlantic Canadians will fight for their rights. In co-op model 2, Atlantians have created an entirely different business system than the global market system that is about to enter their territory. The question of justice in their economy is very real to them: Will these people be able to negotiate with these transnational corporations to maintain their autonomy?

To put the problem metaphorically: Will people be able to create a Magna Carta in this feudal war between kingdoms? Will they be able to set a new direction for business to recognize their productivity through cooperation? Can the co-ops make social contracts with global firms? Can both Atlantic Canadians and global firms win in the new market? In sum, can this sector of the global market remain both accountable and profitable?

Co-op Model 2. Co-op Atlantic

Co-op Atlantic is a cooperative system serving Canada's Atlantic Provinces: Newfoundland, New Brunswick, Nova Scotia, and Prince Edward Island. It was founded in 1927; today it serves the needs of its owners, 161 retail, producer, agricultural, housing, and fishing cooperatives and a co-op newspaper. It wholesales groceries, hardware, petroleum, dry goods, and livestock supplies, provides assistance with management training, and operates Atlantic People Housing, a subsidiary that manages and constructs co-op housing. In 1993, Co-op Atlantic wholesale sales to member co-ops exceeded $440 million. Co-op membership includes over 168,000 families of primary producers and consumers representing more than 500,000 people. Member co-ops have over 5,000 workers and over $300 million in assets. Co-op food stores now account for 19 percent of all food sales in Atlantic Canada. Efforts are under way to expand into other business and production areas. Each co-op is self-governing and democratic in operation.[17]

While we wait and see whether Co-op Atlantic is able to cope with the changing scene of global markets, there are similar cooperatives facing the same situation all over the world. According to the National Cooperative Business Association, there are 47,000 cooperatives in the United States that generate more than $100 billion in annual economic activity. As many as 100 million Americans—40 percent of the population—are directly served by some type of cooperative endeavor.

The cooperative movement is not all rosy in the United States. Some co-ops have become bureaucracies and look like regular businesses. The big mutual insurance companies, for example, began as customer (policyholder) co-ops but lost their original purpose and mission. Some of this shift toward bureaucracy and pure business can be attributed to the competitive environment in which co-ops must develop to survive.[18]

Producer co-ops and consumer co-ops have competitive interests as represented in our next case on the Swiss dairy industry (co-op model 3). Producer (worker) co-ops seek the highest prices possible in the context of a free market; consumer- (customer-) owned co-ops seek the lowest possible prices in the market. They have a natural conflict of interest, but in some countries co-op markets are organized to negotiate prices and purchases with a sense of ethics and fairness. The practice is notable especially where there are a balance of power and established procedures for negotiation. Producer and consumer co-operatives work best when they are both powerful, as in this case of the Swiss dairy market.

Co-op Model 3. Swiss Dairy Market

Swiss milk producers are organized into more than 4,000 local cooperatives, 13 regional associations of cooperatives, and the Central Association of Swiss Milk Producers, a confederation of associations representing all milk producers and, hence, a large share of all Swiss farmers. In addition to engaging in milk production, the local cooperatives and the regional associations are active in milk processing.

Milk processors are organized into six business associations divided into two large groups. One consists of cheese manufacturers, with more than 1,000 members in all, organized into a complex system of three interlocking associations, two of which represent independent cheese makers. The other group, with about 10–20 member firms, consists of industrialized dairies. The Central Association of Milk-Producers and an Association of Milk Buyers jointly regulate the general conditions of purchase between buyers and sellers of raw milk. Regional and local associations of milk producers and milk buyers negotiate contracts that regulate both prices and various services. This matching between supply and demand takes place through democratic associations outside government. The two main retailers, MIGROS and COOP, represent the consumers directly; together they have 39 percent of the market. In other cases, producer-consumer co-ops successfully "self-regulate" product quality, safety, and level of output without major government control.[19]

The cooperative movement grows quietly in free markets around the world—in South America, North America, Japan, India, and Africa. Now what is the connection between people in civic movements and people in conventional business?

Most CEOs would not connect these civic protests with the "cooperative movement." Civic protests look dangerous, and "cooperatives" are perceived as part of the Third Sector, different from business. But the two sectors are moving closer, perhaps evolving toward a more civil order of markets.

Business Strategies: Decentralizing Corporations
and Markets

The spirit of cooperation is recognized by CEOs today as essential for a business enterprise to succeed. The concept of cooperation is now within the culture of competitive enterprise, and the frictional difference between old ideologies of "competitive market vs. the co-operative market" is disappearing. Viewing together these two different principles helps us understand how a "civil economy" may be the most profitable and humane direction to go in the twenty-first century.

There is a profit-minded reason for decentralization. CEOs in big firms find that a centralized bureaucracy can cause problems in efficiency and lower revenue. For these reasons, they have begun experiments to localize authority in global firms, that is, decentralize their operations. CEOs hope to gain efficiency along with accountability to people in localities. These trends in business show some kinship with the century-and-a-half-old "cooperative movement" growing quietly in capitalist markets. We argue that the principles of competition in capitalism and the principles of cooperation in grassroots cooperative movements show a potential for building a more community-oriented and profitable economy. A community-oriented economy requires cooperation among competitors for the common good.

A trend toward "partnerships" and corporate decentralization is taking place paradoxically at the same time that there is a trend toward mergers and giant conglomerates. CEOs in big corporations are restructuring their "line management systems" (based on strict command/obedience) by delegating more authority to lower managers and stakeholders. They are also subcontracting with localities overseas. These corporate policies could allow Atlantic Canadians to sustain their autonomy and increase cooperation and partnerships. The two systems match in principle—the ideals of people in many grassroots organizations and the plans of CEOs.[20]

Businesses today are entering strategic alliances for research and development or for competitive advantage in a chain from production to consumption. The desire of a firm to create such an alliance also shows a willingness to give up some autonomy and control in exchange for partnership benefits.

To put this another way, U.S. firms are forming coalitions with other organizations as part of business strategy. These strategic partnerships become a leverage allowing each firm to increase its reach without adding fixed capacity and to gain a measure of stability in a turbulent environment. Joining with organizations at different points on the value chain provides the financial benefits of sharing costs and gaining economies of scale. Business firms achieve these gains by pooling resources with companies in pursuit of common ends by way of a consortium or an alliance with other firms in a field where they may lack competence themselves. There are profits to be made by linking closely with stakeholders, such as suppliers, customers, and communities. There may be a new deal in the making.

Research suggests that such partnerships have a significant impact on the social organization of each company. The desire of a firm to create an alliance means a willingness to give up some autonomy and control for partnership benefits. Significant partnerships include stakeholder agreements, supplier and customer contracts, and joint ventures. These alliances show overall changes in the command system of the corporation. For example, managers in closer contact with the organization's partners become more central to the strategic communication flow, and their power inside the organization increases; as the importance of the outside partnership grows, the subunit managing the relationship gains power; the staff role changes from "control" to "consultation." The cooperative process becomes more significant to the corporation.

Partnerships require a new set of skills for executives and managers. A type of cooperative problem solving replaces the old adversarial bargaining. Threats to cut off a customer's shipment or cancel a supplier's order or similar acts of brinkmanship are seen to be no longer the best tactical alternative. Managers are learning to resolve points of contention and deal with real issues instead of taking the easy option of avoiding a problematic situation. Partnership is a commitment not to end the relationship abruptly. It means subsequent investments will reinforce that commitment. It is a new path.[21]

There is optimism about the possible results of corporate partnerships and decentralization, but the question is whether this partnership can occur with people in grassroots movements. The details are unfolding, slowly. Local corporations like community land trusts, community development corporations, and customer-owned banks are making contracts with global corporations, thereby keeping big "centralized mergers" accountable through this Third-Sector link. But at present, social contracts between NGOs and community corporations and global corporations are few in number. Can global firms continue to see the benefits of collaborating with the Third Sector? How can this collaboration make everyone profitable and accountable?

A Business Movement: Decentralized
Management through Cooperation

There is an allied management movement to reckon with here in contemplating strategic cooperation with civic movements. CEOs in leading-edge companies are surrendering selected portions of their authority to managers in lower divisions of the hierarchy. They are reorganizing their companies into profit centers, encouraging competition and cooperation among them. Managers in lower divisions are building markets and alliances inside and outside the firm, which become a substitute for the old administrative fiat and direct "command authority." Hewlett-Packard's corporate policy, for example, is for its executives to "guide by persuasive leadership" rather than by "command and demand." MCI executives stimulate "creative argument" between top and lower managers in an effort to preserve the autonomy of operating managers. Johnson and Johnson encourages coalitions of business subsidiaries by creating separate companies with their own boards of directors, hoping to provide a measure of local control and ownership.

While pressure to localize authority grows from grassroots movements, some big corporations and whole market sectors are proceeding independently toward decentralization. In addition, corporations are writing codes of conduct, protecting stakeholders, setting health norms, writing safety rules and environmental standards, and establishing procedures for self-monitoring. Some trade associations have done this while they advance the purpose of business. Let us look at some examples in the business sector.

Decentralizing Business: Cases of Firms,
Market Sectors, and Customer Relations

Business is decentralizing strategically to advance the participation of employees in firms in ways that are influencing changes in the organization of whole market sectors. The strategic logic of this management policy is to advance greater powers of self-direction by lower managers and create more local stability and self-reliance and more money.

We begin first with models of decentralization among firms in which employees gain self-management and ownership, evolving toward producer co-ops. Second, we move to market sectors that are trending toward market co-ops. Third, we look at business-customer relations, moving toward consumer co-ops. Fourth, we look at "horizontal business ecology" in which the private sector and communities together take account of the environment.

Firms

The Milwaukee Journal at first sought to develop a centralized command system but then reversed its direction and created a decentralized association of locally managed subsidiaries, giving more power to their local employees in distant cities (model 1).

Business Firm Model 1. The Milwaukee Journal

The Milwaukee Journal is an employee-owned company in the state of Wisconsin with over 2,000 employees. In the 1940s, the original owner gave the employees ownership shares in the company, and the company subsequently grew in size and productivity, eventually buying subsidiary firms in allied markets. Company headquarters in Milwaukee had a "community council" of employee representatives (organized by departments) to offer advice to management appointed by the employee-elected board of directors. But when the Journal began buying new companies, management did not practice the same mode of democracy in these subsidiary firms. As they bought out independent firms in different parts of the country, they made them part of their command systems of management in Milwaukee headquarters.

When employees in the Journal's subsidiaries learned about the democratic practices in Milwaukee, they complained to the board of directors. The issue was whether to extend the democratic ideas across the country to the Journal's extended business system.

The board discussed whether the subsidiary employees should remain under the command of the Milwaukee firm or whether local subsidiary employees should have the option to buy shares and be given representation on the Milwaukee board of directors. The board decided that subsidiary employees should be given the right to buy into the ownership, to buy shares in the main company.

Today the Milwaukee company takes these geographically distant employees seriously in its management policies. When deciding whether to shut down or transfer its work in subsidiaries overseas, it must consult with representatives of these subsidiaries on the top board. The result is a greater concern for and interest in maintaining local relations in this growing firm.[22]

Where is employee ownership going in the future? If employee ownership is combined with employee self-management, the preceding case suggests a trend toward localizing authority, although the company is expanding itself and building subsidiaries. Employee-owners in distant subsidiaries will need to be consulted whenever a big company moves overseas.

When a company is very large, it is not sufficient simply to include representatives of employees on the board of directors. The structure of co-determination (Germany) and producer cooperatives (Mondragon) is not adequate by itself to stop strikes. If there is no worker participation at lower levels of the corporate hierarchy, there will be labor-management problems. This is illustrated in the case of Ularco, a Mondragon cooperative that grew into a bureaucracy (model 2).

Business Firm Model 2. Ularco in Mondragon

Ulgor was a Mondragon firm of 2,000 workers. Although its board of directors was employee elected, management had a strong line of command over workers. At one point, dissident workers under this strict command system went on strike. The employee-elected board was embarrassed by a strike among its own workers. After some deliberation, the board crafted a federation of companies and restructured their "departments and divisions" into autonomous companies, each with its own corporate board. A new corporate structure emerged and was called Ularco. Ularco became a federation of company subsidiaries, each of which had employee representation on a separate board.

The new Ularco organization included a higher board to represent all the autonomous companies (former departments in the one company). The powers of this higher board were restricted to administrative matters, such as uniform bookkeeping, and marketing products for the autonomous firms. The overarching board of this Ularco federation had no power to intervene in local management or local systems of work. By centralizing their accounting and marketing operations, however, they kept their corporate community and the necessary uniformity in accounting, as well as their sales power in European markets. Simultaneously, they preserved job autonomy and self-direction in local work systems.[23]

There is a similarity between the U.S. business firm (the Milwaukee Journal) and Mondragon's cooperative. *They were both the same size and they both found improvements by decentralizing their organization.*

Market Sectors

Experimenting with new systems of worker self-management is often persuasive ("catching") within an industry. A whole industry or trade sector can begin to practice self-management, firm by firm. This happened with the airline industry, but it is a slow process to change the management systems, create new training programs, and design a different order of administration. Model 1 illustrates what happened in U.S. steel companies.

Market Sector Model 1. Decentralizing the Steel Industry

1. Weirton Steel was a division of the National Steel Corporation in 1982 during a decline of industrywide profits. Other nations were becoming fierce competitors. The U.S. steel industry was suffering. A divestiture program at National was designed to sell less profitable segments. On March 2, 1982, Jack Redline, then president of the Weirton Division, announced that National Steel had presented the Weirton Division with a pair of alternatives: one was to close the plant; the other was an "employee buyout" of the plant. A local committee formed and decided to hire attorneys to evaluate the possibilities of success. The signing of a buyout agreement with National Steel occurred January 11, 1984. The projections of profits for that year were $8 million, but the employees earned $62 million on sales of $1 billion. The high profits resulted from wage and benefit reductions, aggressive marketing, reductions in operating costs, and overall employee mutual trust—contributing to higher productivity and pride in accomplishment. Local people said, "Without the buyout, this place would be a ghost town."[24]

The United Steelworkers of America much later negotiated an agreement with the National Steel Corporation allowing it to name a director to the company board. In addition, the deal permitted a greater amount of power sharing from factory floor to the boardroom.

2. Other steel companies, including the Wheeling-Pittsburgh Steel Corporation and the LTV Corporation, now allow union board representation. These firms needed union cooperation to emerge from bankruptcy. A new mood for employee self-governance is moving across market sectors; the hoped-for results are to avoid unemployment, improve employee well-being, and save communities.[25]

There is a close connection between employee ownership and achieving more authority for communities. Employee-owners are less likely to move their enterprise to other nations where wages are lower. They will more likely think of creative alternatives. Hence, this movement within a whole industry has its place in building a community-oriented economy.

Now let us look at an entirely different market sector. Sports in the

United States have become big business. The owners of teams want to maximize profits, regardless of how people in the local community see their teams as "their own." Teams are bought, sold, and transferred from one community to the next according to the principle of profitability. The business is going global. Residents in Seattle, Washington, had to fight to keep Japanese investors from buying its baseball team, the Mariners. But that will not be the last time a global firm will try to purchase a local recreational company.

For almost a half century, people in Cleveland took their football team seriously. They endured rain and bitter cold to support their home team, the Cleveland Browns. Then, owner Art Modell moved the football team to Baltimore. Clevelanders were furious and felt deceived, cheated. But a few hundred miles away in Green Bay, Wisconsin, a city of 97,000 people, there was no worry about their team relocating to another city. This case will help explain the importance of the "normative order" that can arise between a local company and its national trade organization (model 2).

Market Sector Model 2. Decentralizing National Sports

In 1922, the Green Bay Packers were bordering on bankruptcy. Gate receipts were lower than expected. Then four fans decided to help. They reorganized the franchise into a nonprofit corporation whose 15 directors would be elected by local shareholders. With help from the city and the school board, the nonprofit built the team's first stadium. During the depression, the team stumbled, but nonprofit leaders came up with a novel idea. Pointing to how important the team was for local business, the Packer's Executive Committee convinced the Green Bay Chamber of Commerce to organize its members into neighborhood teams and sell $25 shares, door to door. At this moment, 1,915 shareholders own 4,634 shares of the team, and 60 percent live in Green Bay. Shareholders can trade shares within their families or sell them back to the corporation for $25. But nobody can own more than 20 shares. The direct benefits to Green Bay are about $60 million per year, and local charities earn about $400,000 each year operating concession stands. The team's victory in the 1997 Super Bowl boosted these numbers.

Because the football team is a nonprofit corporation, shareholders receive neither annual dividends nor capital gains on resale, though they do control the enterprise by voting for the board of directors. When the team runs a financial surplus, as it has in recent years, net revenues are reinvested in the stadium and the players. If the team were to experience a loss (it has not failed to sell out a game since 1958), the corporation could sell additional stock to members of the community to rejuvenate finances.[26]

It is vital to understand this case because of its connection to its larger profit corporation, the National Football League (NFL). A critical connection lies in the fact that the NFL maintains certain rules for all its 30 franchises. The "rules" in business federations can increase self-governance, lessen it, or even destroy a member firm.

One positive rule in the NFL for Green Bay is that revenues from the sales of television rights, tickets, T-shirts, and knickknacks are shared among all NFL teams and limits ("caps") are placed on the sum of the salaries a team can pay. Without these rules, the Packers would have lower revenues and be less able to compete for top players. But a negative rule is that the NFL also made it impossible for other teams to follow Green Bay's example. A single individual must own every franchise, with the exception of the Packers, at least 51 percent. Green Bay happened to have moved to "community ownership" before the rule was made.

This profit-oriented (NFL) corporation has the power to write the rules for its members. A larger federation in this case can maximize or minimize the power of self-governance for its members. It maximized the power of self-governance (local sustainability) of the Packers by sharing revenues. It reduced the options of members for local self-governance by forbidding any team to follow Green Bay's example. This is why *the kind* of "social governance" and *the kind* of rules that shape the market system are so important. The Supreme Court exempted this business corporation from being a monopoly. It could be pressured by the Justice Department to break up into competing leagues. This is a political decision, but it is also an issue in the social organization of markets. The department could require a restructuring of the sports market so that such leagues become mutually governed associations. They could be organized like a confederation in the same manner as trade associations.

Now let us look at how business has been active in bringing customers into its organization, very much like consumer co-ops but not exactly the same.

Business Customer Relations

We have discussed vertical-to-local decentralization with greater authority among lower-level employees and communities in firms and markets. Now let us look at decentralization in which the clients (or customers) of companies are given more attention and power in making decisions. Model 1 shows some examples of companies working closely with customer-stakeholders.

Customer Participation Model 1

Herman Miller sends its design teams to work at clients' offices to understand their furniture needs and produce prototypes to test on site, thereby speeding development time, reducing costs, and increasing client satisfaction. One manager said, "We bring customers in at the very beginning to become partners in design."

Black and Decker assigned a design team to work with 50 typical "do-it-yourself" homeowners around their homes and workshops and to accompany them on shopping trips to learn what they wanted in tools. This fresh understanding produced an award-winning product line, "Quantum," with interchangeable power sources, new safety features, free maintenance checkups, and a toll-free hot line for advice.

Honda videotaped customers testing new cars and had line workers call 4,700 Honda owners to get their criticisms and suggestions. The results were used to make thousands of changes over the past few years that made Honda the top-selling auto in the United States.

Westinghouse has developed such a close working relationship with the public utilities it serves that some managers exchange business plans and engage in joint reviews of each other's operations. "We work with the utilities in partnership arrangements to share our responsibilities," said a Westinghouse program manager.

Baxter Laboratories provide on-site inventory management of medical supplies for hospitals, sharing in both losses and gains. "This goes beyond loyalty," said a Baxter executive. "We share a common P&L [profit and loss]. You both make money by keeping costs down."

General Electric (GE) creates cross-company teams of its own employees and those of its clients to handle tough technical problems, even sending teams to training programs together. "Working as a single entity enhanced communications," said a GE vice president.[27]

These firms are single examples of small steps in civil development in a giant picture puzzle of capitalism in transition. Has the business system altered fundamentally? "No," say most analysts. Business leaders simply see that it is profitable to decentralize, to work and meet with stakeholders regularly, to set ecological standards. Yet, critics say that if managers really want to serve their customers better, they should have them serve on corporate boards.

When Louis Gestner replaced John Akers as CEO of IBM in 1993 and was exploring ways to revitalize the corporation, a prominent analyst advised the following.

If Gerstner is sincere, he should create a new board made up of IBM customers, suppliers, partners, employees . . . a new kind of IBM that couldn't help but be more responsible because the people in charge represent the company's future . . . and clearly signal that business as usual is dead at IBM.[28]

The business sector is slowly moving toward realizing a value in the principle of cooperation. The question now is whether civic movements and business can get together and produce still more accountability with profitability than now exists in the world economy.

Now let us look at how business is building horizontal/ecological relationships so that companies need not go outside their localities to obtain supplies but rather can utilize the wastes of other local companies as energy resources for themselves. Such activities, representing a movement toward ecological communities, are another facet of business that links with the cooperative movement.

Horizontal Business Ecology

The next cases describe how CEOs and local people planned "horizontal" and "local" decentralization to protect the environment and strengthen communities. In model 1, unusable waste products of local companies became the raw materials and organic feedstock for other local companies, creating an ecologically oriented community.

Horizontal Ecology Model 1. An Ecological Community in Denmark

The Danish town of Kalundborg is about 80 miles west of Copenhagen. Kalundborg is a model of what is called "industrial symbiosis," or "industrial ecology," involving a coal-fired electric power-generating plant, an oil refinery, a biotechnology product plant, a plasterboard factory, a sulfuric acid producer, cement producers, a local heating company, and local agricultural and horticultural interests. Asnaes, the electricity-generating plant, supplies process steam to the oil refinery and a pharmaceutical plant.

These local industries in Kalundborg have made innovative cost-benefit decisions that factored in an ecological social responsibility component. By working together, they synthesized local and human values with their need to maximize profits. Gyproc, the plasterboard producer, buys surplus gas from the refinery, reducing the need to burn coal. The refinery removes excess sulfur from the gas to make it cleaner burning: the removed sulfur is sold to the sulfuric acid plant. Asnaes has desulfurized its smoke, using a process that yields calcium sulfate as a side product, which is sold as "industrial gypsum" to Gyproc. In addition, fly ash from the desulfurization process is used for cement making and road building.

Asnaes uses its surplus heat to warm its own seawater fish farm, which produces 200 tons of trout and turbot a year for the French market. Local farmers use sludge from the fish farm as fertilizer. Novo Nordisk, which runs the pharmaceutical plant, also provides hundreds of thousands of tons of "nutritious sludge" used as a liquid fertilizer by local farmers. Previously, the sludge had been disposed of as waste, but Novo Nordisk began adding chalk lime and heating it to neutralize remaining microorganisms.[29]

This was a voluntary process. Government law required none of the actions taken by companies in this community; each exchange was negotiated independently between the firms themselves. Collectively these companies represent a synthesis of human and economic values by creating a network of local market interdependencies to sustain community life. Firms in other locales interested in building a civil, ecologically friendly local economy can imitate this example.

The development of civil society involves a creative synthesis of the values of government (justice and democracy), business (competition and efficiency), and voluntary organizations (cooperation and human purpose). A good example of this synthesis is illustrated by Sweden's innovative "Natural Step." Natural Step is a national movement building a consensus around environmental sustainability. Some 10,000 government officials are active in 16 specialized networks developing and carrying out action programs to achieve many environmental objectives. These objectives include 100 percent recycling of metals, eliminating the release of compounds that do not break down naturally in the environment, maintaining biological diversity, and reducing energy use to levels of sustainability. Forty-nine local governments, members of the Swedish Farmers Federation, and 22 large Swedish companies are working to align themselves with these objectives.

The next examples (model 2) are from the United States and concern energy conservation. In a typical U.S. community, 70 to 80 cents of every dollar spent on energy immediately leaves the local economy.[30] When local businesses, governments, schools, and households cut energy expenses, they have more disposable dollars to spend on other priorities. The money saved from reduced energy bills circulates in the community economy, strengthening its economic base.

Horizontal Ecology Model 2. Sustainable Energy in Local Economies

Osage, Iowa (population 3,500), started an energy efficiency program in 1974 through their public utility, which resulted in keeping an additional $1 million a year in the local economy. This program, relying on simple tools like caulk guns, duct tape, insulation, lightbulbs, and education, created an annual community economic stimulus equal to $1,000 per household.

Ellensburg, Washington (population 12,000), started energy efficiency programs in 1989 that resulted in an additional $6.84 million in industrial output. This saving was enough to support many more jobs for the community.

San Jose, California, established an energy management program in the early 1980s. Residents, businesses, and agencies cut more than $5.5 million from annual energy bills and saved enough energy each year to power 7,600 homes. San Jose predicts its sustainable energy programs will produce a countywide $33 million increase in wages and salaries and a net employment gain of 1,753 job years over a 10-year period.

Davis, California, is a university town of about 40,000 people. More than half of its population consists of students, faculty, or staff at the Davis campus of the University of California. When the city council refused to construct bike lanes, Davis faculty got themselves elected to the council and worked with others to construct more than 28 miles of bike paths. Today there are more than 28,000 bicycles in Davis, which comprise an important part of the transportation system. In addition, the council helped to organize the Energy Conservation Project, which took account of the unique local climate. An energy conservation code was devised that led to the restructuring of buildings to better utilize solar energy.[31]

These examples are related to what sociologist James Coleman calls "social capital." Social capital is a "sharing and a trust" among people that becomes related to efficiency and productivity; in these cases social capital has developed through cooperative structures created by the nonprofit and business sectors.[32]

In other cases, social capital is developed through codes of conduct constructed by employees and executives for the common good. Take model 3 as an example.

Horizontal Ecology Model 3.   Code of Conduct in a Chemical Company

Scott-Bader is a plastic resin manufacturing company in Wallaston, England, employing over 500 people. It is a worker-owned firm, civic-oriented, decentralized, productive, profitable, self-accountable, self-regulated, and democratic. It calls itself a "Commonwealth," and membership is open to all employees after a probationary period of one year. Each member of the "Commonwealth" has one vote. The main legislative body is the "General Meeting," which meets quarterly. The following principles are excerpted from its corporate code.

Code of Practice for Members

A. We recognize that we are first a working community and that it is our basic attitude to our work and to our fellow workers that gives life and meaning to the Commonwealth.

B. We have agreed that as a community our work involves four tasks, economic, technical, social and political, neglect of any one of which will in the long term diminish the Commonwealth. . . .

C. We recognize that since management by consent rather than coercion is an appropriate style for the Company, a corresponding effort to accept responsibility is required from all. . . .

D. We are agreed that in the event of a downturn in trade we will share all remaining work rather than expect any of our fellow members to be deprived of employment. . . .

E. We recognize that we have a responsibility to the society in which we live and believe that where we have some special talent or interest we should offer this to a wider community. . . .

F. We are agreed that . . . our social responsibility extends to:
    1. Limiting the products of our labour to those beneficial to the community, in particular, excluding any products for the specific purpose of manufacturing weapons of war.
    2. Reducing any harmful effect of our work on the natural environment by rigorously avoiding the negligent discharge of pollutants.
    3. Questioning constantly whether any of our activities are unnecessarily wasteful of the earth's natural resources.[33]

A firm such as Scott-Bader expresses principles of democracy as well as productivity and profitability. Employees build mutual trust and cooperation along with the values of the market: competition and efficiency.

Summary: Co-op and Business Strategies

Robert Monks, president of Institutional Shareholder Partners in Washington, D.C., sees the need for studies on effective governance for corporations. "No set of laws can ensure an adequate system of corporate gov-

ernance," he contends, "without supporting culture and institutional structure. The informed and active involvement of owners is essential."[34]

Ordinary businesses are integrating stakeholders into their management strategies and are increasingly capable of connecting and contracting
with civic (cooperative) movements. The integration of contrary ideas, such
as "profitability" *and* "accountability," is paying off. "Cooperation" once
had a bad name in business because it was associated with "collusion" (il-
legalities), but it is now a vital part of good business. Companies and associations, which build on the synergy of contrary ideas, are now mirroring
what is done in the cooperative movement.

The Swiss dairy industry has gone virtually all the way. In this Swiss
market, producer and consumer associations represent opposite interests
and resolve differences routinely. Producer associations wish to sell at high
prices and are thus in conflict with consumer associations, who wish to buy
at low prices. Distributors are "middle negotiators" who engage in conflict
resolution between the two sectors. Though we did not mention it in our
case (co-op model 3), the Swiss were also solving the problem of supply and
demand. The associations anticipate the demand for dairy products for the
coming year and send the message down to producers to make the adjust-
ment. The point is that these competing associations cooperated to facilitate solutions to tough questions in the marketplace: a fair wage/price system and "supply matching demand."[35]

Mondragon followed a different model for conflict resolution based on
stakeholder representation: retail stores put their stakeholders (customers,
employees, and producers) on their board of directors. The conflict resolution (negotiation) took place at the board level of retail stores. In turn,
Mondragon schools included teachers on their boards, and housing co-ops
included employees and residents on their boards, unlike in the United
States. Such top board "representation" of opposing parties deserves attention. These firms (e.g., business firm model 2) exemplify how stakeholders reduce the need for government to solve their problems.

The ecology of "exchange relationships" created at Kalundborg, Denmark, illustrates how competitors cooperated to maximize economic returns at local levels, strengthening community life (horizontal ecology
model 1). Other cases told us how cooperation works to reduce government
costs and decentralize corporate bureaucracies, making local life healthier.
The Seikatsu system, the Mondragon system, the Atlantic Co-op system,
and the Swiss dairy markets are experiments in building a strong local economy. Civic and co-op leaders resolved problems based on the principle of
"subsidiarity," where power is transferred down the corporate hierarchy
into the lowest level of effective authority.

In sum, a community-oriented economy depends upon putting together contrary principles in markets: *cooperation/competition, productivity/accountability, sociability/profitability,* and other opposing concepts such as *private/public* and *local/global.* Such opposing concepts can become complementary. They can work together to advance the purposes of people in civic movements and business.

Our three sectors of the economy—government, business, and nonprofits—build the base structure of a civil economy. Capitalism is socially and politically changing, perhaps evolving. Business and Third Sector leaders have shown a capacity to advance a civil economy. A civil economy is a system of self-governing firms and markets that are accountable, profitable, humane, and competitive for the good of stakeholders. Civic leaders in business and the Third Sector have been collaborating, and as we shall see in Part 2, government can assist this development for the common good.

II A Developing Economy

4 A Theory of Civil Privatization

Sometimes it is said that a man cannot be trusted with the government of himself. Can he, then, be trusted with the government of others? Or, have we found angels in the form of kings to govern him? Let history answer this question.

—Thomas Jefferson, first inaugural address, March 4, 1801

Patricia Annez, chief of the Urban Development Division of the World Bank, speaks of an increase in privatization worldwide. She says that national and local governments are unable to meet both "social and infrastructure needs" on their own, hence, many are turning to the private sector to manage and/or finance their infrastructure investments and infrastructure companies.

Latin American cities, for example, are increasingly using concessions as a tool to bring domestic and even foreign equity and loans into urban finance. Buenos Aires and Mexico City have managed to privatize their water companies by attracting financing in the form of concessionaire equity and syndicated bank loans from foreign and local banks. Concessions, leases to private companies that require some equity financing, are also becoming more prevalent in the delivery of solid waste services in a number of cities from Accra, Ghana, and Sfax, Tunisia, to São Paulo, Brazil. The available evidence shows that cities like Buenos Aires, Caracas, and São Paulo that have allowed competitive private operation of solid waste services have been able to provide this service at half the cost of public sector companies and to operate it with lower subsidies.[1]

"Privatization" is the planned transferal of government activities into the business sector. We should look at this process—sponsored by the World Bank and Third World countries as well as by federal and state governments in the United States—from the perspective of constructing civil society. This transformation of government agencies into private firms has taken place in all types of nations but with many problems. Our task in this chapter is to look at those problems and examine civil solutions.

First, we will look at arguments for conventional privatization. They include contentions that it is more efficient and reduces government bureaucracy. Second, we will investigate social, political, and moral problems created by privatization in postcommunist European nations, Asian nations, and Western nations. We see that when privatization is done in the capitalist tradition, it results in social problems and more government.

Finally, we will propose that success in privatization depends on planning civil governance, networking, and management training in the competitive market. We will propose a theory of civil privatization designed to solve problems that cause government growth. Civil privatization means helping people in competitive firms establish public standards (e.g., safety, health, and honesty) for the common good. We will give examples of how governments privatize by building a social infrastructure for competition.

The Arguments for Privatization

The argument for privatizing government has been advanced for some time by conservative analysts, but today the subject is discussed widely across the political spectrum. We summarize these arguments before looking at the problems evoked by the conventional practice.

First, the position of "laissez-faire" economics is that the private sector works more efficiently than the government. Privatization saves money by reducing government and taxes, and its success can be tested by economic criteria—the capacity for markets to be more productive and profitable than a bureaucratic government.[2]

Second, some political economists argue that governments have grown too large, become bureaucratic and monopolistic. Government is the largest corporate monopoly in society. The U.S. federal government employs about 3 million people and owns one-third of U.S. land. It annually purchases more than $130 billion in goods and services and issues 4.8 billion publications. In the last 50 years, government expenditures have grown a hundredfold, from an eighth to more than a third of the gross national product. Even after subtracting the costs of national defense, foreign aid, and veterans' benefits, the growth pattern of government persists. Per capita expenditures, expressed in constant dollars, have increased more than sevenfold during this period. The federal government has grown more rapidly than the states, which, in turn, have grown more rapidly than the cities. There have been an increasing centralization of power at higher levels of government and a waning of power in the local government. A goal of privatization is to reduce that top-heavy bureaucracy.[3]

Third, free-market economists object to what they see as government's overregulation of business. Big government inhibits the growth of enterprise and free association and destroys the capacity of the economy to develop new jobs. The government's size and power to control the economy should be reduced to protect people from its imperial tendencies.[4]

The fourth argument, coming out of international economics, is that free markets reduce the destructive tendency for nationalist movements to expand state territory. Multinational firms, not bound by territorial self-interests, transcend nationalism through their networks and help create a global community. Social-political ties of global companies and their markets restrain the fanatical actions of national leaders. Free markets help keep the nation-state within its proper limits of power and authority.[5]

David Osborne and Ted Gaebler have popularized the idea of privatization, saying that government's "administered programs" are driven by constituencies, not customers, and thus fail to meet the needs of people they are intended to help. These programs are motivated by politics, not by policy, so that by the time a legislative bill has passed through the U.S. Congress its original goals are watered down so far as to be meaningless. They also create fragmented and overlapping service delivery systems and at the same time rarely achieve the scale necessary to make a significant impact. Finally, they use "commands" to get things done, not incentives, and consequently are ineffective in cases where coercion does not work. It is proposed that government programs can learn from the market by decentralizing their authority around economic principles.[6]

In sum, governments can become large and inefficient, too costly, even abusive and oppressive. Governments should be restrained from oppressive practices, from extremist and narrow ideologies, and from bureaucratic growth that achieves monopolistic power and fails to serve the public interest.

The Problems of Conventional Privatization

These arguments for privatization are compelling, but the actual practice does not solve the problems in capitalist markets. Privatization has been tried in many different countries, yet the record is dismal for producing economies that are vital and self-regulating. The development of civil society has suffered in postcommunist, Asian, and Western countries. We offer a few examples here to illustrate the difficulty in relying on this approach to create a self-governing economy.

Postcommunist Nations: Blunders
in Abundance

Most observers agree that privatization has not worked well in Eastern Europe and Russia. To be sure, market conditions offer a better system than the former authoritarian regimes, but privatization has not produced energetic economies. There are many reasons for this failure, including political corruption and self-dealing, but we want to emphasize a few problems related to creating a mature, self-regulating private sector.

Our story begins with a false image of capitalism. Capitalism is not composed simply of private enterprises. Privatization in postcommunist countries took off from this mistaken image. The assumption was that each company is an independent entity, rather than part of a social system of supply-buyer networks. Researchers now realize that success in privatization depends upon taking account of social networks. Economic sociologists argue that every independent firm is "socially embedded."[7]

Researchers in Eastern Europe conclude that privatization does not work without "social networking." Sociologist David Stark documents the problems of privatizing individual firms in Hungary and Czechoslovakia. In Hungary, state property officials measured success by the amount of profit brought back into the state treasury when selling individual firms on the market. *Transaction officers* were rewarded according to the amount of revenue received from sales of individual government agencies. The concept of networking had no place in this planning. Indeed, Stark talked at length with a transaction officer who was privatizing a firm manufacturing steel cable. He found that the officer was completely ignorant of the work of officers *down the hall* who were dealing with the agency's upstream suppliers in basic metallurgy and also unaware of the dealings of officers *across the hall* handling privatization of a downstream customer in the manufacture of motors. Things did not work well without coordinating buyer-seller networks.

Stark found that the successful entrepreneurs were those who were aware of this intercompany network. An example of an economic success in Hungary was the Fotex Group. The company began by acquiring the Azúr network chain of cosmetics and household goods. Then it acquired other related firms, such as a wholesaler of photographic equipment and optical products and a small manufacturer of spectacle frames. Fotex renovated flagship outlets in the capital city, centralized its warehousing and inventory control, upgraded products, and made exclusive agreements for products and distribution. The common name "Fotex Group" became recognized as an interlinked chain of company operations. It became a major force in the market, with a dozen subsidiaries, over 4,500 employees, and 378 outlets and facilities. The entrepreneur in this case knew, better than the state officials did, how networks work in capitalism.[8]

Fotex was an economic success, but it produced a social problem that was not discussed in Stark's study. Fotex was building a vertical monopoly when Hungary did not have the public infrastructure to deal with it. In the United States, Fotex would be subject to investigation by the Antitrust Division of the Justice Department. Organizing such vertical controls through one company can be against the law. This capitalist networking results in unfair competition that can attract more government supervision over the market.[9]

We conclude that researchers need to study the *kind* of networking that leads to success in reducing government controls. In this case, researchers found that financial success depends on social networking, but they failed to observe the long-term problem. Stark and colleagues saw the larger social reality going beyond individualism, but social networking can be anything—conniving, collusive, or civil.

We define civil networking as that organizational restructuring that reduces the need for government. It is done by building cooperative relations between firms in a manner that allows them to compete with standards in the public interest. Civil networks are organized with norms that encourage firms to compete for the common good as well as in their own corporate interest. Let us take a parallel case in the United States.

U.S. trade associations are part of the market infrastructure. They are organized as federations, or as affiliated networks with autonomous members. The Vision Council of America and the Better Vision Institute (VICA/BVI) is an association of businesses in the optical field that parallels the Fotex case. VICA/BVI is a nonprofit trade association composed of U.S. manufacturers, distributors, and service people in optical products. The association holds trade shows, conducts public education campaigns, is concerned with ethical issues, and provides journals and research for its members. Such trade associations support their independent firm members and subassociations. In sum, this is a decentralized association of competitors, not one big business monopoly.

This example of a vertical association is a start for thinking about civil development. These associative (democratic) networks of independent firms—where competitors collaborate to advance their own interests in the context of common norms—should be part of the privatization practice in postcommunist nations. As we shall see later in this chapter, it is easier to work through them to build private markets with public accountability.

Now let us take another country. Privatization in the Czech Republic was organized differently but also with defective markets. The Czech policymakers favored transferring assets of state enterprises into the market though a voucher auction offered to millions of citizen-investors. State officials encouraged citizens to sign up by promising a 1,000 percent return on their investment, hoping to promote a popular capitalism. It did not work. The unintended outcome was an elite oligarchy in the financial system. In a complicated social interaction, six of the nine largest funds became state owned. Back to ground zero.[10]

A common problem in postcommunist countries in their attempt to build a market economy was that members of the former state hierarchy got an "inside track" into stock ownership, for example, when the old political elite would purchase vouchers from workers and retired people.

Marshall Goldman, professor of Russian Economics at Wellesley College, states that Russian privatization was "perverse and disappointing." Privatization began almost immediately after the dissolution of the Soviet Union in 1992, and soon reformers claimed that 70 percent of the nonagricultural economy had been privatized. Privatization planners assumed that if the government provided every citizen with a voucher convertible into shares of stock in newly privatized industries, the public would then feel it had a stake in supporting the private sector. However, the rapid and often corrupt manner in which this was done did little to strengthen the market or competitive forces. State monopolies were "privatized" into corporate monopolies. Abolishing Russia's industrial ministries did not deter the newly privatized enterprises from requesting and receiving subsidies from the state budget. It also did not mean that the now-private enterprises would cease to be a source of patronage jobs for governmental cronies. Russia did not have the regulatory institutions to support the privatized sector, nor the legal codes of commerce, nor the trade association infrastructure. The common rule came to be cheating and stealing from the state.[11]

Advocates of this rapid privatization believed that it was essential to curb excessive government interference and terminate government restrictions on the operation of market prices. Wealth had been held in the name of the state, but when the USSR began to disintegrate, there was a frenzy to seize a share of that wealth before someone else stole it. Largely the members of the Communist Party seized the wealth. According to one survey, 61 percent of the new enterprise owners had formerly been listed as *nomenklatura*, the old political and managerial elite. Other studies showed the figure closer to 90–95 percent. Many new banks were chartered in 1991 and 1992, but they were often designed as slush funds for enterprise directors who joined together to underwrite the stock in the new ventures. These banks were used to issue credit to the factory directors (often

officers of the bank) so they could increase their holdings in their enterprises.

While most of the public gained little from this, some members of the
former nomenklatura profited a great deal. A special tragedy in this process
is in the fact that a small group of bankers and industrialists in Moscow now
supplies the capital for political campaigns. In this respect, they are copy-
ing the U.S. tradition. The political winners owe their victory to the contributions of the financial elite. The big money spenders on political campaigns are subsequently appointed to top positions in government.

Although many problems are evident in the privatization of the former
Soviet Union, a study by Logue, Plekhanov, and Simmons cites some
beneficial civil development. These researchers studied cases of worker
ownership and found them successful. The authors emphasize that the self-
managed firms were atypical of the prevailing system but that their achievement is noteworthy. The broader base of interests represented within the
self-managed firm allowed for advantageous connections in the marketplace.[12]

The following is my summary of their conclusions that are relevant to
building a corporate infrastructure in postcommunist countries.

> Decentralization inside the firm was generally tied to new incentive
> systems, which provided substantial material rewards for workers above
> and beyond whatever distant material rewards that ownership might
> provide. Furthermore, despite the fact that all the firms in question were
> majority employee owned (and five of six were 100 percent employee
> owned), there is no evidence of "the triumph of the new owners' desire
> for consumption over investment." The firms combined a general cul-
> ture of economic egalitarianism and formal democratic structures with
> significant real authority for the management that transcended the for-
> mal structure. The general directors of the firms studied seemed de-
> voted to promoting the welfare of their employees. In addition, there
> was significant understanding of the process of democratization among
> workers who had gone through the process. The firms generally sought
> to create an internal market for employee stock, at least for those who
> left the company or retired. Most significantly, a number of the firms re-
> stored something of "the traditional integration of the planning system"
> by having customers and suppliers hold joint ownership in them.

The researchers concluded that every firm in their study undertook a
radical, and successful, decentralization of authority in a relatively short
time after privatization. However, top government officials, the Yeltsin reform team, were ideologically opposed to employee ownership. Yeltsin pro-

moted "voucher funds" as though they were American-style mutual funds with professional management, but many turned out to be gigantic pyramid schemes. The "mutual funds" promised incredible rates of return in massive advertising campaigns; those returns were actually paid to early investors out of the flow of vouchers subsequently coming into the funds. In the virtually unregulated conditions that the government created, a number of fund managers simply stole the funds and shuttered their offices.

This team of researchers concluded:

> Employee ownership is likely to recede in the voucher privatization sector, where it now predominates. As a result, there is a clear tendency toward concentration of ownership in the hands of a few managers and their outside associates in firms already privatized. . . . Had the rest of the Russian economy performed as well as this worker-ownership sector did, perhaps economic reform would be perceived as a success by ordinary Russians.[13]

Asian Nations: More Lessons

The problems of postcommunist nations are similar to those of other nations that are in the early stages of capitalism. These countries develop a type of networking within former clans, extended families, and groups of friends, often called "crony capitalism." Many Asian countries fall into such postfeudal (or postclan) organization of the private sector, but the story is complex because each case is different. The Japanese *keiretsu*, the South Korean *chaebol*, and other types of networking in Southeast Asia had appeared to some researchers as effective grounds for organizing business, but these "social networks" are not the same as the associations in "late-stage" capitalism.[14]

This "early-stage capitalism" can show remarkable success in the beginning, especially with big consumer markets in the United States and friendly foreign investors. Many students of Asian markets have claimed economic success based on these types of social networks. But such studies do not examine the modes of self-governance and accountability systems in these networks. Closely organized kinship systems and oligarchies organize the networks, while the larger economy is composed of market oligopolies. One cause for the mid-1990s downfall of Asian markets can be attributed to extended family ethnic ties combined with an authoritarian control over markets.

Most Asian countries broke the civil norms of a mature business system. They overborrowed, overinvested, and failed to tackle corruption. Japan was guilty of failing for years to deal with its ailing banking system.

By mid-January 1998, stock markets in Indonesia, Malaysia, and Thailand had lost about 75 percent of their value on December 31, 1996. In the Philippines and South Korea, the loss was 65 percent. In the first two weeks of January, holders with claims in the Indonesian rupiah lost 70 percent of their value. The Thai baht, South Korean won, and Malaysian ringgit fell 40 to 50 percent in the same period.[15]

Peter Hartcher is an economic analyst who studies the Japanese economy. He states bluntly that the government's Ministry of International Trade and Industry (MITI) was composed of high-powered bureaucrats who virtually controlled the economy. He explains how imprudent behavior of executives in protected firms, isolated from competition, was a major factor in Japan's market problems. For example, the banks, which the Ministry supervised, were allowed to collude in setting rates. Then, brokerage firms that the Ministry regulated guaranteed the investments of large clients. And insurance companies were permitted to slice pension fund payouts.

Hartcher tells of one individual, Harunori Takahashi, whose personal connections got him a blank check for billions of dollars from an under-regulated bank to build an empire of hotels, golf courses, personal jets, and French paintings. In effect, the Ministry was more comfortable with cartels than with competition. It believed such collusion to be in the national interest because Japan's markets were global. It was "Japan Incorporated" competing with the rest of the world. But the collusion of big firms and the support of government's friends in business with unregulated loans and reckless financing were important factors in Japan's recession of the 1990s.[16]

Yet, the problems in the Asian region were not caused solely by the domestic organization of markets. International investors and their lack of "prudent behavior" also caused them. The word *prudent* is part of the vocabulary of finance and is an example of what we call "civil norms" governing the economy. One big problem in these cases was that *no one monitored the capital flows between countries.*

Three rules of prudent behavior were ignored in Asian markets. First, Asian banks and other Asian borrowers used short-term renewable credits from foreign banks to finance long-term loans. All banks break this rule occasionally, but *the extent* to which this rule was broken in this case made a huge difference. When foreign loans are not renewed, Asian banks and corporations face large defaults.

Second, Asian banks and corporations borrowed in foreign currencies—yen, marks, and dollars—and then loaned in local currency. They accepted the exchange risk without "hedging." They failed to realize that interest rates were lower abroad, and this difference included the risk of currency depreciation. Foreign lenders also did not show prudent concern in making short-term dollar or yen loans to borrowers that financed long-term domestic assets.

Third, most U.S. and other bankers did not ask to see consolidated market sheets. They did not monitor the total assets and liabilities of the borrowers. The lack of "transparency" in bookkeeping was a reason for failing to anticipate market problems.

Fourth, Asian bankers may have assumed the International Monetary Fund (IMF) and world banks would always bail them out. This is an allegation, and if it were true, it would have increased the tendency for Asians to be imprudent in their investment practices. The continuing practice of the IMF and U.S. Treasury of lending to Asian countries produces a type of dependent relationship, not a system of self-governance.

Asia is not alone in this problem. The savings and loan (S&L) crisis in the United States during the 1980s was due in part to a reliance on government regulations and protection by the Federal Deposit Insurance Corporation (FDIC). The FDIC was created under the Glass-Stegall Act of 1933 during the Great Depression. It required commercial banks to conform to certain standards of responsibility: to maintain adequate reserves, limit interest payments, and use deposits exclusively for low-risk loans, not investments. In 1980, Congress expanded federal insurance from $40,000 to $100,000 per depositor. In 1982, Congress (the Garn–St. Germain Act) loosened restrictions on who could own S&Ls, what constituted prudent investment, and how much capitalization was necessary for operations. The industry was not prepared with its own rules and structures for self-regulation.

To continue one part of this sad story, unscrupulous investors took over, created, or bought out S&Ls. They redirected loans from housing to junk bonds, stock purchases, and real estate. They knew that they would be protected by federal government insurance and thought about ways to drain the assets in their favor—to finance personal schemes, pay for political campaigns, and become rich. The market failure of S&Ls cost the government (and taxpayers) over a half trillion dollars. Although the story is more complex than we can reference here, this market failure was rooted in a regulatory problem.

This cost should be a lesson for future policymakers. Government deregulation should never proceed without preparing the market for self-regulation. A self-regulating market is not composed of single firms. It is a system of civil norms, associations, collective attitudes, and mores—a culture in itself. In sum, the social-cultural organization of private markets and industries is critical to their success or failure.

The IMF has the power to pressure governments to "restructure markets," but the question is how to do it. This world agency has a power, like domestic governments, to "structure" markets into self-regulating (civil) systems, but it has no theory of civil privatization. *Civil* privatization is a process in which government officials work with entrepreneurs, trade associations, and trade unions in a manner similar to the way private consultants work with companies in organizational development. When corporations experience problems, outside consultants help explain what is happening, provide models for self-directed change, offer advice, think with their constituencies about the consequences of different strategies for action, and ask the people involved how they might solve their own problems.

The solution to the problem of a market failure is not only financial but also equally social. Our word to describe the social alternative is *civil.* Civil privatization is not taught in the fields of management, economics, and finance. It does not lead to corruption and collusion but rather to cooperation and competition in the public interest.

When firms fail, they affect people socially, not just financially. Market failures produce instabilities and political unrest, and they inhibit the development of civil society. Authoritarian governments grow from a people's discontent. People suffer personally when the economy fails. Scientific studies show an increase in suicides, divorces, and crime, as well as cases of political rebellion. Following recessions and mass layoffs, there is an increase in the medical costs for treating everything from heart attacks to diseases brought about by increased levels of poverty.[17]

In sum, planners of privatization in postcommunist and nascent capitalist nations should take account of the social market structure. Planners should create conditions for self-organization and accountability. With proper consultation and training, competitors can create ethical norms for their industry, and with help from government, business leaders can initiate juridical systems, establish models of fair contracts, organize customer courts or advisory boards, and formulate a common set of norms for safety and warranties. Democratic governments can encourage these practices by tax incentives, temporary subsidies, loans, and penalties. "Civil privatization" is measured by the degree to which accountability systems guarantee honesty, fairness, and due process in the market.

Western Nations: Lessons Close to Home

Privatization in many Western nations has met with greater success than in communist nations, partly because it has developed a relatively civil (moral) infrastructure. But the long-range social problems are hidden by the government and paid for by citizens. Privatization produced a lot of money for Western governments and made some people wealthy, but it has also produced injustices, inequalities, and more government to regulate markets with added costs to taxpayers.

In Great Britain, between 1980 and 1988, more than 40 percent of the state sector was transformed into private enterprise. Sixteen state-controlled enterprises, including such essential industries as communications, gas, automobiles, and airlines, were privatized. More than 600,000 former government employees now work in the private sector. The process amassed more than $11 billion in the U.K. treasury.

In the United Kingdom, privatizing for employee ownership seemed desirable because it could increase the level of a firm's accountability to workers. With the dismantling of government agencies in the United Kingdom, over 400,000 workers bought shares in companies on favorable terms. During the flotation of British Telecom stock, 96 percent of the Telecom workers bought shares. At the time of the sale of the National Freight Consortium, about 10,000 workers bought shares, and soon stock was held by more than 27,000 employees—almost the entire workforce. The shares became worth 47 times the original price.

This was a financial windfall to employees, but there were problems of equity in a new concentration of power. In all the major utilities the proportions of share capital of the privatized company reserved for employees were small, never greater then 10 percent, although the percentage of employees buying them was high. The sale was financially successful, but employees felt that the inequalities in power and wealth remained. This kept them alienated in the organization of their firm.[18]

The extent to which privatizing for employee ownership is successful depends upon many factors, such as the price paid by outside investors, the strength of the management team, the way stock is organized, and the outlook of future profitability for the business. Broadly, the smaller the amount of external funding required, the greater the opportunity for employees to acquire control of the business. In the United Kingdom, for example, bus companies were successful (socially and financially) when employees acquired a controlling interest in them.[19]

But if employees in a profitable firm can sell their stock on the market, the company can be easily taken over by outsiders. In the province of Alberta, Canada, the government accepted a bid in 1975 from the employees to buy its bus operations. The government agency, Byers Transport, became a highly successful employee-owned firm. But the firm lost its worker ownership about four years later when the employee shareholders were unable to resist the temptation to realize a fiftyfold increase on their original investment. They sold out to a much larger trucking firm. This would seem logical in the culture of capitalism, but the firm is now under outside management and no longer self-managed.[20]

Outsiders have bought many "successful" employee-owned firms. In the United States, the *Kansas City Star* newspaper was once owned by its employees. The firm was so successful financially that the employees were persuaded by outside financiers to sell it to a corporation located in New York. Employees became wealthy, but their company was now a subsidiary under the command of a distant large corporation. All the gains in self-management were lost.

In our theory of civil privatization, the way to avoid sellout and gain long-term success in self-management is to organize employee stock so that it must be sold back to the firm. The repurchase of stock becomes a supplementary pension for all the employees. The corporate charter or the by-laws should state that each employee has one vote in the system of governance. When government agencies are privatized in the capitalist tradition, the shares are secured for employees to vote *per share* rather than *per person*. Money becomes the way to power for wealthier managers through stock buyouts. Executives "buy control" over the firm. The dignity and individuality of employees in the company are lost or diminished. Wealthy insiders run the corporate board. When the self-governing authority of employees is lost, the company loses in the long run.

A Theory of Civil Privatization

Conventional ("free") markets are not organized to regulate excessive rivalries among firms and to stop labor or consumer exploitation. Hence, conventional privatization perpetuates problems that are inherent in capitalism—at least, as we know the system up to now. The market invites ever more government intervention.

Hence, we pose these questions: Can privatization help solve the market's perennial problems? Can the creation of dangerous products and wanton environmental destruction be avoided inside the market system? Can "privatization" help entrepreneurs organize self-regulating markets? Can the success of privatization be judged by the degree to which people create a system that protects workers, maintains safe products, and solves consumer problems? If so, privatization will not repeat the problems that require big government. Problems will be solved at the point where they originate—in the market organization itself.

The sociologist Alan Wolfe describes the way politicians and social scientists dichotomize the market and state "while forgetting society." He argues that we should turn our attention toward *markets as a part of the society,* where people have a sense of cooperation and moral obligation as well as a sense of competition and self-interest.[21]

A Civil Theory: Current Systems of Thought

Two types of professional orientations connect with this theory of civil privatization. The first is an intellectual movement that bears on public policy, and the second is an evolving form of discipline in the university.

First, leaders in the communitarian movement in the United States have argued for a "moral infrastructure" in the market. They call for a sense of rights *and* responsibility in the business system. They argue that the two sides of the dyad "community vs. individual" are not purely separate or opposed but rather intersect and can be complementary. Indeed, the way people increase (or decrease) personal autonomy is determined by the way they organize a community. The moral order of the business community is a vital part of this organization.

Amitai Etzioni, a major advocate of communitarianism, contends that

> *law in a good society is first and foremost the continuation of morality by other means.* The law may sometimes lead to societal change to some extent, but if the moral culture (shared values and commitment to them) does not closely follow, the social order will not be voluntarily heeded and the society will be pushed toward the edge of the communitarian pattern—and, ultimately, beyond the limits of tolerance, transforming into an authoritarian society.[22]

Etzioni notes that when the communitarian platform was translated into German, the term *member* was translated as *burger.* When he noted that *burger,* translated back into English, means "citizen," he was told that in German there is no word for it, that is, none that fully captures the notion of membership. The word *mitglieder,* for example, is closer to "dues payer" than to "member." But the idea of "membership" in civil society is different from "citizenship." This communitarian thought, like a theory of "civil markets," requires special concepts to explain a new frontier.

The concept of "membership" is relevant here. Civic associations are constructed on the idea of equality among their members. Being a "member" of an association is notably different from being an employee, a worker, a laborer, a manager, or an executive. Being a member implies a status of equality in an association. To put this another way, the concept of citizen refers to people who are equal within a democratic government, but "member" refers to people who have a common status within an association. People are citizens of a government and members of an association and, altogether, members of a society.

Second, this theory of "civil privatization" connects with university subjects created between economics and sociology. The subjects have been given different names in this century, such as welfare economics, institutional economics, evolutionary economics, socioeconomics, social economics, economic sociology, and contextual economics. Contextual economists today include "welfare" as a concept within this field. Economist Neva Goodwin suggests that "welfare" has four principal aspects: survival, happiness, self-actualization, and moral/spiritual development. These goals are broadly stated and are ends in themselves, hard to define with any precision, but they are guideposts for civil privatization.[23]

Civil privatization is designed to increase public welfare in the private sector. The difference in meaning between "government welfare" and "private welfare" is transformed into a broader concept of public welfare. In this context, the purpose of privatization is to establish a system of civil markets where firms and associations define standards for the public welfare, including the welfare of member-competitors.

The government helps competitors set up the game rules, so to speak. Competitors create norms of fair competition and standards of conduct that can be monitored by their own paid umpires. This self-regulation is done in both business and nonbusiness sectors of the economy in a multitude of ways. A trade association, for example, organizes a professional tribunal whose members are selected by the members of the trade association. By consensus, the umpires may report violations of standards to third parties for action. Third party monitors may report violations to the association's tribunal for judgment and penalty, or to customers for awareness, or to the mass media for public pressure. The last resort is of course to report violations to government agencies.[24]

To put this another way, competitors define public norms on safety, environmental protection, truth in advertising, and so forth, through their associations and set up the means for self-enforcement. Civil privatization advances this practice, but we note that it already exists in many associations of business (e.g., manufacturing, banking, retailing), the professions (e.g., medical, legal, accounting), the sciences (e.g., physics, biology, sociology), religious groups, and so on.

In other words, this principle of self-regulation exists currently within both business and nonbusiness associations. In the business sector, if a competitor violates a joint agreement, it pays a penalty. In other words, if a firm fails to stop using a prohibited toxic chemical because it wants to save on production costs and lower its price to win a bigger share of the market, competitors are motivated to enforce penalties in their own interest. In the sciences, there are similar standards of honesty for reporting data. In medicine, human rights standards protect patients. In the social sciences, standards exist to protect experimental subjects from injury or exploitation. This practice of self-regulation has been developing in all sectors of society for over a century.[25]

We propose that associations can be more self-regulating at all levels of the economy—in workplaces, firms, market sectors, the national economy, and the global market. Our proposal is that people at each level of association have the power to become more self-governing (more self-directing, self-reliant, self-accountable) by creating new forms of governance where a consensus is reached on the rules of the game. In other words, competitors or colleagues must cooperate with one another to increase the power of their own freedom for self-governance. A major goal of civil privatization is then to enable this "progression" of self-governance to take place at all levels of the economy.[26]

In civil privatization, the culture of capitalism changes step by step and case by case. In theory, the progression of self-governance requires a synthesis of seeming opposites (or a rejoining of apparent binaries) into a higher level of thought. This higher thought requires inventing a new organization to fit it. The process requires people to put together ideas often isolated in their minds, such as freedom vs. order, private vs. public, competition vs. cooperation, individual vs. community, and so on, into a more elevated synthesis than exists at the present time. If an organizational invention is done right, people can enhance both values at the same time in ways never before imagined.[27]

Civil privatization helps to transform these binaries (as isolated ideas) into new organizations that represent a higher value. This is done contextually in a way that integrates elements on opposing sides. Thus, the government, following this theory, helps entrepreneurs cooperate to design norms of justice to enhance their free and competitive market instead of imposing more laws on it. In theory, more civil justice in the market should provide more freedom for enterprises to operate without government controls.

Theoretically, if the work is done right, establishing more cooperation for the public good among strong competitors should increase market freedom and effectiveness without increasing government controls. The private sector develops its own civil society as people agree on principles to advance honesty, safety, and environmental protection in the midst of their competition.

The dialectical aspect of this theory is discussed in a forthcoming book, but our point here is that civil privatization promotes this dual optimization of values.[28] Government planners work with entrepreneurs to create civil markets and associations. Markets can be synergistically free and just, competitive and cooperative, efficient and self-regulating. To put this broadly, a civil market is developed when it augments *cooperation* and *competition* in a way that strengthens the *private* sector for the *public* good.

In sum, government agencies are selectively reorganized into a system of civil, self-regulating markets. The purpose is to cultivate competition between firms who create public standards to advance civil justice and freedom. Civil privatization organizes markets to be accountable *and* profitable. In this way, government policies seek to develop public welfare in the private sector. This theory proposes that some government agencies can be reduced in number and expense (or even slowly eliminated) by creating civil markets. As competing sectors become more civil and accountable, people develop a common culture of norms and structures that represents a new way of doing business.

Applying a Civil Theory: Three Levels of Organization

In this section, we suggest three levels for civil privatization: first, at the level of corporations; second, at the level of communities; and third, at the level of nationwide (public) corporations. We looked at systems of accountability in chapter 3, and now we imagine how a theory of civil privatization applies to this same mode of development.[29]

Level 1. Accountability within Firms

At the level of organization within firms, government can use training programs for participatory management and civil networking when privatizing its services or production facilities. Self-managed firms are organized internally with tribunals and social standards, as well as other structures that participants find important. Company shares are kept from unlimited purchase by predatory outsiders. As such firms keep emerging, they need to organize a cooperative network for mutual support.

Self-management training is different from training in management schools or in government administration. Governments do not normally have officials trained in self-management and therefore need a special department with staff specialized for this purpose. Governments can contract with private consultants who know how to organize self-managed firms— including company owners who have sold their enterprises successfully to employees. They have experienced the trials and tribulations of civil-

development training. The transformation of a public agency into a self-managed private firm—or into a market of competing firms—requires skill and a different management theory.

The cost of privatization should pay for itself. The government should at best make money selling its production facilities. If a government does not conduct the sale itself and provide its own self-management training, it can allow others who have the skill to bid for the job. The government then judges the ability of a private firm (e.g., a bank) to organize self-managed firms in the bidding process. In the Mondragon system, the bank made a lot of money organizing cooperatives.

Models 1 and 2, which follow, illustrate how social entrepreneurs have been accomplishing this kind of task on their own. There are a thousand ways to develop such firms, but the right skills and attitudes are critical to success. The following cases show aspects of self-management that government officials need to know. The last case (model 3) illustrates how a national government is proceeding to privatize its agencies into employee-owned firms.

Model 1. Carris Reels: Gradual Training and a Global Perspective

Carris Reels manufactures cable reels, plastics, and wood furniture and is headquartered in Rutland, Vermont, with 1,770 employees. The owner, William Carris, anticipated some of the problems that might arise with employee ownership and made plans to transfer the ownership of his company to employees on a gradual basis. He is transferring 10 percent ownership each year for the next decade. The employees choose the type of ownership plan they want and participate in long-term decisions about the company's mission and management. Carris says, "It's not a giveaway. It just seems like a better way to run a business from an efficiency, profitability and employees standpoint."

Mr. Carris started with a few rules about gradual development that he shared with employees. First, he would sell 100 percent of the firm over time without borrowing. Second, the employees should own the company but should become trained as professionals to manage it. Third, employees should vote on a one person/one vote basis, not one share/one vote. Carris believed that one-share voting becomes too conservative over time. Fourth, Carris said he was concerned about global issues and initiated a program for employees to travel to a third-world country.

The company has offered employees all-expense-paid trips to Africa and Central America because "We believe a program like this not only empowers employees in their own life and their work, it also makes you a world citizen." "The trips are not vacations," Carris says, "but working seminars during which employees travel and live with people whose experiences and needs may be drastically different from those of the average working American." The company's Full Circle Travel Seminars are organized and hosted by the Center for Global Education, an alternative travel program headquartered at Augsburg College in Minneapolis. At Carris Reels, employees are picked through a lottery system to ensure that anyone at any level of pay or authority has equal access to the program. Many individual attitudes have changed in the process of implementing these programs.[30]

Model 2. The SRC: Special Training for Financial Accountability

When Jack Stack started the employee-owned Springfield ReManufacturing Corporation (SRC), he applied an open-book policy, sharing financial and production data with all employees. To make the data meaningful, Stack put everyone through training courses to help them understand balance sheets, profit-and-loss statements, and other financial reports. This was not easy. When he began to teach others about the financial issues of the company, he realized that before he could educate his employees about retained earnings, he would first need to help them master long division and compound fractions.

Now everyone in the firm can read the financial statements, as well as their own stock-ownership accounts. Their accounts told them on one occasion that shares of the company, after three stock splits, had climbed from 10 cents to over $18 each, making the employees' stock fund worth about $5.5 million, up from a mere $6,000 at its inception in 1983. Those figures amount to over 9,000 percent annual growth rate over 10 years. Beyond that, the firm has spun off more than a dozen new businesses, conceived—and operated—by former employees. The spin-offs are part of a strategy to "transform SRC into a diversified collection of enterprises and an ongoing business incubator." In other words, a great deal of personal effort and individual education was involved in developing this employee-owned firm.[31]

Model 3. Egyptian Firms: National Privatization in Embryo

Egypt has 60 million people. Gamal Abdul Nasser nationalized most of the nation's significant businesses in the 1960s. After many delays, the government has now started to privatize, and employee ownership is playing an important role. In all privatization, employees must obtain at least a 5 percent to 10 percent stake in the company through an employee share-holder association (ESA), an employee-run organization authorized to buy and hold shares for employees.

The roots of employee ownership go back to 1989, when Alexander Tire set up the first plan. An Egyptian attorney created the structure of this first employee-ownership plan with advice from U.S. ESOP specialist Norman Kurland. Alexandria Tire was a new tire company set up as a joint venture between an existing Egyptian tire company and Pirelli Tire. To help finance the transaction, the Egyptian company's chair, Fathy El-Feky, contacted the U.S. Agency for International Development (U.S. AID). AID agreed to invest the LE40 million (about $13 million) but wanted to do it through an ESOP. The AID official explained how ESOPs work and helped them raise funds.

As of July 1997, ESA had 280 firms. A board of directors and a General Assembly, whose powers are defined by the trust document, run the ESA. The ESA board is made up of employees represented by the different firms. At this point, ESA remains highly experimental. Employee participation in management at workplace levels is low, and programs in worker education are limited, but the government remains a strong supporter of the idea. The Minister of Manpower and Education sees employee ownership as a long-run part of development in the Egyptian economy.[32]

In our first case, the owner, William Carris, knew that it would take time for employees to understand the changes involved in self-management. He knew how to give incentives and teach workers about the problems of overseas business, imaginatively introducing them to a global, intercultural perspective.

In the second case, Jack Stack believed that employee ownership is best achieved through training in financial accountability. Not all training programs emphasize this, but it paid off in this case. Patience was Stack's virtue. Stack taught the employees not only accounting procedures but also how to assume responsibility for "transparency." He trained employees so well that they invested as entrepreneurs in new self-managed firms. They have been creating an association of self-managed firms in different markets with a mutual-support system.

The details in these cases are too complex to review here, but it would be helpful for government officials to visit such companies. Governments need to learn about this form of self-managed organization.

The third model exemplifies privatization by a national government. Such privatization has been a spur toward the growth of employee ownership internationally, but in almost every country, this method of rapidly producing employee ownership has had problems. Widespread attempts often lead back to concentrated capitalist ownership in the hands of top managers. Egypt may prove to be an exception. In any case, model 3 shows how a national government seeks to ensure success in this form of privatization by organizing a network of like-minded firms for mutual support.

Our point is that self-governance in firms requires special training that, if done right, should advance the public welfare. When this form of social management is implemented, it reduces the need for federal laws to protect employees in matters of safety, health, drug inspections, locker privacy, parental leaves, and so on. The firm becomes self-accountable. Employees assume responsibility for these matters, not the government.

Self-management consultants know that there is much more to success. They list the following principles that are fundamental to this form of consultation.

1. Deepen the trust of all employees of the enterprise.
2. Sell stock to outsiders but retain control.
3. Involve future employee-owners in design decisions.
4. Employees should pay for and vote their stock.
5. All stockholders participate in the election of the board.
6. Retain a significant share of the profits in the firm.
7. Majority ownership by employees is better than minority ownership.
8. The company should buy back stock when employees retire.
9. Include all new employees as owners after a probationary period.
10. Develop laws that encourage rather than discourage employee ownership.
11. Design a process for the enterprise to continuously improve its performance.
12. Employees have to learn to be owners.
13. Communicate so that everyone understands the business.
14. Continuous learning is the key to continuous improvement.
15. No cookbook exists.
16. Nothing is more important than leadership.[33]

Privatizing for employee ownership can include collaboration with trade unions. Trade unions carry a public purpose when they are providing pension funds, offering consultation to employees in big corporations, defending exploited workers overseas, or supporting employees in poorly organized self-managed firms.[34]

Level 2. Accountability in Local Communities

Civil privatization includes many different methods of selling government property and services to stakeholders. Some examples include the following: First, *government land is sold to community land trusts* where local residents are elected to the board, along with resident businesses who pay rent on the land and follow public standards set for the locality. Second, *government hospitals are sold to a proper mix of stakeholders* (doctors, nurses, administrators, and former patients) on the board. Third, *government utilities (gas, electric) are sold to customers* who are supplied with training programs to teach the responsibilities of ownership in shareholding and monitoring. Fourth, *government housing is sold to renters* who govern their own apartment building or housing complex. In all cases, management-training programs are essential for stakeholders who participate in the new civic enterprise.[35]

Let's take the fourth example (sale of government housing to renters) and stress the importance of management training. In the following case, an important element to success was training through teamwork. The training involved residents in learning how to maintain a civil order in their own community. The practice led to residents starting their own businesses.

Model 1. King's Lynne

Eleanor Wessell was a resident of America Park, a public housing project in Lynn, Massachusetts, in the 1960s. She lived with cockroaches, leaky walls, teen-age gangs, and hundreds of dogs that overran one of the state's worst public housing projects. In a transformation that spanned nearly a decade and many personal efforts, the project was reborn as King's Lynne, a $21 million, 441 unit mixed income complex that rivaled any upscale housing community.

The public project's boarded buildings in this case were razed to make way for wood frame townhouses and mid-rises with balconies. Trees were planted along the bare streets of the 58-acre complex. Tennis courts, swimming pools, tot lots, and a recreation center were built on the site that once invited vandalism. Eleanor Wessell now tells her story of how she participated in the process. "The stigma of living here was horrendous," she says, "but the change has been a miracle."

The key to success was organizing an intertenant community. The tenant community then sets standards, enforces them, and oversees the property. Brian De Lorey, asset management director at the Massachusetts Housing Finance Administration, says, "Privatization requires developers willing to enter a partnership with tenants, a strong tenant organization."[36]

A program that changes government housing into civic housing requires "resident conferences" and "self-management training" for renters who become common owners. The project cannot be left to a distant government or left in the hands of private developers.

Michael Schuman, an attorney, recommends that local governments could improve all of their operations by encouraging community corporations to bid on public contracts or franchises.

> Many environmental initiatives undertaken by cities might be creatively reframed as contracts for community corporations. Recent studies indicate that if Los Angeles planted trees and covered its rooftops and roads with reflective material, it could reduce the ground-level temperature by five degrees and cut annual air-conditioning costs by more than $150 million. This simple measure would reduce temperature-sensitive pollution by 10 percent and create an estimated $300 million worth of health benefits—as much as removing three out of every four cars from the road would accomplish. Los Angeles might open a bidding process to community corporations to perform the various pieces of work, including planting trees and manufacturing reflective materials and installing them on roads and roofs.[37]

Civil planners are concerned with how the government's work can be most effectively performed by a private (civil) corporation. A municipality that privatizes department work to community corporations by competitive bidding takes a big step toward local self-reliance and self-accountability.

Level 3. Accountability in Public (Nationwide) Corporations

This theory of "civil privatization" is for policymakers who want to disengage state corporations from collapsed authoritarian regimes but also to cultivate a public orientation to the marketplace in mature capitalist countries. Our question at this nationwide level is whether there are structural alternatives to big capitalist and government corporations. Can publicly chartered enterprises function in the private sector for the common good? We look first at civil privatization in the mass media and then briefly at the field of public education.

The Mass Media   Can mass-media corporations (whether owned privately or by government) be structured for the common good? Can media in the private sector be publicly governed without elite ownership? Are there civil-society solutions here?

Most people in the United States view the media as a business, but others view it as a public service industry. The mass media are a vast net-work of communication companies that sends millions of messages to watchers, listeners, and readers on a daily basis. People have overlapping media exposure because on any given day they may view television, read newspapers, listen to the radio, view videotapes, read books and magazines, attend the theater, see films, and listen to musical recordings. The power of the media is overwhelming in shaping public opinion.

James Ledbetter tells a sad story about the "death of public broad-casting." He offers a short history of U.S. mass media as a system of pub-lic communications. The U.S. government, he says, has always had a com-munications policy, running back and forth between public (government) control vs. great freedom for the media to operate in the private sector. But public (government-sponsored) broadcasting has its shortcomings. Led-better describes subjects that you will not see on public networks—for ex-ample, how to organize unions, or how to make serious critiques of the United States' most powerful corporations, or how the federal bureau-cracy exploits people, or how the military establishment operates secretly in foreign countries. People do not notice how certain subjects are care-fully selected—or avoided—in both the private and public media.[38]

All private media corporations claim to work in the public interest be-cause they (a) act according to professional (journalism) ethics, (b) com-pete against one another for the best programming, and (c) provide regu-lar polls on audience opinion. Critics point out that the public media corporations in the United States—NBC, ABC, and CBS—are owned by General Electric, Disney, and Westinghouse. These megacorporations are in many business sectors; hence, critics argue, they cannot represent the public, though they claim to do so.

The goal of these corporations is to maximize profits in their own in-terest. This interest includes pleasing business advertisers as their source of income as well as not offending their business owners. Critics argue that this private structure poisons the neutrality and the civic purpose of public broadcasting. What should be done? The answer may be civil privatization—or finding the capital to structure new models.

The question is how to establish public accountability in the private sector. Is it possible to organize media corporations in the public interest without government controls? Again, we must pay due attention to both sides of the great principles of modernity: individuality and community, freedom and justice, private and public.

The following case describes a private structure designed to serve the public welfare.

Model 1. Public Television Organized in Society

A special kind of "public television" began in the private sector of former West Germany during the early 1950s when an association of radio stations created the First Channel Television. The Second Channel Television in Germany was organized in 1961 with a television board designed to represent "society." The board includes 8 representatives from various political parties who were appointed according to their electoral proportions in the government. The remaining representatives were drawn from civic, religious, and professional associations. They included 1 representative of the Press Association; 3 from major religious groups (Catholic, Protestant, Jewish); 4 from universities; 2 from labor unions; 1 from the employers' (trade) association; 1 from the Chamber of Industry and Commerce; 1 from youth organizations; 2 from employees at the television station; and 1 from a "citizens' initiatives" group representing dissent expressed through new organizations emerging in Germany.

Apart from the First and Second Channel TV channels, the broadcasting firms have a trade association that produces "Third Channels" alongside regional programs. The dominant topics are education, public information, and the arts. Thus, the media's trade association has broadened the basis for firms to act in the public interest although it was designed primarily to serve the media industry.[39]

In effect, the First Channel Television is "governed by society." It is managed by representatives drawn from the public arena, the civil society, not controlled by government and not by corporate self-interest.

Is this model applicable to the United States? Could the U.S. Public Broadcasting System (PBS) support itself in the private sector? Many political conservatives have argued that PBS is already self-sustaining, including income from advertising and gifts from listeners. But could it be privatized democratically with representatives from civic and professional associations representing the public? Could it be endowed with capital that is socially invested and publicly managed as a civil-society corporation? Could it screen commercials in the public interest? Could it compete with other mass-media corporations?

Could government-subsidized agencies, like the National Endowment for the Arts (NEA), be privatized as civil corporations? Could the NEA board of directors include representatives from appropriate civic groups—art associations, university associations, craft associations, its own employees, and so on? Could the public company be given a "start-up" subsidy endowment by the government? Could it apply for grants from private foundations for special research projects (in the manner of nonprofit universities) to help it become financially self-sustainable?

We are talking about the broad voluntary sector of civic-oriented companies, not ordinary business. Could such government agencies be privatized to finance themselves from professional fees and charges for their consultation with other firms on management organization? Could the public company finance itself by commercials screened by professionals—paid to work in the public interest? Can a market be organized so firms compete directly in the public interest? Can we imagine a time when advertisers compete against one another on the basis of their quality record in environmental protection, safety, health, and quality of work life?

This step toward civil privatization in the United States would be an experiment in civic business. PBS or the NEA would then be organized in the *private sector* while maintaining a *public structure* and *civic purpose* organized to express the public welfare. Such a mass-media corporation is tantamount to being in the Third Sector. It is a self-financing corporation designed to fulfill the essential purpose of government, that is, to serve the public good.

Let us review the organization of such Third-Sector corporations—or shall we say, such civic-structured firms? They have a unique mode of being accountable and profitable at the same time.

The civic firm could be a television station, a radio station, a national periodical, or a national newspaper. The board members of this (Third-Sector) "civic corporation" would represent nationwide groups in society, appropriately in religion, science, government, labor, business, and the professions. The board representatives then would decide on professional criteria for programming. The task of the board would be to determine whether a nationwide news program (or an art exhibit) is "obscene" or "too violent." The decision of the board would normally be put into practice by "public executives" selected by the civic board. The questions for executives in such corporations would be constantly: What is news? What is art? What is right? What is wrong? What is fair? What criteria should guide the writing of a new comedy program? What moral/aesthetic principles should be considered in producing a new drama series?

In civil privatization—or in the civic restructuring of today's media firms—the mass-media market remains open and competitive. The new competition now is simply a civil corporation designed to answer ultimately to a "board of societal representatives."

The answers to some social issues could require consultation with professionals on an advisory board. Corporate (public) executives would base their judgments on issues in ethics, aesthetics, law and medicine, public responsibility, international significance, and the like, not primarily on commercial interests and profit maximizing. This board is not a group of financial investors or a group of government commissioners with political agendas but rather a group that keeps its eye on self-financing while representing the larger society.

A public conference on Media and Democracy was held in San Francisco in 1996 to discuss how to break big corporation control over the U.S. mass media. Lawrence Grossman, former chief of PBS and former president of NBC news, suggested that the nation needs a nonprofit information consortium to provide "the kind of information that society needs, but commercial broadcasting is not providing." The gaps that he felt needed to be filled were subjects like education, public issues, culture, and the arts. The kind of consortium he envisioned included universities, museums, science institutions, and public library systems, organized to serve "all the people, all the time" beyond the demands of the market. To pay for the consortium, Grossman proposed "spectrum-use fees," electronic tuition charges, viewer contributions, and some advertising that does not influence program content. The fees and charges would not be filtered through the government.

At this same conference, Jerold Starr of West Virginia University announced the launching of a grassroots campaign to push for the creation of a Public Broadcasting Trust Fund, to be paid for by spectrum fees on commercial broadcasters. Starr said that a tax of just 2 percent on those broadcasters would yield $1 billion a year. The airwaves are a public space. Mark Crispin Miller of Johns Hopkins University advocated a 5 to 7 percent tax on all advertisers or carriers of advertising to generate up to $10 billion a year to subsidize public broadcasting, including national public radio.[40]

In sum, all these different forms of civil privatization require experimentation. Some of the key issues include the following: organizing management training for the public board and employees; finding a solid basis for self-financing in order to compete in the market; developing a strategy for civil networking; resolving conflicts among those values ruling the sectors of commerce, religion, government, and professional and civic life. The dispute issues and decisions of the board could be the subject of periodic reports to its audience, the public. This could mean a scheduled hour on national television or radio or a column in a nationwide newspaper where audiences debate the issues with the public board. This civil corporation might be a competitive model for others to follow in the capitalist system.

Higher Education   In communist, fascist, and other authoritarian regimes, the privatization of state-controlled education runs into obstacles because there is no perfect alternative in capitalist societies. Privatization of public education in authoritarian regimes would at best decentralize authority in government schools and universities. But we need examples that show a new direction for civil society.

A great accomplishment in civil society has been the creation of public schools and state universities, while maintaining the opportunity for private schools and universities to operate at the same time. But is this the end of the story? Could civic experiments begin with the cooperation of both private and government sectors? We will examine this question in the next chapter, but here we point briefly to the positive accomplishment in the sector of higher education in the United States. We see this private sector as offering a foundation for more civil development.

Many educators believe that the transmission of culture should be socially governed, not state governed, not politically ruled, not territorially bounded and defined by one municipality or one nation. The purpose of general education includes government interests, yet transcends them. Many teachers argue that they should never be required to take an oath of allegiance to the government or teach courses approved only by the city or the state. Rather, teachers should meet professional standards, public standards, academic standards, and human rights standards that are defined by civil associations.

How has higher education developed civil self-governance in the United States? The answer is largely through private professional associations chartered by the state with great freedom to develop diversity and self-governance. The model of private-public associations that follows can point the way toward the formation of a new system.

A high-rise building is situated at One Dupont Circle in Washington, D.C., and houses several dozen higher educational associations.[41]

Model 1. Civil Education

The educational associations represent and coordinate the work of 4,000 institutions of higher learning, lobby for various forms of federal aid to higher education, and define national educational issues and priorities through conferences, publications, and special projects. Many people are not aware of the activities of the American Council on Education, the National Association of State Universities and Land Grant Colleges, the American Association of State and College Universities, or the Association of American Colleges or of the differences between them. But professional educators and college presidents and deans know these associations are vital in maintaining a civil society. They are important to the establishment of public standards in the same way that professional associations of faculty establish standards for their own subject. Each profession also has its own associations—for example, the American Sociological Association, the American Historical Association, and the Modern Language Association—which set learned standards within the broad field of education. This complex array of independent academic and professional associations is part of the contemporary organization of civil society.

In this array of associations, public accountability is not defined completely by the government. Indeed, the original founders of educational associations were committed to a philosophy of "associationalism" that justified a multiplicity of power centers in society. This part of the U.S. system of higher education is relatively self-governing, guided by its academic standards. It is part of a civil order of markets operating in the public interest. We will look further at modeling civil education in chapter 6. The moral infrastructure in this system of free association is much better than what privatization can achieve quickly in a communist nation, but it still has much ahead for civil development.

Summary: What Is Ahead?

Successful privatization is dependent upon creating civil markets and networks. Most people start at the grassroots level, but the civil action goes higher and higher.

Privatizing a government factory into a self-managed private firm with voting rights for employees, or divesting a government utility by transforming it into a civic company owned by customers, or converting a government housing complex for low-income families into a residence of self-organized owners, or disconnecting a national agency from government control and transforming it into a society-managed firm are all vital ways to build toward a civil economy.[42]

To put this another way, organizing a self-managed firm, a customer-owned utility, a self-managed housing complex, a society-based corporation is important to making a private economy become more socially accountable, but at the same time these cases are not adequate by themselves to express that larger public accountability across all markets in society. The long-range task is to keep building connections with regional and nationwide associations. People in society-wide associations need to think about how the principles freedom and justice come together in the local market-place. Thus, an economy-wide system of answerability to stakeholders builds slowly by the multiplication of associations—from the lowest to the highest level.

Many economists recognize that the old system of privatization did not work in postcommunist countries and are raising questions about domestic policy. Joseph Stiglitz, the chief economist at the World Bank, upon viewing the financial failures beginning in 1998 said, "The emphasis on privatization over the past decade has stemmed less from concern over lack of competition than from a focus on profit incentives . . . the privatization in the transition [developing] economies was, in several instances at least, badly flawed [i.e., without an effective legal structure covering contracts, bankruptcy, corporate governance, and competition]." Stiglitz went on, "From today's vantage point, the advocates of privatization . . . underestimated the costs, particularly the political costs of the process itself and the impediments it has posed to further reform."[43]

Our question in the next chapter is: How do we put into practice this theory of civil privatization? We will examine how "civil economy" is developed from the bottom up by shifting agencies from government control into a self-governing sector of civil markets.

5 The Practice of Civil Privatization

Market competition is the only form of organization which can afford a large measure of freedom to the individual.
—Frank H. Knight, economist, *Freedom and Reform* (1947)

We have before us the fiendishness of business competition.
—Karl Barth, theologian, *The Word of God and the Word of Man* (1957)

Now that we have seen the arguments for privatization and the social problems that result from conventional practice and we have developed the rudiments of a theory to solve these problems, we can look more closely at the civil alternatives. Our contention is that privatization is made legitimate and possible by financial studies and then it becomes executed by planning civil markets.

John Weicher, a senior fellow with the Hudson Institute, notes that privatization is on the increase in U.S. and third-world cities because it provides better municipal services for less money. Among his examples, we find the following:

In Indianapolis, Mayor Stephen Goldsmith has privatized the management of a large wastewater treatment plant . . . and has contracted for maintenance services on the city's fleet of trucks and heavy equipment.

In Chicago, Mayor Richard Daley has hired private firms to provide janitors and parking lot attendants at O'Hare Airport, and privatized the management of city-owned golf courses.[1]

Advocates of privatization, however, do not explain how conventional business produces social problems, ultimately requiring more government expenditures. Why do businesses and markets literally require government regulations? The answer is simply that state and federal agencies (e.g., the Environmental Protection Agency, the Federal Trade Commission, and the Food and Drug Administration) are created to protect people from in-jury, unfair competition, and exploitation in these markets.

To put this another way, the framework of economics that is used to evaluate successful privatization does not show the reasons why govern-ment agencies are created in the first place. They do not show the loss in public accountability under privatization. Conventional privatization leads back to business as usual and results eventually in more government. The social costs we addressed in the last chapter are not included in the eco-nomic (business-oriented) framework for evaluating productivity and cost savings.

In the first half of this chapter, we will look at economic studies on cost and productivity in privatizing a local government's *physical facilities* (waste disposal, water supply, street maintenance, and public transporta-tion). This is a start for civil planning, but these studies do not show how the business sector creates the need for more government regulations. Ac-cordingly, we will suggest civil alternatives for privatization in these market sectors. In the second half, we will look at economic studies of privatization in the government's *human services* (police, fire protection, hospitals, housing, and education) and point again to the social problems before we propose civil alternatives.

Civil alternatives refer to the organization of firms and markets that are accountable to stakeholders. For a government to sign a contract with a conventional firm to do street maintenance or run public buses is easy. But to set up a civil arrangement in which the firms are both profitable and accountable requires more thought and planning. We make the argument for civil alternatives because they are designed not only to save govern-ment costs but also to prevent government from regulating firms after they have been established. These firms and markets are designed to be self-regulatory.

Civil privatization is no easy task because it is a new frontier. The idea is not conventional, certainly not written in college textbooks; hence, it re-quires special planning and leadership. To prevent the social problems that normally occur in privatization requires imagination. For example, imagine how to maintain local authority in the context of global markets. How can a local firm take advantage of global markets and still establish lo-cal accountability? The idea for localizing global markets is relatively new and requires much thought. Then, there are other factors to consider in civil planning, such as the opinions of local business, union, and commu-nity leaders. In some cases, training and educational programs may be re-quired. We will address these issues as we look at each market sector for privatization.

Our purpose is not to review all privatization studies, nor to catalog all the problems of converting government agencies to business in these sectors, but rather to invigorate our imagination about how governments can practice civil privatization.

Converting Physical Facilities from Government to Civil Management

Overall, economic research on converting a government's physical facilities into private enterprise has shown cost advantages. It appears that privatization can often save government money at least initially, but economic researchers do not study how the practice has eventually caused more governmental regulation. We have noted that social problems caused by business lead to government regulations because of poor quality of work life, lack of safety in the workplace, invasion of worker privacy, and much more, requiring state labor departments and legislation. This economic research also does not tell us about how customers may be deprived of basic protections regarding product safety, deception, and fraud. It does not tell us about how business can cause environmental pollution, again demanding more government agencies and laws. The purpose of civil privatization is to encourage firms and markets to take account of these problems.

Waste Disposal

Economic Studies of Cost and Productivity
The practice of privatization begins by assessing whether it will save money for the taxpayer. Both government and private firms manage waste (refuse, trash, and garbage) across the country, so professional studies can compare costs in each sector. The scientific findings in waste disposal are complex; some are contradictory, but most studies indicate that privatization is cost effective.[2]

Data from Monmouth County, New Jersey, showed the average cost per person of trash collection was 70 percent higher when services were provided by the government.[3] Research in Canada suggests that private sector collection of garbage was less costly than municipal collection in 48 Canadian communities.[4] The National Center on Productivity inquired into municipal systems and reported that the majority of city-run trash collection routes were designed inefficiently, creating the necessity for more working hours and extra fuel, thus raising maintenance costs. The center also stated that some cities retained fleets of collection vehicles that were not adequately serviced and maintained.[5]

At the same time, a University of California, Los Angeles (UCLA) economist found there was no major difference between government and private costs of residential waste collection.[6] A Connecticut study concluded that private collection appeared to be about 30 percent more expensive than municipal collection, which, in turn, was about 25 percent more expensive than contract collection.[7]

James Bennett and Manuel Johnson suggest that most studies of trash collection have failed to recognize that municipalities use different accounting practices than do private collectors, causing certain studies to become biased in favor of the municipality. For example, figures for refuse collection in Hartford, Connecticut, underestimated the actual cost by 41 percent, because the costs of vehicle operation and maintenance, interest, and depreciation were not included. Furthermore, none of the conventional studies of trash collection considered the future cost of pension payments to retiring municipal employees. Leaving out such costs can make the city collection look like a bargain.[8]

E. S. Savas, professor of public management at Baruch College, summarized nationwide solid-waste collection research covering the United States, Canada, Switzerland, and Japan. He found that municipal collection was about 35 percent more costly than "contract collection." Savas listed the following problems that contribute to the lower productivity of government: the use of more people to do the same amount of work, more absences by workers, fewer households served per hour, and less efficient vehicles.[9]

None of these studies, however, deal with the social problems of privatization. Hence, our question: How can privatization avoid causing social problems and "externalizing costs?"

Options for Civil Privatization
We have defined "civil alternatives" to include firms that are accountable to stakeholders—employees, customers, owners, governments, and the public at large. The development of a civil system of markets is a process of experimentation. Entrepreneurs learn to fulfill stakeholder needs and increase profitability at the same time.

Let us begin with employees as stakeholders and see what progress has been made so far. City planners can define and measure progress by the quality and degrees of worker participation and ownership in their own agency.

Several cities have been at the forefront of this kind of experimentation. The New York City Sanitation Department, for example, has made a strong effort to develop degrees of employee participation—helping workers learn self-reliance and self-direction on the job through the auspices of labor-management committees. Management created an atmosphere where workers felt they were represented in the decision-making process, having a direct voice to the top. Gradually, as workers became more skilled, more day-to-day operations were handed over to them. The same process of participatory management, developed in Madison, Wisconsin, reducing average vehicle downtime from nine days to three. The effort of governments to do this can be a first step toward civil privatization.[10]

Sociologist Stewart Perry studied the way employees "own and govern" private refuse collection in the city of San Francisco. Workers in this case are involved at all levels of management and ownership. Perry interviewed worker-owners in trash collection companies that contracted with the city and found that they performed extremely well. There was no need for the municipality to become involved in labor negotiations. Yes, squabbles among worker-owners were part of this history, but the members took care of their own problems.[11]

The workers in this case treated their customers well; hence, there was no need for any system of accountability to the residents they served. However, each community is different. Worker-owned firms may not always be accountable to customers unless there is local competition to keep them alert. Therefore, let us consider customers and the community as a whole in the context of trash collection for a city.

A city that is privatizing can require competing firms to set public standards and self-enforcing systems for local residents in a number of ways. Their options include the following: (1) ask for competing bids from private firms who offer plans for worker training in self-management over a specific period of time, along with joint employee/customer ownership; (2) insist that nonparticipatory trash firms constitutionalize their trade association with a self-enforcing system of accountability to stakeholders, with bylaw statements outlining their method for handling "civil rights" for employees and customers, including work safety standards and a method for responding to customer complaints; (3) recommend that customers be represented on the board of directors in the privatizing process, consulting with residents themselves about this process; and (4) offer local residents the option to own the firm as a consumer cooperative.

These are only a few choices with the broad concept of civil alternatives. Every community is different in terms of its needs, its capacity for resident leadership, and its capital resources. Some villages and neighborhoods have residents who enjoy taking leadership on a voluntary basis, while residents in other communities would not want to become involved—

they are already overcommitted. In the more cosmopolitan community, residents may be paid a fee by the trade association for their board membership, just as executives are paid fees when they serve on big corporate boards. A rotation system for resident representatives on a local board can be devised to prevent local collusion or to thwart an oligarchy from developing in a municipal region.

There are hundreds of creative combinations for such alternatives, designed purposely to fit local needs. For example, suppose a small city government decides to transfer its trash collection to a single self-managed enterprise—a monopoly. This single firm could be required to have customer representation on its board. In this case, customers could be given the contractual right to make influential complaints, not only through their board representative but also to an outside set of professional arbiters.

Another variation: suppose a city offers a contract to competing companies on the condition that they organize a trade association. The municipality would require that the association of competitors be organized with a code of ethics on employee and customer relations. Competing firms in this case would establish due process and judicial arrangements to govern themselves in conflict disputes, even when not all companies are employee owned. Such firms could be quite varied in their internal makeup, including family-owned firms, proprietorships, corporations, and subsidiaries of outside firms. Nevertheless, members of the trade association could write a social constitution (a contract backed by government courts) that allocates equal powers to member-competitors on the governing board, whatever the type of firm. The constitution's bylaws would define each competitor's obligation to operate with rules of safety for employees, to achieve customer satisfaction, and to work in the interest of the community. The trade association could elect a board that would formulate a code of conduct on "fair competition" and arrange for an independent tribunal of arbitrators. To assure that the association is working efficiently, the municipality could require it to pay an outside consultant to make annual reports to compare customer fees with those in comparable cities.

At the same time, trash collection customers could be given the right to elect watchdog representatives to the board of the trade association, which guarantees the customers' right to be heard and the right to company information. They could also have the right to establish an advisory board that would publish a regular newsletter at the cost of the business association. The newsletter would report customer complaints, and the board would set up adjudication procedures for unhappy customers.

There are hundreds of ways to organize social accountability; the foregoing are just a few examples for this particular industry under discussion.

The formality depends upon the level of management skills and the greater the sense of civic duty already existing among owners and managers of companies, as well as the special concerns of customers. The more management skills and sense of personal responsibility in the trash collection firms, the less formal structure is required to integrate efficiency and lower costs without compromising customer satisfaction.

Finally, let us look at accountability to the environment and the public at large. Whatever type of civic-oriented organization is operating—a conscientious worker-managed firm, a trade association with civic purposes and tribunals, a customer-owned company—accountability to the public brings up the question of environmental protection. This covers the disposal of waste through landfills as well as wastewater treatment plans. Without going into too much detail, we can mention that, as the technology for transforming waste improves, city planners should know that many private firms have begun to finance, construct, and operate plants for the recovery of natural resources that have been lost in conventional business. For example, a civic-oriented firm called Solar Aquatics in Providence, Rhode Island, experimented with restoring wastewater through natural methods. It now treats 20,000 gallons daily, including toxin-laden city sewage, with an outcome of excellent water quality. The example serves the public at large because the effects of waste go beyond the confines of the community. This company serves as a model as the owner consults regularly with nonprofit environmental organizations.

Water Supply and Street Maintenance

Economic Studies on Costs and Productivity

Many people think that water supply and delivery to households are government responsibilities, but in the United States, private water companies serve about 31 million people while government agencies serve about 180 million. This contrasts with other countries like France, where private companies are the main suppliers.[12]

The data on differences in costs in this sector are not perfectly consistent, but the overall conclusion seems to be that the business sector has the cost advantage. One study of 24 private and 88 government water supply systems in the United States concluded that government costs are about a third higher than private, due to lower labor productivity and an underutilization of capital by the government sector. By contrast, a later careful study found no difference in cost.[13]

A study in 20 cities found that the cost of municipal street sweeping was 43 percent greater (per curb mile) than the cost of private contract sweeping when the frequency and quality of service were kept constant. The lower cost of the contract sweeping was attributed to greater productivity by contract crews (i.e., more miles swept per hour), more paid time off for municipal crews, more supervision in government agencies, and better equipment maintenance by contractors.[14]

But again these studies do not address social problems or cost externalization. To what extent are employees underpaid and personally oppressed by supervisors? To what extent do they lack safety equipment? To what extent are customers treated unfairly? How is the environment protected? In business as usual, government picks up many of these costs through its regulatory system.

There is also the issue of a loss of local control. Local officials see their economic future connected to global markets. Government officials are creating a favorable business environment to attract global, export-oriented firms. They offer extravagant financing and tax breaks to big outside firms. Stores and shops that have been managed by families for generations are shutting down because of the proliferation of chain stores like Wal-Mart, Barnes and Noble, and Home Depot, which offer less expensive products. In the quest to find lower-wage venues elsewhere in the world, local industries have taken thousands of high-paying manufacturing jobs out of cities since the 1980s, with offsetting employment growth occurring primarily in low-pay jobs like sales and clerking.

Options for Civil Privatization
We have mentioned some civil alternatives that apply generally to all public utilities, but the correct choice of an alternative depends on the preference of people in a particular locality. For example, customers in one community may want to elect a water utility's board of directors and have the power to demand that managers be responsible to local needs. Another community may want to offer bids to start a community corporation. There is a special advantage to this latter case. The Local Initiative and Support Corporation offers grants and loans for the organization of community development corporations (CDCs).[15]

A CDC can do a number of things. It could oversee new technologies for those civic-oriented companies that take over municipal utility systems. It could organize a private subsidiary of its own with a code for environmental protection. It could even plan for employee participation in its own subsidiary.

Top government officials in a metropolis are often not concerned about supporting the economic development of a neighborhood, much less maintaining its appearance and contributing to its beautification. A local CDC carries that responsibility for civic development. For example, aesthetic principles and cost principles need to be combined in contracting for street maintenance. It becomes the responsibility of the community (not hired private firms) to imagine how excess storm water can irrigate lawns and gardens with architectural designs that beautify the locality. Community corporations (CCs) can exercise more power in big city policy-making than a group of unorganized and economically disadvantaged residents.

Community involvement—through carefully organized CDCs, worker-owned firms, and civic-minded firms—is more likely to result in social and economic development in big cities. This social self-development is an added value too often overlooked by economists who persuade big city governments to privatize agencies into conventional firms.

Public Transportation

Economic Studies on Costs and Productivity

With respect to bus service, researchers in the United States, Australia, and England have analyzed the average cost per vehicle mile of public vs. private urban bus services that were identical in size and amenities. Findings were similar: government costs were 54 to 100 percent higher than private costs. Where private firms in the United States (in competitive bidding) were awarded contracts to take over public transit service, cost reductions of 50 to 60 percent were achieved. Private bus firms were more motivated to make quick repairs and have fewer out-of-commission buses. Studies of school bus systems reached similar conclusions. A study of 275 school districts in Indiana concluded that government-owned and -operated buses were 12 percent more costly than contract buses.[16]

These studies cover mainly issues of efficiency and cost. They say nothing about fair compensation, worker equity, or the quality of working life. Indeed, some so-called improvement studies are worrisome. They show that labor costs are higher in government than in private operations. This is judged an economic advantage, but such cases could hide a practice of labor exploitation among private firms. Similarly, private bus companies were able to hire and fire easily and substitute part-time employees for full-time workers; again, there is the unexamined question of labor exploitation. Labor costs in Calcutta's government buses were twice those of similar private buses, reducing economic efficiency for the government, but we are told nothing about the accountability of the owners to workers.[17]

Options for Civil Privatization

One privatization study showed that private buses made more money because drivers were more vigilant about avoiding fare evasions—letting customers have free rides. In this case, employees collected a percentage of the revenues. It follows logically that drivers in employee-owned firms would do the same thing because employees share the profits.

When we look more carefully, we find the busing issues are city specific. In Puerto Rico, local citizens buy station wagons and minivans that function like taxis. The minitransport vehicles do not always come on schedule, but there are so many of them, one does not have to wait long. The fees are low. Years ago, I noticed those private drivers would let poor people ride free. Is this good or bad?

The question for each locality is whether stakeholders should be represented in the privatization process. In some localities, citizens may want to organize a bus company that is owned and managed by the community, including bus employees and customers. It could be financed partly by socially screened advertisements on vehicles.

David Pett, head of the English law firm of Pinsent Curtis, who devised some of the earliest ESOP arrangements in the United Kingdom, reports worker-owned public transport buses to be one of the success stories within the limits of U.K. law.[18]

In chapter 4, we mentioned a privatized employee-owned bus company in Alberta, Canada. The company did not last because it became *too* successful financially. Outsiders purchased it. We spoke of the need for governments to help people organize stock ownership so that a bigger company or wealthy financier does not buy out a profitable local company. The organization of stock and management training are both critical to this particular type of civil privatization.

We have said that civil privatization involves the divestiture of government agencies in such a way that firms and markets become accountable to their stakeholders. In this case of government-owned buses, a variety of other alternatives is again possible. The bus system could become a subsidiary of a CDC, which gives workers participatory-management training. The CDC would get a normal economic return off the firm's profits. Or, the firm could be independently owned and monitored by a CDC. In such ways, local residents have some assurance that their private company would perform with greater efficiency and accountability than a conventional capitalist firm.

If a government acts carefully, selectively, and experimentally with civil privatization, the result could lead, with special planning, to a decrease in metropolitan bureaucracy, a reduction in taxes, and a stronger and healthier self-regulating economy.

Converting Human Services from Government to Private Control

The human services covered in this section include police, fire protection, hospitals, housing, and education. Studies by economists are important when they show overall gains in efficiency, but they are not designed to show the gain/loss in civic responsibility. The competition between types of health services today (government, commercial, nonprofit) is based on comparative statistics on efficiency without consideration for public responsibility. Studies of private police systems show greater safety measures taken to protect people than government police systems, but they do not mention that these systems are organized exclusively for rich, not economically disadvantaged, communities. In fact, creating bigger police departments is not the best (or only) way to reduce violence in city neighborhoods. Other options are more effective in preventing destructive behavior. They involve increasing the skill of citizens to solve their own problems and augmenting the power of self-governance in community life.

Municipal Police

Studies of Costs and Productivity
It is hard to believe that the number of private police departments in the United States has been outgrowing the number of government police, but it is true. Guards in the private security industry during the 1980s numbered 680,000, in contrast to law-enforcement officers amounting to 580,000. Expenditures in 1980 for private security forces in the United States were $21.7 billion, compared to $13.8 billion for government police forces. Government agencies paid an estimated $3.3 billion to private security companies for their services.

City, state, and federal governments even resort to private guard systems instead of using their own police. Boston City Hall, for example, uses private police to guard equipment and property. The U.S. General Services Administration makes extensive use of contract guard services, using them to supply 41 percent of their needs. Private security firms conduct passenger and baggage screening at airports, protect stores against shoplifters, and provide security at banks and hotels.[19]

The growth in government police forces and the creation of private security forces for wealthy "gated communities" could be attributed to many things: the *growing inequality of income and wealth; city police* who lack the training to deal with drug addiction and violent gangs; *the decline of solidarity* in community life, with neighbors no longer knowing each other; absentee *parents* whose work keeps them away from their children; *absentee landlords* who collect rent on deteriorating buildings; and *absentee executives* who work in distant metropolitan centers and never visit the neighborhoods in which their subsidiaries are located. Under these conditions, city streets become brutal as gangs rule them, and city police become more distant from people in these neighborhoods.[20]

Do alternatives exist in the form of civic development, local capital accumulation, and social control by residents? In this section, we emphasize decreasing the costs of city police and private security systems by "community building," encouraging citizen participation in the civil development of markets, accumulating community capital, and changing municipal policies.

Options for Civil Privatization
Residents in city neighborhoods have begun to organize against the forces of violence with street patrols and new forms of community enterprise. Some experiments have the title "community policing," where public safety becomes a local resident responsibility rather than merely a professional responsibility.

This community-building approach changes the role of the police officer from that of an "enforcer" to that of catalyst for community development. Police officers help neighborhood residents clean up vacant lots and move rusting cars, help residents organize marches on crack houses, and assist parents in their efforts to keep kids in school. This approach has begun in more than 300 U.S. cities. According to the National Association of Town Watch, some 18,000 neighborhood groups are organized, with a million members working with local police forces.[21]

A local program featuring self-reliance, self-policing, and community development is the Quaker Project on Community Conflict in New York City, which began to work on crime prevention without requiring police. The community devised a training program to "use street theater and puppet shows as tools to enable aggrieved groups to dramatize their grievances and help to bring about needed changes nonviolently." The program reduced crime by introducing delinquent teens and "disaffected groups" into a program of street theater.

A similar program in Philadelphia cited four goals.

1. To place in the hands of aggrieved groups powerful tools of the dramatic arts as a means for the nonviolent education of the public and the authorities on the [local] suffering and needs.
2. To establish a model for training members of such groups to present in public places short dramatic skits which will have a persuasive impact on viewers, and to follow these up with discussions and leaflets designed to further persuade viewers . . . to take other action to get grievances redressed.
3. To spread this model of training and organizing both regionally and nationally by training groups, printing manuals, creating videotapes, . . . distributing the material to interested groups.
4. To interest people concerned with conventional theater to become involved in this type of street theater . . . to contribute their talents and know-how to its improvements.[22]

These experiments in crime prevention hark back to programs created in the 1930s depression era. They were shown highly effective in low-income neighborhoods. The Chicago Area Project, for example, organized neighborhood councils to reduce and eliminate delinquency, drugs, and crime. Drug addicts were helped to break their dependency on drugs and trained and employed as community organizers and "delinquency prevention workers." The rates of crime, drug use, mental disorder, and alcoholism went down dramatically. Ex-convicts helped rehabilitate local neighborhoods. Such programs should be reviewed for their applicability to reconstruct city neighborhoods today.[23]

But local efforts to prevent crime are not enough. To get at other causes for local crime, economic development is needed—creating jobs and providing greater opportunities for self-empowerment in the local economy. When we look carefully at the roots of the problem in the structure of markets, there is much more to be done through public policy.

Many civic leaders believe that it is possible to restructure the market system through government itself. Richard Moe, president of the National Trust for Historic Preservation, and Carter Wilkie, an advisor to the mayor of Boston, argue that cities have capitulated to the demands of big business. Current policies have devastated local neighborhoods in the following ways: giving government subsidies to housing and automobile industries; single use suburban zoning; tax codes that turn buildings into wasting assets after 31 years; slash-and-burn urban redevelopment projects that favor cars, not people; mortgage lending that rewards racial segregation and architectural conformity. Such policies support the interests of powerful economic groups. Changing public policies can eliminate the causes of this "loss of community control."

Restoring capital to local communities also reduces the need for municipal police. Municipal policies that favor the large chain stores drain capital from local merchants and local customers and redistribute it to distant corporate headquarters. The current trend toward sprawl, private security police, and gated communities can be reversed. The reversal is taking place now in the Garden District of New Orleans, Chippewa Falls, Wisconsin, and Pittsburgh's Manchester neighborhood. Their answer: reverse the steady accumulation of power and wealth in big corporations so that it comes back into local hands. Then the rising rates of crime in neighborhoods and communities can be solved.

The development of "community control" is closely linked with building a civil economy. Author Michael Schuman gives many examples. Let me summarize a few of them.

Municipal governments can mandate their agencies to purchase products from local producers and community corporations. They can require that special labels be put on products that are manufactured primarily with local capital, labor, and resources. General-obligation and industrial development bonds can be restricted to projects undertaken by community corporations. Limiting tax-exempt bonds to community corporations would spur entrepreneurs to form such corporations. Public-employee pension funds can be invested in local economic development, giving preference to community-oriented firms. When municipalities invite multinational corporations into their locality, they should write carefully drafted contracts that clarify the firm's obligations to the community.[24]

Finally, municipalities can encourage the development of community land trusts (chap. 2) where subsidiaries of global corporations pay rent to use local land under specified conditions, such as rules for environmental protection.

Fire Protection

In the early nineteenth century, private firms organized fire fighting, but by midcentury, fire departments were organized largely by municipal governments. Today a modest reversal is taking place through privatization; private fire department companies operate in 14 states and have their own civic trade association.

A pioneer has been the Rural/Metro Fire Department, founded in Scottsdale, Arizona, serving 20 percent of Arizona's population and operating 50 fire departments in five states. When the city of Scottsdale contracted for the company's service, the aftertax profit rate of the firm was regulated, not to exceed 7 percent of gross revenue. This government regulation against making too much money presents an interesting question about motivation for business ventures. In theory, the capping of profits should take away a company's incentives to go into this business.[25]

But motivation was not reduced. The company saw its competitors as governments and its work as a public service. Other fire-fighting companies were not the competitors of Rural/Metro, but the local governments were. The question was whether Rural/Metro could demonstrate that it could do the job better than government in terms of efficiency and safety. Competition remained; it was between government and business, thus providing an incentive to keep costs in check while remaining civic oriented and keeping the community protected.[26]

Health Care: Nonprofits vs. For-Profits vs. Governments

Studies of Costs and Productivity

Health care represents 11 percent of the gross national product (GNP) in the United States, the highest proportion in any industrial nation. Hospital corporations have grown rapidly in the private sector as they buy, lease, or contract to manage formerly public hospitals. For-profit hospital chains took over 180 government hospitals 20 years ago. Today they face competitive pressures from one another and from firms that provide contract management for specific services within government hospitals, such as housekeeping, food service, emergency room, plant operations and maintenance, respiratory therapy, pharmacy, laundry, and data processing. This is a fast-changing market sector.[27]

Some of the advantages of profit-based hospitals (compared to government hospitals) include the ability to raise money for physical modernization and new technology. They do not need voter approval for bonds, and they have greater access to capital markets. They can achieve greater efficiency through computerization, bulk purchasing, and the flexibility to attract new physicians and services.

There is a hot debate over the ability of profit-based hospitals to promote quality health care. Many professionals question the motivation of a firm to make money while trying to meet human needs. Data are still being gathered to make the right judgment. A comprehensive study by the National Academy of Sciences compared for-profit and nonprofit hospitals and found no difference in the quality of care. But they also found that the former had costs ranging up to 10 percent higher than the latter. Critics of the study argue, in turn, that the study did not take into account the taxes required of the companies and the need to amortize more recent capital investments. In other words, the study was not comparative.[28] Hence, the reader should be cautious of these conclusions.

The testimonies of professionals who have worked in profit-making hospitals convey harsh realities of cutbacks and understaffing. Members of a statewide group of 3,000 doctors and nurses in Massachusetts protested by tossing annual reports of for-profit hospitals from the Boston Tea Party Ship on December 2, 1997, after a "call to action" published by the *Journal of the American Medical Association.*[29]

The battle is strong—indeed, raging—at this point. Hospital management, controlled traditionally by professional administrators, is shifting to control by physicians who are creating corporations. Medical doctors have been buying health maintenance organizations (HMOs), constructing their own hospitals, and managing their own clinics. It is a struggle for power in a competitive business market.

Great Barrington, Massachusetts, a town of 2,810 residents, has a community hospital (called Fairview) that is threatened by a group of 80 local doctors (Berkshire Physicians and Surgeons) who want to put up a medical building to treat their patients about a mile and a half away. If the doctors construct this building, Fairview officials argue, it will drain patients and business from the community hospital. State Representative Christopher Hodgkins says, "Any service that makes money, they'll try to steal from the [Fairview] hospital. . . . And any service that loses money, they'll leave to the [Fairview] hospital." The Berkshire struggle is a microcosm of what is happening nationwide.[30]

Third-Sector critics have called doctors "the new capitalists," but there is an added moral factor to examine here. We do not know the extent to which professional codes might become a moderating factor in calculating profits. These physicians say they want clinics and hospitals to show both efficiency *and* better health care, but if they act simply as individual entrepreneurs and do not develop public accountability systems, they will create high-profit-making clinics. It is a battle between quality health care and profit making.

HMOs have tried to cut down on hospital stays in an effort to trim health care costs. Big hospitals are fighting to obtain affiliations with them in order to get patients. Hospitals have promised millions of dollars in cash and other forms of support to woo health centers. Consider the following case.

South Boston Community Health Center has two giant hospital suitors. The rivals for its attention are New England Medical Center (NEMC), which has had a long-standing relationship with the health center, and Partners Healthcare System, which is trying to woo the center into its own camp. NEMC claims that it has contributed hundreds of thousands of dollars to the South Boston Center in the form of subsidized rent, staff, and clinical and outreach programs as well as cash. As the center considered switching its affiliation to Partners, NEMC is closing its subsidized rental contract with the South Boston Center, threatening to remove the center's space where its counselors treat thousands of patients each year. John Northridge, a program manager at the South Boston Center, said, "This is happening everywhere. When you change one relationship, it affects another. It's just business."[31]

This rivalry will likely continue for some time in the United States. Local issues are complexly related to the changing nationwide system of health care. There are no definitive answers for building a civil system nationally that operates for the common good; however, we can propose a few examples of hospitals and health care centers that have become relatively self-governing outside formal government structures. The process of getting there requires negotiation—emphasizing cooperation along with competition in this health market.

The health care struggle spotlights the role of nonprofits as part of the capitalist system. It reveals the increasing power of physician-managed corporations in the competitive struggle for power. Other professionals (lawyers, dentists, educators, nurses, social workers, etc.) are also deeply involved in this competitive capitalist system.

Options for Civil Privatization

In a civil plan, the privatization of a city hospital into a nonprofit or profit-based hospital should require corporate bylaws that outline its responsibility and accountability to stakeholders. Cities should give stakeholders (e.g., doctors, administrators, nurses, former patients, government representatives) the option to organize the board of directors. In other words, the city publishes guidelines for organization and then asks for competitive bids for a civic hospital. The guidelines include plans for self-financing, appropriate systems of disclosure, and accountability for employees, patients, and the community. Such plans would parallel the idea of a "public corporation" (chap. 4).

Some governments have solved the problem of indigent people being rejected by hospitals. For example, the East Cambridge Health Center in Cambridge, Massachusetts, did not have much money, and most of its patients did not have health insurance in 1989, yet for many years uninsured patients had no trouble seeing doctors or nurses at the clinic. For serious medical problems, they were referred to the parent hospital, Cambridge Hospital, which ran the center. The cost of this clinic, $35 million a year for the Cambridge Hospital, was covered by a fund called the "uncompensated care pool," a safety net that guaranteed everyone in Massachusetts access to health care.[32]

Massachusetts hospitals under state law must provide free care to those who cannot afford to pay, but physician groups do not come under that law. The physicians and surgeons that we mentioned previously as part of a corporation in the Berkshire region planning to build a clinic to compete with a community hospital are not obliged to follow this law. Local people may have to argue in court that this is "unfair competition."[33]

The health maintenance organizations can affect the survival of hospitals, whether they are nonprofit, for-profit, or government owned. This is a new issue for privatization and civil development. HMOs and physician groups "favor" certain hospitals with their patient referrals. It is a competitive process based on the best contract offered. The Harvard Pilgrim HMO in Massachusetts has arranged to send patients to Brigham and Women's Hospital for in-patient care, allowing for exceptions in emergency cases. The physician groups and boards of trustees of corporate HMOs decide on the choice of hospitals; thus, the organization of health care organizations is important to examine in a market jungle that includes for-profits and nonprofits. We favor "stakeholder" models of self-governance to enhance the probability that the work is done for the entire community.

The following case exemplifies a relatively self-managed (nonprofit) care center.

Harvard Vanguard Medical Associates: The Harvard Pilgrim HMO In an effort to devolve authority and give doctors increased ownership over clinical (customer) service and financial outcomes, the Harvard Pilgrim HMO spun off Harvard Vanguard Medical Associates (HVMA) in January 1998, a nonprofit health care provider incorporated with a board of trustees. It has 14 clinical centers. The overall corporate board is composed of three representative groups: (1) HVMA employees, (2) the HMO insurance company, and (3) "community representatives."

First, the HVMA is formally composed of nine members of the health care organization: three board members are elected from its Primary Care Unit (chosen by all physicians who have final responsibility for their own patients), three members elected from the Medical Specialties Unit (chosen by medical specialists), and three members elected from Advanced Practice (chosen by nurse-practitioners and physicians' assistants). Second, the Harvard Pilgrim HMO has four trustees, who for some purposes control 50 percent of the votes. This 50–50 split gives incentives both to the parent company and to the new entity to put the social well-being of their relationship ahead of their individual preferences. Third, "community representatives" are recommended by employees and selected by the board. Currently, there are one government official, one leader in private industry, and one professional consultant. Representatives on the board are elected within a staggered time frame from one to three years.

Finally, the 14 different local clinics are incorporated as associates in different locations, each with its own board. These boards are advisory to the corporate board and include representatives of all employees: professionals, administrative personnel (record keepers, buildings and grounds, etc.), and nursing and medical staff.[34]

Hospitals have become dependent upon HMOs, government, and insurance companies that together are changing the health care system in the nation, but it is clear that options for self-governing structures exist for HMOs and hospitals. Their corporate boards need not exclude stakeholders (doctors, nurses, administrators, and civic leaders) who together seek to balance and integrate the contrary values (e.g., health vs. profits) in this sector of the market economy.

There are too many facets to the organization of health care to cover all of them here, but let us conclude with one more example of how issues of self-governance cross between the profit and nonprofit sectors. Ambulance services represent one aspect of hospital services. A survey of cities in the United States showed that 25 percent of the cities contracted with business firms for ambulance service, and 11 percent contracted with not-for-profit agencies or neighborhood organizations, with the remaining percentage run by hospitals themselves.[35] In civil privatization, an association of ambulance services would be organized with professional guidelines for operations, a code of ethics, safety rules, and an internal tribunal allowing access for appropriate stakeholders—employees, patients, community members. Stakeholders would be heard according to "due process" within each member company in the association.

Housing

Studies of Costs and Outcome: Vouchers and Rent Control

The market system is not designed to help the poor and protect the homeless. Hence, the government has created programs to regulate the location,

construction, and pricing of housing. It supports urban economic development related to housing the poor. Unfortunately, government housing programs have been wasteful and sometimes irresponsible. Public housing
projects have become "warehouses" for troubled families. Vandalism, ar-
son, delinquency, and crime have damaged government projects. Public
housing has been touted as one of the most dysfunctional systems in U.S.
government. One-fifth of all government housing was once officially labeled "riddled with problems" by the federal housing agency. A symbol of
the seriousness of these problems was the razing of Pruitt-Igoe houses in
St. Louis 15 years after they were built, because they had become too di-
lapidated and dangerous for occupancy.

Many alternatives to public (government) housing have been tried
with varying degrees of success. Two of these controversial alternatives are
the voucher system and rent control. Some research has shown that building a new housing unit for a needy family costs about three times as much
as supplying that family with a housing voucher; consequently, the federal
government has promoted housing vouchers. The Report of the President's Commission on Privatization (1988) states, "Rather than financing
housing construction, the government should provide housing subsidies to
eligible low-income households in the form of vouchers enabling them to
rent acceptable housing in the private marketplace."[36]

Vouchers are intended to augment a family's purchasing power, so
that people can make their own decisions on location and types of housing.
The idea is to strengthen the viability of conventional mortgage institutions,
attract more lenders into the mortgage market, and redirect government
credit agencies toward supporting private investment rather than merely
competing with it. Housing vouchers, based on income, family structure,
and relative costs in a specific area, could be applied toward rent or toward
the purchase of a house. As a family's income goes up, the subsidy goes
down. If tenants can find bargains in good quality housing, they may pocket
the difference from lower rent; if they accept higher prices, they must be
willing to pay the extra amount themselves. In a voucher system, families
(theoretically) have more choice about where they want to live, but the system remains controversial.[37]

Government rent control has been controversial for decades. Although rent control *can* help residents who are unable to pay escalating
costs in rents, it can also backfire and hurt them. For example, economists
have shown that rent control creates a shortage of housing because inex-
pensive existing units are overconsumed and new ones are not built. Rent
control can lead to striking inequities among families in equivalent housing—well-to-do people instead of the economically disadvantaged being

subsidized or young people being blocked from rent-controlled apartments because the apartments are already occupied by middle-aged or elderly people who have been living there for many years. Also, when two families live in adjacent, identical units and one family pays less than the other does because they have lived there longer, problems arise. If new tenants have less income than the longer-term residents, then they are (ironically) subsidizing their wealthier neighbors. Because older, long-term residents are more often without children, they need less space, but they have larger units while younger couples with children have to pay more for smaller units.

Options for Civil Privatization

One issue in civil privatization is how to bring the government-owned housing under the ownership and civil control of the residents. In some cities, tenant-management associations have helped to develop residents' skills and encouraged them to plan for home ownership. Here we offer a case that demonstrates how human and financial problems were solved in a system of self-governance.[38]

Rent-paying residents transformed the Kenilworth-Parkside development in northeast Washington, D.C., once an active drug market, with violence common and bulletproof barriers around administrative offices. Under the leadership of Kimi Gray, an African American welfare mother with five children, residents pressured the mayor to let them manage the property. The tenants wrote their own constitution and bylaws, decided on their own personnel and policy procedures, and defined their own job descriptions. They trained residents to manage property and do maintenance; they set up fines for violations of the rules, including littering and loitering in halls, sitting on fences, not cutting the grass. They elected building captains and court captains to enforce the rules; they started classes to teach housekeeping, budgeting, home repair, and parenting. They started an after-school homework and tutorial program for children whose mothers work full time and set up courses to help adults get high school degrees. They contracted with a doctor and a dentist to set up part-time office hours and make house calls at the housing development. They set up an employment office to help people find jobs and began to create their own businesses, to keep money and jobs within the community.

Their first enterprise was a shop to replace windows, screens, and doors, owned by a man who could neither read nor write. Then, residents hired their own garbage collection service and organized a co-op store, a snack bar, two laundromats, a beauty salon, a barber shop, a clothes boutique, a thrift shop, a catering service, a moving company, and a construction company that helped renovate vacant apartments. All the new businesses employed residents, and all were required to hire young people to work with the adults.

The accounting firm Cooper and Lybrand released an audit of Kenilworth-Parkside. During the first four years of tenant management, rent collections increased 77 percent, seven times the increase of public housing citywide. Vacancy rates fell from 18 percent to 5.4 percent. The resident management corporation helped at least 132 residents get off welfare: it hired 10 as staff and 92 to run the businesses it started. Its employment office found training and jobs for 30 or more. The resident community had saved the city government at least $785,000. In 1990, the residents then bought the whole development. A community of 3,000, once typified by single-parent families on welfare, is now a community of homeowners.[39]

This is social self-development initiated by the residents themselves. It is organized self-direction and self-reliance in the context of the market. The role of government in privatization is to provide guidance and incentives for such programs.

Another type of civil alternative is "cohousing." A civic movement for cohousing was started in Denmark after World War II by people who had become disenchanted with the anonymous life of high-rise apartment buildings. After spreading across Europe, the movement came to the United States in the 1980s. There are now as many as 150 cohousing communities that have been built or are in the planning process. In a cohousing community, members live in private homes that are self-sufficient, but some have adopted a cooperative form of ownership. In either case, members share a common facility known as a "common house." Here people can sit around a fire, hold meetings or share meals when they want, or use facilities like laundry rooms that everyone needs but no one needs all the time. Sites are designed to encourage social life while respecting privacy and to preserve open space for gardens, walkways, and play areas. Cohousing communities attract a diverse mix of households (including singles, couples, families with children, and elders) and a variety of ethnic and racial groups.[40]

We referred earlier (chap. 2) to community land trusts (CLTs), but city planners, to my knowledge, have never applied the concept to privatization. The CLT board, representing a community within a specific area of land, controls the policies and operations of rental housing. It offers everyone an opportunity to make decisions on the right and privileges of tenants.

The CLT determines rents, basing its decisions on the principles of fairness, not on speculative profit making. It accumulates capital through its rents and can organize educational programs among the residents about how and when to use land held in common.

In summary, housing problems have not been solved adequately either by government or by conventional "privatization." Civil privatization may evolve from policies such as the following:

Further experimentation with housing vouchers, leading to home ownership

Opportunities for low-income people in public housing to purchase their apartments with rent payments

The construction of housing cooperatives in the private sector with training programs for new residents in social management techniques

Experimentation with community land trusts

The construction of cohousing communities where privacy and community are maximized together

The construction of community corporations with networks of people working together for a safe and secure place to live

Education

Public Education

"Public education" has been under the mandate of governments in the United States since the eighteenth century, but the local system has been a disaster in many cities. Community-oriented experiments have begun but still have a long way to go. A significant change is happening in public education at every level: elementary, secondary, and higher learning.

During the 1980s, although total spending on public education increased by 29 percent and major education reform bills in 47 states were passed, school dropout rates were higher in the 1990s than they had been in the 1980s. Subsequently, educators decided to place more responsibility on parents and communities than upon top-down decision making, which led to experiments with charter schools. The jury is still out on the success of these experiments, but an alternative is developing as governments are giving new options for communities. Our focus in this section is on the philosophical issues of private vs. public education and the potential for civil privatization.

Let us look at the major changes taking place in public education today. We will look first at charter schools that have begun because of social problems in public schools. Then we will look at the changing context of private vs. public higher education. Finally, we examine how civil privatization is a basis for thinking about solving educational problems in this sector of the economy.

Charter School Experiments: From Government to Private Sector
Fifteen years ago a national commission on educational excellence released "A Nation at Risk," a report that said, "Our schools are being eroded by a rising tide of mediocrity that threatens our very future as a nation and a people." Since that time, news reports on what is happening suggest that "you just might hear the walls of an American monolithic public education—starting to crack." As of January 1998, there were 784 charter schools operating, 143 approved to open, and 241 awaiting approval.[41]

Charter schools cannot be viewed in isolation from state and local reform efforts, from the communities in which they operate, or from the politics of their sponsoring agencies—school districts, county offices of education, and the state. In chartering new schools, there are academic and organizational legacies to take into account. The motivation to establish charter schools arises in the context of existing institutional arrangements.

Different sets of stakeholders have opinions about charter school practices at each school level, as well as about state and district policies and practices. Some charter schools have drawn strong opposition from people with collective bargaining interests or concerns about job security and teacher rights. Other community groups have opposed charter schools as too selective in student admissions. Many financial problems have yet to be solved. Charter schools have had varying degrees of interest in financial independence, but many leaders have now questioned the possibility of reaching their goal of being fully independent. They cannot cover costs without help from an outside agency. Leaders in this civic movement have not always been clear about how to monitor the impact of the new organization on students and measure the achievement of charter goals. In some cases, a lack of oversight can be due to indifference by the sponsoring agency or to the fact that the district was not accustomed to monitoring academic progress at individual schools.

Charter school developers have usually addressed the proper areas of their new school's program, including the governance structure, the means by which the school will achieve a racial and ethnic balance, and the public school alternatives for students residing in the area who choose not to attend the charter school. Charter documents vary from detailed descriptions of every aspect of the school's operation to a broad outline of the school's plan. The charter school approval process usually requires that teachers, parents, and/or administrators petition a sponsor, often a local district.

The financial relationship between charter schools and their sponsors is a critical issue. The relationships vary in a range from being fully dependent on the sponsoring agency to having a great deal of freedom and autonomy. But some schools are so dependent that the advantages of their charter status are obscured. In some cases, charter schools are held accountable by their sponsors for academic outcomes while in other cases, sponsors are more concerned with financial outcomes. Studies show that some sponsoring agencies have held charter schools more accountable for their fiscal operations than for their educational outcomes. Most schools hold themselves accountable to parents, but the role of the sponsor is critical in terms of administrative authority. Hence, the relationships between charter schools and their sponsoring districts are still under evaluation on matters of civil rights and responsibilities.[42]

Charter (private) schools can draw students away from public schools, depleting their resources. Their organization can be a class conflict between the rich and poor, similar in this respect to the health care system. But it also raises special questions in the philosophy of education. These are questions of substance: Who is the final authority in making decisions on school programs and course content? Is the school dependent wholly upon the state or some private benefactor? Could there be a proper mix?

In sum, charter schools are developing a new domain between government, religion, and business. These schools may force new settlements between the values found within these sectors. Could the antagonism between these sectors produce a new civic domain? Charter schools are competing against the long-held government control over education.

In higher education, however, we see the reverse. The long-held private domain of education is challenged by the growth of government universities and colleges. Is something new happening here?

Higher Education: From Private to Government Sector Universities and colleges were private in the "early American" period. Private institutions dominated the first hundred years of the Republic, but now this situation is reversing toward government domination. The trend toward government-funded universities is increasing worldwide and shows no signs of slowing its pace.[43]

The major shift from private to state higher education in the United States began with the establishment of land-grant universities. States acquired a strong influence over education in the United States. They financed extension services and recruited students with career interests in the professions. The growth of state universities resulted in a greater separation of education from religious influences and in a corresponding leaning toward science, commerce, and politics, emphasizing public service themes. By the 1960s, the college and university systems had become very big, more political, dependent upon government financing, and more closely associated with the state than ever before in U.S. history.

From 1960 to 1980 the number of students enrolled in higher education jumped from 3.5 million to 12 million. Clark Kerr, one of the nation's foremost educators, describes the system moving from "nearly half private in terms of enrollment to one 80 percent public." Community college enrollments grew from fewer than 400,000 to more than 4 million. During this 20-year period the professorate nearly tripled in size, jumping from 235,000 to 685,000 instructors; the number of doctoral degrees awarded each year more than tripled (10,000 in 1960; 33,000 in 1980); the number of new M.D. degrees rose from 7,000 to 15,000 per annum. Federal spending on university-based R&D increased from $1,250 million to $3,000 million (in 1980 dollars), while federal expenditures on student aid rose from $300 million to $10 billion. The university went from a curriculum dominated by letters and science to one ruled by professional schools. As Kerr says, it was "the last and conclusive triumph of the Sophists over the Philosophers, of the proponents of the commercially useful over the defenders of the intellectually essential."[44]

In the United States since the 1990s, the costs of privately funded schools have become prohibitive. One study showed that by the time a kindergartner in 1992 was ready to attend a first-rate private university, costs would exceed $267,000; the senior year alone would cost $75,000 for tuition, fees, books, and housing expenses. Costs at more typical liberal arts colleges would be $200,000. If these trends continue (as they appear likely to do), they will shape a continuing decline in private school enrollments, leading, in the long run, to a system of higher education run almost exclusively by the state.[45]

Educators realize that allowing the state to become the primary source of financial support could undermine the purpose of higher education. When the state becomes the final arbiter over the transmission of knowledge, answering all the "ultimate questions," a crisis emerges around institutional freedom and the personal integrity of faculty.

Some questions in the civil development of education in the economy are these: Does general education have its own goals, its own philosophy, its own method, its own values? Can education become its own institution, standing apart from being dependent upon other institutions, such as government, business, or religion? Can education convey societal and cultural values and still serve its own ends? Can it come under its own authority? If the answers were yes to these questions, there should still be room for educational programs to fulfill the specific needs and values of the state, church, and business.

In a civil society, the government is one body, one "corporation" with its own systems of belief, its own version of truth. States are competing with private universities and colleges in ways that threaten the independent sector, raising these philosophical questions. In the last two centuries, private education, dominated by religious colleges, has become secularized. Might the next century witness a desecularization into a new form of civil education? Can a theory of civil privatization reconcile these issues?

Possibilities for Civil Privatization

On September 10, 1997, the National Collegiate Honors Council (NCHC) participated in a press conference at the National Press Club in Washington, D.C., on the purpose of education. On the same day, representatives of the NCHC met with representatives of the American Association of Universities, the American Association of Community Colleges, the College Board, the American Association of State Colleges and Universities, the American Association of University Women, the National Association of Student Personnel Professionals, the Educational Testing Service, the Coalition for Student Loan Reform, and the Council for the Advancement and Support of Education. Their discussion was a "public's concern" about the nature of education itself—that is, "What kind of education do we need?" Susanna Finnell, executive director of the NCHC, called "this give-and-take around one table a watershed event in our history."[46]

There are many different philosophies of education. Some scholars define education as *a method of learning.* An emphasis on this philosophy is called, pejoratively, "instrumentalist" (or "utilitarian") because the content of a curriculum is dependent on the authority of an outside agency, like a church or government. It implies that "education" has no substance of its own. Some scholars believe that education does not have its own purpose, apart from serving the values of an outside authority from which it obtains financial support and to which it owes allegiance. Charter schools are facing this issue at elementary and secondary levels, but the issue extends as well to this higher level.[47]

Today this means experimenting with different systems of "civil education" that serve the needs of the individual and the public and bring together the values of different sectors of the economy. This form of education respects multicultural differences, national values, and cultures around the world while acknowledging that certain values transcend all cultures. A thousand experimental steps are ahead for building such an educational system. It is a constant search for a higher sense of culture in society. Culture keeps transcending each historical epoch.[48]

A new system of education is always linked with the economy. It requires a self-financing system like that of Berea College in Kentucky, which operates a restaurant, the elegant Daniel Boone Inn, and a retail furniture and crafts store in which products are made and sold by the students from Appalachia as they work their way through college. It shares some profits with business in those cases where experiments done in a campus laboratory show some commercial and societal value. Yet, this is a delicate balance between commercial and societal values. The culture of society remains primary in any thought about changing systems of learning.[49]

Hundreds upon hundreds of issues need to be addressed in organizing a publicly oriented civil association in the educational field. They include the following: finding the basis for self-financing, keeping professional traditions, maintaining autonomous systems in each school, maintaining fair competition, encouraging separate and common scholarships, managing the differences in fees as students choose advanced work in their chosen institutions, keeping costs low, maintaining academic excellence, discussing questions of vouchers and other modes of financial support for students, solving the problem of substantive values in core courses, outlining the geographic boundary of such an association, and defining criteria for membership.

Summary: Into the Future

Civil privatization is designed to fit the conditions of each community as well as those who bid for city contracts or the new entrepreneurs. We have discussed how government agencies can be transformed into self-governing and accountable enterprises. There is much experimentation ahead for the transfer of government operations into civil enterprises, whether profit or nonprofit. (See a few areas in the list that follows.) The future requires "trial runs" to determine how more civil markets save money, reduce taxes, enhance the standard of living, and advance the common good.

Our purpose is to arouse thought about civil privatization as a direction for local planning. Social problems need to be solved in the economy where they originate, not solved *only* by adding more laws and agencies to government. Democratic governments exist to support a self-regulating market as well as to promote public safety, national defense, and the general welfare. Governments should continue to protect the public but also advance civil development.

A democratic government can help people govern themselves with greater freedom, civic responsibility, and accountability. The organized economy is not simply a private system of markets; it is part of a public domain designed for the common good. It is self-organized through multiple types and layers of associations, and it is self-creating. In the next chapter, we speak of competitive firms in civil associations at the national level.

Areas for Civil Privatization: Cities and Counties

Adoption, air-pollution abatement, airport operation, airport services, alarm-system maintenance, ambulance, animal control, appraisals, architectural, auditorium management, auditing

Beach management, billing and collection, bridge (construction, inspection, and maintenance), building demolition, building rehabilitation, buildings and grounds (janitorial, maintenance, security), building and mechanical inspection, burial of indigents, bus operation, bus-shelter maintenance

Cafeteria and restaurant operation, catch-basin cleaning, cemetery administration, child protection, civil defense communication, clerical, communication maintenance, community center operation, computer operations, consultant services, convention center management, crime laboratory, crime prevention and patrol, custodial

Data entry, data processing, day care, document preparation, drug and alcohol programs

Economic development, election administration, electrical inspection, electric power, elevator inspection, emergency maintenance, environmental services

Educational development, schools, universities, colleges

Family counseling, financial services, fire communication, fire-hydrant maintenance, fire prevention and suppression, flood-control planning, foster-home care

Golf-course operation, graphic arts, guard service

Health inspection, health services, homemaker service, hospital management, hospital services, housing inspection and code enforcement, housing management

Housing (government apartments, rental controls, regulations)

Industrial development, insect and rodent control, institutional care, insurance administration, irrigation

Jail and detention, janitorial, juvenile delinquency programs

Labor relations, laboratory, landscaping, laundry, lawn maintenance, leaf collection, legal aid, library operation, licensing

Management consulting, mapping, marina services, median-strip maintenance, mosquito control, moving and storage, museum and cultural

Noise abatement, nursing, nutrition

Office-machine maintenance, opinion polling

Paratransit system operation, park maintenance, parking enforcement, parking lot and garage operation, parking lot cleaning, parking meter servicing, parking ticket processing, patrol, payroll processing, personal services, photographic services, physician services, planning, plumbing inspection, police communication, port and harbor management, printing, prisoner transportation, probation, property acquisition, public administrator services, public health, public relations and information, public works

Records maintenance, recreation services and facility operation, rehabilitation, resource recovery, risk management

School bus, secretarial, security, sewage treatment, sewer maintenance, sidewalk repair, snow (plowing, sanding, removal), social services, soil conservation, solid waste (collection, transfer, disposal), street services (construction, maintenance), test scoring, traffic control (markings, signs, and signal installation and maintenance), training (of government employees), transit management, transportation of elderly and disabled, treasury functions, tree services (planting, pruning, removal)

Utility billing, utility meter reading

Vehicle fleet management, vehicle maintenance, vehicle towing and storage, voter registration

Water-meter reading and maintenance, water-pollution abatement, water supply and distribution, water treatment, weed abatement, welfare

Zoning and subdivision control

6 Civil Associations

Associative democracy has two fundamental distinctive features: it bridges and transforms the division between state and civil society . . . [and] . . . it promotes the democratic governance of corporate bodies in both public and private spheres, aiming to restrict the scope of hierarchical management and offering a new model of organizational efficiency.

—Paul Hirst, *Associative Democracy* (1994)

In this chapter, we argue that the internalization of social costs is an activity performed best by associations in the private sector. Public standards for fair competition, safety, health, and transparency can be established in associations where members agree on rules of the game. As this rule-making activity develops, the private economy should become a more public affair where essential norms are held in common and exchange systems are designed to be as open as possible. The economy becomes recognized as a system of cooperative and competitive firms in standard-making associations.

We developed the logic of a self-governing economy in previous chapters. We said capitalism began with the principle of self-regulation. Then, during the eighteenth century, the unrestricted rise of corporations made it difficult to realize this principle. On the positive side, we said that people had developed associations to settle their own problems in all sectors of the economy. We noted that when competitors set standards for their common good through a more civil association, they increase their capacity for self-governance. Market rules are socially constructed, not simply rules that are government constructed and imposed through agencies.

Thus, we have argued that civil "freedom" cannot exist without civil "order." We illustrated systems of accountability that have been evolving to supply social standards at different levels of market organization. We pointed to the synergy that could be created between people in civic movements seeking justice and business seeking profits. We argued that, in a decentralized order of associations, people could increase justice *and* profits.

Finally, we discussed how privatization could happen through civil associations that create a system of fair, productive, and reliable competition.

In this chapter, we continue this proposal for civil development in the marketplace. We contend that competitors can create even greater measures of self-regulation in their associations. People in all sorts of positions—as business leaders, corporate consultants, public officials, public interest lawyers, union stewards, consumers, employees, and citizens—can build more civil organizations in the economy.

A civil association develops when competitors in the economy set standards that work for themselves and the public good. Civil associations provide an order within which members compete with public standards. A more civil economy is created through associations that help members create space to internalize social costs, maintain market competition, and offer more transactional transparency. In our theory of civil governance, this should save taxpayer money, keep capital circulating in the private sector, and offer a greater moral integrity for everyone doing business.

There are many angles to this discussion, but we propose the following points for readers to consider: (1) Government cannot regulate the conduct of millions of national and global firms; (2) Corporate competition costs too much to regulate by government alone—without civil associations; and (3) Civil associations are a frontier for a free-market economy; they increase the market's competitiveness, efficiency, and profitability and make it more possible for industries to work effectively for the public good.

Government Cannot Regulate Millions of Firms

There is a strong reality behind our argument for civil associations. Governments can no longer regulate and monitor corporate conduct in any effective way, as important as that task remains today. Government regulation has become unworkable by itself, given the growing number of firms and the market's rapidly changing technology. There are over 15 million business establishments in the United States and millions more in the global marketplace. The government cannot monitor all of them. There are too many firms devising too many schemes to advance their own self-interest.

Adding to the difficulty of large numbers, there are many firms using or producing exotic technologies for which only they have the expertise. In some industries, only the experts in firms are in a position to judge the negative impact of chemicals, bacteria, gases, and technology. Government officials, without comparable expertise to make assessments, must rely on scientists working in corporations. The government's dependency on private sector experts was a cause for the terrible disaster of the *Challenger* space shuttle (see chap. 1); there are many cases of a similar sort. The growth in technology in the free market points to a dim future, unless responsible self-regulation can be established.

An April 1998 report by the General Accounting Office (GAO) concluded that federal regulatory efforts in food safety are inconsistent and unreliable. The report warned that federal agencies could not ensure that the growing volume of imported foods is safe for consumers. The GAO report said that the number of imported food entries into the United States more than doubled between 1992 and 1997, from 1.1 million to 2.7 million. Yet, during the same period, Food and Drug Administration inspections declined from 8 percent of the total imports to less than 2 percent.

There is also the issue of monitoring imports. The Washington, D.C.–based Center for Science in the Public Interest issued a summary on "Ensuring Safe Food," stating that "globalization of the food system brings food from all over the world in the US marketplace, and with it the potential for food-borne infection or other hazards." The report cites outdated safety laws and a fragmented federal regulatory structure with 12 federal agencies responsible for implementing 35 food safety statutes.[1]

Leaving all environmental problems for governments to solve does not work. One failed attempt to have government regulate on environmental issues must suffice to illustrate our point.

When some environmentalists wanted to protect children from carcinogens, a coalition of nonprofit groups (e.g., the Natural Resources Defense Council and the Environmental Working Group in Washington, D.C.) helped pass the Food Quality Act of 1996, a pesticide reform law. But in 1997, it became clear that this attempt to "regulate" corporate behavior had failed for many reasons. (1) It will take decades before the EPA, which already has 10,000 tolerances to work on, can adjust the new legal "tolerances" established; (2) The EPA's "tolerances" only affect pesticides on food, but children encounter pesticides in drinking water, the home, schools, day-care centers, lawns, gardens, swimming pools, paints, lumber, and so on, all not covered by the law; (3) The EPA does not know who is using what pesticides in what quantities on which crops or in which locations; indeed, there is no record of pesticide use in the United States; (4) The EPA has no idea how contaminated the environment is with pesticides; (5) The EPA has no way of establishing methods of testing for pesticide effects (e.g., nervous system, immune system, genetic damage, etc.); (6) There is a problem of proprietary rights in the marketplace; that is, businesses do not like to open their accounting systems and private information for public review.[2]

Government agencies cannot fulfill the task set out for them by the U.S. Congress, not by a long shot. The Occupational Safety and Health Act was written "to assure as far as possible every working man and woman in the nation safe and healthful working conditions," but thousands of workers are killed and millions injured each year in on-the-job accidents. Data from the National Safety Council show the problems are mounting around issues of both health and safety. There are too many companies with too many products for the government to inspect, monitor, and regulate.

This is not just a moral problem. Economists Russell Settle and Burton Weisbrod looked at the costs and benefits entailed in the operations of the Occupational Safety and Health Administration by analyzing efficiency and wrote about a market failure and government inefficiency.[3]

The Chemical Industry: One Example

The chemical industry continues to grow at the rate of 3.5 percent each year, doubling in size every 20 years. Of the 70,000 chemicals in commercial use in 1995, only 2 percent had been fully tested for human health effects. At least 1,000 new chemicals are introduced into commercial use each year, largely untested. If all the laboratory capacity currently available in the United States were devoted to testing new chemicals, only 500 could be tested each year. Hence, even if the necessary funding were made available, there would be no way of ever testing all the chemicals that are currently in use or all of the new ones being introduced each year.[4]

The scientific data on the injurious effects of chemicals is growing. Scientists have begun to discover that toxic substances are linked to high rates of asthma, learning deficiencies, cancer, birth defects, and species extinction. Since 1995, scientists have been trying to explain why frogs are being deformed in large numbers. Worldwide, frog populations are declining. Among the suspected causes is toxic contamination, such as pesticides, heavy metals, and acidification. It is known that detergents interfere with the ability of frogs to breathe through their skin and tadpoles to breathe through their gills. Another class of industrial compounds, called retinoids, has been implicated in frog deformities, but the case is not airtight.[5]

Hundreds of other chemicals show toxin risks that are not absolutely confirmed. Teams of researchers are working on whether the declining proportion of male births is linked to an increase in birth defects of the penis and testicles and are also investigating increases in testicular cancer. Two groups of scientists hypothesize that these patterns are linked to exposures to hormone-disrupting chemicals, including dioxin, pesticides, lead, solvents, and smokestack emissions from smelters, steel foundries, and incinerators.[6]

The Environmental Protection Agency (EPA) issued a report in 1997 about hormone-disrupting chemicals, stating that no government action was needed to protect the public health and the environment. Reviewing 300 scientific studies of hormone disruptions, Dr. Robert Huggett, EPA's assistant administrator for research, told the *New York Times* that all these studies "demonstrate that exposure to certain endocrine disrupting chemicals can lead to disturbing health effects in animals, including cancer, sterility, and developmental problems." Civic leaders are asking why the EPA does not stop the use of these chemicals.

The answer is that U.S. political and public health authorities rejected what is called "precautionary action" over 70 years ago. Serious questions around the toxic impact of chemicals are mounting with virtually no solutions. In chapter 1 we noted that the EPA could not act against a potentially toxic gasoline additive proposed by the automobile and petroleum industries. It will take decades to establish systems of accountability and self-regulation, even with strong civil movements.

Civil Movements: Precautionary Principles and Green Chemistry

The chemistry industry can serve as an example of the complexity in regulatory activity, but our proposal is that, under the right conditions, competitors, stakeholders, and outside watchdogs could do a better job at regulation. Government controls are essential to maintain today, but better standards can be created with more effective monitoring through civil associations where competing firms pay the cost for outside experts and governments to help them create standards for their industry. They must agree on outside spectators or monitors.

If effective trade/professional standards are not introduced on a voluntary basis, the government can coerce industries to create them. As we will see later in this chapter, when competitors pay professionals to monitor their performance, customers can face a price hike in a product. This standard making and monitoring process costs competitors, but we propose this practice costs less—and is more effective—than turning to government. The government can act as a consultant to business and neutral parties about how to establish market regulation that meets public requirements.

Government agencies can help business create effective self-monitoring and self-enforcing mechanisms.

The Precautionary Movement

A "principle of precautionary action" has been emerging among conscientious scientists and civic leaders for the last 10 years. On January 1998 at Wingspread in Racine, Wisconsin, an international group of scientists, government officials, lawyers, labor, and grassroots activists met to define this precautionary principle in more detail. They argue that environmental decisions based on risk assessment are inadequate. When a product raises threats of harm to human health or the environment, precautionary measures should be taken even if the cause and effect relationship is not fully established scientifically. The proponent of the product, rather than the public, should bear the burden of proof. This civic group believes that corporations, governments, organizations, and scientists should adopt a precautionary approach to all endeavors, including new chemicals.[7]

Author Sandra Steingraber, one participant in the Wingspread meeting, said: "When toxic chemicals enter our bodies—or the bodies of our children—without our informed consent, it is a toxic trespass. Such a trespass is wrong and almost everyone recognizes that it is wrong."[8]

Another Wingspread participant, Robert Costanza of the University of Maryland, proposed an "assurance bond," which he had dubbed the "4P" approach to scientific uncertainty. The "4P" stands for the "precautionary polluter pays principle." This means that before a new technology or chemical could be introduced, the worst-case damage should be estimated in dollar terms. Then the proponent of the new activity would be required to post a bond for the full amount before start-up.

Such "assurance bonds" are common in the construction industry, to make certain that a job will be completed on schedule. A "4P" bond would shift the burden of proof onto the proponent of a high-risk product. If harmlessness could be shown as time passed, the bond would be returned with interest. The bond would also give a financial incentive for proponents to reduce the worst-case damages by adapting less damaging alternatives. Opposition from the chemical industry, however, has already mounted and would most likely prevent any such law from passing the U.S. Congress. It is difficult to estimate the future harm of a product to a society or the whole world.

The precautionary principle, which shifts the burden of proof for harmlessness onto the producers of toxic chemicals, carries a market-based solution. The pharmaceutical industry must show safety and efficacy before marketing a new drug. Peter Montague, a critic of the chemical industry, makes the following argument.

> The rationale for placing such requirements on the drug corporations was that humans would be directly exposed to drugs, so safety had to be shown and the need for the new drug established. Today we know that all landfills leak, incinerators don't fully destroy toxic chemicals, and humans are therefore exposed to low levels of essentially every industrial chemical released into commercial channels (whether as waste or as product). Therefore, the rationale for U.S. pharmaceuticals policy would logically lead to the conclusion that all industrial chemicals should be treated the same as drugs: the burden of proof of harmlessness (and proof of need) should fall on the producer.[9]

Montague argues his point in the language of business. The companies should "put their money where their mouths are," he says. Investors who want to bet on the future should embrace such an "efficient and fiscally-responsible precautionary proposal."

In my judgment, the federal government should search aggressively for solutions through civil associations. Agency officials should support public interest movements that help build enforceable standards in the chemical industry. A special concern about toxic effects has also developed among chemists.

The Green Chemistry Movement

The green chemistry movement focuses on the design, manufacture, and use of chemicals and chemical processes that have little or no pollution potential or environmental risk and are simultaneously economically and technically feasible. The principles of green chemistry can be applied to all areas of chemistry, including "synthesis, catalysis, reaction conditions, separations, analysis, and monitoring." The green chemistry movement includes the practice of teaching alternative chemistries in universities.[10]

The American Chemical Society (ACS) is helping to sponsor this movement in green chemistry. ACS is a self-governed, individual membership organization with 155,000 members—60 percent from industry. It is constantly holding national, regional, and local "section meetings," exchanging information and ideas. The organization seeks to "foster communication and understanding" among its members, as well as the business sector of the chemical industry, governments, and local communities. Its goal is "to insure health and public safety," as well as to keep up with research and other matters. The ACS is aware of the growing safety and environmental problems. Indeed, during the past year, it has held conferences on "Environmental Management," "Chemistry and the Global Environment," "Good Manufacturing Practices in Chemical Development," "Pollution and Environmental Technology," and so on. We are saying, however, that the government should work more closely with such independent associations on specific issues of testing and self-regulation.

There is a sincere interest among business leaders in the chemical industry in solving problems of waste and health risk, but at the same time, they maintain a strong defensive posture against setting environmental standards. This contradictory interest can be seen in the work of the Chemical Manufacturing Association (CMA). World organizations (chap. 8) have recommended that global corporations "report annually on routine emissions of toxic chemicals even in the absence of host country requirements." The response of the Chemical Manufacturers Association was to form the Chlorine Chemistry Council (CCC) to defend the industry on this matter. At the same time, the CMA has positively supported 10 guidelines for "Responsible Care," which are currently under discussion with global environmental organizations.

A Three-Sectored Strategy
If we think carefully, effective solutions will require the collaboration of our three sectors: government, business, and nonprofit associations. Government officials should play a stronger role in urging trade associations in private industries, academic associations in education, and scientific associations to set standards and push alternatives. If government cannot pressure associations into action in critical situations, it must mandate the rules. Let us illustrate how government has already played this vital role.

On January 31, 1990, the Occupational Safety and Health Administration (OSHA) published a rule for "Occupational Exposures to Hazardous Chemicals in Laboratories." The new standard applies to all laboratories meeting OSHA's definition of laboratory use of hazardous chemicals. Each laboratory employer is required to appoint a chemical hygiene officer to develop a written plan to implement. The recommended standard operating procedures identify the safeguards that should be taken when working with hazardous chemicals, including employee management and training, medical surveillance, labeling and hazard identification, use of personal equipment, and record keeping.[11]

Obviously, the first task of government is to protect the public. At the same time, government has another task to encourage more responsibility in the nonprofit sector. Public policies can encourage the integration of a public need for safety and health with corporate needs for efficiency and profitability. We think this integration is best developed through civil associations, not single firms, and not just by government alone. The creation of public standards, accountability, and market efficiency is a responsibility of civil associations. Public policies could encourage the chemical industry to serve as a model.

The chemical industry in the United States releases more than 3 billion tons of chemical waste each year to the environment. Industry then spends $150 billion per year in waste treatment, control, and disposal costs. The challenge for associations of manufacturers, chemists, and educational associations is to examine the public problem as it is constituted in each one of their own fields. The problem exists in all stages of chemical design, manufacture, and use. The challenge for trade associations is to make incremental changes that, when summed, will achieve significant accomplishments in the design of new products and processes that are less polluting and hazardous to the environment. Governments can support appropriate associations in doing this, and in turn, civic associations can help governments advance the cause of public safety at less cost. The type of associations (e.g., the CMA, American Industrial Hygiene Association, Chemical Producers and Distributors Association) that should participate is a matter for government to decide.

Let us illustrate how this "cause" is accomplished through governments, business, Third-Sector organizations, nonprofit associations, and political parties.

First, federal agencies, because of their different responsibilities, can be in conflict about what to do about this problem. Officials in the U.S. Commerce Department support the business sector, in effect saying, if the United States were to stop innovations in the chemical industry by precautionary principles, other nations would obtain a competitive advantage over U.S. business. Consumer and safety agencies argue for precautionary principles, yet, what is actually done is political, depending upon the party in power. Hence, civic movements raise public awareness about the problem in all its complexity.

Civil solutions require setting standards and rules both inside and outside the business sector. There are the associations mentioned previously but also environmental consulting firms and educational associations that are directly involved in these matters. Consulting firms should participate in government negotiations for safety and efficiency. A company called Environmental Standards, for example, provides consulting services to Fortune 500 companies and to private industries. This company helps businesses find cost-effective solutions to meet public standards and solve environmental problems. It is not in business to monitor conduct for the government. But such business consultation can help firms to find ways to meet standards and save money. People in a particular business may know better than government officials how to solve technical problems.[12]

In November 1998, the Chemical Manufacturers Association (CMA) and the Environmental Defense Fund (EDF) announced an unprecedented cooperative program to test nearly 3,000 major industrial chemicals for their effects on health and the environment. This was a battle between the CMA and hundreds of Third-Sector organizations. The Third Sector was concerned about toxic effects of unregulated chemicals on the public. This civil (moral) decision took place among corporate actors. The EDF happened to be an actor in the Third Sector who negotiated a settlement. But the federal government was an essential actor, serving behind the scene, helping to resolve their differences in the public interest.

We discuss procedures for finding solutions at the global level in chapter 8, but markets need to be regulated from inside the private sector and not alone by government. Government cannot do the job by itself, although it plays a role in mandating public disclosure and encouraging business associations to assist in rule making and the enforcement process.[13]

In sum, we need more civil associations in the market system. A civil association is a self-governing body of competitors that is voluntary and carries a public sense of responsibility. Civil associations cultivate certain attributes, such as (1) democratic member participation in decision making; (2) systems of stakeholder accountability; (3) codes of corporate and individual conduct; (4) public standards on such matters as safety, health, and environmental protection; (5) transparent systems of social-financial auditing; (6) impartial monitors of corporate and individual conduct in relation to its own standards; (7) judiciary systems issuing penalties against offenders who break the rules.

We are talking about an economy in which members of an association are free to compete in their own self-interest yet also design themselves to operate in the context of a common good, that broader set of values in society.[14]

Market Competition Costs Too Much to Regulate by Government Alone

Citizens pay for the cost of regulating business in a competitive market. The U.S. government had 14 major regulatory agencies before 1930, over two dozen in 1950, and 57 by the early 1980s. Each year billions of dollars are added to the cost of goods and services because of government regulation. There is an endless flow of forms, reports, and questionnaires for businesses to complete in order to satisfy the requirements of regulatory agencies. One estimate is that, on average, each dollar Congress appropriates for regulation results in an additional $20 in costs imposed on the private sector. A good part of this added cost is the burden of paperwork that business must absorb. Some analysts contend that government regulations reduce innovation and efficiency, delay new investments in plant equipment, and have disproportionately adverse effects on small business. Business leaders have been very concerned with "regulatory unreasonableness."[15]

There are now more than 30 laws that every business executive must know to manage effectively. This includes five antitrust laws, five employment laws, three securities regulations, six labor laws, five environmental laws, and five consumer protection laws, all written for the common good. In the federal budget today, the major costs of regulation are for (1) finance and banking (e.g., Federal Deposit Insurance Corporation), (2) industry-specific regulation (e.g., Federal Communications Commission), and (3) general business (e.g., Securities and Exchange Commission). Certain regulatory agencies are designated as "social," including the Equal Employment Opportunity Commission, the Occupational Health and Safety Commission, and the Consumer Product Safety Commission. Some agencies are industry specific, such as the Highway Traffic Safety Administration and the Food and Drug Administration.[16]

The cost of economic regulation has grown about 100 percent over 25 years, and social regulation has increased about 300 percent over the same years. The numbers of agency staff have increased along with the costs.[17]

In the last decade, corporations have been accused of breaking the law more frequently, and the government has been getting bigger and tougher. Between 1988 and 1991, federal prosecutions increased by 50 percent, and the average fine for corporate crime went from around $200,000 to $1,500,000. Mandatory sentences have raised the number of jail terms for convicted executives. Most corporate crimes go undetected; if effective methods for detecting corporate crime were instituted, the cost and size of government would rise even further.[18]

State supreme courts have been spearheading a movement to protect consumers. Producers are increasingly held responsible for product-related injuries. (Manufacturers have become more concerned about product liability laws today than about the Consumer Product Safety Commission.) Judges have tossed out the old rule that manufacturers and sellers are liable only when they are "negligent" or "unreasonably careless" in making products. They have adopted a tougher standard of "strict liability" in place of the old standard of caveat emptor (buyer beware). Now the product itself, rather than the way consumers use it, is put on trial. The legal concept of "buyer beware" has shifted to "seller beware." The quality of the product itself is now the focus of legal inquiry.

This has meant that government courts become overloaded with pending cases, judges overtaxed in their work. In this case, the issues of justice and efficiency go together. Such costs to the public—to everyone—indicate that an alternative should be considered to reduce the need for government oversight and restraint. The question follows as to whether government costs and burdens like this should continue or whether the conditions can be changed.

Is it possible to cultivate a greater measure of self-regulation in markets? Can public norms be "internalized" within market organization? Can the amount of externalization be reduced? Can rules of fair competition be ratified in social contracts between stakeholders in their associations?

In theory and in business law, the answer is yes, but the answer in practice is—only with strong leadership. Leadership must come from people doing business as well as from the government. In some cases, business leaders know how to establish rules of the playing field better than government officials do, and in other cases government officials have more expertise. The task of self-regulation requires a working relationship between business and government and, where appropriate, among stakeholders, to internalize costs in the private sector and reduce agency expenditures.

We have noted that business competitors establish rules for themselves all the time in the private sector, but they must first cooperate to do it. Such self-discipline is common in many fields of competition. Scientists are very strict on their rules for empirical research. They have a responsibility to themselves and to the public to obtain factual data, to tell the truth. A professional association requires referees, anonymous readers, and experts in the field to evaluate competitive papers submitted to its journal. Outside experts are called upon to evaluate articles and judge reports on research. Professional findings are published in trusted journals—ranging in subject matter from astronomy to medicine to zoology—and go into the public domain. A profession assumes public responsibility for its members' work. With the time required to make agreements, set strong standards, and maintain public responsibility, professional work remains competitive, efficient, and highly productive. Could business do better?

The idea is simple: members make an agreement to play by the rules. Competitors sign a contract to set standards and the procedures by which to judge violations. It is in the interest of each member to create, affirm, and abide by the rules of fair competition.

A New Public Policy

More self-regulation needs to take place in the business system on a wider scale with neutral third parties involved. Government agencies, like the Federal Trade Commission (FTC), regularly negotiate settlements and restructure markets, but we are saying that their *new task* should be to encourage and pressure competitors and stakeholders to solve their own problems. This new pattern of government-business negotiation encourages (or requires) competitors to write social contracts that have rules and agreements for tribunals and final arbitration. The purpose is to reduce the need for more government agencies and laws.

For example, the FTC focuses its attention on six issues: truth in advertising, selling practices, truth in lending, warranties, packaging, and pricing. Competitors and interest groups inform the FTC of violations of the law, and then the agency moves to correct the problem. For example, a baking company was found to be falsely advertising its product by claiming that "Our bread will help you lose weight." The FTC ordered the company to stop making the claim and to spend 25 percent of its advertising budget for six months on corrective advertising.

The change in policy we are proposing would start with the FTC taking such punitive action, but then the agency would work with the baking association to establish self-regulatory mechanisms for the industry to settle its own cases. Some laws are already on the books. The baking association cannot administer such severe penalties that they destroy the business of a competitor. The law already says that the penalties of a trade association cannot interfere with free competition, but they can be serious enough to motivate fair play among all members.

In another case, the FTC ordered Sears, Roebuck and Company to stop its "bait and switch" tactics in selling home appliances. This meant that Sears had violated a rule against advertising a product at a low price and then telling the customer that the advertised product was not available, but that the customer could buy a higher priced product. We are suggesting that the FTC should serve the injunction but then work within retail industry associations to establish civil codes and the appropriate penalties to stop the practice. This rule is in the members' collective self-interest. If bait and switch is widely practiced, it diminishes the value of all advertising. Consumers learn to disregard advertisements.

The FTC would then negotiate the conditions whereby competitors come to agree on the rules, the monitors, the arbiters, and the penalties against violators. Administrative law is very complex, but the FTC has several tools available to it. It may seek a temporary injunction to stop certain practices, seek voluntary compliance with the rules, use consent orders, and proceed to formal adjudication for a hearing or trial before an administrative law judge. The judge's opinion may be appealed to five commissioners at the FTC. Indeed, all major government agencies use this "rule-making" device to establish uniform standards for all companies in the field.

Increasing Transparency, Not Secrecy

This rule making is in the public domain. The Sunshine Act of 1977 says that the public must be allowed to sit in on all meetings of some 50 different federal agencies, including the FTC and the Securities and Exchange Commission (SEC). Public access to meetings is not limited simply to formal sessions where votes are taken; people are entitled to listen at any time that a majority of the agency's board members holds sessions about official business.

Other federal laws in this regard are noteworthy for our purposes. A government regulatory agency has the right to subsidize public participation in its rule-making decisions. Such financing, called "intervenor funding," increases transparency around public issues. The agency provides financial support for people who do not have funds to litigate their case. But this support and openness can also lengthen the legal process; hence, something called "negotiated rule making" has become popular.

This open rule making allows access to regulatory policymakers and offers an alternative to the long, fractious process of safeguarding the public, workers, or the environment. It shackles fewer people and businesses with undue economic burdens. With negotiated rule making, regulators try to quicken the pace and limit the number of lawsuits that would take an extended period.

Thus, the public policy we are proposing has begun to happen; it is partially enacted. Our three sectors (business, government, and nonprofit) have begun to negotiate settlements. Nonprofit consumer groups and automobile makers help the FTC fashion new warranty rules. Nonprofit environmental groups and oil companies meet at the Interior Department to formulate air-pollution standards for offshore drilling rigs. Labor unions and manufacturers meet at the Occupational Safety and Health Administration to decide on new factory exposure limits for widely used toxic solvent.

We are saying that this practice could be extended further into the private sector with the aid of a more sharply defined public policy. The government can require the private sector—with its competitors and countervailing powers—to set up "justice structures" at the association level to set-tle social problems where they originate in the market itself.

It costs money in the private sector to set up a civil system of arbiters and regulatory procedures. Yet, it should be cheaper in the long run as a civil practice than as a government practice. We propose that the cost of a civil regulation should be less expensive in most markets than leaving the whole responsibility to the government. The money stays in the market, as opposed to increasing taxes and the transfer costs to government. A civil process of market regulation, given the existence of countervailing powers, should be cheaper. It is cheaper logically because the settlements are made where the problems arise—among the immediately affected parties.

We are talking about efficiency and effectiveness, not ethical and moral conduct. Market self-regulation, done properly, should be more efficient than government regulation. Setting the rules of fair competition and establishing systems of accountability in market sectors should be a better way of doing business. Self-regulation, as a custom of commerce, a habit of industry, could be very productive. Indeed, it could create more capital in the private sector.

Increasing Cooperation, Not Collusion

Collusion exists when organizations (businesses and governments) collabo-rate to the competitive disadvantage of others and against the public good. For these reasons, many (perhaps most) people do not trust business *or* gov-ernment. Top business leaders and government agencies in the past have col-luded against the public interest. Business competitors have colluded to raise prices and "corner a market," but we are saying that the government sector can help the business sector go further with its own civil development.

The popular image is that government is the only institution (not busi-ness) capable of stopping collusion. In my judgment, this is a popular myth. Collusion between government and business has been documented for over a century. We are simply suggesting that the government can serve the public better by assisting the development of a responsible self-governing economy. Government can always be a monitor, a safety net, and a court of last resort. When associations (competitors and neutral parties) fail to en-act effective procedures, the government is a backup. When the job is done properly and institutionalized, the government is not needed.

Recently, there has been a growth in civil rights laws. The *Equal Pay Act* established that women could not be paid less than men for doing sub-stantially the same work. The *Age Discrimination in Employment Act* made it unlawful to refuse the employment of any individual because of age. The *Americans with Disabilities Act* covered not only people with hearing, sight, or mobility impairments but also those with emotional illness, dyslexia, AIDS, and past drug or alcohol addictions. The *Civil Rights Act of 1991* extended punitive damages of up to $300,000 to victims of employment discrimination based on sex, disability, and race.

Companies that have not supported "equality in employment" have faced expensive lawsuits. The State Farm Insurance Company was accused in 1992 of sex discrimination and negotiated a $240 million settlement. Hughes Aircraft Company was hit with a $89.5 million race discrimination verdict in 1994. Penalties can be severe enough to get the attention of business executives. Ethical issues on "equality" require a new perspective on business responsibility.

Yet the business culture is changing in this era of human rights. Today's top executives say that they have found legally required affirmative action programs helpful in monitoring their own progress for equal job opportunity. General Electric, AT&T, and IBM said that they would continue to use affirmative action goals and timetables *even if they were not required by law.* The fact is, however, that self-regulation requires systems of accountability. Without government laws or civil associations to enforce agreements, companies forget the rule.[19]

In other words, government laws may be essential to get the moral message across to companies, but in our theory of civil practice, agencies should also negotiate rules with trade associations to reduce the government workload. The government has certain mechanisms at its disposal to make such negotiations, such as voluntary consent orders and formal adjudication. It has a process of arranging settlements between public interest groups and whole industries. All major government agencies have the right to use this "rule-making" device to create uniform standards for all companies in a single field. Thus government can build more civil associations in the marketplace.[20]

Government laws are made and agencies are created when the atmosphere of competitive markets pushes companies into acting like hungry lions roaming for the kill. Competitive markets by themselves do not create a sense of the common good. Hence, there is a need for executive self-reflection on the creation of "market communities" that work in their interest and for the common good.

A civil procedure for justice in the private sector requires a search for professionals who can be trusted, establishing an effective means for ousting those who are found violating the trust placed in their professional office and choosing outside monitors who know the field. This reduces the likelihood of collusion. In other words, civil procedures may include paying third parties or neutral arbitrators in those cases where competitors in associations cannot regulate themselves on essential issues.

Members of the Defense Industry Initiative on Business Ethics (DII) have taken a step along this path. DII is a self-regulatory organization for the defense industry that was formed in 1986 in the wake of revelations of widespread fraud and corruption. DII encourages and assists its members in establishing ethics programs to promote high standards of conduct throughout their companies. Members pledge to (1) develop a code of ethics; (2) conduct ethics training; (3) provide for internal reporting of alleged misconduct; (4) practice self-governance through monitoring systems and voluntary disclosure of violations; (5) attend periodic DII Best Practices Forums; and (6) provide for public accountability.

I do not know of any studies on the effectiveness of this example of self-regulation with the DII, but I would imagine that there are problems. It is normal to have successes and failures in an industry that has a reputation for being prone to corruption, but this is not the point. The point is that self-regulation requires practice, success, and failure, as it seeks to make progressive steps. Leaders learn from failure.

Trade associations have been relatively successful (and relatively unsuccessful) in setting standards in different industries. I would view the slow development of self-governance in the economy like the century-long development of civil government. It requires experimentation to form the habits of civil order. Continued practice and experimentation lead eventually to convention and custom. People need to get accustomed to new and civil practices in a competitive society.

All trade associations have rules—from the proper grading of wood to the making of fireproof clothing. In many industries, rules for the common good have become a standard, a custom, let us say, an institutionalized way of life.

Thus, the business sector has already moved in this direction, but to introduce self-regulatory measures on a broad scale—and to move government policies further in this direction—requires a civic movement. In the past, people have organized nationwide to establish laws on environmental protection, consumer protection, and general health and safety for workers. Traditionally, such movements involved citizens demanding that government force (coerce) corporations to be more accountable. Nationwide movements have influenced political parties to take a stand on issues of job safety, health, and environmental protection. Elected representatives try to put these issues into laws.

In the past, civic leaders have looked to the government to solve problems, but we are in a new era. Today the government is in a position to help (or coerce) competitors and stakeholders to find their own solutions. This means working through associations, not adding more laws and government agencies. Government assists owners, managers, workers, and consumers to solve problems at the point where they originate.[21]

We are talking about a public interest movement that includes conservative, liberal, and independent parties, going beyond a single political ideology. This movement should involve responsible business leaders who want to construct accountability systems in their trade associations and scientists who want to advance safe technology. It should interest union leaders who want to see more job safety and consumers who want more protection from toxins. It should interest political leaders who want the business sector to solve its own problems and public interest lawyers who see the logic of moving in this direction.[22]

One final point is of importance to see the larger picture. Business leaders themselves seek more government controls, not simply public interest groups. Historian Gabriel Kolko *(The Triumph of Conservatism)* pointed to this contradiction between business rhetoric and lobby tactics by trade associations to create more government in their own interest. Kolko describes how, despite the large number of mergers and the growth in the size of corporations, the dominant tendency at the beginning of the twentieth century was toward competition, but that was unacceptable to key financial interests. He argues that the merger movement was a reflection of business efforts to bring highly competitive trends under control. Business leaders who do not like competition promoted the growth of regulatory laws and agencies. Influential business leaders believed that for the sake of stability, a rational order in the market was needed. Top business leaders saw that the national government could, as Kolko put it, "rationalize the economy." Internal problems in the market could be solved only by political means.[23]

Trade associations lobby for government laws that protect their members. For the last six years, corporations have been promoting environmental audit bills but negotiating for laws that improve environmental protection and public health according to rules in their own interest. Indeed, big corporations have approved the passage of most major environmental laws.

Environmental "self-audit" proposals have been designed to give immunity to corporations that do their own reporting. Environmental laws impose onerous requirements for gathering and reporting data, and large corporations complain about these features, but in truth, the audit requirements provide immunity and a competitive advantage for large corporations vs. small. All the paperwork that environmental laws entail hurts small businesses. A big company just assigns a team to the task and gets it done.[24]

In other words, governments can demand and/or negotiate self-regulation through trade/professional associations, but they must emphasize the freedom to compete in this civil order. Government agencies can consult with business and civic leaders on how market restructuring should be done to advance competition in the public interest. As we noted in chapters 2 and 3, government can negotiate on decentralizing business, helping big corporations work more effectively as a confederation of competing firms. Confederations are akin to trade associations. A civil confederation of firms, however, would have its own contracted system of public accountability.

If some competitors do not collaborate on public standards, government grows, the financial penalties get bigger, and the courts get tougher in demanding honesty, transparency, fair competition, and civic responsibility in business affairs.

The government has created many laws to restrain and, conversely, to support corporate power. Government has sought to construct more justice in markets and to require firms to operate in the public interest, but it is time to create a system of civil markets. It is time for leaders in business, labor, and the nonprofit sector to work toward public accountability in the private sector.

Civil Associations Are a Frontier for a Free-Market Economy

We forget that leaders in the private sector (business and nonprofit) have found consensus on norms and established procedures for self-regulation for well over a century. Democratic structures already exist in trade associations, labor unions, scientific associations, professional associations, and church denominations. People have developed consensus-making procedures for determining "what is right" and the best "professional norms" or market rules.

A market order is created within both government and civil rules or norms. Government creates "law norms," that is, rules that a democratic legislature decides are important to enforce. An association creates "civil norms," rules that are self-determined or set by some consensus within the voluntary sector. The two types of norms are very close in many ways. Each works best under certain conditions. Civil norms oftentimes can be more powerful and effective than law norms.[25]

Let us look at how civil associations reduce government interference in the market. First, we look at how competitors with government pressures internalize their costs. Second, we suggest that civil associations are a basis for providing space to promote transparency and a more effective way to enforce rules. Third, we suggest that rule making in associations could evolve as custom or a convention, with less need for outside concern.

Civil Associations Create Rules for Competition in the Public Interest

Much government intervention in the marketplace is the result of externalities or spillover effects. Government regulation becomes warranted because "negative externalities," or social costs, fall on society, not on the industry or the person who causes them. For example, the auto industry, which manufactures cars, and people, who drive them, produce degraded air quality. The industry and car drivers do not pay the full cost of production. In other words, firms that cause pollution use the environment as a free input in the production process; hence, the operating costs of the firm do not include the costs of pollution.

In effect, the firm's output is underpriced from a social cost point of view. The free market yields an inefficient solution because the consumer of the goods pays less than the full cost of production and some costs are borne by others who do not derive benefits from the product. Solving this problem of externalities may require new inventions, but it also may require collective rules for honest reporting and careful monitoring. We argue that the problem is capable of being solved through the collaboration of our three sectors. Government collaborates with business and nonprofit (trade, professional, educational) associations.[26]

For example, Toxic Use Reduction (TUR) is an environmental protection program that creates civil rules to reduce social costs. This involves rules for transparency and monitoring by the collaboration of different sectors. It was established in Massachusetts to promote safer and cleaner production processes. It enhances the viability of competitive firms through a common agreement. Let us look at this case.

A Model for the Chemistry Industry: TUR

"The goal of the TUR is to reduce the generation of hazardous wastes without limiting the capacity of local firms to grow and prosper." The program was established in 1989 when the state legislature passed the Toxic Use Reduction Act, the result of a long negotiation between business and environmental interests that resulted in a bill endorsed by both. Firms are encouraged to establish planning teams and engage the workforce in analyzing production processes, conducting materials accounting programs, auditing health and environmental regulations. The program requires thorough financial and technical analyses, which include more than 1,200 toxic chemicals. The firms must file an annual report and pay an annual fee to cover the costs of the program.

The fee was set to provide revenue to support the TUR program without incurring costs to the government and the State University in Massachusetts. Monies raised through the fee are set aside in a special trust fund, which can be used only for that program. The actual fees vary according to the size of the firm and the number of listed chemicals used above the annual threshold.[27]

The Toxic Use Reduction Institute at the University of Massachusetts in Lowell provides education and training in TUR for professionals and the general public, conducts a technology transfer program, and sponsors research in the development of safer materials and cleaner technologies. The funds for environmental protection come collectively from private industry to pay for the cost of regulation. Since the TUR program is self-financing by collective agreement within the industry, it models certain attributes of a civil association. The state could have negotiated an arrangement for TUR to be managed by a professional board in the private sector with minimal state involvement.

In other words, this institute is a model for industries that want to establish a more civil association. It is a civil alternative, an option, and a civil-market method to solve the problem of increasing numbers of dangerous technologies and chemicals.

The TUR program eliminates the ability of competitors to cut costs by noncompliance and, to some extent, predatory pricing, that is, lowering prices to corner a market. Here *all firms in the market pay a fair fee for monitoring and they comply together.* This is a "collective internalization" of cost, as opposed to an "individual externalization" of costs. Customers might pay for this system of public protection, but it is a choice between higher and lower transactional costs. This system costs less than the cost of government to regulate it. It is self-financing and a self-accountable system.

Unfair competition usually happens when one firm internalizes costs (e.g., maintaining worker safety or environmental protection) and its competitors do not. The former loses in market pricing. But in this Massachusetts model, business associations are in a joint venture. We are suggesting that TUR works better than government control.

When all association members compete by the same rules (e.g., disclosing information that was formerly "proprietary"), they monitor the program in everyone's interest. There is a motive to be honest by their common rules, not by common law. Thus, the government can encourage trade and nonprofit associations to create common rules for disclosure and for the well-being of the whole marketplace.

Creating norms through civil associations requires consultation with government officials, business leaders, stakeholders, and experts. Then, voluntary commitments among members to rules and outside arbitrators make a difference. The process takes away the cost of government monitoring and control.

The following list, Are You Y2K OK? is a list of associations that had worked to prepare for the year 2000. They advertised in newspapers to help one another. They realized that they were interdependent in the whole economy. They worked to make a Y2K date change on their computers. The associations listed were committed to helping small and medium-sized companies prepare for January 1, 2000. This work was done in their interest but also for the common good of everyone in the economy.[28]

Are You Y2K OK?

These organizations urged small and medium-sized businesses to prepare for the year 2000.

Aerospace Industries Association
Air Conditioning Contractors of America
Air Transport Association
Alliance of American Insurers
American Ambulance Association
American Association of Community Colleges
American Association of Engineering Societies
American Association of Exporters and Importers
American Association of Orthodontists
American Association of Pharmaceutical Scientists
American Bankers Association
American College of Cardiology
American Council of Life Insurance
American Crop Protection Association
American Electronics Association
American Financial Services Association
American Frozen Food Institute
American Gas Association
American Hardware Manufacturers Association

American Hospital Association
American Hotel and Motel Association
American Industrial Hygiene Association
American Institute of Certified Public Accountants
American Insurance Association
American Iron and Steel Institute
American Meat Institute
American Medical Association
American Paper Machinery Association
American Petroleum Institute
American Pipe Fittings Association
American Public Power Association
American Public Transit Association
American Public Works Association
American School Food Service Association
American Short Line and Regional Railroad Association
American Society of Association Executives
American Textile Machinery Association
American Water Works Association
America's Community Bankers

The Arlington Institute
Armed Forces Communications and
  Electronics Association
Association for Computing Machinery
Association for Financial Technology
Association of American Railroads
Association of Metropolitan Water
  Agencies
Association of School Business Officials
The Bankers Roundtable
Building Owners and Managers
  Association, International
Business Software Alliance
Cellular Telecommunications Industry
  Association
Chemical Manufacturers Association
Chemical Producers and Distributors
  Association
Community Associations Institute
Computer & Communications Industry
  Association
Computing Technology Industry
  Association
Consumer Bankers Association
Consumer Electronics Manufacturers
  Association
Council of Insurance Agents and Brokers
Council of State Governments
Council on Foundations
Direct Marketing Association
Edison Electric Institute
Financial Executives Institute
Food Distributors International
Food Marketing Institute
Gifts in Kind, International
Greater Washington Society of
  Association Executives
Grocery Manufacturers of America
Health Industry Manufacturers
  Association
Independent Bankers Association of
  America
Independent Petroleum Association of
  America
Independent Sector
Industrial Research Institute
Information Technology Association of
  America
Information Technology Industry Council
Institute for Interconnecting and
  Packaging Electronic Circuits
Institute of Electrical & Electronics
  Engineers

Intelligent Transportation Society of
  America
International Association of Emergency
  Managers
International Association of Food
  Industry Suppliers
International City/County Management
  Association
International Council of Shopping
  Centers
International Franchise Association
International Insurance Council
International Sign Association
International Sleep Products Association
International Trade Council
Internet Society
Interstate Natural Gas Association of
  America
Investment Company Institute
Joint Commission on Accreditation of
  Health Care Organizations
Local Initiatives Support Corporation
Luggage and Leather Goods
  Manufacturers
Measurement, Control & Automation
  Association
Million Dollar Round Table Insurance
  Agents
Motor Freight Carriers Association
National Association for the Self-
  Employed
National Association of Broadcasters
National Association of Chain Drug
  Stores
National Association of Counties
National Association of Federal Credit
  Unions
National Association of Government
  Labor Officials
National Association of Manufacturers
National Association of Mutual Insurance
  Companies
National Association of Professional
  Insurance Agents
National Association of State
  Departments of Agriculture
National Association of State Fire
  Marshals
National Association of State Information
  Resource Executives
National Association of Water Companies
National Automobile Dealers Association
National Cable Television Association

National Cattlemen's Beef Association
National Consumers League
National Electrical Manufacturers
  Association
National Emergency Management
  Association
National Farmers Union
National Food Processors Association
National Governors Association
National Grain and Feed Association
National Grain Trade Council
National Home Equity Mortgage
  Association
National League of Cities
National Meat Association
National Milk Producers Federation
National Retail Federation
National Rural Electric Cooperative
  Association
National Rural Health Association
National School Boards Association
National Stone Association
National Telephone Cooperative
  Association
National Turkey Federation
National Voluntary Health Agencies
National Waterways Conference
National Y2K Civic Leadership Initiative
Natural Gas Council
Natural Gas Supply Association
Newspaper Association of America
North American Electric Reliability
  Council

North American Fire Training Directors
Nuclear Energy Institute Organization
  for the Protection and Advancement of
  Small Telecommunications Companies
Personal Communications Industry
  Association
Process Equipment Manufacturers
  Association
Professional Convention Management
  Association
Public Technology, Inc.
Regional Airline Association
Reinsurance Association of America
Responsible Industry for a Sound
  Environment
Securities Industry Association
Semiconductor Equipment and Materials
  International
Society for Information Management
  Year 2000 Working Group
Society of Manufacturing Engineers
Software Publishers Association
State Emergency Medical Services
  Directors
State Information Technology
  Consortium
Uniform & Textile Service Association
U.S. Chamber of Commerce
United States Council for International
  Business
United Way of America
Wholesale Florists & Florist Suppliers of
  America

Source: Advertisement; October 19, 1998, by the U.S. Small Business Administration. Reprinted by permission.

Antitrust laws are a set of government rules that have been forged for the common good of the economy. Since the turn of this century, they have become virtual "commandments," moral principles that are followed strategically by wise business leaders. In the future, the common good may be considered a function of civil associations.

Following are examples of seven "negative commandments" established by legislation and enforced through agency policy. Executives today must *not* engage in the following types of activity.[29]

Government Rules for Fair Competition: Examples of "Taboos"

- Dividing markets with competitors geographically ("you sell west of the Mississippi, I'll sell east of it");
- Manufacturers requiring stores (that sell their products) to charge a certain minimum price and taking retaliatory action if they do not;
- Manufacturers guaranteeing a distributor or retailer an *exclusive territory* arrangement, that is, an exclusive right to sell in a particular area;
- Large companies offering their products below costs, engaging in any *predatory practices* in order to force small companies out of business;
- Group of competitors agreeing to boycott, or not deal with, a person or firm outside the group;
- Suppliers selling gidgets only if buyer also agrees to buy some gadgets; these *tying arrangements* obviously limit competition in the gadget market;
- Manufacturers or suppliers selling a product to retailer A at one price and to retailer B at another price.

Laws like those just listed are written to civilize (rationalize) market competition, but our question is whether future law norms can be anticipated and be self-written as civil norms by nationwide associations. They then become "norms of consent" among member-competitors or they become part of a civil constitution that is evolving in the market economy.

Civil Associations Create Transparency

The lack of transparency in business was one cause for the collapse of Asian markets in 1998, as well as a cause for other crashes, like the stock market in the 1930s and the failure of the savings and loan industry during the 1980s. Secrecy and overzealous proprietary rights are two reasons for market failures. In some measure, everyone pays the cost for secrecy, as it becomes a cause in market failures. In a theory of civil associations, market transactions can invoke questions of transparency vs. secrecy at every level of organization.

At the corporate level, studies have shown that open book management (OBM) increases corporate performance. Hence, corporations have begun "open book" policies for employees to increase productivity and profitability. The National Center for Employee Ownership conducted a study of OBM and concluded that it is "more than a gesture of participative management"; it increases corporate performance. They used the following criteria in their comparative study.

1. Sharing the income statement and balance sheet with most of the employees, 2. Sharing other data with employees (such as productivity and plant utilization/quality data), 3. Encouraging employees to use the data in their daily work, 4. Training employees to understand financial numbers, and 5. Maintaining the presence of a gainsharing program based on the numbers.[30]

The center found that employee-owned companies with OBM had better sales figures and performance than their non-OBM competitors. In chapter 4, we described how the employee-owned Springfield ReManufacturing Corporation trains employees for open book accounting and shares financial and production data with all employees.

In the field of finance, professional auditors across the nation assess the fiscal status of firms. This nationwide practice of *financial auditing* is a "civil structure," to which professionals want to add *social auditing*. For years, members of the accounting profession looked for ways to link social accounting with financial accounting. The movement began in the mid-1970s when firms like Bank of America, Arco, Dayton Hudson, and others pushed the idea of social audits.[31]

In 1986, the National Association of Accountants issued new guidelines to measure company performance that place less emphasis on financial measures like earnings per share and return on investment. The new guidelines sought to improve the value and potential of the company's assets. The term *value accounting* then replaced the term *social accounting* to distinguish hard-nosed worries that accounting may not measure real value. In 1994, Walker Research, a business unit of the Walker Group based in Indianapolis, Indiana, made a strong case for responsible business practices along these lines. Government agencies, they note, have been interested in supporting the social-audit practice. The Labor Department in 1994 issued a discussion guide to help business groups examine corporate performance measures based on workplace practices. Various professional accountants have argued for the integration of social standards with financial standards in the business sector.[32]

Accounting professor Ralph Estes argues that the "right to know" through a system of open audits and transparency in markets is a basic principle of the market. It is a "cost effective way" to be responsible in business without government regulations. He believes that the "piecemeal approach" to disclosure through government laws is too costly for everyone.

Congress takes this piecemeal approach by creating dozens of laws administered by dozens of government agencies. Estes's research indicates that the total social cost externalized by business exceeds $2.6 trillion every year. Hence, Estes argues that the market needs a new system of social-financial accounting that enables stakeholders to make informed economic decisions. A free-market economy rests on the assumption that *all decision makers have full and accurate information.*[33]

In 1994, the SEC issued a major report, *Market 2000,*[34] that called for major changes in the regulation of securities markets, including rules requiring better training for stockbrokers and investment advisers, more complete disclosure for the buyers of mutual funds, and tougher policing of municipal bond markets.[35]

Civil self-regulatory practices are becoming more legitimate today. Marc Epstein, writing in *Management Accounting,* describes how senior corporate managers agree that U.S. companies will be held responsible for the ultimate reuse, recycling, and proper disposal of the goods they produce. A large field study—on how companies can integrate environmental impacts into management decisions—concluded that managers are now beginning to accept responsibility for "postconsumer waste." Company managers are figuring out how to internalize (not externalize) costs that result in government regulations.

> While governments have been pressing ahead with take-back regulations, many companies have been moving forward rapidly with voluntary programs. Most manufacturers are preparing to calculate the costs of reuse, recycling, remanufacturing, or proper disposal (including transportation and handling costs); to offset the costs with potential revenues and reduced expenditures for raw material and other inputs; and to reflect all these impacts in the prices of new products.[36]

The business sector is not alone in this problem of information disclosure. Big government itself often does not provide access to information relevant to public decision making. A government can be as much at fault as a big corporation. Consider the following cases.

When Dean Wenel and his family smelled something odd near the Vulcan Chemicals facility outside Wichita, Kansas, and sought to find out if the odor was harmful, they were given no right to know. Even the Community Right to Know Act and the EPA's risk assessment would not tell them.

When an African American clerical employee suspected that she was making a wage below the two dozen white workers holding the same job, she was not given the right to know. The EEOC report on the company was filed with the federal government. It covered broad categories, but employees were not allowed to see it.

When city officials in Ypsilanti, Michigan, granted GM generous tax abatements amounting to $1.3 billion over 20 years—in return for a promise to keep 8,000 jobs in the city—GM refused to report publicly on job retention and much later closed the facility to move production to Texas.[37]

Nonprofits also have problems with transparency, just like business. The transparency idea is applicable within the whole voluntary sector, including medical, legal, dental, art, civic, recreational, and scientific associations. Jean Field, a lawyer and former public information associate at the American Civil Liberties Union, is concerned about the Third Sector, especially about setting disclosure standards for nonprofits. Field sees nonprofits as "big business." There are 120,000 nonprofit corporations in California, ranging from condominium associations and chambers of commerce to religious associations and charities with total assets at $100 billion.

Field recommends that all nonprofits disclose annual reports on goals and accomplishments, a list of board members, and detailed financial records. In the final analysis, she admits that it takes personal initiatives from national leaders to establish norms across the nonprofit sector. For example, the National Center for Nonprofit Boards is starting a California Governance Project that has taken leadership in promoting more awareness on nonprofit issues, including disclosure standards.[38]

Some government services are being privatized into the nonprofit sector—from social services to running national parks—but nonprofits are not subject to the same laws that apply to business. Not all nonprofit organizations are subject under the law to disclosure requirements; rules vary depending on their legal classification. The practice of responsible self-regulation should apply equally to the Third Sector.

In sum, increasing disclosure in all sectors is a goal in civil governance. Business corporations and nonprofits need a better accounting system and more transparency. We are saying that the government can require disclosure most effectively through trade, nonprofit, and professional associations. This reduces the likelihood of firms engaging in unfair competition. In certain cases, professionals in the Third Sector should serve as monitors. Regulatory authority often requires a balance of inside (private sector) and outside (government sector) authority for monitoring, but today the great need is to cultivate more public standards in the private sector.[39]

Civil Associations Are in the Public Domain

What is the public domain? Clearly, the meaning of the term *public* is in transition.[40] Political scientists say that the dichotomy of public vs. private in U.S. society is a "grand myth" defined in modern culture. The words we use to describe the business sector define our mental reality today. Yet, they are not sufficiently accurate to designate the problem of government growth. In popular terms, people describe the private sector as composed of *firms* that *compete,* but we could say that it is composed of *associations* that *cooperate.* Both statements are true.

Jeff Weintraub, a research fellow in sociology and political science at Leheigh University, sees this public/private dichotomy used to hide a wide range of important distinctions. We cannot determine what is meant by the terms because they are given such a variety of meanings. The literature on "public goods," for example, takes its lead from neoclassical economics. This term addresses quite a different subject from the "public sphere of dialogue" delineated by the philosopher Jürgen Habermas and different again from the "public life" of sociability on city streets charted by Jane Jacobs and Richard Sennett. Hence, there is much ahead for people to clarify about the meaning of this so-called private/public opposition.[41]

The irony is that markets and corporations are both public and private at the same time. But the greater the impact corporations have on stakeholders, the more people think about the economy in the public domain. Our proposition is that the economy is changing in general discourse to being considered more in the public domain.[42]

The banking industry underwent rapid deregulation between 1977 and 1984. We noted in chapter 4 that savings and loans had greater freedom in the marketplace but without any training for self-accountability in their associations. The government deregulated too quickly without setting rules for disclosure. Such costly failures speak dramatically about how the market system is part of the public domain.[43]

Yet, something positive began to happen during the 1970s to push private banking into the public domain. A civic movement began among people in economically disadvantaged communities. They accused financial institutions of blanket credit denials, a practice called "redlining." Low-income people were being discriminated against in their neighborhoods, and their complaints led to the passage of the Community Reinvestment Act (CRA). This legislation empowered federal agencies to consider a bank's service to the neighborhoods in which it operated before approving its application for a new depository facility, such as a retail branch. This began as a government regulation, but in this case, the nonprofit sector became involved. Nonprofits became monitors, connected now with banking, moving this market sector more into a public domain.

When the government requires corporate transparency, it allows non-profit groups to be monitors of a business sector. When this happens, the economy moves further toward being considered public. The popular term *private economy* refers to business, but when nonprofits are engaged in the same market sector as a countervailing power, the idea of the economy broadens to gain a more public character.

In our case with the CRA, nonprofit groups were engaged in tracking developments in private banking, assessing their effect on lower-income neighborhoods. These organizations had the advantage of greater trans-parency by virtue of the CRA law, which provided more public access to bank information. Thus, the injustice perpetrated by banks on low-income neighborhoods was being addressed by the participation of nonprofits, not just government. Nonprofits become outside monitors under rights of pub-lic disclosure.

The right to public disclosure allowed the Center for Community Change (CCC), a nonprofit organization founded to support grassroots groups, to offer its expertise and strategic guidance to the government. Nonprofits now had access to private bank information on the allocation of loans. The work of nonprofits like the CCC, given transparent accounting, went far to stabilize and civilize this sector of a market that was producing social problems. Banking now had a measure of public accountability.[44]

Many nonprofit organizations, like the CCC, view banks as part of the public domain because they receive government benefits from deposit in-surance and guaranteed access to emergency funds during crises of illiq-uidity. Furthermore, nonprofit groups of this sort view all corporations as having a public responsibility to be transparent in accounting by virtue of the government support they receive in legislation, subsidies, and liberal charters. This view seems to be part of a growing opinion in wider sectors of U.S. society.[45]

Some lawyers argued in the 1970s that big corporations should go pub-lic, which meant that they should be federally chartered. They based their argument on a proposal by James Madison during the Constitutional Con-vention in 1787. Madison wanted national charters based on the idea of public accountability. In the ensuing years, this public-charter idea was given to states, which competed fiercely to get corporate charters, and the popular notion of a federal charter for corporations virtually disappeared. Some scholars still argue for federal (national) charters today, contending that giant corporations should be required legally to operate in the public interest.[46]

Adam Smith said that corporations couldn't function in competition for long without a loss of civic responsibility. Hence, Smith was against the rise of corporations because he saw their excesses leading to government control over the market. In turn, excessive government would destroy civil society. We have argued that the corporate actor has largely replaced the individual actor in the market system of Smith's time. As an alternative to federal charters and government controls, the members of an association can preserve their self-interest and compete while they create public standards. This civil process provides an opportunity for corporations to develop a measure of self-regulation that Smith believed defined a civil society.

Summary

First, governments cannot regulate millions of firms. Governments are vital to maintain order, but they do not have the power to monitor the growing number of firms. They do not have the expertise to oversee the multitude of specialized markets. Government agencies are like kings in feudal times. They have too many subjects to watch under too many circumstances. It follows that companies must learn to govern themselves in a civil economy.

The lack of social accountability in business and the rate of growth in state bureaucracy are sufficient reasons to structure markets for greater self-regulation and to lessen the need for outside intervention. Market competition by itself cannot sustain a civil society.

Second, market competition by itself costs too much. Without some cooperation among competitors for the common good, the market increases the number of government laws and enforcement agencies. In every competitive sport—whether it is baseball, basketball, football, or tennis—civil order is required. A civil association exists so that members can compete, create rules of competition for their common good, and appoint an umpire, a referee, or a final arbitrator to make decisions about rule violations and disagreements. This associative practice for competing with rules and penalties is done in all major fields of nonbusiness activity—science, art, education, religion, medicine, and law. This practice needs to be developed further in the business sector.[47]

Third, civil associations should be constructed to increase freedom as a civil frontier for self-regulation in society. Business organizations, unions, and professional and scientific associations have invented standards for themselves during the past century. This spontaneous activity has already reduced the need for laws. Now, however, we are talking about this self-development supported by government policies and a public more conscious of the need for a nationwide system of accountability and profitability.

In civil development, competitors pay the cost of market freedom by regulating themselves. Many business associations now pay for trade journals, trade fairs, training in management and uniform accounting, professional mediation, outside arbiters, and so on. We are saying that the associative practice of self-regulation requires members to internalize social costs. The internalization of costs is the key to building a civil economy.[48]

The private economy is part of a public domain. The private market affects everybody; hence, the marketplace is a public affair, even as it remains autonomous from government. Civil associations are an avenue for competitors and Third-Sector organizations to guide free markets.[49]

In conclusion, market rules are self-constructed, as well as government constructed. The internalization of social costs is not a problem to be solved by one firm in the midst of market competition. The setting of public standards, such as fair competition and transparency, can be established at the level of associations where everyone agrees on the rules of the game. The civil economy develops with human values and civil networks within which people compete against one another in their own interest and work for the common good.

III A Global Economy

7 Problems in Global Markets

> There was a time when corporations played a very minor part in our business affairs, but now they play the chief part, and most men are the servants of corporations.
>
> —Woodrow Wilson, "The Older Order Changeth," in *The New Freedom* (1913)

> The new electronic interdependence recreates the world in the image of a global village.
>
> —Marshall Herbert McLuhan, *The Medium Is the Massage* (1967)

After the collapse of communism, free trade became the mantra of governments and businesses around the world. Since 1991 some 600 changes have been made in the regulatory regimes of countries worldwide to make them more open to foreign trade and investment. The global reach of business markets, however, has given rise to fears that decision-making powers are passing from governments to boardrooms.[1]

The globalization of markets is therefore critical to understand if we want to anticipate the future of nations and the environmental well-being of the planet. The power of global corporations has grown rapidly because of their capacity to do something nations cannot do—integrate economic resources (technology, production, finance, marketing) on a worldwide scale. Nations cannot integrate material resources in the same manner; hence, they lose power to global firms. Global firms now compete with nations to influence the direction of global governance.[2]

Bennett Harrison of Carnegie Mellon University asserts that the destructive features of global markets are serious. Conglomerate corporations and their allies have gained control over regional and local markets. Global corporations are beginning to determine the future of civil society. Indeed, they threaten the existence of the nation-state with their power to move freely across political boundaries in a way never seen before in history.[3]

Robert Reich, former secretary of labor, explains how this new global system could have dire consequences.

We are living through a transformation that will rearrange the politics and economics of the coming century. There will be no *national* products or technologies, no national corporations, no national industries. There will no longer be national economies at least as we have come to understand that concept. All that will remain rooted within national borders are the people who comprise a nation. Each nation's primary assets will be its citizens' skills and insights. Each nation's primary political task will be to cope with the centrifugal forces of the global economy which tear at the ties binding citizens together—bestowing ever greater wealth on the most skilled and insightful, while consigning the less skilled to a declining standard of living.[4]

In this chapter, we illustrate global problems that we propose are due to a lack of regulation in world markets. First, the problems stem from a lack of *government regulation.* Second, they stem from a lack of civil *self-regulation.* The absence of these two kinds of regulation can create serious crises.

In the first section of this chapter, "Civil Problems," we contend that unregulated global markets are causing the following problems: (1) a downward leveling of public standards in corporate products and markets, (2) destruction of the environment, (3) the global diffusion of a commercial culture, (4) dangerous technological consequences, and (5) the likelihood of recurring financial disasters around the world. Our purpose is not to prioritize the problems or attempt to describe their details, nor do we intend to cast blame on corporations themselves. The goal is simply to indicate the serious need for global regulations.

In the second section, "The Need for a System of Global Governance," we conclude that nations by themselves do not have sufficient power to regulate global markets; hence, a new path toward international regulation must be developed. We explain why current modes of business self-regulation are not adequate by themselves and point to the need for broader involvement of world leaders. In chapter 8, we will discuss ways to solve these problems through the collaboration of our three sectors: governments, business, and nongovernmental associations.

There are more problems than we have space to cover here. The solutions are constructed by applying the theme of this book: Competitors require a common playing field with rules based on fairness, justice, safety, and transparency. To maintain market freedom, the solution requires new modes of mutual governance that optimize self-governance. This is the key to a civil economy.

Civil Problems

The growth of global firms has been dramatic. In 1970, there were 7,000 global companies in the world, and more than half of them were based in the United States and Britain. By the 1990s, there were 35,000 global companies.

The combined assets of the top 300 firms make up a quarter of the productive assets of the world. These big companies are so powerful with respect to national economies that they can veto a range of crucial political decisions across the planet.[5]

In many cases, political strategies are dictated by financial markets that are increasingly difficult to monitor. Nationalism is still popular among citizens of every country, but nations are losing power under the weight of debt and bureaucracy. Global business, on the other hand, is gaining power as big firms move into the vacuum. Global corporations are outpacing the power of nations to regulate them.[6]

The development of capitalism in the past has been attended by economic depressions, political rebellions, communist movements, and the rise of authoritarian governments around the world. Some of the old problems of capitalism are repeating themselves today on a world scale, but global firms are also producing new problems.[7]

The Downward Leveling of Public Standards

The public standards set by national governments are being lowered on the world scene. Standards are lowered because nations compete against one another to get multinational subsidiaries into their territories. In the process of this competition to attract global firms, domestic regimes reduce their regulatory controls.[8]

Corporations in production, telecommunications, finance, banking, and transportation easily cross national boundaries in this competition. Global firms seek low costs for labor and the fewest government regulations over their operations. Host governments that need economic development will go to great lengths to meet the demands of corporate executives. There is no appeal to a world court when global firms close down and move to other countries with lower wages and lower taxes. There is no world government to limit the freedom to pollute. National power declines in the same way that the power of towns and villages declined at the early part of the century when corporations moved from being local to national in scope.

To put this another way, when nations compete to attract the sub-sidiaries of multinational firms, they often give away land and property, lower (or eliminate) taxes, receive corporate contributions to political parties that promise to stop unionization, overlook problems in the workplace, and fail to implement laws on protecting the environment. The result is a worldwide "downward leveling" of standards. The protective conditions for labor, consumers, and the environment fall toward the lowest/poorest standards.[9]

This "downward leveling" is the consequence of (1) millions of un-connected (nonconspiratorial) decisions made by individuals; (2) busi-nesses pursuing private self-interest; (3) a lack of common standards and ethics for businesses operating in world markets; (4) a deliberate policy of global corporations to reduce all barriers to this downward leveling; (5) trade agreements based solely on the principle of free markets; and (6) strategies of the IMF and World Bank.

The downward spiral is encouraged by trade agreements like the North American Free Trade Agreement (NAFTA) that foster free trade without addressing international standards for workers, consumers, and en-vironmental protection. The IMF and the World Bank also advance the downward spiral by requiring "shock therapy" and "structural adjust-ment." These world agencies want to fulfill the dream of developing na-tions to produce more goods for the world market and raise their standard of living, but "adjustment programs" make demands of the host nation to become market oriented. These demands include a reduction of social spending, a practice of deregulation, a devaluation of national currencies, and the privatization of state-owned segments of the economy.

A major problem drawing worldwide attention is the lowering of stan-dards for worker protection. Even companies with good employee prac-tices in their home country find themselves contracting with third-world factories or farms that operate under exploitative conditions. The trend for global firms to subcontract production activities abroad has increased the prevalence of such exploitation. The exploitation is carried out by local en-trepreneurs and government elites who have little regard for human rights or ecology. Some global firms have developed codes of conduct, but inde-pendent local contractors may fail to monitor and enforce them.

Destruction of the Environment

The worldwide downward leveling includes severe damages to the envi-ronment resulting from industrial processes. Damages include soil erosion, increased levels of greenhouse gases, ozone-depleting chemicals, acid rain, forest destruction, and toxic pollutants. Petrochemical plants, oil refineries, steel smelters, and coal-fired electric power plants are constructed in countries to create jobs and capital development, but also result in a loss of global oxygen. Let us detail some of these problems.

Soil Erosion

Agricultural practices by corporations in North America today are destroying topsoil at the rate of 6 billion tons per year. The rate of loss, and the consequences for local people, is even greater in China. Topsoil is the matrix of all our lives—the lives of plants, the animals who eat the plants, and the humans who eat both animals and plants. It takes nature 10,000 years to produce one inch of topsoil, but the planet's fertile land will be reduced by one-third in 15 years. This means that, as the human population expands, the demands for food will increase; yet the amount of fertile land will shrink by 33 percent.

The green revolution introduced in the 1960s to enhance crop-seed production requires intense use of fossil energy for fertilizers, pesticides, and irrigation. Global firms are part of this scene. Their technology has enhanced soil erosion and polluted groundwater and surface water resources, while the use of pesticides has caused serious public health and environmental problems.

Forest Destruction

Almost half the forests that once covered the earth—3 billion hectares—are gone. Between 1980 and 1995, the world lost at least 200 million hectares of forest. In recent years, the world has been losing an estimated 16 million hectares a year. Environmentalists agree that the world's forests are disappearing at an alarming rate—one-third of the planet's remaining forests will be destroyed in the next 15 years.[10]

The clear-cutting of tropical hardwood forests by lumber companies has almost completely destroyed valuable forests in developing countries and devastated their economies at the same time. Forest destruction in tropical countries has led to industry collapse and to losses in jobs, incomes, and exports. Nigeria was once a major exporter of logs, but by 1988, the nation was spending $100 million importing forest products.

The island of Puerto Rico and the 7,000 Philippine Islands were once endowed with rich rain forests, fertile lowlands, and extensive mineral deposits, but today, the land and the forests are endangered. The proportion of the Philippines that is forested has decreased from 35 percent to 20 percent, less than half the amount needed to maintain a stable ecosystem.[11]

Deforestation was once a local problem, but it now affects the entire planet. The global market, without international rules, bears some of the responsibility for this calamity. The people clearing vast tracts of land today are generally the ones engaged in maximizing short-term profits to satisfy distant markets, rather than those who know the land and have a long-term commitment to it.

The world's forests now lose more carbon to the atmosphere than they absorb—a recent shift in the functioning of these ecosystems, fueling global climate change. One-quarter of all the atmospheric carbon produced by human activities comes from cutting and burning forests. Those that burned in Indonesia sent as much carbon into the atmosphere in a few months as all of Europe's industrial activity did in a year.[12]

Toxicity

There is a growing concern about industrial pollution by substances that are toxic to human beings and other living things. For example, dioxin is the common name for a family of chemicals with similar properties; 75 different forms of dioxin exist. Dioxins are *not deliberately manufactured*— they are the unintended by-products of industrial processes that involve chlorine. The Citizens Clearinghouse for Hazardous Waste lists the social costs and problems created by dioxin around the world.[13]

Reporters on the dioxin story describe cover-ups, lies, deception, and data manipulation by corporations and governments, as well as fraudulent claims and faked studies. For many people it has been a story of pain, suffering, anger, and betrayal. It has meant birth defects, cancer, and other health problems. It is a story about what happens when business operates in a global market without regulation or pollution prevention practices.[14]

Richard Barnet and John Cavanaugh tell the story of attempts to dump toxins in the oceans:

> The fourteen-month globe-circling voyage of the *Khian Sea* is but one of over 1,000 documented efforts to export toxics to faraway places. In this case, the vessel set sail in October 1987 with more than 13,000 tons of toxic incinerator ash from Philadelphia bound for Haiti, which had agreed to accept the ash under the impression that it was fertilizer. The ash was dumped on a beach. When the Haitian government discovered what it really was and complained, the crew shoveled most of the ash back onto the ship, leaving 2,000 tons or so on the sands. The *Khian Sea* then put in at ports on five continents seeking to unload its poisonous cargo, but fourteen countries, including Senegal, Cape Verde, Sri Lanka, and Yugoslavia, turned the ship back and the toxic ash was eventually dumped into the Indian Ocean.[15]

There is no enforceable law of the open seas. The Law of the Sea Convention entered into force only in 1995, and the United States refused to ratify it. A business corporation can do virtually anything it wants to do on the oceans.

Governments also sign international agreements to prevent environmental damages and then exercise little or no control over corporations in their own borders. For example, the Basel Convention on hazardous waste says governments will take measures to prevent firms from exporting hazardous waste, but prevention seldom happens. Even the United States does not have an export review system, except for military-related products. So, the United States does not have the capacity to control waste exports directly. (For more on toxicity, see chap. 6.)

Fisheries

Fisheries around the world collapse when the global demand for seafood overruns their sustainable yield and when pollution destroys their productivity. The collapse of fisheries has raised seafood prices, eliminated jobs, and contracted this sector of the market. In Newfoundland, the collapse of the cod and haddock fishery has left 33,000 fishers and fish-processing workers unemployed, crippling the province's economy.[16]

Big commercial vessels bear a large share of the responsibility for overexploitation of world fishery resources. In the early 1950s, European shipyards began to build huge, mechanized vessels that could catch up to 500 tons of fish a day. Known as factory trawlers, for the enormous trawl nets that are hauled up the ship's stern to onboard processing and freezing, these floating factories allowed corporations to process, freeze, and package huge quantities of fish at sea. They were then free to roam the globe in search of profits. The efficiency of the more expensive gear made it even harder for the "little guy" to compete; fisheries have been increasingly dominated by corporate vessels and absentee boat owners.

Kjell Inge Rokke, a Norwegian-based conglomerate, controls almost 10 percent of the world's whitefish (cod, hake, and pollock) production, with operations concentrated in the North Pacific and Russia. A Spanish firm, Pescanova, accounts for 20 percent of world hake production, with ventures in South Africa, Namibia, and Mozambique. Yamaha Motor Company buys fish feed from Dutch producers to sell to Japanese aquaculturists. Large multinational companies such as these have financial backing and political power to influence their own governments and to persuade foreign governments to give them cheap access.[17]

Climate Disaster on the Horizon

A number of governments have adopted the Montreal Protocol on Ozone Depletion, but companies in many of those countries still manufacture and use ozone-depleting compounds. The Montreal Protocol states that member governments should take actions to reduce and eliminate certain classes of ozone-depleting compounds within their national boundaries, but there is no effective corporate verification procedure to implement the agreement. Furthermore, some countries have chosen not to become members of the Montreal Protocol, in order to encourage foreign investment in their countries.

The 1990s have been the hottest decade since record keeping began in 1866. Ice core records from Antarctica show that temperatures in the twentieth century are higher than any since at least 1400 A.D. Ice caps in the Andes have been melting more quickly since the 1970s; glaciers atop the European Alps have lost half their volume since 1850. The scientific data on global warming continues to accumulate at North Greenland's ice cap, the South Pole, and other locations around the globe. The U.S. National Oceanic and Atmospheric Administration has linked the sustained trend in global warming to "heat-trapping" greenhouse gases released by human activities, such as the burning of fossil fuels. This is the consensus of the world's top climate scientists, assembled by the United Nations in the Intergovernmental Panel on Climate Change.[18]

If average temperatures continue to rise as projected, the consequences are likely to include a greater incidence of floods and droughts, diminished food production, and an expanded range for disease vectors. Warmer thresholds could push ecosystems past tolerable thresholds. These conditions may already be causing the decline of amphibians, the large-scale growth of toxic algae in the oceans, and the death of coral reefs.[19]

The financial resources of the oil and coal lobbies are extensive. Over the last seven years these industries have spent millions of dollars to wage a public campaign to downplay the threat of climate change. The Information Council on the Environment (ICE) was the creation of a group of utility and coal companies. In 1991, using the ICE, the coal industry, mainly Western Fuels, launched a campaign to find scientists who could argue that global warming was "theory rather than fact." The campaign was more clever than accurate, asking in one newspaper advertisement prepared by the ICE, "If the earth is getting warmer, why is Minneapolis getting colder?" (Data indicate that the Minneapolis area has actually warmed between 1 and 1.5 degrees Celsius in the last century.) Another industry lobbying group, Global Climate Coalition (GCC), disseminated a report declaring that there had been no increase in severe weather events. The report was dismissed by prestigious scientists, who noted that the report contradicted the findings of researchers from the NOAA National Climate Data Center earlier that year.[20]

This is a battle among nonprofit associations as well as business firms. The fuel industry has established and funded nonprofit organizations designed to furnish their own explanations. At the same time, in addition to nonprofit scientific associations that have been active in disclosing the facts as they see them, the insurance industry has trade associations that support the warning given by prominent scientists about a major climate change. Insurance associations have published statistics in their own interest—showing that the annual weather-related disaster claims have increased sixfold since the 1980s, from $5 billion to $30 billion in the first half of the 1990s.

Prominent business and political leaders recognize that civil society cannot survive the coming onslaught of climate change. William Ruckelshaus, former head of the EPA and now CEO of Browning-Ferris Industries, and Dr. Henry Kendall of MIT, recipient of the 1990 Nobel Prize for physics, have seen the consequences of climate change with the unregulated growth of greenhouse gases and other environmental problems. For MIT's Kendall, it is the precarious nations of the developing world who will first revert to dictatorship. Democracy is too clumsy to respond to sudden disruptions in food supplies, water sources, and human health and a flood tide of refugees from homelands that cannot feed their populations.[21]

The Global Diffusion of Commercial Culture

Richard Barnet and John Cavanaugh say the issues are even more subtle and complex. Global firms are shaping worldwide cultures in their own self-interest. The advertisements of Coca-Cola in mass media reach billions of people globally at the same instant. A commercial culture is transmitted instantaneously by mass media, movies, TV programs, videos, records, cassettes, books, and CDs around the world. Disneyland is a global empire, drawing 300,000 visitors a week in Tokyo. There are no government agencies monitoring these international "entertainment centers" and planetary advertisements—in general, this traffic in commercial culture.[22]

Critics protest the way CEOs push global "entertainment" as "education." CEOs describe their theme parks as "educational experiences," but critics ask: Should business corporations decide what children should experience around the world? Big corporations create world heroes, such as Michael Jackson, to sell millions of records and videos (e.g.,"Thriller"). Critics object to Madonna and her leather-and-lace image as a worldwide model for young women. They are suspicious of the impact of billion-dollar records, like "Purple Rain" by Prince, the 22 million copies of the sound track of *Dirty Dancing*, and so on. They ask: Is this global education? Where is this new corporate power going? What does it mean when a few standardized products (from toys to chemicals) dominate world consumption?

A major problem in this global commerce, critics say, is the lack of interchange between producer and consumer. There are a need for more feedback from consumers, a need to present countermodels, and a need for public forums to debate the values eclipsed by global firms. The global entertainment centers now under construction by multinational firms for the twenty-first century have no public input.

Commercial products, and the habits, values, and signs of prestige that go with them, can have a negative effect on people's health and well-being. Look at the U.S. tobacco industry. As tobacco industry sales slow down in the United States because of regulatory action, the industry is moving to foreign markets. The use of U.S. manufactured tobacco then injures and kills people in nations around the world. Philip Morris Corporation today operates in more than 170 countries, with annual corporate earnings larger than the budget of New Zealand.

The Dangerous Consequences of Technology

Global firms are centralizing power through technology. Worldwide webs of corporate computer activity have attained a level of global integration not achieved by any political world empire. Unilever has a computer network involving 500 separate companies in 75 countries. Increasingly, global firms are contracting out the running of their data networks to IBM, Digital Equipment, and other companies with global telecommunication services. As information technology becomes more important to nonprofit corporations (churches, universities, and governments), they hire outside global companies to organize their private data networks. The Roman Catholic Church employs GE to run its global data network linking the Holy See with dioceses and church installations around the world.[23] A new rather profit-oriented, corporate-based global sovereignty is evolving through this technology. What does this mean for the future?

A major concern among world scientists and UN leaders is the management of genetic engineering and biotechnology by global firms. Genetic engineering bypasses conventional breeding by using artificially constructed "vectors" to multiply copies of genes and, in many cases, to carry and insert genes into cells. Once inside cells, these vectors fit themselves into the host genome. In this way, transgenic organisms are made carrying the desired transgenes. Such technologies are raising many questions.

There are now 1,400 biotech companies in the United States, with a total of $13 billion in annual revenues. Development is proceeding in an astonishing number of areas, and many universities are involved. Scientists at Harvard University have grown human bladders and kidneys in laboratory jars. University of Wisconsin scientists have genetically altered brooding turkey hens to increase their productivity by eliminating the "brooding" instinct: the desire to sit on and hatch eggs. Other researchers are experimenting with the creation of sterile salmon who will not have the suicidal urge to spawn but will remain in the open sea, to be commercially harvested. University of Michigan scientists say that by breaking the spawning cycle of chinook salmon, they can produce 70-pound salmon compared to less than 18 pounds for a fish returning to spawn. The mothering instincts and the mating instincts are being bred out of birds and fish.

Genes are gold to the biotech industry, and companies that control them will exercise enormous power over the world economy. The U.S. Supreme Court and the Patent Office have both given the green light for this market. The Patent Office ruled that all genetically engineered multicellular living organisms—including animals—are potentially patentable. Global firms are scouting the continents in search of microbes, plants, animals, and humans with rare genetic traits that might have future market potential. After locating the desired traits, biotech companies modify them and seek patent protection for their new "inventions."[24]

Scientists and political leaders are questioning the global "right" to clone animals, the right of multinationals to patent seeds that farmers must then buy in order to grow plants. Global patents on seeds could, in the future, require farmers around the world to purchase productive seeds from global corporations rather than being allowed to harvest their own seeds for planting. Dr. Mae-Wan Ho, head of the Bio-Electronic Laboratory of the Open University in Milton Keynes in the U.K., speaks of this new mode of biotechnology. He says that its purpose is to accommodate problems that reductionist science and industry have created in the first place—widespread environmental deterioration from the intensive, high-input agriculture of the green revolution, and accumulation of toxic wastes from chemical industries. It leads to discriminatory and other unethical practices that are against the moral values of a community of nations. Worst of all, it is pushing a technology that is untried, and, according to existing knowledge, is inherently hazardous to health and biodiversity.[25]

Peter Montague, editor of the Environmental Research Foundation, says that government regulation and self-regulation in biochemistry does not work. For example, the Toxic Substance Control Act (TSCA) was passed by Congress in 1976. The basic idea of the law is that government should decide which chemicals, among the 70,000 or so now in use, are dangerous, and, second, how to protect workers and the general public from their dangers. "But the entire result of 21 years of steady effort under the TSCA has been to remove nine chemicals from the market. We could multiply the size of our federal government by ten (a truly frightening thought) and it would still be no match for the Fortune 500."[26]

The Likelihood of Repeatable Financial Disasters around the World

Trillions of dollars move speedily back and forth between nations without government monitoring. Over $1 trillion—roughly the equivalent of the annual GNP of the entire globe—travels every day among banking systems as bits of electronic information. Electronic networks permit securities trading overnight around the world. People buy and sell on electronic screens, dealing with people they have never seen. This electronic system saves money for banks, but it has inherent dangers: a flash of lightning, an episode of widespread fraud, or a computer virus could trigger power failure. Scrambled money messages could bring gridlock and breakdown in a large part of the global finance system. It could lead to the world's first computer-driven panic and an economic depression. There is no overall government with the power to monitor these transactions.

Global financial markets in 1998 became deeply involved in causing the collapse of fragile economies in Southeast Asia, Russia, Eastern Europe, and Latin America. Imprudent, unwatchful investments by U.S. banks led to a meltdown in the early 1980s when Latin American governments were unable to repay loans to U.S. banks, but the financial crisis starting in the late 1990s has been immensely worse by comparison. Total equity loans and investments to 29 emerging countries surged to a peak of $305 billion in 1996. Financial markets became fluid and interwoven, with big banks and mutual funds moving billions into small, unprepared economies; the consequences have become a showcase for how the current market system can move quickly into chaos.

New and emerging markets are always characterized by weak regulations and poor accounting practices. Without public rules, people will hide a company's true financial condition, making it impossible for outside investors to assess the risks. In Malaysia, for example, there were no credible rating agencies. South Korea borrowed heavily from Western and Japanese banks in the two years before its currency crisis, loaning the money to domestic companies, but without prudent norms. When the currency crisis occurred, international banks pulled out. In Russia, high-interest government bonds, known as GKOs, were a magnet for banks, at one point yielding 200 percent. Hedge funds from foreign banks were also drawn into the trap. The short-term GKOs then became a destabilizing force. The Russian ruble fell, and political instability followed. The government, unable to repay the GKOs, devalued its currency and defaulted on $40 billion in ruble-denominated debt. The social and political consequences are evident today.

As the collapse of markets around the world—Hong Kong, Taiwan, Thailand, Japan, Russia—then reverberates back to the United States, each country increases government controls over the economy. Russia's market failure and its default on billions of dollars of debt have raised the specter of another authoritarian regime. The government in Japan has taken over its major banks. It is not simply a communist plot or an anticapitalist ideology that is forcing government controls over the economy. It is the sheer need for nations to survive economic disasters.

The Complexity of the Stock Market:
The Widening Inequality of Wealth

Robert Kuttner describes a very important change in the character of the stock market today. As recently as 1960, only 12 percent of the whole New York Stock Exchange turned over in a year. There were virtually no derivative instruments other than old-fashioned futures markets. Everything was based on custom and regulation. Today, financial markets turn over their entire value many times in a year. This rapid and volatile movement is a destabilizing force.

Kuttner argues that the trading market is a zero-sum game. It adds no real value to the economy but diverts many billions of dollars from the real economy. It also diverts expert attention from the legitimate task of carefully analyzing and valuing the underlying assets, not to mention building real enterprises.[27]

Kuttner reminds us that most of the financial activity in stocks and bonds is a secondary market; that is, the shares being traded are *previous issues*, not new demands for investment capital. In effect, this market has become more like a gambling casino. Day-to-day share prices are driven by guesses of changes in perception of other investors.

The lack of public accountability in private finance continues, and many of the best economists play the game. Market mechanisms called "arbitrage," "hedge funds," "leveraging," "margin calls," "short selling," and "derivatives" have all developed to quicken financial returns without accountability to the public. These mechanisms are legal, but they are ways to avoid prudent investments. They are profiteering techniques that lead to market instability.

Arbitrage is employed by the rich to profit from the discrepancy in price between equivalent assets, including stocks, bonds, currencies, and commodities. If one corporation trades stock in New York at $20 a share and $19.50 in Chicago, a smart arbitrage investor can buy in Chicago and quickly sell the shares in New York, keeping the profit. This requires special computers and a professional skill that most investors do not possess.

Hedge funds are shrouded in secrecy. Many wealthy investors use hedge funds that are publicly unregulated and privately administered. They have grown to an estimated $175 billion in assets. Private financiers hunt for high-risk investments to make big money. High-risk investments in 1997–98 included short selling on stocks and investments in Russian government bonds, with investors often borrowing large amounts of money to gamble on the future. The hedge funds are not required to report to federal regulatory agencies—hence there is no definitive estimate on their size—but they are known to have grown webs of debt throughout the conventional financial world. All the trusted names in finance—Goldman Sachs and Company, Bankers Trust, Chase, J. P. Morgan, and Merrill and Company have been involved in these mechanisms.

The volatile history of international currency and stock markets has been well documented by Charles Geisst, a professor of finance at Manhattan College. He says that Wall Street has become very complex over the last two centuries and it still operates on the same principles, showing the same problems of volatility over its history. New markets have developed and their functions divided, and the trading volume has expanded tremendously. But a nineteenth-century trader would still recognize the core of the Street's business. The extreme fluctuations remain the same.[28]

In other words, this history of failures is systemic. We contend that the problems are now repeating themselves on a global scale. The market must be globally monitored and regulated. We are in global markets where new stock exchanges are emerging for the first time in a number of countries, without sufficient regulation. Global rule making and greater transparency will be the agenda for the next century.

The problems are even evident in mature capitalist countries. The U.S. Federal Reserve Bank in 1998 had to bail out private financial investors. It was reminiscent of the imprudence producing the savings and loan debacle in the 1980s, but this time the failure of a single firm could have caused major harm to the economy. The Federal Reserve arranged for a financial rescue of a private investment group called Long Term Capital (LTC), helping to manage the takeover by a group of lenders at $3.5 billion. This action on behalf of one investment firm was unprecedented. Big investors in LTC had borrowed large amounts of money and put most of it into those complex instruments we called derivatives. Derivatives in this case allowed private investors to control huge financial positions at a relatively low cost. LTC had borrowed heavily from Wall Street's biggest securities firms and banks to make its bets on the financial market. If LTC had to dump its assets at very low prices, the entire financial system could have been at risk. The ripple effects of its collapse would have had a greater impact than simply its own investors' losses.

In the recent financial crisis, big investors placed much of their money in crony capitalism, immature economies, not thinking about what happens to loans under conditions of oligarchy, oligopoly, monopoly, dictatorships, and similar adverse conditions of social and political organization. They did not think about the need to cultivate management skills in emerging nations, or about training for prudence in allocating capital, or about establishing systems of social accountability in overseas markets. Mainstream economists, government leaders, and agency heads do not think seriously and systematically about helping associations in the financial sector of developing countries to set self-governing standards to avoid economic instability. The concept of a civil economy is not in their agenda. Financial investors do not calculate the need for social development in market systems, or plan for systems of responsible self-governance.[29]

Policymakers are now talking about solving problems with more government control over the "financial flows in and out of emerging markets." Some top analysts believe that the United States should control all the financial flows, as though one nation could solve the problem. They are not thinking about global systems of enforceable self-regulation and systems of social accountability.

The best economists guide the U.S. market system, but their framework for making decisions does not include civil development in the economy. The participants in the Long Term Capital Fund included Harvard Business School economist and Nobel Prize winner Myron Scholes and former Fed vice chair David Mullins. Harvard economist Jeffrey Sachs blamed the problem of this market failure on "unfettered, rapid, and large capital movements," but he did not see the problem as due to a lack of social development and civil self-regulation.

The Inequality of Wealth and Difficulties
with Taxation

According to the UN Development Program's *Human Development Report 1992*, in 1970 the richest fifth of the world's people received 30 times more income than the bottom fifth; by 1989 they received nearly 60 times more. The richest fifth now receive more than 80 percent of the world's income, while the poorest fifth receive 1.4 percent.[30]

David Korten *(When Corporations Rule the World)* notes that the $20 million that Nike paid the basketball star Michael Jordan to endorse its shoes was more than the entire annual payroll of the Indonesian workers who made them. Historian David Landes argues that the biggest challenge and threat today is the gap in wealth and health that separates the rich and the poor. It is the greatest single problem and danger facing the world of the third millennium. It is in the interest of rich and economically disadvantaged peoples to see this gap narrowed.[31]

Civil society depends on the fair application of taxes. Taxes on business and employees pay for public services. But tax havens provide opportunities for individuals to reduce their tax liabilities substantially and provide tax advantages for companies. The taxation of global firms is becoming too complex for nations to monitor and regulate.

"Transfer pricing" refers to the ability of global firms to manipulate prices on systems of exchange between their subsidiaries so they do not have to pay taxes anywhere. Global firms move profits from a high-tax country to a low-tax country and reduce overall tax liability. In 1992 the IRS introduced extensive documentation requirements on firms to ensure that the transfer pricing system was not being abused, but according to a recent survey of major companies by Ernst and Young, transfer pricing is now the hottest tax issue facing global firms as well as tax collectors.

Donald Barlett and James Steele, Pulitzer Prize–winning investigative reporters for the *Philadelphia Inquirer*, have studied taxation for 25 years. They are appalled at the way global corporations are able to avoid paying taxes. Their recent study shows how most of the United States' most profitable corporations pay little or nothing in taxes, while middle-income taxpayers pick up a growing share of the nation's tax bill. They argue that tax policy is now affected more by how many lawyers and lobbyists one can afford than by questions of either equity or efficiency.

They document how the job of tracking the income and expenses of global firms across national boundaries is impossible under current government audit procedures. The issues involve arcane terms, like *worldwide combined reporting, water's edge, domestic disclosure spreadsheet,* and *unitary formula apportionment.* The problem is that states (or national governments) cannot determine the amount of tax that should be paid by a global firm with many subsidiaries in different countries.[32]

For the most part, the IRS takes the word of the global companies. There is no choice. With thousands of global firms, and tens of thousands of subsidiaries, and millions upon millions of transactions each year, it is impossible to track each transfer of goods.

Failure of Fiscal/Monetary Policy: The Lack of Countercyclical Solutions

Since the 1930s depression, economists have relied on a mix of monetary and fiscal policies to control extreme fluctuations in the economy, but these policies no longer work straightforwardly in this global market. "Monetary policy" refers to all actions of governments, central banks, and other public authorities that influence the quantity of money, interest rates, and bank credit. The U.S. Federal Reserve Bank has played an essential role in monetary policy by influencing interest rates and the legal reserves of commercial banks, hoping to avoid both economic contractions and inflations. These policies seek a high level of employment and output, a sustainable rate for economic growth, and stable price levels and exchange rates for the nation's currency.

Fiscal policy is connected to government expenditures and tax policies that promote these same objectives. Most economists believe in combining fiscal and monetary policies, but there is disagreement on the proper mix. Conservative economists, such as Milton Friedman, believe that monetary actions taken deliberately to counter cyclical fluctuations may actually produce or accentuate the problem. Expansionary policy actions, such as reducing interest rates to stop a recession, can have too slow an impact; their effect may occur perversely when the next boom phase is happening. Members of this school oppose all discretionary countercyclical monetary policies. At the same time, many economists believe that no expansionary monetary policy could help recovery from a deep depression and that fiscal policy is the only alternative. Some economists believe it is important to reduce taxes or increase government expenditures to support aggregate demand.

But we are in a new era. No longer can domestic governments confidently respond to aggregate economic fluctuations simply with a combination of these two kinds of policies. Foreign trade in goods and services, the international movement of physical and financial capital, and changes in the international value of currencies (influencing, among other things, the size of international debts) are all significantly affected by the use of these domestic policy instruments, and they in turn affect economic activity in many ways, quite often counteracting the intended direct effects of macroeconomic policy. The complexity of these overall interactions is enormously increased, and both the ability to predict their ultimate net direction and size and the confidence that this net direction will be favorable are considerably weakened.

When domestic governments try to combat recessions and stimulate their economies today with domestic policies such as lower interest rates, and then rising prices and other direct effects occur, these worsen the country's balance of payments and induce the nation's currency to decline in value. The former (worsening the balance of payments) offsets economic expansion. The latter (currency decline) increases the debt burden and leads to an outflow of financial and physical capital, again decreasing the expansionary effects of the policies. Lowering the price of the dollar on the foreign exchange makes the price of U.S. exports abroad cheaper, thereby increasing the amount of exports. But this also increases the price of U.S. imports, thereby decreasing U.S. imports. Raising the price of the dollar on the foreign exchange does the reverse: decreases exports and increases the price of U.S. imports. International currency speculation has increased with the broadening and deepening of the global market system. This can seriously aggravate these adjustments by augmenting the volatility of exchange rate changes. It can add to crisis situations and even create them.

Walter Wriston, former CEO of Citibank, has emphasized the degree to which currency traders now can manipulate the global economy and drive domestic policy. Currency traders have become so big today that their actions can have a major consequence on domestic economies.[33]

The recent collapse of many East Asian currencies has increased the burden of their large debts to other countries, especially Japan, which significantly worsened the situation of Japanese banks, already burdened with their own domestic bad debts, paralyzing them from lending for investment and/or providing liquidity. Japan is thus unable to serve as a support of international commodity demand and liquidity for monetary crises, therefore deepening the real overall crisis involving Asian currencies.

John Maynard Keynes once referred to a condition of this sort in domestic economies as a liquidity trap. Consumers are too fearful to spend, and creditors are too fearful to lend. The consequence is that the economy implodes despite plenty of money. Keynes said this was a major cause for the Great Depression. Now a similar trap is happening at the global level on a larger, multinational scale, but the solution requires more than just macroeconomics applied on the domestic scene.

Unless global regulations within the financial system are set into place, the wild fluctuations can and will occur again. We are arguing that regulations must be written as civil agreements inside markets and as intergovernmental agreements outside markets. Civil agreements require competitors to establish rules on transparency, monitoring rights, and arbiters in the private markets. Civil freedom requires civil order inside markets.

Financial Lawlessness and the Social Consequences

A continued danger in these worldwide changes is increased lawlessness in world finance. Global computer networks make it easier to hide money. Organized crime has created its own financial networks at the global level. Crime is made easier because electronic transfers are kept secret. Anyone who wants to hide funds from regulators, creditors, or partners can communicate with a bank by fax or modem and order wire transfers across the globe without ever speaking to a bank officer. Some nations are tax havens, nesting grounds for criminal gains and untaxed profits. Many "off-shore" deposits are there to avoid scrutiny by regulatory and taxing authorities.

These market forces are always bound with political forces, in this case resulting in great human tragedy. The World Bank estimates that soon half the entire population will barely be able to scrape together one meal per day; up to 50 million adults are unemployed; at least 20 million children are out of school. The close affiliation of the political economy (conventional capitalism) and immoral politics—including genocidal government policies— is visible in countries like Indonesia. The sale of weapons to dictators in impoverished countries in the developing world is part of the problem, not the solution to capitalist development. The 1996 Nobel Peace Prize winner, José Ramos-Horta, sees the Indonesian economy in tatters, while for the past two decades the United States and Great Britain have been the two largest providers of military hardware to Indonesia. The corrupt and despotic military regime of President Suharto was supported by major countries around the world.[34]

Let us summarize facts that require attention in a global civil society.

Today 300 global corporations own an estimated one-quarter of the productive assets of the world, suggesting that a new transnational force is shaping the future of people in all nations.

Global corporations typically move their operations to nations with the lowest labor costs, the least regulation over the environment, and the lowest health/safety standards for workers and consumers.

The global market produces environmental problems beyond the power of any single nation to control—lowering the quality of the air we breathe, creating problems with lakes, streams, and drinking water, lowering the nutrition of food products sold globally.

Financial markets are global: Foreign exchange approaches $1 trillion per day. Global foreign direct investment has grown at an average of 29 percent a year, causing an unprecedented increase in the imprudent allocation of money and also more currency speculation.[35]

Global issues are mounting in number and complexity: there are disputes about deforestation, greenhouse gases, biotechnology, and biogenetics, which are beyond the control of any single national government.

Domestic fiscal and monetary policies are no longer adequate by themselves to solve the problems of global finance; they are no longer sufficient to serve as countercyclical policies in the face of the growing interdependence of world trade and finance.

The Need for a System of Global Governance

The threat of global markets to nations and local communities is real, and solutions to world problems require new systems of accountability. We have argued that the economy requires mutual self-governance—the development of civil markets. This requires social inventions. The global economy needs civil contracts, civil partnerships, civil monitors, civil transparency, and civil arbiters for settling disputes. To accomplish this task requires collaboration among our three sectors, business, nonprofits, and government.

Government laws and agencies are needed to regulate markets, but there is no world government with enforceable laws for markets. Hence, international agreements are needed to develop civil governance. We will explain how this can happen in the next chapter, that is, how rules can be established and enforced through the aid of intergovernmental agencies and by nongovernmental organizations through the United Nations. Our argument in this final section is that "business self-regulation" by itself is not the way to solve all these problems.

Unworkable Business Self-Regulation: Worsening the Problem

The World Trade Organization (WTO) was born quietly during the Uruguay round of the General Agreement on Tariffs and Trade (GATT) in 1995. It is a trade body with an independent legal identity and staff similar to that of the World Bank and the IMF. Its mandate is to eliminate barriers to international trade. This global body represents the world's largest corporations and is committed to ensuring their "rights" against the intrusion of nations into their activities. The special danger of the WTO is that its New World trade rules can override national and local laws on political policy. The WTO endangers the right of nations to protect their domestic economies through their own effort to set environmental, health, and safety standards.

WTO is mandated to work with the World Bank and the IMF but not with other UN agencies and citizen groups. GATT excludes the UN General Assembly and other UN bodies from global economic policy-making. Furthermore, world trade policy and regulations will not be made "democratically" but on the basis of "state trading power." This new force for free trade adds to the likelihood of lower labor and environmental standards. For example, workers' unemployment compensation, pensions, and health care could be ruled as "unfair trade barriers." Global standards, initiated by many UN affiliates (e.g., the World Health Organization, International Labor Organization) on water purity, pesticide formulas, and worker exposure levels, could be attacked as too stringent.[36]

WTO is charged with harmonizing the rules of commerce and creating a uniform environment to carry out global trade. It has the power to seek enforcement of its own rules under a private dispute settlement process rooted in corporate power. But world watchers say that there are more dangers ahead. Here are some examples of what has happened in the last few years.

U.S.-based Ethyl Corporation sued the Canadian government for $350 million for banning the import of MMT (a potentially toxic fuel additive banned in the United States). The company said the ban was "tantamount to expropriation," since it threatened to reduce the value of Ethyl's MMT manufacturing plant, hurt its future sales, harm its corporate reputation, and have a "chilling effect" by encouraging other countries to review their use of MMT.[37]

The United States sued, and the WTO overturned the European Union (EU) ban on importing hormone-treated beef.

Venezuela and Brazil challenged aspects of the U.S. Clean Air Act before WTO, and the regulation was changed.

The EU rule banning the import of fur from leg-hold traps was delayed in response to a threatened U.S./Canada challenge.

The U.S. House of Representatives voted to gut U.S. dolphin protection to avoid a WTO challenge.[38]

The Organization for Economic Cooperation and Development (OECD) worked on what was called a "multilateral agreement on investment" (MAI) to advance "trade harmonization." Public interest groups obtained drafts of the agreement and protested that the free trade agreement would lower public standards worldwide. At this point of writing, the formal work on the MAI has been suspended. Yet the public interest groups assert that the original purpose and design of the MAI is still on the agenda of the OECD.[39]

In sum, global markets are growing, and social problems are growing with them. There are no world authorities to create checks and balances, no world government to enforce standards, no international "justice department" or "antitrust agency" to regulate competition, no global "security exchange commission" to require disclosure, no enforceable world law for governing fair trade. The result is an aggressive free-for-all where big corporations fight to corner markets, with the consequence of a mounting series of human and environmental problems.

Workable Mutual Governance: Toward the Solution

Civil solutions are more possible today because the financial problems in the world economy are so serious. Joseph Stiglitz, chief economist at the World Bank, has described lessons derived from the East Asian financial crisis. In effect, he says that the social system is vital to the solution of these problems but that "changing the system (e.g., through institutional development, transformations in credit culture, and creation of regulatory structures which reduce the likelihood of excessive risk-taking) has proved more intractable than finding short-term solutions, such as recapitalizing the banking system."[40]

National governments need to move together to establish regulations through intergovernmental agreements, but my argument in the next chapter will be that we need a comparable level of civil self-regulation. This means better social governance in global markets as well as better economic governance. We have spoken about the principle of self-governance at other levels of market organization throughout the book, but let us make this principle very clear at the global level. The parallel is important to observe.

By mid–twentieth century, at the *global level,* the Bretton Woods Agreement played a key role in stabilizing world markets, but in global competition at the end of the twentieth century it no longer works as a solution. A new global agreement on civil markets is needed to replace it. This means a new strategy for mutual management and cogovernance of the world economy. This action is mandatory to maintain economic stability and growth.

Michael Best has pointed to the importance of cooperation—as well as competition—through "industrial restructuring." He sees an "enduring tension" between competition and cooperation.[41] A market cannot exist without some balance of cooperation with competition. Now, we suggest that a certain kind of cooperation is needed to maintain stable markets and to make best use of competition. This kind of cooperation is among competitors who make agreements on public standards in ways that allow their market to flourish without government intervention. Civil action requires a specific type of cooperation on standards in the midst of competition.

Is there a message in all this? It required the Great Depression in the United States for people to realize the need for regulations, that is, to create the Securities and Exchange Commission (SEC). The SEC maintains those old rules and still creates new rules on transparency, insider trading, and stockholder resolutions. The regulations are essential for the market to operate successfully. Now, the recipe for stabilizing world stock trading and financial markets requires international monitoring and global rules for transparency and enforceability. The most cynical, yet most critical, question to ask now is, How much of a financial disaster is needed to convince global leaders to set up the needed world organization and civil rules for international finance?

Summary and Looking Ahead

If there are no democratic federation of nations, no world law to keep corporations from polluting the seas, no international agency to maintain safety and health standards, no suitable world agency to regulate the ever-volatile global stock market and/or stabilize financial markets, no law to protect the world's forests from being destroyed, and no international group to monitor the Internet and global media, then what can be done about corporations operating in global markets without constraint?

There are solutions to be found through the collaboration of government, business, and the nonprofit sectors. Solutions will depend on the existence of approximately 400 public and 5,000 private international organizations. Nearly all of them have been established within the past century, most of them growing since World War II. They are usually classified as intergovernmental agencies (IGOs) and nongovernmental agencies

(NGOs).[42] The IGO sector involves diplomacy, treaties, conferences, rules of warfare, the regulation of the use of force, peaceful settlement of disputes, the development of global law, trade, travel, and economic cooperation. The NGO sector is often called the Third Sector and is still being defined through the United Nations. We argue in the next chapter that solving global problems involves the collaboration of all these sectors. The facilitator could be the United Nations, a fair meeting ground for the three sectors to work out civic solutions on the world scene.[43]

8 Toward a Global Civil Economy

Custom reconciles us to everything.
—Edmund Burke, *On the Sublime and the Beautiful* (1756)

We, the peoples of the United Nations
Determined to save succeeding generations from the
scourge of war . . . To reaffirm faith in fundamental
human rights, in the dignity and worth of the human
person . . . have resolved to combine our efforts to
accomplish these ends.
—Charter of the United Nations, June 1945 (preamble)

Every nation in the world has found it necessary to regulate markets to protect consumers, workers, and the public, but there are no plans to regulate the global market. After World War II, some authors spoke of creating a democratic world federal government in order to inaugurate the rule of enforceable law. Grenville Clark and Louis B. Sohn's plan, *World Peace through World Law* (1958), was typical of such ambitious plans. But this idea is not supported widely because the principle of national sovereignty remains strong, while world federation is untested and risky. Hence, the hope for market regulations through agencies of a strengthened United Nations or of a novel world federation seems unrealistic. What has emerged instead is the rapid advance of unmonitored and unregulated global markets.

National leaders have no recourse to a world government that could resolve international problems of unemployment, stabilize a global stock market crash, protect the planet's ecological deterioration, prevent the corrosive effects of chronic poverty in world regions, and monitor the growth of genetic engineering. The UN Draft Code of Conduct for Transnational Corporations was abandoned in 1992 after 18 years of negotiations, since no major group of states any longer wanted it and since international business doubted that the code would be uniformly enforced. The New International Economic Order, proposed in 1974, did not lead to a meaningful North-South dialogue by the Cancún summit of 1981, and the proposed New

World Information and Communications Order only provoked the withdrawal of the United States and Great Britain from UNESCO in 1984.[1]

This chapter presents an action strategy to create a global civil economy. The time has come to think about a planetary self-governing system of markets, discuss the idea in UN conferences, and implement experiments in a more just economy. Many world leaders and business executives are joining with community leaders in a shared concern that the global market is a threat as well as a boon to long-term human interests. Research on the creation of a global civil economy should be on the agenda. Leaders in the United Nations are starting to play a role in conceptualizing civil self-governing markets, organizing public forums on the subject of a global civil society.

We will look at three steps to treat the destructive forces in business markets.

Step 1.   Conceptualize a global civil economy

Step 2.   Experiment with civil market solutions

Step 3.   Organize global workshops

Step 1. Conceptualize a Global Civil Economy

Imagine a global economy that is healthy and self-governing. Imagine markets that are organized to empower people. Imagine an economy that is free, humane, competitive, productive, profitable, decentralized, nonbureaucratic, and socially accountable. Imagine a global economy that operates for the common good, a market that develops local-to-global structures to build sustainable communities.

This sort of economy is what we are talking about in civil development. It requires a new order of thinking about global markets characterized by freedom and accountability.

A Theory of Civil Markets and Structures

A theory of civil markets starts with the premise that buyers and sellers must not become too unequal in power on the world scene. If global monopolies and oligopolies develop, regulation for the common good is virtually impossible. In chapter 7, we said that there were no antitrust organizations at the global level to ensure fair competition. A balance of power must be cultivated among associations acting across markets and countries. Without a relative balance of power, "civil markets" are almost impossible.

By civil markets, we mean *systems of exchange in which competing actors agree to standards for the common good and are capable of enforcing them.* This means situations in which trade, professional, labor, and community associations set codes of conduct, require certification procedures, and establish neutral observers (monitors) and regulatory systems that are authorized to issue penalties for members who break contracts. For a "free market" to operate with civility, then, it must be based on certain principles of justice and rules of fair competition.

Civil markets have yet to be carefully defined, studied, tested, and practiced in the global economy. A civil market, as we have defined it, must have the following: (1) "accountability systems" that require corporations to be answerable to the people they affect and (2) "civil structures" that solve problems of justice and fairness in the higher levels of a global market system.

These two concepts are associated with civil corporations that (a) have their own self-enforcing codes of conduct—giving them a capacity to respond effectively to their stakeholders and (b) participate in civil trade associations that have ethical standards written by members, including tribunals designed to induce compliance. In major markets, monitors or neutral outsiders report on how civil agreements are followed in a market. Neutral outsiders can be international lawyers appointed jointly by competitors, countervailing powers, impartial observers in the UN, the Third Sector, or national governments. Let us look in more detail at both accountability systems and civil structures.

Accountability Systems

Accountability systems are designed in the private sector to operate for the common good of all member-participants. They do so by contracts, standards, monitors, and regulators to whom enterprises are answerable.

1. *Contracts* are written agreements between people that set standards for civil conduct in the marketplace.
2. *Standards* are guidelines (norms, rules, and principles) for conduct, which are written into contracts. In contracts, we include broadly corporate charters, bylaws, constitutions, mission statements, and corporate codes of ethics.
3. *Monitors* are watchdogs and countervailing organizations that keep the stakeholders and the public informed on how well the standards are maintained. We have argued that monitors cannot do their job adequately without transparency. Monitors include NGOs, social-financial

auditors, public interest groups, consumer federations, social investment firms, and UN agencies.

4. *Authorities* are judges and rule enforcers in the private sector. They operate at different levels of organization and can be called tribunals, arbiters, courts, judiciaries, boards of directors, final decision makers, and enforcement groups that are empowered by stakeholder agreement to make judgments and issue penalties for misconduct. They are designated groups who judge offenders, issuing fines or specific punishments against offenders and helping bring them toward conformity with the agreed standards. A national government has been the traditional regulator, using courts and judges to decide on penalties such as probation, restitution, fees, and jail and prison sentences, but the private sector has developed a different tradition.

"Regulatory systems" in the private sector are more varied in their organization. For example, standards are in written contracts and formal agreements, not in statutes. Violators of agreements must face "tribunals" and "final arbiters" that are established by consent among the people involved. The penalties are also made by their consent. Regulators include civil (nongovernment) courts where, based on prior agreements, representatives of competing groups issue judgments, prescribe corrective actions, and levy penalties. Consenting groups at different levels of organization enforce judgments against offenders. They may be peers, managers, executives, stakeholders, or trade and professional associations.

Violators are not sent to prison, but it is important to recognize the power of norms of consent—folkways, traditions, conventions, customs, and mores in the private sector. These guides to conduct often rule the market more powerfully than any government. In some cases, the judgment of a trade group can have more power than a government regulator. The judgment of friends can be more powerful than an official court of justice. Peers may punish offenders by social isolation and have a stronger impact than offenders facing a court sentence. If an agreement or a contract is breached, stakeholders (unions, suppliers, customers, workers, etc.) can virtually destroy a corporation.

Stakeholders protest in a government court. Customers boycott, suppliers refuse to sell products, workers go on strike, and so on. A responsible tribunal in the private sector is necessary to ensure that the rules of fair competition and civility are followed. Such councils are organized inside corporations (e.g., labor-management committees) but business associations also write codes of conduct and establish tribunals. If a member firm breaks a formal agreement, the participant members have given themselves the power to make their own judgments. If the system does not work, there are alternatives. The government is a last resort in case things go wrong. A hundred different types of enforcement mechanisms already exist in the private sector, depending upon the nature of the contract, the formal agreement, the level of organization, and the particular market sector. Examples of accountability systems are summarized in the following. We have discussed all of them in earlier chapters.

Examples of Accountability Systems

I. Accountability to *Buyers*
Example: Grading of Lumber Quality
    A. Contract: democratic agreement among competing members of a lumber association

    B. Standard: grading code for wood products

    C. Monitor: buyers in construction firms and customers who are affected by grading

    D. Authority: lumber associations with tribunals to hear cases about offenders breaking the rules

    E. Example: Southern Pine Lumber Association[2] (see chap. 1)

    F. Civil function: the system eliminates the need for a state agency to make lumber standards.

II. Accountability to *Employees*
Example: Enterprise Self Management
    A. Contract: labor agreement on democratic (electoral) structures inside the firm

    B. Standard: written principles on types and degrees of participation/ownership

    C. Monitor: the governing board of employees; sometimes watchdogs are trade unions and appointed ombudsmen

    D. Authority: representative board of directors chosen by employees

    E. Example: Mondragon co-op boards; Milwaukee Journal board[3] (see chaps. 2 and 3)

    F. Civil function: employee self-management reduces the need for government labor departments

III. Accountability to *Residents*
Example: Community Corporations (CDCs, CDFCs, and CLTs)
    A. Contract: bylaws for elections and distribution of authority

    B. Standard: written constitution/bylaws on community norms

    C. Monitor: citizens act through periodic elections

    D. Authority: a resident board and judiciary in the community corporation

    E. Example: San Bernadino CDC, CA[4] (see chap. 2)

    F. Civil function: CDCs reduce the need for government protection agencies for local citizens

IV. Accountability to *Customers*
Example: Consumer Co-ops and Customer Boards

    A. Contract: bylaws and elections

    B. Standard: member and public norms written in bylaws

    C. Monitor: customer-owners

    D. Authority: elected board powers and due process in decision making

    E. Example: (customer-owned) Seikatsu (see chap. 3)

    F. Civil function: consumer governance reduces need for government utilities and bureaucracies

V. Accountability to the *Public*
Example: Public (Nongovernmental) Corporations

    A. Contract: social constitution/bylaws

    B. Standard: professional codes of member associations and standards in bylaws

    C. Monitor: elected NGO groups on board of directors tempered by audience polls

    D. Authority: elected board deciding on programs; power to judge and fire executives

    E. Example: German Television Station, Second Channel[5] (see chap. 5)

    F. Civil function: societal governance on board avoids private oligopoly and government media

VI. Accountability to *Students and Parents*
Example: Colleges and Universities

    A. Contract: accrediting agreements between institutions and professional associations

    B. Standard: academic excellence, accreditation norms

    C. Monitor: watchdogs are students, teachers, parents, alumnae associations

    D. Authority: elected boards of associations of colleges and universities, guided by state charters

    E. Example: American Council on Education, Association of American Colleges (see chap. 4)

    F. Civil function: professional associations avoid the need for state accreditation agencies

Civil Structures

A civil structure is a group of accountability systems (contracts, standards, monitors, and arbiters) that solves stakeholder problems in a larger market system. A self-governing system of organizations requires firms to be accountable to the people they affect at the level of a nation or the global society.

An example of a civil structure is the technical classification and grading of products in the whole economy, not just one system of accountability in a specific firm or industry. Standards for size and the grading of thousands of consumer goods, like shoes, lightbulbs, circular saws, and lumber, are defined and maintained through the cooperation of competitors in trade associations. These structures also function at global levels.

Another civil structure is the system of public accounting in the private sector. Keeping proper company books is done with the aid of a society-wide set of professional rules supported by associations whose job it is to monitor the fiscal status and reliability of the firm. There is a system of agreements and standards for accounting procedures that is taught professionally in schools of management. Its latent function is to eliminate the need for government agencies to assess the bookkeeping of firms and to judge their financial credibility. Certified professionals do the job. Governments support the procedure and serve as a last resort if the system breaks down.

The Southern Pine Lumber Association has its own accountability system for grading, but it represents only one part of a civil structure in which thousands of products are graded in the U.S. economy. Systems of accountability in this grading process include democratic trade associations, codes of conduct, jointly managed tribunals, and countervailing organizations. Countervailing organizations in the case of the lumber industry include construction firms and real estate associations who depend upon (thus, monitor) the grading of lumber. The nationwide grading of lumber is then a civil, self-governing structure in the market that eliminates the need for governments to intervene on behalf of the public. Civil structures provide for fair competition at the national and international levels.

Civil structures are usually produced through the pressures of competition and conflict in the market. Solutions are privately negotiated. Structures are organized just to solve mutual problems, not particularly with an intention to fulfill civil-society values, such as justice and freedom. Nonetheless, the presence of these arrangements within a market expresses such values in the market. Indeed, new accountability systems develop to become part of these structures, without public attention. For example, social audits are coming to be included with financial audits of global corporations. As we shall see shortly, global environmental standards are developing today that relate to the grading and classification of products.

In other words, competing corporations become civil through accountability systems and civil structures. The extent of their existence is a study in itself, but we can say summarily that corporations become responsible through their associations. Through their associations, they operate collectively in the public interest as well as in their own self-interest. They construct a market system that functions, in effect, like a civil commonwealth. They synthesize social goals (e.g., fairness) with economic goals (e.g., efficiency) to operate for the good of the whole society.

Global Civil Structures and Accountability Systems

The creation of accountability systems enhances the viability of a global civil society. They avoid market interventions by governments, reduce social costs, and decrease the need for a world government with enforceable laws. International government organizations (IGOs) and business leaders—who do not want a "world state" managing a global market—have reason to develop self-accountable structures.

Broadly speaking, accountability systems and civil structures require companies and trade associations to write statements about ethical standards, principles, and fair-competition rules in market sectors; they require transparency in decision making, honest reporting of resource use, and a fair appraisal process for regulators to judge whether results are satisfactory. They are concrete mechanisms for holding offenders accountable by issuing penalties for poor performance. Their purpose is to advance sustainable development for communities in a global economy.

Now the question is how to advance social standards and enforce them better in the future.

Step 2. Experiment with Civil Market Solutions

There are many ways to develop civil structures at the global level, but we will limit ourselves to two examples. First, we will describe the current effort of the International Organization for Standardization to set global standards to protect the environment. ISO is composed of business associations attempting to work with governments and NGOs to organize procedures for monitoring and enforcing global standards. Second, we will describe how the United Nations could cultivate a system to advance accountability systems and civil structures. We take the United Nations Conference on Trade and Development (UNCTAD) as our case. Later in the chapter, we will make an argument for UN public workshops on the creation of civil markets.

The International Organization for Standardization (ISO)

The ISO represents the efforts of business competitors to set standards to protect the environment. Their experiment is ongoing and has not been fully tested. It needs to be studied as an intersectoral experiment (business, government, and nonprofits) in setting environmental standards, self-monitoring, and self-enforcement mechanisms. This effort to establish environmental standards exemplifies how the three sectors work together. Let us look at its progress, before we assess its future.

ISO Steps toward Standard Making and Enforcement

ISO is a worldwide federation of businesses founded in 1947 to promote development of international manufacturing, trade, and communication standards. ISO is composed of member bodies from more than 110 countries. It receives information from government, industry, and other parties before developing a standard. It develops standards that mediate between the interests of business, NGOs, and international governmental organizations (IGOs).[6]

Although standards developed by ISO are voluntary and no legal requirements force countries to adopt them, countries and industries are adopting ISO standards in ways that make them virtually mandatory. They could become part of the evolving "world mores" as well as the law of individual nations.[7]

ISO represents (by its own estimate) more than 95 percent of the world's industrial production; it has more than 200 technical committees and almost 3,000 technical bodies that develop and publish standards. Governments are invited to have observer status at ISO committee meetings. Decision making in ISO is by member associations and firms.

ISO 14000 is a series of standards being tested in selected markets for managing environmental impacts of business. The standards include basic management systems, auditing, performance evaluation, labeling, and life-cycle assessment. An environmental management system (EMS) is de-

signed for *third-party certification as a method of monitoring compliance.*
It addresses the immediate and long-term impact of products, services, and
processes on the environment. EMS is an organizational method that works
toward compliance with national and international requirements.

The effort to create a single, generic, internationally recognized environmental management system is motivated by the desire among corporations to avoid duplicative and sometimes competitive corporate and governmental programs.

EMS is intended to achieve

> a commitment to prevention of pollution . . . management and employee
> commitment to the protection of the environment with clear assignment
> of accountability and responsibility . . . encourage environmental planning throughout the full range of the organization's activities, from raw
> material acquisition through product distribution . . . establish a disciplined management process for achieving targeted performance levels
> . . . establish a management process to review and audit the EMS and to
> identify opportunities for improvement of the system and resulting environmental performance . . . establish and maintain appropriate communications with internal and external interested parties.[8]

The development of these standards involves the participation of government, business, and professional associations. It is a start in the direction for civil management, but it is not a perfect example. As we shall see
later in this chapter, better collaboration may be necessary between the
three sectors of a global society (government, business, and nonprofits) before a fully enforceable self-regulatory system of standards can be established.

The positive side of this global effort is that ISO 14000 represents a
change in focus from ISO's technical engineering standard making as it
moves into the realm of public policy-making. ISO 14000 comes under the
international trade rules of the World Trade Organization (WTO) and is a
demonstration of the potential that industry has to create world trade standards without government participation.[9]

This effort suggests that global markets cannot be characterized as
composed simply of corporations hungry for profits, exploiting environments, and dominating market sectors of small nations. Business is attempting to formulate a set of jointly managed social standards and humane
rules. The standards require public study and criticism through a global forum. The public needs to know how they may be flawed and yet may develop in a constructive direction with assistance from environmentalists.

An Assessment on Enforcement: ISO 14000

The issues of global code enforcement are especially complex. Critics say that there are many problems to be solved in this pathbreaking effort to self-manage markets. For example, Benchmark Environmental Consulting, located in Maine, USA, is concerned that ISO 14000 does not make reference to Agenda 21, the Montreal Protocol, the Basel Convention, the Convention on Climate Change, the Convention on Biological Diversity, or the OECD Guidelines on Hazardous Technologies.[10]

This is important because Agenda 21 recommended that transnational corporations "report annually on routine emissions of toxic chemicals even in the absence of host country requirements," drawing on the model of the U.S. Toxic Release Inventory. It contained recommendations to global corporations to "introduce policies and commitments to adopt equivalent or not less stringent standards as in the country of origin" and "be encouraged to establish worldwide corporate policies on sustainable development."[11]

Later in this chapter, we will note the need for a global forum on the way the standards of ISO 14000 were established, which was largely by industry collaboration through trade associations. The agreement requires "conformance" to standards, but many observers say that there is no clear measure of corporate "performance." There are still issues to be clarified (e.g., labels "conformance" vs. "performance") and terms to be defined more explicitly. For example, at this stage ISO does not test for environmental "impacts" but only on their "aspects." ISO does not require a "verifier" of a firm's environmental management system, only a "certifier." These technical terms (in quotes) refer to subtle distinctions that need to be debated by professionals in public bodies. The meaning of civil *command, control,* and *compliance* in ISO 14000 should be studied further. The industry-wide establishment of standards should give companies the opportunity to internalize costs and still compete in a global market. The UN can work on standard making only through negotiation and consensus building with all major stakeholders. But there are also other essential issues on enforcement.

Even with their shortcomings, ISO standards are still very significant because they may be used by national governments for official enforcement. Some countries plan to adopt them as law or use them as a basis for contracting. In other words, ISO 14000 standards are not "law," but they become a moral imperative to survive in the marketplace. The EPA in the United States may use ISO 14000 as a basis for its voluntary compliance program, which means that ISO's certified companies could face less regulatory oversight and smaller fines for environmental lapses, a reward for global certification. There is much more to be seen as this experimental effort goes forward.[12]

The United Nations Conference on Trade and Development (UNCTAD)

Our second illustration of how civil-market experiments may develop is associated with the United Nations. The civil strategies cited are my own proposals offered in conversations with UNCTAD officials, but they also apply to other UN affiliates and world groups.

UNCTAD is the principal organ of the General Assembly of the United Nations in the field of trade and development. It was established as a permanent intergovernmental body in 1964 with a view to accelerating economic growth and development. UNCTAD discharges its mandate through policy analysis, intergovernmental deliberations, consensus building, negotiation, monitoring, implementation, and follow-up. It is comprised of representatives from 188 member states, but many intergovernmental and NGO organizations participate in its work as observers. It has a staff of about 480 and is located at Geneva.

Following are examples of how civil-market options could become part of UNCTAD's consulting work with nations and global firms. The official activities of UNCTAD are described in *italics* and the opportunities for UNCTAD to promote accountability systems are proposed as Civil Strategies. These are my recommendations submitted to UNCTAD officials in New York. I see them as policies that could help build a civil economy.

UNCTAD: Recommendations for Building Civil Markets

UNCTAD seeks to help solve social problems created by the enterprise system. For example, the expected closure of diamond mines in the province of Namaqualand (South Africa) placed thousands of miners and their families in critical situations. Negotiation and consultation have been the main approach to deal with these problems.

Civil Strategy: **UNCTAD should examine "employee-community buyouts" before a host plant is closed.** UNCTAD in this case makes itself available for consultation to host-society governments, employees, and multinational executives for the purchase of "expected closures" of a global firm's subsidiary. In the United States, a subsidiary that makes a profit, but not with sufficient margins for a big firm to maintain it, is often "shut down." Yet, when the firm is still valuable to the locality with its limited profits, factories have been successfully purchased by employees and civic groups, and managed sometimes through business-government partnerships. In those cases where a firm can survive and still be useful to a community, UNCTAD can recommend a market study and a civic purchase for the benefit of all parties. A new firm can be created with public (health, safety, environmental) standards.

UNCTAD can consult with governments about providing tax incentives to firms' saving funds as a reserve for job creation during budget crises and recessions that cause shutdowns and employee layoffs.

UNCTAD seeks sustainable development for communities and aims to reduce inequities in trade and commerce.

Civil Strategy: **UNCTAD should promote community-based organizations (CBOs) for local development and global accountability.** UNCTAD can provide information about CBOs to local leaders and business groups. CBOs offer opportunities for businesses to participate in social development. A community land trust (CLT), for example, allows land to be owned by residents and leased at fair market value to the subsidiaries of multinational firms. Residents are trained for the responsible use of their land, leasing it to global firms for development. In this case, UNCTAD training teams would work with local people and business executives (e.g., mining companies entering rural areas) to think together about making a social contract. People in poor neighborhoods can write contracts with enterprises for social development, promoting environmentally safe industrial parks and quality circles in assembly plants that feature safety and health standards. Other CBOs, such as community development corporations and customer-owned banks, can design civil contracts with global firms for socioeconomic development.

UNCTAD encourages the creation of small- and medium-sized enterprises (SMEs).

Civil Strategy: **UNCTAD should encourage ethical codes in trade associations and SMEs.** UNCTAD can help business organize trade groups to establish standards for the common good. This involves consultation with IGOs and NGOs. When global firms enter developing countries, they are then encouraged to join a trade (industry) association with social standards. The area-wide trade group defines corporate codes of conduct and organizes tribunals for conflict resolution. UNCTAD in this case provides models of codes, tribunal structures, and legal information on code enforcement in the private sector. The global firm's own adjustments to local cultures remains a priority for success.

The UNCTAD secretariat proposed that UNCTAD IX initiate a one-year pilot phase of the "Trade Efficiency Review Mechanism (TERM)." The ultimate goal of TERM is to contribute to lowering the cost of trade transactions, and to lower barriers to participation in world trade. Efficiency is related to the quality and cost of services in business practices, customs, transport, trade information, telecommunications, and the like. UNCTAD has been at the forefront of offering assistance of this sort.

<u>Civil Strategy</u>: **UNCTAD should help global firms reduce externalities as part of an efficiency program.** When global firms reduce external costs (e.g., environmental damage) that result in lawsuits, government reprisals, and grass roots protests, they add to their own efficiency. UNCTAD can discuss how common labor and environmental standards advance trade efficiency.

When an UNCTAD team reports on a country's trade efficiency, it can promote competitiveness through systems of social accountability. When accountability systems are held in common by competitors, the market becomes more reliable and self-sustainable. The UNCTAD Team Report can offer suggestions for setting public standards that have been shown to reduce the costs of doing business overseas.

UNCTAD's TERM Reviews state that they *require close cooperation between public and private sectors.* The reviews *seek a better synergy between government and entrepreneurial cultures.* With these UNCTAD goals in mind, the staff's countrywide reports should include the idea of building "civil structures" toward a secure, dependable, profitable, independent, and self-regulating economy.

NGOs and IGOs interact through the auspices of UNCTAD.

<u>Civil Strategy</u>: **UNCTAD encourages transparency in market transactions and provides models for monitors and arbiters in global business.** UNCTAD staff should promote "civil structures" in the private sector between business, nonprofits, and professional associations. Imagine, for example, that there is no "environmental protection agency" in a developing country. (Few small nations are able to monitor a global firm proposing, say, a mining operation.) With UNCTAD consultation, people in the host locality can sign a contract with the global company to work in partnership with a competent NGO. The NGO, by transparent and objective standards, *monitors* the firm's effects on the environment. The NGO could be the host country's university. University scientists then do the monitoring. The faculty in university departments (e.g., biology and

chemistry) contract with the government to study the local mining process and assess the environmental effects of the firm with respect to the air, water, trees, etc. Thus, a global firm is working in partnership with the host government and a host nonprofit (e.g., a university) that conducts impact studies.

Another example: NGOs and business leaders create a partnership in a television station reaching the population of a whole country. Representatives of the nation's civil-society organizations invest in it. These organizations are of the highest order, such as tribal federations, groups of religious institutions, business associations, and labor unions, etc. Civil-society organizations hire professional staff for the TV station and assist in writing the public-interest objectives. Financial investors—and social investors—provide capital at low interest rates. NGOs serve with investors on the board of directors of the mass-media corporation.

UNCTAD plans to work on international telecommunication systems. It proposes to become the forum for creating intergovernmental consensus on developmental aspects of the Global Information Infrastructure (GII). This is in line with the Ministerial Declaration adopted at the UN International Symposium on Trade Efficiency. UNCTAD's role here complements the programs launched by the International Telecommunications Union (ITU) and the World Bank, focused on the financing and privatization of telecommunications infrastructures and on the promotion of the use of "universal norms and standards for equipment and signals."

Civil Strategy: **UNCTAD encourages public standards in telecommunication systems and GII.** UNCTAD staff view "universal norms and standards" to include civic/public standards in the development of global communications. Introducing public standards with technical standards follows the example of ISO 14000 and other code-making organizations. Thus, UNCTAD helps build codes of conduct and systems of accountability for enterprises seeking to enter developing countries.

UNCTAD offers training packages (TRAINFORTRADE) on trade-related services. They are written for policymakers in developing countries. Such training programs have been organized on "trade and environment," "national trade policies," and "competition policies," as well as "trade perspectives" with EU single market countries.

Civil Strategy: UNCTAD creates information on accountability systems in TRAINFORTRADE. UNCTAD writes training packages on the development of civil-market structures.

UNCTAD's annual World Investment Report *is the world's main source of comprehensive information on trends in foreign direct investment and on the activities of transnational corporations (TNCs). Recent editions of the* Report *have focused on subjects such as the economic restructuring impact of TNCs—on TNCs, employment, and the workplace—and on TNCs and competitiveness.*

Civil Strategy: **UNCTAD identifies social investment criteria in its *World Investment Report.*** UNCTAD has the option of adding sections to the *Report* which include ethical criteria used by global investors who make portfolio decisions on standards for health, safety, and environmental protection. In the *Report,* UNCTAD staff would review code principles and standards from NGOs and UN affiliates such as the International Labor Organization (ILO) and the World Health Organiation (WHO). Thus, UNCTAD opens an opportunity for collaboration on codes of conduct among different UN agencies.

In 1995, UNCTAD co-organized an international business conference on privatization in Uzbekistan, at which some 15 business agreements and understandings were signed. About 200 participants from the business community participated in the meeting and were informed about the investment opportunities in Uzbekistan. The conference brought together government representatives and international business executives and organizations.

Civil Strategy: **UNCTAD holds global conferences on civic partnerships between business, IGOs, and NGO sectors.** IGOs, NGOs, and business leaders in this case should study civil privatization as a form of social development. Future conferences can examine how civic standards are part of enterprise development in the private sector. Privatizing a government agency into a stakeholder-oriented company makes a civic contribution to the organization of a civil society.

UNCTAD has been a forum for intergovernmental conferences on commodities. It has facilitated international agreements on trade in sugar, olive oil, cocoa, timber, and rubber.

Civil Strategy: **UNCTAD advances the idea of public standards in world trade agreements.** UNCTAD, at best, should organize conferences on the subject of world standards for safety, health, and environmental protection. These conferences could include industries such as automobiles, oil, and steel. Co-organized conferences on international agreements in this case would include representatives from other UN affiliates (e.g., ILO, WHO, the United Nations Environmental Programme) and selective NGOs. These "observer-participants" could become advisors to the writing of associated standards in these industries.

UNCTAD can work with interested industry leaders to write a model for "internalizing social costs" for the purpose of self-regulation. Each company in this case pays its proportionate share to finance a global monitoring agency overseeing their agreement on standards appropriate to their industry. Contracting firms would fund a professionally staffed agency and, with UNCTAD as an outside observer, have the power of on-site inspection for all member companies. A tribunal could be established to conduct fact-finding inquiries and issue penalties (fees) against offenders. Global firms would then compete as strongly as they may wish within these industry-wide standards.

In September–October 1995, a number of national governments carried out a review of an action program for "least developed countries." They adopted a declaration stating their determination to accelerate economic and social progress together. UNCTAD is entrusted with the international monitoring of this program.

Civil Strategy: **UNCTAD recommends civil associations as a basis for monitoring "social progress."** UNCTAD staff could discuss civic-oriented firms and public/private partnerships as part of the process of accelerating economic and social progress in these least developed countries.

UNCTAD is taking initiatives to establish GII "nodes" in Africa at trade points proposed by the secretariat. "Nodes" are points at which information can be collected and received and from which it can be disseminated. They are locations where information, training, and contacts can be obtained. Through these nodes, local communities can be linked to international networks. Nodes function as centers for exchanges of experience, training, and research.

Civil Strategy: **UNCTAD disseminates information on accountability systems in these GII nodes.** UNCTAD staff should discuss how these nodes could be organized for the collection and dissemination of model accountability systems in the private sector.

UNCTAD has a database for trade control measures (TRAINS) and offers computerized information on all measures affecting trade for more than 50 countries. The objectives are to increase transparency in trading conditions and to facilitate trade.

Civil Strategy: **UNCTAD creates a public database on ecological impacts for TRAINS.** UNCTAD in this case develops a database for measuring the ecological impact of business. The database then helps business competitors to establish civil associations.

UNCTAD creates documentaries.

Civil Strategy: **UNCTAD produces documentaries on accountability systems designed for the public in developing countries.** In this case UNCTAD prepares documentaries that refer to model codes of civil conduct for corporations. They would demonstrate the principles and techniques for competing fairly and preserving the cultural values of host countries.

If UN agencies help build accountability systems, they will seed a new kind of global market. A mission for creating civil markets could be part of an overall UN plan. Such a plan would include what we shall call "global partnership workshops."

Step 3. Organize Global Workshops: Building Civil Partnerships

The UN Commission on Global Governance, an independent group of 28 world leaders, studied how "a global community could better manage its affairs in a new time of human history." The commission recommended in 1995 that an annual Forum on Civil Society should be composed of representatives of organizations accredited to the General Assembly as "civil society organizations."

In the spirit of this recommendation, we propose that a series of global forums should begin with the support of world leaders. The purpose would be to gather data on what is needed to create global markets—given the growing number of international associations working on standards for social justice in the world economy. The growth of codes of conduct and enforcement mechanisms is significant but so complex that no one knows fully what is happening. World leaders need to know how global associations might serve as a foundation for civil markets.

We suggest that the UN hold a series of forums on civil partnerships, bringing representatives from business, labor, government, and NGOs to help coordinate Third-Sector and business interests. We have given illustrations earlier in the chapter about the International Standards Organization (ISO) and strategies for creating civil markets through UNCTAD. The proposed forums would encourage global actors to coordinate civic action in the business sector.

The number of agreements on global codes of conduct is growing, but there are problems of monitoring and enforcement. Nonprofit monitors of global codes and agreements have developed in ways that are too numerous in their purpose to describe in detail here, but the following case suggests the direction of this code movement.[13]

In 1989, several immense institutional investors (such as the public pension funds of New York City and the California Public Employees' Retirement System (CALPERs) came together with some of the United States' largest environmental groups (such as the Sierra Club and the National Wildlife Federation) to form the Coalition for the Environmentally Responsible Economies (CERES). The original intent was to encourage companies to adopt a positive environmental ethic. CERES designed a set of principles that asked companies to integrate environmental concerns into their planning and reporting to protect the biosphere. It worked as a new strategy, and it continues to open new avenues of cooperative action. Today more than 60 companies have endorsed CERES principles and taken steps to meet its goals. Executives from these companies work with CERES to tackle tough problems of environmental management. CERES is a monitor and a "certifier," not a regulator in the full sense of the concept, but it is developing in that direction.[14]

A series of global partnership workshops on market standards and the issues of enforcement should lead to data gathering and to better practices on self-regulation. The creation of industry-wide codes of conduct is a worldwide strategy that carries questions for world leaders to discuss together.

Planning Workshops: Global Partnerships for Business, NGOs, and Governments

The outline that follows lays out some of the global associations that could be involved in these workshops and offers questions for public discussion.[15] Such workshops should be a basis for gathering data and for building a theory around civil markets, and participants should take steps to implement civil partnerships with effective global standards. Descriptions of organizations named in the following outline cannot be detailed here, but their presence and the schedule of questions for discussion represent what I think lies ahead for world leaders to consider in this trend toward globalization.

The purpose of these workshops would be to encourage participants in the three sectors to talk with one another about standards in a global economy. First, we see global business, defined by profit making, efficiency, productivity, and competition; second, civil governments, defined by democracy, justice, equity, welfare, and cooperation; and last, the Third Sector, defined by other values, such as those found in ethics, art, medicine, law, religion, charity, and education.

PROPOSAL: GLOBAL PUBLIC WORKSHOPS

A project for the collaboration of governments, NGOs, and business organized with UN support. The panels are to be held in locations likely to attract the public and the press. Representatives are invited from each program listed.

Global Workshop I
Technical and Environmental Standards

Question: How are global competitors developing social standards?

International Organization for Standardization: ISO 14000
What are the ISO 14000 series standards? What is behind the EMS (environmental management standards) movement? How did it start? What is the guidance document? What is included in ISO 14001? Is ISO 14001 a product certification standard? Is ISO 14001 applicable to all industries? What are ISO 14010 audit standards? ISO labeling standards? Performance standard? Life-cycle assessment standards? Are government bodies adopting ISO 14001? What is the role of ISO 14000 in the European Union?

The Chemical Manufacturers Association
What are the 10 guidelines for responsible care adopted by the CMA board of directors in 1988? What is the relationship between ISO 14001 and responsible care?

American National Standards Institute (ANSI)
How are ANSI standards established? How are government and industry leaders jointly involved in setting global standards? Is there a balloted consensus by a special technical committee composed of government regulators, users, manufacturers, and ANSI staff? What is the relationship of ANSI to other standards organizations (e.g., NSF, ISO 14000)? To what extent are environmental and consumer protection guiding principles behind these standards?

Commentaries from leaders representing Agenda 21, the Montreal Protocol, the Basel Convention, the Convention on Climate Change, the Convention on Biological Diversity, the OECD Guidelines on Hazardous Technologies, and government agencies like the U.S. Environmental Protection Agency

Global Workshop II
On Cooperation between Competing Companies

Question: How have business competitors established effective codes?

International Chamber of Commerce: Codes and Tribunals
Key Presenter: ICC

Why did corporate codes develop? On what theory of business are they based? What relation do the codes have to the UN Code? How are they enforced? What is their success? Is there a business ethic here?

The Caux Principles, 1994
Key Presenter: The Minnesota Center for Corporate Responsibility

How did chief executives from key TNCs in Europe, the United States, and Japan write these principles? How do these principles connect with others developing in the global market? Does any monitoring of corporate conduct take place?

Keidanren Global Environmental Charter
Key Presenter: Japan Federation of Economic Organizations

How did the charter develop? Who is involved? How is it enforced?

Commentaries from business scholars, UN analysts, and organizational theorists

Global Workshop III
Allocating Social Capital: Professional Criteria

Question: How are investment professionals creating standards?

The CERES Principles
Key Presenter: Trillium Corporation

How did the goals for excellence develop? Who are members? How are the codes enforced? How do firms develop social audits? What is a "disclosure form"?

Principles for Global Corporate Responsibility: Benchmarks for Measuring Business Performance
Key Presenters: Interfaith Center on Corporate Responsibility (United States), Ecumenical Committee for Corporate Responsibility (Britain, Ireland), and the Task Force on the Churches and Corporate Responsibility (Canada)

How did the measures for responsibility develop? What are "benchmarks"? What is unique about this code? How is it implemented?

Commentaries from representatives of the Council of Institutional Investors, International Chamber of Commerce, Council for a Parliament of the World's Religions, Council on Economic Priorities, International Labor Organization

Global Workshop IV
Corporate Codes of Conduct: The Salience of Subsidiary Systems

Questions: How do corporations introduce social standards in their global subsidiaries? How do companies enforce their own standards?

General Motors Board Guidelines on Corporate Governance
How are the guidelines enforced? How can appeals be made from the public?

Levi Strauss and Co.
With sales approaching $6 billion a year and 36,000 worldwide employees, how is the three-part mission statement implemented? How can the mission hold in the face of serious competition?

Cadbury Committee on the Financial Aspects of Corporate Governance
What is the "Code of Best Practice"? How is it implemented?

Commentaries from the ILO, Association for Social Economics, American Sociological Association, and American Management Association

Global Workshop V
Connecting Global Codes with UN Affiliates

Questions: What is the relationship of the UN in helping to advance codes of conduct in the global market? How can the UN assist business and stakeholders to organize codes and enforcement procedures?

International Labor Organization (ILO)
How can existing guidelines and codes become more effective? For example, the Field Guide to Labor Rights, the Tripartite Declaration of Principles Concerning Multinational Enterprises and Social Policy.

OECD: Guidelines for Multinational Enterprises, 1991 UN Draft Code of Conduct
What was the status of the corporate code of conduct created by the UN? How does the code now operate under the authority of UNCTAD?

Putting Together UN Human Rights with Corporate Codes
1. The Universal Declaration of Human Rights
2. Convention on the Elimination of All Forms of Discrimination against Women (adopted by UN, 1979)
3. The Wood-Sheppard Principles for Race Equality in Employment (Race

Equality Project, Ecumenical Committee for Corporate Responsibility, December 1993)
4. The United Nations Draft Declaration on Gender Equity (July 1985, Nairobi)
5. A Code of Practice for the Employment of Disabled People (Manpower Services Commission, 1984, Britain)

How do these past codes connect with new standards being established?

Commentaries from world organizations that represent women and minorities

Global Workshop VI
Special Industry and Market-Based Codes

Advertising Codes
Key Presenter: British Committee of Advertising Practices (CAP)

What application do national codes have to international codes of advertising? What role do media associations play in curbing malpractice? Can trade associations of broadcasters and newspapers set standards on advertising?

UN Affiliates' Codes
1. International Code of Marketing of Breast Milk Substitutes (WHO/UNICEF)
2. International Code of Conduct on the Distribution and Use of Pesticides (Food and Agriculture Organization of the United Nations [FAO])

How do these codes fit into codes of conduct within the communications industry? How can codes become a guide for policies in corporate radio, television, and newspaper associations?

Commentaries from international news media and professional associations

In the preceding proposal, keynote speeches can be given by world leaders—the secretary general of the United Nations, the presidents of major nations, major global firms, and other major global groups. Global workshops can help form UN policies that implement civil partnerships and accountability systems.

Avenues to Civil Enforcement: Global Forum Preparations and Follow-up

Civic leaders who have created partnerships across the sectors of business, labor, government, and voluntary organizations can offer models on how inter-sector collaboration has been accomplished. Two essential questions are the following: (1) How do partnerships combine profitability with account-ability? (2) How do they integrate self-interest with the common good?

Ideas for the answers to such questions need to be discussed in prepa-ration for these global workshops, and a UN follow-up on forum outcomes should be planned. This effort to build systems of accountability is vital to Workshop I, but it applies equally to others. Questions of accountability concern social/technical audits, codes of conduct, certified examiners, and effective methods of code enforcement.

Harris Gleckman and Riva Krut have listed major instruments for us-ing civil systems for enforcement purposes. These include the following:

- An effective enforced regulatory system that sets costs for previously free goods (e.g., land damaged by waste disposal is given a cleanup cost);

- a civil liability system that "punishes" firms/executives for not taking care of health, safety, and the environment (e.g., the polluter pays health damages);

- a corporate accounting system that reflects "real" environmental costs during the internal decision-making process (e.g., recycling costs are included in budget forecasts);

- an eco-labeling system that encourages consumers to make purchases on the basis of the product's environmental impact (e.g., labels would publicize unacceptable environmental business decisions);

- a national tax system based on the use of natural resources rather than on income flows (e.g., taxes are charged on the consumption of nonrenewable resources rather than on income flows);

- a mandated requirement that manufacturers have a responsibility for their products' full life-cycle uses (e.g., costs for a public recycling plan are paid for by the manufacturer); and

- an end to government programs that underprice natural resources and therefore encourage their over-use or misuse (e.g., costs for soil depletion are not subsidized by agricultural programs).[16]

In the past, national governments let professional bodies certify whether organizations were complying with standards, such as the Finan-cial Advisory Standards Board (FASB) in the United States. The "environ-mental field" has yet to establish such a board, but one point is clear: En-vironmental costs need to be internalized within global firms on an industry-wide basis. In order to do this, businesses need industry-wide accountability systems built into trade associations to create a "common playing field" in world markets.

Without world law, there are still many paths to "global enforcement." Regional organizations, like the EU, help set rules that become standard for other world regions. The EU has the power to encourage corporations to become advocates for a "common playing field" on world markets. NGOs also have a role as a monitor in the making of civil markets.

Social investors will likely play a role as global monitors. Twenty-five years ago, U.S. business took a new turn when John Hines, the presiding bishop of the Episcopal Church, stood up at the General Motors annual meeting in Detroit and asked the board of directors to withdraw its operations from South Africa. The action marked the beginning of a wave of shareholder activism that is part of the history of social investment. Today hundreds of institutional investors exercise their rights as owners of firms to express their views on everything from executive compensation and corporate governance to employment practices and environmental responsibility.

In late 1993 the Governing Council of the American Public Health Association (APHA) unanimously approved Policy Statement 9304 urging U.S. industry to stop using the chemical chlorine. APHA is a professional society, founded in 1872, representing all disciplines and specialties in public health. It is the heart of the U.S. public health establishment. The APHA said, in effect: We cannot study all the possible toxic effects of 15,000 individual chlorinated chemicals. Therefore, based on the weight of the evidence, we should assume all chlorinated chemicals are dangerous and avoid all exposures in order to prevent harm. This issue needs to be discussed at the global level.[17]

Summary and Looking Ahead

Something new is happening in global markets. The first steps on standard making have been taken. The following organizations exemplify standard-setting efforts that are ongoing.

> The Global Charter of the Keidanren, Japan Federation of Economic Organizations, International Chamber of Commerce Business Charter on Sustainable Development, the Caux Principles, the CERES Principles, the ILO Tripartite Principles Concerning MNCs and Social Policy, the work of the OECD (representing industrial nations), the UN Draft Code of Conduct, the single issue codes, like the International Code of Marketing of Breast Milk Substitutes (with the help of WHO/UNICEF, the World Health Assembly, and the six nations adopting it), and the International Code of Conduct on Distribution and Use of Pesticides (FAO).

Special civil agreements are important to recognize as part of this process of civil development. World leaders have begun to integrate environmental standards into regional trade agreements. In North America, the

North American Free Trade Agreement (NAFTA) set up the North American Commission on Environmental Cooperation in a side agreement, a fair beginning but needing enforcement that is much more adequate. In the Pacific, negotiations within the Asia Pacific Economic Cooperation (APEC) Forum propose to integrate key commitments in Agenda 21, but the issues are still to be worked out. The governments of Trinidad and Tobago, Chile, Jamaica, and Bolivia are setting up environmental infrastructures in the belief that this is a "rite of entry" to the Free Trade Agreement for the Americas, but we must yet see how this becomes implemented.[18] There is much ahead in the organization of civil markets.

A theory of civil markets is building from these independent efforts to guide corporate conduct on the world scene. We know that social standards by themselves are important but not sufficient without a method of enforcement. Civil enforcement is at best backed by a legal system that supports code making. Without the existence of a world government and enforceable law, social self-governance in the global market is the only alternative. When properly organized, accountability systems—defined by agreements, contracts, standards, monitors, and final arbiters—can do a good job. Market self-governance requires transparency and the collaboration of trade associations, trade unions, NGOs, IGOs, and the United Nations.

In sum, the construction of an effective global economy requires linking social principles (e.g., democracy and justice) with economic principles (e.g., productivity and efficiency). Problems in the current market require global workshops to study the creation of standards and enforcement mechanisms to protect people from exploitation and unruly players on the global scene. Business leaders need to learn more about how civil structures become effective in global markets. And government leaders need to learn more about social contracts, codes, monitors, and final arbiters, which ensure compliance to standards in this emergent world economy.

People in the era of feudalism struggled for centuries to produce democratic governments. Now, people living in an era of global markets have their own struggle. A global economy with no enforceable regulations can be a hazardous place, but it can also be designed on principles of civil development. The development of local-to-global markets should, at best, have all the ingredients of civil society. A civil society has mechanisms of conflict resolution and, in the long run, collaboration among competing parties for higher purposes. This is the essential battle ahead for the coming century—transforming market systems into a civil economy.

Appendix: Great Ideas in the Academy

Philosophers first defined civil society as *government*, and then later Adam Smith identified it as a system of *business*. Now, scholars identify civil society as the *Third Sector*, not typified by government or business. Hence, our task has been to examine how all three sectors coexist in society. This task has brought us to view the economy from a broad perspective. This appendix is provided for those readers who want to look at this broad perspective in a way that points toward future studies on the economy.

Today it is popular to think of the economy as the business sector. Some scholars, however, have defined the economy as the way people allocate scarce goods and resources. Others view the subject as a specific set of ideas, such as efficiency, competition, productivity, and profitability. For still others, the economy is the way people are guided by rational self-interest to organize systems of exchange or the way people produce, distribute, and consume goods and create services. Here we contend that the subject of the economy crosses all these subjects and more. In our sense, the subject is interdisciplinary and should lead students ultimately to questions about nature and the meaning of life itself.

In this appendix, we see how great ideas have defined the economy. This endeavor should point to an entirely different picture of the economy as it links with society and culture. These ideas are complex and beyond our scope to examine carefully here. Nonetheless, we refer to them in order to entice curious readers to think about an economy that keeps evolving in every new century.

Great Ideas: Moral, Social, Political, and Cultural

While philosophers studied the *nature of the state* two centuries ago, we think social scientists should study the *nature of the economy* in the twenty-first century. We imagine here that the economy has moral, social, political, and cultural dimensions. These ideas are not prioritized in any order of importance. They can be simultaneous in the mind, yet also seen as separate and interweaving in their application to the economy.

Smith wrote about the moral idea in the eighteenth century, but today the economy is explained in secular terms. The ideas of moral philosophy are separated into subjects of different university departments. Moral thought in Smith's day was overarching in its reference to human society, but moral ideas today have been secularized into departments of economics, sociology, political science, and anthropology. Moral thought has been privatized, so to speak, into different systems of belief among religious organizations. It can be taught in a department of philosophy or a school of theology but not with the same significance that it had in the time of Smith. Hence, we examine Smith's idea as though secular terms were hidden in it. We propose that moral sentiments still exist in corporations and the politics of associations, obscured by the vocabulary of finance and commerce.

The Moral Idea

We noted that Adam Smith saw the new European class of bourgeoisie evolving in the late eighteenth century and called it "civil society." He envisioned the free world of commerce as an alternative to feudal rule, a path toward individual freedom and progress. Individual competition could then be combined with a moral conscience in the marketplace. Free enterprise was a realm of personal autonomy where people could develop personal accountability and become responsible for their own action in a moral sense. The enterprise system required personal reflection that was more advanced than the feudal system. The new commercial system created a space in which people could be free from monarchal rule and could organize their own systems of exchange.

Adam Smith (*The Theory of Moral Sentiments* [1759]) thought that a moral idea was essential to civil society. The economy originated in nature, guided by a Creator. Indeed, this business economy was like nature in the sense that it was not always "rational"; the whole human enterprise reflected great passions and moral sentiments. Moral sentiments referred to passions in the whole range of human feeling, from rage and fear to love and suffering, but Smith saw such emotions experienced inwardly and conditioned by a private, rather concealed identity with others.

People in civilization carried deep feelings, but the original passion, he said, was mutual sympathy. A sense of mutuality was screened from immediate view, speechless as it were, but part of the development of a moral life in society. An inner social dialogue took place between one's self and the image one had of other people. The vast range of human passions felt and observed by the individual had an inner spectator. People were participant observers of their experience with other people. They made moral decisions based on their judgment about what they felt to be right within their limited range of experience.

Smith introduced his concept of "spectators" to show how moral sentiments socialize individuals and fashion them into communities. He distinguished two main types. First, there is the spectator external to one's self, that is, a type of observer who, by showing some approval or disapproval of a person's conduct, exercises an influence on a person. Second, an internal spectator operates on two levels. There is the spectator of one's imagination, that is, what one imagines another person's reaction would be to one's behavior, that social image of another person apart from one's self. Another level of the internal spectator operates through one's own moral judgment. It is one's own conscience, so to speak, that person "within one's breast." He saw the latter to be an "impartial spectator." A social self was civilizing the primitive nature within each individual. In essence, Smith was saying that the whole economy had a natural and social foundation.[1]

Smith's theory of moral sentiments and his idea of "justice" in *The Theory of Moral Sentiments* are important to understand as background for his later book *The Wealth of Nations* (1776). Putting together Smith's ideas in his two books helps explain how he could view markets as self-regulating.

For Smith, "moral sentiments" operate at different levels of intensity. They vary according to the nature and strength of stimuli affecting people from the outside. Smith describes the way in which the strength of "passions" varies with the closeness of a relationship. He viewed this closeness in regard to duration, space, kinship, nationality, occupation, rank, and so forth. A contemporary philosopher, David Hume, thought like Smith in some ways. Hume repeatedly used the term *distance* metaphorically to signify factors separating individuals from each other, a usage that goes back to both Aristotle and Thomas Aquinas. This subtle relationship between closeness and distance becomes part of the study of social self-regulation (see discussion of NASA's *Challenger* space shuttle disaster in chap. 1).[2]

Smith assumed that social relations existed in the marketplace. Thus, we propose that social relations formed his concept of self-regulation. We propose the idea that Smith's mutual sympathy, or a joining of the self and other, could be applied to the situation in which competitors find a common identity to join their different interests. Indeed, this human propensity for mutual identity could be a driving force behind "all the toil and bustle of the world." In free markets, competitors must establish a basis for a mutual self-governance among themselves.

Smith saw a social self existing unnoticeably with inner reflecting mirrors. A moral economy develops from social relations where a common identity is evoked with others, and at some point a sense of justice is summoned. This sense of justice requires a constant construction of who am "I" and who are "we." The answer to these questions seems to be at the heart of Smith's theory of a self-regulating market. It is not the whole story, but it could be part of the reason why he saw a competitive market as self-regulating.

Smith said that people needed to establish a government when this civil life was inadequate to meet the needs of a society. He argued that the natural expression of moral passions leads eventually to a just order in the marketplace. The human tendency toward civil order and justice is not strong enough by itself, among ordinary people, to meet the demands of the larger society. Hence, a government at some point must enforce certain rules through law and magistrates.

Smith's proposition on self-regulation is about the way people civilize their primitive instincts and socialize their passions. Human instincts are in a perpetual strain to become civilized. Thus, we have argued that rules are created in the private sector to civilize markets and to develop a greater freedom through a civil order in the economy.[3]

For Smith, the individual was the basis for self-reflection, and his moral philosophy was based on a social idea. In turn, this social idea gained prominence among other philosophers. The word *social* appeared between the 1820s and 1840s in opposition to the idea of *individual.* Philosophers saw people divided into rich and poor classes. In Robert Owen's *London Cooperative Magazine*, the word *socialism* appeared in 1826 as opposed to *individualism.* Utopian experiments in community and revolutionary movements sought to create a different social order. Most failed, but the social idea never disappeared. "Social" is simply a fact of life.[4]

The Social Idea

The social idea refers to the way people in the economy interact, organize groups, and orient to one another in making decisions. Great philosophers, like Rousseau, Locke, Montesquieu, Saint-Simon, Mill, and others, were interested in the social idea, not just Smith.

In the eighteenth century, the field of political economy was prominent as a study about government and commerce, but critics soon realized that the subject rested in society. Comte Henri de Saint-Simon (1760–1825) described an order of associations in society, as opposed to an order of individuals, not a society based on "egoism." John Stuart Mill (*Principles of Political Economy* [1848]) suggested that Saint-Simon had sown the seeds for socialist thought. Mill wrote about "states of society like different constitutions or different ages in the physical frame." He welcomed the ideas of Auguste Comte, who became one of the founders of sociology. Marx's *Critique of Political Economy* (1857) argued that the capitalist system was rooted in society, not in an individual or political idea.[5]

On occasion, this social idea was interchangeable with the moral. Herbert Spencer (1820–1903) differed with Marx and spoke of "The Morals of Trade" (1859) as though the market system represented freedom from bondage. Social development in the trades, he said, was produced from a spontaneous energy, observed in voluntary and cooperative associations in the market system.

Smith's theory of mutual sympathy can also be interpreted, as it happens, from an organizational perspective. In this case, organizations operate as though they were individuals, as autonomous and in mutual sympathy. Our theory of civil economy is based on the idea that organizations are in "mutual self-development" while in a competitive market. This organizational concept is not exactly the same as mutual sympathy, but it is close enough by metaphor to be worthy of research. This idea does not profess to account for all facts about the economy, but it is about how people live in communities. We can see the idea unfold in the thought of sociologists.[6]

Émile Durkheim (1855–1917) critiqued the moral ideas of Utilitarian philosophers, like Hume and Smith. He said the Utilitarians assumed that moral values were the products of individual adults, possessed of language and intelligence, who judged the actions of other individuals. People made moral judgments on a belief about the consequences of their actions that are harmful or painful, arousing anger or punitive tendencies, and actions whose consequences are beneficial or pleasant, arousing affection or approving tendencies. But Durkheim contended that in society, a rule becomes part of an organization and is then institutionalized. Thus, it becomes sanctified; it assumes a sacred character. Then the rule is followed regardless of its human-welfare consequences. Individuals are in organizations (governments, churches, corporations) in specific roles where they follow the rules. Thus, moral rules, and their attitudes and consequences, originate in the group, rather than at the individual level. The values most sacred to the individual are those most widely shared by, and most closely binding people in, associations.

Durkheim said that the capitalist system was in a state of anomie (normlessness), full of human insecurity. He studied the rapid changes in market life, such as sudden wealth, economic depression, the rise or fall of a social class. He found these changes associated with the changing rates of suicide.

For Durkheim, no state could write the rules that govern a whole economy. The economy was too complex. Authorities and rules that become sacred can be harmful. No single authority can be a perfect judge, he might say today. But because of the anomic condition of the market, Durkheim saw the need for greater coordination of "economic functions with the directing and knowing organs of society."[7]

Georg Simmel (1858–1918) objected to Durkheim's emphasis on the idea of a "group mind." Rather, he saw society emerging out of group interaction. Society was created from within itself, so to speak. People made their own rules of order. To enter society, individuals become "categorized"; indeed, they would experience a generalization of themselves as they took roles given to them by associations. For example, a new infant is born into "the Smith family" and is called a "child." It plays its role according to the rules of the Smith family. Some part of the individual is sacrificed (and a part retained) in this social process, according to Simmel.

For Simmel, society develops directly through people's experience in associations. The first rules for any association arise out of *sociability*. Sociability is a "play form" of association; in other words, it is "human association for its own sake," not for profit (as in a business) or for a supernatural purpose (as in a religious group). It is an association with its own reward; it may exist for the sheer enjoyment of people being together. We might understand it today as a "social," or a "sociable" gathering in which the personalities of the individuals, not their formal interests or roles (as "president" or "worker"), are prominent in guiding a conversation. People are in (partly) spontaneous interaction when they create society.[8]

Simmel saw society as a process of self-creation. Individuals remain in their discreteness, yet undergo a higher unity through a synthesis of mutual identity in associated life. One can only speculate on how this idea of social self-creation would be connected to Smith's "mutual sympathy" or imagine how sociability would connect as an idea with what Herbert Spencer saw as "spontaneity" in the marketplace.[9]

Following Simmel in a theory of civil economy, we would say "societal groups" are composed of people who are both inside and outside them, simultaneously. People retain a certain individuality while following the rules of a social group. Keeping Simmel's theory of group self-creation in mind, we would contend that people are in a self-organizing market, thus government can help stakeholders in markets invent solutions to their disputes in the marketplace.

In this outlook on a social economy, we see employees that work for the Boston Gas Company abiding by its organizational rules. As individual employees, they experience a change (gain or loss) in self-identity. But, in turn, this corporation becomes a member of the American Gas Association and abides by the rules of its larger association. Each corporation is unique and has its special interest within a self-organizing association.

Let us put these ideas together in the sociology of a civil economy. For Durkheim, rules in established associations can acquire a sacred (inviolable) quality. Trade associations, unions, governments, and professional and church associations establish rules that can develop a hallowed character. If certain rules are broken, the violation may be considered not only wrong and illegal but immoral. On the other hand, for Simmel, when a local shoe manufacturer joins a trade association (or a local nondenominational church joins a national denomination), it changes (loses/gains) something of its identity by integrating its corporate self-interest with a larger association interest. It finds a new social identity (perhaps, mutual sympathy) by associating with other corporations in the same field.

Thus, the theories of Durkheim and Simmel apply to the life of individuals and organizations across society. All associations develop rules and collective self-identities. People have identities as "retailers" or "bankers" or "scientists." They say, "We are grocers," or "We are in frozen foods," or "We are in the computer business," or "We are women." They act corporately with a mutual sympathy. Metaphorically, they are like Smith's individual person, reflecting on their experience in the marketplace.[10]

This not a tidy picture of morality. In this perspective, some civil order exists in all groups. The members of a violent gang set rules for themselves when they fight a gang down the street. Certain rules are inviolable. The members of a local church make agreements among themselves in their battle for autonomy within a denomination. A group of workers set their rules as they combat other groups within unions, and so on. All groups act with a set of agreements in their associated life. All associations are self-governing in some measure while interdependent with others. Each individual and each association has its self-interest, yet shows the potential to become part of a larger associated interest. As the associations become larger, common interests become "common values."

People civilize themselves in associations, even as they, as individuals, might be discourteous or obnoxious to one another. Separate associations can become offensive, abusive, and damaging to one another. Each association develops its own corporate ego, in a manner of speaking, as it competes in the economy. Smith saw some big egos in his day and called them corporations.

Thus, we are expanding the social idea in Smith's moral philosophy. Each individual's (personal) interest is disciplined and then is potentially re-created within a body of associations. Individual interests may change variously as they become suppressed, compromised, partially fulfilled, or more completely fulfilled through associations. At this associative level, people can also be more bonded and work in common "structures of feeling." They are in a context of reproducing, overcoming, and transforming old systems, maintaining and inventing new systems of governance in the economy.

The social idea has its objective and subjective poles of thought. At the objective end of this continuum between poles, Karl Marx had a theory about class conflict that he thought was complete and true; it was an omniscient view of society and history. Postmodernists label such theories as "totalism" or "objectivism." Very differently, Durkheim studied business cycles in terms of the rate of suicide. His findings could be tested as a "social fact," a statistical reality. Finally, at the other end of these poles of thought, the social idea is conceived in more subjective terms. Simmel saw individuals as vital to the creation of group rules, and viewed people engaging in a process of self-creation. And later sociologists, like Max Weber, saw reality in the subjective life of people.

In sum, organizations in markets develop through mutual sympathy and identity as well as through conflict and competition. This is true for all sectors of the economy. And in memory of Adam Smith, individual associations can be passionate in their corporate life, especially in a fight for survival in the marketplace or when a corporation lobbies a legislature to advance its religious beliefs. This perspective on social life then allows us to view the economy as a political idea.[11]

The Political Idea

The political idea refers to the way power is exercised in a polity. A polity is any organization or community that is administered like a government. In this idea, the economic order is composed of a network of organizations that administer some form of power in relation to the state. The economy, as a political idea, changes our image of market organization.[12]

Some political analysts find that corporations rose to their place of dominance on the basis of "power," not on the basis of "efficiency." Small manufacturers emerged at the beginning of the twentieth century because powerful actors made their development possible. The state, for example, used its power to promote railroad developments by issuing bonds that drew entrepreneurs to this form of transportation. And financiers used their power to build huge manufacturing enterprises by deciding to finance these mergers. This outlook on corporate history is based on a political idea more than on a moral, a social, or an economic idea. It describes the economy in terms of power and a sense of justice, not in terms of efficiency and a sense of freedom.[13]

A concept of justice is part of every political order. Nothing rivals the passion of a corporation to "win the game," yet each game has its system of justice. In the battle over "what is right" between the Detroit Lions and the Pittsburgh Steelers, the final decisions are made in the National Football League. In the battle between the Microsoft Corporation and its opponents, the final judgments are made in government courts. Some measure of civil order, some degree of justice, operates in this context of people in a political economy. In this mode of thought, everyone is a political actor.

Organized labor has its own political history that is defined as a power struggle with business corporations. The original purpose of the labor movement in the nineteenth century was to fight for human dignity and social justice. But organized labor was forced to compromise. In the United States, during the Great Depression, the federal government legalized the basis for labor to organize, negotiate, and make binding contracts with management. Labor and trade associations, both political actors, relied on government for a solution called "collective bargaining." Some labor leaders argue that the New Deal was only a political idea, a compromise. Labor had settled for the opportunity to advance wages and benefits in a capitalist system, losing something of their original identity and purpose. Collective bargaining was a historic moment, a political and legal contract to be sure, but for some leaders, a pause in a larger struggle for social justice. In the original organization of labor, justice had meant "shared power" in the corporate economy, but that goal was not fulfilled. The idea of social justice is still a quest for labor leaders today.[14]

Municipal and state governments are also political actors who compete in the market. We illustrated earlier how governments compete against one another to attract business to localities for economic revenue, but here we offer one example of how governments are both corporations and political actors concerned with power, justice, and money in the marketplace.

The National Football League (NFL)

The National Football League (NFL) is a for-profit corporation that has been exempted by the Supreme Court from being viewed legally as a monopoly. Yet, the problem is that state governments, such as those of Washington, Missouri, Florida, and Ohio, have faced the loss of professional teams that move from state to state. States and big cities lose business when famous teams relocate. The problem for cities is similar to what happens to the economy of small nations where global businesses have the power to move to another nation.

States have challenged the NFL's antitrust exemption because the opportunity to have famous teams in their locality helps their economy. Every government has to make a cost/benefit analysis in making a decision about whether to give money to a team to locate in their territory. The team itself also makes those economic calculations in making its decision about location. Thus, the subject of economics applies to all organizations that seek to survive in the marketplace, but we are emphasizing how the idea of power and justice applies to *organizations* in the economy.

Governments and corporations are both political actors looking for money. Today an attorney general of any state could go to court and demand the breakup of the NFL into two leagues, thereby opening professional football to competitive forces, as in the 1960s when the American Football League existed. Competition between leagues would create more teams and allow more cities to host them without such great cost to the taxpayers. *Teams would then compete for the right to capitalize the local economy, rather than the present situation, in which governments compete to capitalize teams.* At this moment, governments give away local land and build lavish stadiums for sports teams. This is done largely at the expense of the taxpayer, but it happens because of the social/political organization of markets.

In the case of the New England Patriots, part of the public debate has been an apparent promise to Robert Kraft, the Patriots' owner, by which the NFL would not allow any other team to move into New England after the Patriots move to Connecticut. In other words, no other NFL team would be allowed to take its place in New England. The Supreme Court decision remains ambiguous about how actions of the NFL might become unlawful. An antitrust lawsuit could result if the Patriots relocated and the NFL would not allow another team to enter New England.[15]

Thus, the market system is a subject of political science as well as economics. We are talking about corporations that exist autonomously within a broad economy. One corporation is the state. Another is the business firm. This subject is not simply about government-market relations.

State and city governments are geographically based competitors. They make financial decisions about how to attract these teams and strengthen their corporate economy. It is one part of this larger polity of associations. At the same time, the NFL calculates its economic decision and has its own way of administering justice by the way it organizes and administers power in its own association.

The political idea usually refers to a state; hence, political scientists do not study how people create a self-governing economy. The idea of "self-government" hangs in the public mind as though it were related only to the state. Yet, the idea of self-governance applies to the market economy.

Political scientists could and should view the market system as a battle for power as much as for profit; the power struggle keeps going higher and higher to global arenas. The essential motives (power vs. profit) of business can be debatable, but the question we raise is whether the economy is a basic subject of political science, raising questions of justice in a polity of associations.

When pork farmers in a trade association lose money and go bankrupt, while members of distributor and retail associations reap profits, it is not simply a problem to solve in the economics department. These organizations are all interdependent in a game of rules and fair play, that is, rules of competition. It is a game for profits and power, yet all organizations are dependent upon one another; trade members are in a delicate balance of power that involves the survival of all. The political idea raises issues on how an economy of organizations balances power and works with rules of fairness for all stakeholders.

All these questions of polity are raised in the framework of civil society. Philosophers in the eighteenth century raised questions of power and justice in a system of monarchies. They saw the need to establish a civil government. Political scientists in the twenty-first century, in turn, should raise questions of power and justice in a system of organized markets. They should study markets as part of a civil economy.[16]

The market system is composed of organized power in such systems as *franchises, partnerships, alliances, confederations,* and *federations.* Each of these systems represents a decentralized vs. centralized order of authority. Each has different rules of order that raise or lower the autonomy of members.

Today, competing corporations, unregulated, could destroy civil society, as we know it. Or, they could examine themselves as self-governing bodies in competition for a larger good. Political scholars do not study the effectiveness of trade associations as federations, as decentralized systems of power. Nonetheless, the economic order has its polity, its series of administered governments, standing separate from the state. The economy, as a self-governing order of organizations, is a subject waiting for research by political scientists.

The Cultural Idea

Some scholars have begun to study the economy as a cultural idea. This idea connects with the changes taking place among our three sectors, government, business, and nonprofit/grassroots organizations. In the interaction between these sectors, a cultural dynamic becomes significant. The symbols and values of the market economy become viewed as ruling powers.

Cultural scholars ask, Does "civil society" hold a capitalist economy in its womb? Or, does a capitalist system hold civil society in its womb?

Many writers are in a critical mood. They see the fields of music, painting, the arts, architecture, the professions, and intellectual work itself as products of the capitalist market. Many of these observations are true, although some writers are not fully conscious of the meaning of culture as an idea. Superb writers, nonetheless, open our mind to a hidden violence in the perpetuation of the capitalist culture connected with physical violence and the destruction of community life.

Mike Davis teaches urban theory at the Southern California Institute of Architecture. He sees the city of Los Angeles symbolizing capitalism. He paints a picture of decay, violence, and death. For him, capitalist power is like a meatcutter chopping a body into pieces or like a mammoth truck careening out of control down the highway with a crowd of people ahead. All organizations are hierarchies of power and dominance. The less empowered actors, the unions, churches, artists, and grassroots organizations, are hierarchies struggling for power, battling helplessly within the capitalist system. This is a story of market madness and the destruction of community life. Davis tells us about the market forces that do not allow for rational choice and civility.[17]

Our view of a trisectored economy is the opening for more exploration of the cultural idea. In the twenty-first century, the cultural intersection between nonprofit and business sectors could become an issue in the governance of society. It could become a question of symbolic (not just financial) power in the economy. The cultural idea evolves as a theory when these different sectors bring very different values to the marketplace. The cultural idea cannot remain an esoteric part of university studies because trisectored associations hold conflicting values and symbols. Business interests compete (or combine) with associated interests in art, science, education, and religion. At this intersection, we see crucial changes in governance ahead. The trisectored economy is a cultural phenomenon.[18]

The most sophisticated notion of a "cultural economy" is in the work of Pierre Bourdieu. His central concepts, called "habitus," "capital," and "field," are terms that describe the economy as a multidimensional phenomenon. Bourdieu wants to overcome the gap between subjective and objective dimensions of the economy. In his discussion of social structure and practice, people live in a world that is "embodied" with practical knowledge and structures.

We can only point suggestively in the direction Bourdieu takes his study of the economy as a cultural idea. For Bourdieu, the concept of habitus assumes that social life is a "mutually constituting interaction" of structures, dispositions, and actions. Social life, however, is also a "structured improvisation" that has an enduring character. It is in a process of self-construction in subjective and objective terms. The notion of "capital" is thus multidimensional. Bourdieu sees an interplay between social, cultural, and economic capital. Economic capital is the most efficient form, easily convertible into social and cultural capital, and vice versa. The notion of "field" is a framework for a "relational analysis" that takes account of these different dimensions. Bourdieu wants to reconstitute the "objects of analysis" as a crucial part of each research effort.

For Bourdieu, specific markets are sites of collective symbolic struggles and individual strategies to produce valuable goods. The value of a symbolic good depends upon the preference assigned to it by a consumer community. Value judgments are made in most fields by the amount of symbolic capital accumulated by producers. Victory in this cultural struggle means that one's symbolic goods have been judged to possess more value than those of one's competitors. Thus, Bourdieu characterizes the multidimensional character of the economy that we describe as trisectored.

Bourdieu speaks of "institutions of culture" as though they were instances of "conservation and consecration." Law and politics (ordinarily perceived as coercive institutions) are symbolic powers. Hence, for him, symbolic fields of power organize the world into "objective relations." Capital is derived from the relationships between positions that people occupy in the distribution of resources, that is, economic, symbolic, and cultural capital. Thus, the dominant class has the greatest portion of multidimensional capital. Economic capital (e.g., money), rather than symbolic capital (e.g., prestige), is the dominant principle in modern societies. This is because it is so easy to transfer and "objectify." It possesses "liquidity" and is easy to calculate.

Bourdieu is concerned with social self-reflection that is intricately anthropological. For Bourdieu, a reflexive subject can be an individual, a social class, or a entire society. The object of reflection can be rules that organize a society or part of a society. Bourdieu's work is focused on rules that become embodied in people's lives. His work is significant for our purposes because of its focus on the reification of rules in the practice of self-regulation. In a sense, a concept of civil economy helps define the social structures developing in Bourdieu's theory.[19]

Let us make one last point about the idea of culture. Most people have forgotten that the word *culture* began in the fifteenth century. The idea was transferred from French to English at a time when it referred to tillage of soil and cultivating the earth. It took a century or more to lose that meaning and distinguish a new meaning—from husbandry and tillage—to the "cultivation of the mind." A new word *agriculture* had to be coined to distinguish the difference from this great idea of "cultivating" the mind. Culture has a historical form, and it also goes beyond any single period of history.[20]

Every society expresses a historical myth. People live in an unspoken set of principles and beliefs. Nonetheless, modern society is still composed of individuals, associations, and, we would argue, a polity in commercial life. Thus, our three sectors of society—government, business, and voluntary groups—embody subcultures in the overall myth and the legend of modernity. Subcultures are embodied in corporate structures that carry strong feelings and moral passions; people live simultaneously in different roles and associations. We all stand in the tension of differences in a cultural economy.

In sum, the cultural ideal has both historical and universal meanings, not altogether dependent upon the structure of a capitalist system yet entrenched specifically within it. Each locality and each sector of society has a subculture; each association has its rules and moral sentiments. Cultural critiques and literary novels help us to identify the destructive forces of capitalism in our time, and anthropological treatises give us distance to observe the change.

The Unfinished Work

Great ideas in the past centuries carry special messages today. Adam Smith and Karl Marx saw nature and humanity in tension, joining somehow, somewhere, some time in the future.[21]

Smith said boldly, sounding like Marx, "Laws and government may be considered . . . as a combination of the rich to oppress the poor." He argued that merchants and manufacturers are "an order of [people], whose interest is never exactly the same with that of the public, who generally have an interest to deceive and even to oppress the public, and who accordingly have, upon many occasions, both deceived and oppressed it." Smith's word *public* should become defined more tidily in the coming century.[22]

Marx said boldly, sounding like Smith, that each individual should act with humanity in transforming this capitalist system. He was worried about "political man." He said, "Political emancipation is the reduction of man, on the one hand to a member of civil society, an egoistic and independent individual, on the other hand to a citizen, a moral person." Individuals in their actual material lives must take "the abstract citizen back into [himself/herself] . . . [people] must recognize [their] own forces as *social forces,* organize them, and thus no longer separate *social forces* from [one's self] in the form of political forces. Only when this is achieved will human emancipation be completed."[23]

The nature of this market economy remains filled with contradictions, still a mystery, and still evolving. Smith and Marx were studying the structure of markets in their time, yielding truths, giving us deep insight into this evolving system. But the market economy is more complex than either one ever imagined. Nor is it explained adequately today by mainstream economics. By now we should know that the subject of the economy goes beyond the province of economics. Today the subject should be studied through the lens of all great ideas. Moral, social, political, and cultural ideas have developed in systematic ways since the time of Smith and Marx. They should become a basis for understanding the market from a human perspective. We have been saying that *the market economy is human nature trying to civilize itself.* The task for interpreting the development of a civil economy will be a major challenge for students in the third millennium.

Notes

Chapter 1

1. Jean Cohen and Andrew Arato, political theorists of civil society, say:

On the whole, in neither Latin America nor Eastern Europe has the "interface" of civil society and market economy been adequately analyzed. Such an analysis, however, is a precondition for any really serious conceptual alternative to the dangers of economic liberalism and the false promises of utopian socialism. Without such an alternative, one can expect more vacillation between market and state as agents of liberation and renewed neglect of the destructive effects of both on social solidarity and individual autonomy (*Civil Society and Political Theory* [Cambridge, Mass.: MIT Press, 1997], 77).

2. Adam Smith, *The Theory of Moral Sentiments,* ed. D. D. Raphael and A. L. Macfie (Oxford: Clarendon Press, 1976), 9, 61. Adam Smith, *An Inquiry into the Nature and Causes of the Wealth of Nations* (Chicago: University of Chicago, Encyclopedia Britannica, 1952). David Hume also sketched a theory of the "moral sciences." In his *Treatise,* Hume discusses "the rise and progress of commerce" (*A Treatise of Human Nature* [London: Clarendon Press, 1958]).

The new moral economy was interpreted partly in the eye of the beholder. William Blake, a poet and a contemporary of Smith, was the first to notice the "Dark Satanic mills" beginning to wipe out the cottage industry and jamming workers into ugly new factory towns. The weaker and less efficient firms cut corners and began to hire children at low wages and long hours. The social consequences of industrialization made the appalling aspects of work life more visible.

3. For the tendency of corporations to achieve exclusive privileges, see Smith, *Wealth of Nations,* 26, 51; on the idea that corporations work against the forces of competition as well as on how their "combinations" work against the public, see ibid., 55. Adam Smith said that *if* this new civil society encouraged selfishness, it risked destroying its moral foundation. He argued that people must try to put themselves "in the situation of the other" and become aware of each other's distress and suffering. The new order of the eighteenth century strengthened individual freedom, but a danger existed in that corporations could emerge, undercutting the interdependency fostered by the market society. As we will indicate later in chapter 1, Smith's negative opinion of corporations was borne also by early U.S. leaders, who made corporate charters very restrictive. By the time of Andrew Jackson's presidency, the business corporation had become a matter of intense political dispute, crystallizing around the so-called War on the Bank. Jackson argued in 1836 that the

Second Bank of the United States concentrated power in the hands of a few men failing to be responsible to the people. The evidence of moral deterioration in corporate conspiracy and restraint of trade mounted so high that the Sherman Antitrust Act was enacted in 1890, followed later by other regulatory legislation.

4. In the nineteenth century, working conditions in some regions were appalling. Child labor was widespread. Wildcat strikes were common, as was industrial sabotage. Employers used every means to break strikes, including the use of private security forces and state troops. Violence brought more violence, and many died in the "industrial wars." The early attempts to regulate the economy through government came after states reduced their restrictions for corporate charters.

5. This early government growth includes the creation of the Interstate Commerce Commission (1887), Antitrust Division (1890), Federal Reserve Board (1913), Federal Trade Commission (1914), and dozens of agencies created during the Great Depression. Government regulations continued around new issues in each decade. A moral concern for human rights began in the 1960s, producing the Equal Pay Act (1963), Civil Rights Act (1964), Age Discrimination in Employment Act (1967), Vocational Rehabilitation Act (1973), Americans with Disabilities Act (1990), and Civil Rights Act (1993). For more details on this history, see James Post et al., *Business and Society* (New York: McGraw Hill, 1996), 411ff.

6. For key references on social capital, see James Coleman, "Social Capital in the Creation of Human Capital," *American Journal of Sociology* 94 (Supplement) 1988: S95–S120; Robert. D. Putnam, *Making Democracy Work: Civic Traditions in Modern Italy* (Princeton, N.J.: Princeton University Press, 1993).

Civil-society theorists today give special attention to the fact of interdependence in the human community. Civil law has come to refer to human rights and protection from the state. To be civil once meant to come out of savagery, to refine oneself, to learn the proper rules and habits of society. Civility has meant being considerate and courteous. Civic life has a slightly different connotation but also equally applies to the common rules of people living together. "Civic" points to what is socially required to live in a peaceful local community. A "civic center" refers to public buildings and landscaped spaces at the center of a town, including an auditorium, a library, a band shell, shops, and hotels as well as government office buildings. It represents the core of the community, not the core of government. A course in civics would focus on democratic principles, not merely on government and the duties of citizenship. See also Stephen L. Carter, *Civility: Manners, Morals, and the Etiquette of Democracy* (New York: Basic Books, 1998).

7. Morton Horowitz, *The Transformation of American Law, 1780–1860* (Cambridge, Mass.: Harvard University Press, 1977), 112.

8. Edwin Merrick Dodd, *American Business Corporations until 1860* (Cambridge, Mass.: Harvard University Press, 1934), 395. For further examination of these issues, see the pamphlet by Richard Grossman and Frank T. Adams, *Taking Care of Business* (Charter, Inc., CSPP, P.O. Box 806, Cambridge, Mass. 02140, 1993).

9. Louis Hartz, *Economic Policy and Democratic Thought, Pennsylvania, 1776–1860* (Cambridge, Mass.: Harvard University Press, 1948), 240.

10. The details of this history are explained in Ralph Nader, Mark Green, and Joel Seligman, *Taming the Giant Corporation* (New York: W. W. Norton, 1976), 33ff.

11. William Roy addresses the question of why corporations emerged in the United States. He challenges the conventional theory that corporations were more

efficient. Roy contends that the rise was a question of "power"—defined as the capacity to shape the alternatives that others choose from. Powerful actors (not the principle of efficiency) shaped this history (*Socializing Capital: The Rise of the Large Industrial Corporation in America* [Princeton, N.J.: Princeton University Press, 1997]).

12. Adam Smith's sense of "interdependence" among individuals was critical to philosophers in this period. German philosophers were especially fascinated by this rise of civil society in the eighteenth and early nineteenth century. In the early nineteenth century, philosopher G. W. F. Hegel argued that selfish energies unleashed by the market created "a system of complete interdependence, wherein the livelihood, happiness, and legal status of one man is interwoven with the livelihood, happiness, and rights of all." Hegel, writing later than Smith, saw a growing selfishness in the commercial system as a problem in the development of a moral society. He said that civil society was developing more around individual *(particular)* self-interests and could not be reconciled with *universal* morality. This was not a moral economy. Hence, the state was the final moral authority (T. M. Knox, *Hegel's* Philosophy of Right [New York: Oxford University Press, 1967], 123). Karl Marx then opposed Hegel's view of the state as the ultimate moral authority. Publishing his critique of bourgeoisie (civil) society in 1845, he said that social forces would replace both capitalism and the state. Property owners would never give up their rights to ownership. The only way to freedom, he said, was through a proletarian revolution. Once this class conflict was resolved in the economy, the state would "wither away."

13. Vladmir O. Pechatnov, the first secretary in the embassy of the USSR, in Washington, D.C., argued that "Civil society is the most natural, organic form of social self-organization, and it would be ideally the only such form—hence, the famous notion of the withering away of the state ('the absorption of state power by society') as an ultimate ideal of socialism" ("Civil Society in the United States and the Soviet Union," *Kettering Review* [Winter 1990]: 6–8). Pechatnov said that the special feature of U.S. history was that civil society preceded big government and developed under very favorable conditions. In the early American colonies, there were a high density of horizontal societal associations of a robust and muscular nature and a strong antielitist tradition. Freedom from government intervention was seen to be most important. The Russian situation was almost the opposite. A strongly autocratic central state preceded civil society and capitalism, thwarting social development. Because of the lack of self-regulation by an active society, the predominant pattern of sociopolitical change became one of stagnation, followed by revolution. There was no long-term progression in the development of civil society. The essential meaning of perestroika was the emancipation of civil society and of the individual from excessive interference and control by the state, as the only way of unleashing the creative energies of the people. The logic of the future is a movement away from encompassing state ownership to more plural forms of ownership, a redistribution of powers among central, national, and local authorities (ibid., 6–8).

14. Lester Salamon and Helmut Anheier, "The Civil Society Sector," *Society*, 34, no. 2 (January/February 1997): 60; see also Salamon and Anheier, *The Emerging Nonprofit Sector* (New York: Manchester University Press, 1996).

15. On the conservative view, contact the Cato Institute, 1000 Massachusetts Ave., N.W., Washington, D.C. 20001. On philosophers, see Jürgen Habermas, *The Structural Transformation of the Public Sphere* (Cambridge, Mass.: MIT Press,

1989). On cultural theorists, see Adam Seligman, *The Idea of Civil Society* (New York: Free Press, 1992).

16. Sociologist Alan Wolfe argues today that the political economists of the eighteenth century were not justifying a capitalist society. "[T]heir aim was to provide the rationale for a capitalist economy within a *society* held together by a nonbourgeois (or more precisely, an early bourgeois) morality." Wolfe says that the difference between a realm of morality organized solely by economic principles and one organized by the principles of civil society becomes clear in Adam Smith's treatment of friendship (*Whose Keeper?* [Berkeley: University of California Press, 1989], 29–30). Under feudalism, Wolfe argues, friendships were formed out of what Smith called "necessitudo"; that is, they were imposed by the necessity of the situation. In the more "modern" countries of Smith's time, people joined around "a natural sympathy" that would enrich and deepen their moral obligations to one another. Smith saw civil markets based on mutuality and friendship, very different from the calculating and utilitarian economics for which Smith is often cited today. In specific marketplaces, economic exchange would reenforce mutual trust and respect. In this context, civil society defined economic transactions in a moral light. In a specific market, people could barter and exchange until they made the best *mutual* agreement. Friends could rely on their knowledge of one another during an economic transaction. Conversely, in *the* market system of today, people are forced generally to treat one another as potential threats to their own self-interest. Unfair play, suspicion, and deceit arise in excessive and impersonal competition. Specific markets could be reconciled with morality and civility in Smith's vision but not *the* market system.

17. On this history, see Edgar Heermance, *Can Business Govern Itself?* (New York: Harper and Brothers, 1933), 93.

18. *American Brands, Inc. v. National Association of Broadcasters*, 308 F. Sup 1166 (D.D.C. 1969). Some people think that "business self-regulation" became unconstitutional when the government relied so heavily on it during the Great Depression. The essential court decision in this case involved a trade code in the poultry industry. The Supreme Court decided against the trade code because it was (1) deemed as law through presidential authorization; (2) all infractions involved intrastate trade, not interstate trade; and (3) as a private code, it did not have the effect of law enforced by the federal government. None of these conditions apply to our cases, which are all voluntary. *A. L. A. Schechter Poultry Corp. v. United States*, 295 U.S. 495 (1935).

19. Burton Weisbrod, *The Nonprofit Economy* (Cambridge, Mass.: Harvard University Press, 1988), 172. For-profits have complained that permitting nonprofits to be in competition with them puts them at a disadvantage since they have special access to tax-deductible contributions, but a study by the Roberts Foundation suggests the reverse. In many cases, nonprofits are under pressure to offer wages above the market rate, something a for-profit would do only to secure a highly productive employee (Jed Emerson, ed., *New Social Entrepreneurs* (San Francisco, Calif.: Roberts Foundation, 1996).

20. Economists were not conscious of the Third Sector before the 1970s. They did not make any effort to categorize the vast literature on nonprofits before that decade. These points are elaborated in Jon Van Til and associates, *Critical Issues in American Philanthropy* (Oxford: Jossey-Bass, 1990). Today, government could give incentives to business associations to express civic purposes, that is, to establish stan-

dards of safety, health, environmental protection, and the like, with self-enforceable procedures of due process. Altering the tax laws could provide incentives for trade associations to include a clear civic purpose. In effect, certain trade associations would then overlap in purposes with the Third Sector. Just as we said nonprofits are rechartering themselves to join the business sector, so trade associations, as non-profits, could recharter themselves under special tax laws *to advance civic purposes.* Under the right tax conditions, trade associations could be recategorized so that members who chartered their association to protect stakeholders by self-enforceable codes of conduct and effective tribunals would fall under this code designed for them.

21. This evolution of judicial systems in business associations remains largely un-studied. In 1958, the U.S. Chamber of Commerce conducted a survey of 634 trade associations and found that 195 were engaged in commercial arbitration; such asso-ciations hear and settle controversies between themselves (as competitors) and also for their customers. At the same time, churches, unions, professional associations, and other types of nonprofit groups also have codes of conduct with tribunals and self-enforcement systems.

The Chamber of Commerce and the National Association of Manufacturers are nonprofit associations that have advanced the cause of business. The American Med-ical Association and the American Bar Association are nonprofit associations that have advanced the cause of their professions, becoming great corporations them-selves. Dissidents criticize such associations as unfair and too powerful. Nonethe-less, they were part of this civilizing process that meant going beyond petty and per-sonal interests to professional and collective interests and values, as in the formation of legal and medical ethics within their own competitive market. They now face new ethical problems as big corporations and new responsibilities at this higher level of organization. The National Education Association and the National Council of Churches grew to giant size, presenting problems for people opposed to their prac-tices, but they were similarly engaged in organizing a relatively civil sector in their own field of activity. All these nonprofit associations constructed powerful lobbies in Congress and have not always acted in the public interest, but they have been part of an important socializing process as competitors in the market.

Today these associations are becoming more significant in the public mind. About a third of the graduates of the Kennedy School of Government at Harvard Univer-sity now take jobs with nonprofit corporations. The estimated 1.4 million nonprofit organizations have become a significant part of the market economy. Harvard was given a $10 million grant in April 1997 to create a new center for the study of non-profit institutions. Other universities are moving in this same direction.

22. This is my short summary. See George Lamb and Sumner Kettele, *Trade As-sociation Law and Practice* (Boston, Mass.: Little, Brown, 1956), 92–93. The formal organization of these civil associations is democratic, but the informal organization varies in terms of some members being more dominant, not always perfectly demo-cratic. But then, nations are formally democratic but not always perfectly democratic in practice.

23. Let us apply this theory in the context of all organizations in all sectors. The proposition is that resolving the tension between "self and other" is central to the civil development of markets. In the resolution of this tension, a form of social gov-ernance develops at each level of organization: work circles, corporations, industries,

nations, and international organizations. Theoretically, individual interests become optimized through systems of mutual governance. The way markets become self-regulating is through a constant recreation of mutually self-governing associations. In a theory of civil society, people work toward the lowest common denominator of power that is most effective for civil order.

24. John Kenneth Galbraith, *American Capitalism: The Concept of Countervailing Power* (Boston: Houghton Mifflin, 1962).

25. *Marjorie Webster Junior College, Inc. v. Middle States Association of Colleges and Secondary Schools*, No. 23, 351, USCA (DC Cir.) 1970. The trial record takes up 14 volumes in which the MSA declared the Sherman Act did not apply to them.

26. Diane Vaughan, "Autonomy, Interdependence, and Social Control: NASA and the Space Shuttle Challenger," *Administrative Science Quarterly* (June 1990): 230.

27. Vaughan states that the character of internal-external relationships between the regulators and regulated is the basis for assessing corporate performance. She cites Barry Turner's studies of the "failure of foresight" of catastrophes as due to special norms and culturally accepted beliefs about hazards that develop in the too-close relationship, including poor communication systems, inadequate information, and other problems (ibid., 225).

28. There is no empirical data on the "motives" of philanthropy in this case, and there is much more to be learned about influence and collusion. But there is also the irony that occurs in changing generations. For example, the modest W. Alton Jones Foundation was elevated into the ranks of the top 100 charities when Occidental Petroleum bought out Cities Service Oil, sending the value of stock owned by the foundation sky high. The founder, W. Alton Jones, a chief executive of Cities Service, had created the foundation out of a "big heart," and he was no environmentalist. Yet his widow, Nettie Marie Jones, and their two daughters had a different opinion and focused their gifts on protecting the environment as well as stopping the nuclear arms race. Today the Jones Foundation, which had benefited from the petroleum industry, is a major thorn in the side of that same industry (Scott Allen, "The Greening of a Movement," *Boston Sunday Globe,* October 19, 1997, pp. A1, A30; Allen discusses more illustrations of these "contradictions").

29. J. J. Boddewyn, "Advertising Self-Regulation: Private Government and Agent of Public Policy," *Journal of Public Policy and Marketing* (1985): 129.

30. Ibid., 135.

31. Contextual economist Neva Goodwin speaks of the motives in the economy. "The role of profits in contributing to a well-functioning market can perhaps be better understood if we distinguish between the *profit motive* and *profit discipline.*" She introduces a new set of questions for economists to ask in their analysis of markets (*As If the Future Mattered: Translating Social and Economic Theory into Human Behavior* [Ann Arbor: University of Michigan Press, 1996], 61).

32. The American Automobile Manufacturers Association has adopted new specifications for U.S. gasoline that would preclude MMT use. According to the association, MMT harms automotive systems. Fifteen oil companies have taken a first step to not use MMT, but four (Amoco, Anchor, ARCO, and Sunoco) have taken a second step by promising *to notify the Environmental Defense Fund,* a nonprofit association, if they change their plans. This is my summary of information in an *EDF Letter,* 27, no. 3 (May 1996): 1, 5.

33. David Osborne and Ted Gaebler, *Reinventing Government* (Reading, Mass.: Addison-Wesley, 1992). The authors point out that nonprofit organizations were the fastest growing parts of the economy, in terms of employment (45, 281).

34. For a list of members and a description of what they do, see Joel Makower, *Beyond the Bottom Line* (New York: Simon and Schuster, 1994).

35. The Tufts University study also calls for greater cooperation among nonprofit organizations and proposes a common agenda to advance their purposes and to settle problems. According to this study, there is a lack of management training and rampant internecine warfare. Also, people who are trained in social work, museum conservation, or medicine frequently lack business training and management skills. Nonetheless, the study anticipates a very positive development in this sector for the future. Editorial, "Doing Better at Doing Good," *Boston Globe,* July 9, 1998, p. A14, and July 10, p. E5.

36. A total of 182 major financial institutions (pension funds, community development funds, foundations, etc.) are making socially responsible investments of one type or another, totaling $639 billion in assets, or roughly 9 percent of the $7 trillion in funds under management in the United States. An estimated $473 billion of the total is controlled by investors who either sponsor shareholder resolutions or vote their proxies on the basis of formal policies embodying socially responsible goals. Three out of four U.S. money managers who handled investments for clients opposing apartheid in South Africa continue to manage "responsibly invested" portfolios today. An estimated $162 billion is under management in socially screened investment portfolios. Socially and environmentally concerned investors are on a rapid rise today. Apart from traditional criteria in screens called "avoidance investment" (e.g., tobacco, alcohol, weapons), there is a growing emphasis on "positive investing," encouraging improvements in company practices in the use of screens for human rights, the environment, animal rights, and employee rights, including workplace treatment of women and minorities. For further information, see *After South Africa: Responsible Investing Trends in the U.S.* (A Report of the Social Investment Forum, P.O. Box 57216, Washington, D.C. 20037 [Tel. 202-872-5319]). See also Peter Kinder, Steven Lydenberg, and Ami Domini, *The Social Investment Almanac* (New York: Henry Holt, 1992).

37. Robert A. G. Monks, Nell Minow, *Watching the Watchers: Corporate Governance for the Twenty-first Century* (Cambridge, Mass.: Blackwell, 1996), 125–26.

38. Local Initiatives Support Corporation, 733 Third Ave., New York, N.Y., 10017.

39. The Commission on Global Governance has seen the significance of this inter-sector relationship for building a world society. Its members argue that there must be a place in the UN system for individuals and organizations to petition action to redress wrongs that imperil people's security. To be an effective instrument of global governance, the United Nations must take greater account of the emergence of global civil society (the nonprofit or Third Sector). New global actors will play a crucial role in the management of global affairs. A reassessment is under way of the relationship between the UN and its family of organizations and the growing array of organized nonstate activity (*Our Global Neighborhood: The Report of the Commission on Global Governance* [New York: Oxford University Press, 1995], 253). The commission examines the possibility of a new system of world governance that takes account of this growing body of voluntary organizations.

40. Carmen Sirianni and Lewis Friedlander, "Civic Innovation and American Democracy," *Change* (January/February 1997): 16.

41. As we indicated earlier, social investment began in the Third Sector with churches, foundations, and universities and then spread into the business sector. Teacher pension funds, such as the Teachers Insurance and Annuity Association and College Retirement Equities Fund (TIAA-CREF), act in certain moral concerns, for example, avoiding investment in the tobacco industry. For more discussion on the innovative practices of social investment, see Ritchie Lowry, *Good Money: A Guide to Profitable Social Investing in the 90s* (New York: W. W. Norton, 1993). For examples on the activities of socially responsible firms and their associations, see Makower, *Beyond the Bottom Line.*

42. Archie Carroll, *Business and Society* (Cincinnati, Ohio: South-Western College Publishing, 1996), 76. Business scholars use the term *social accountability* to refer to the "actively responsible" conduct of business leaders. It is perhaps management's closest term today for the Scottish philosophers' idea of moral order founded on the ideas of self-interest and human interdependence. The study of the social interdependence of people in the enterprise system has introduced a stakeholder theory of governance in the corporate economy, taught in business schools.

43. Although several companies were engaged in these questionable market practices, the Swiss conglomerate Nestlé was singled out by a Swiss social activist group in an article published in 1974 entitled "Nestlé Kills Babies." At about the same time, an article appeared in Great Britain entitled "The Baby Killers" (Rogene Bucholz, Willam Evans, and Robert Wagley, *Management Response to Public Issues* [Englewood Cliffs, N.J.: Prentice-Hall, 1985], 80).

44. Ibid., 84ff.

45. Neva R. Goodwin, *Social Economics: An Alternative Theory, Building Anew on Marshall's Principles,* vol. 1 (New York: St. Martin's Press, 1991), 55. Goodwin says that the threads of her argument are already woven into the field of economics. She starts with the neoclassical economist Alfred Marshall, who believed that the principle of cooperation needs to be taken seriously, going beyond the "profit motive and competition," to enable the market economy to fulfill societal values. She continues to say that the issue is how to link causally the benefits that an economic actor confers on its environment and the benefits that it derives from the environment (ibid., 56).

46. We use "self-regulation" and "self-governance" interchangeably in this book. The terms refer to the capacity for people to be independent of outside control, or supervision, or excessive influence. The power of self-governance diminishes or increases according to the way people organize themselves in the economy. We use "civil" in both a factual and an ideal sense. "Civil" is a fact insofar as it refers to the way people already set rules in associations and thus conduct their affairs without physical violence. It is a fact that people cannot live in freedom without civil order. One group, nonetheless, acting nonviolently with its common (civil) rules, can act injuriously against another group with a different set of rules. It is easy to see how members in one group are civil to themselves but would be seen by others as uncivil or perhaps as acting unjustly against them. We also refer to "civil" in an ideal sense. We see groups that are competing or in conflict yet are able to negotiate a set of rules to work together through an overarching association. In a more civil association, they can compete while also working for their common good. They remain as individuals

who compete within a larger community of interest. When conflicting parties are able to set new rules of governance together, and account for the identity and well-being of individual members, they become in this sense "more civil."

Chapter 2

1. Keith Davis and Robert Blomstrom, *Business and Society,* 3d ed. (New York: McGraw-Hill, 1975), 39.

2. Neva Goodwin, a contextual economist at Tufts University, says that, "accounting systems are methods for counting up what matters to us—what 'counts.'" She suggests that we need new systems to assess what is most important. Many social-economic indicators were developed in the 1960s, deducting some of the costs of urbanization, congestion, crime, and so on, from the GNP, bringing more sober assessments of the "goods" and "bads" of development. For more, see Goodwin, *Social Economics,* 43ff. See also Richard N. England and Jonathan M. Harris, eds., *Alternatives to the Gross National Product: A Critical Survey,* discussion paper no. 5, Global Development and Environmental Institute, 1997, <http://www.Tufts.edu/GDAE>.

3. For current information on employee-owned firms, see the National Center for Employee Ownership at <http://www.nceo.org>. In 1998, employees in employee stock ownership plans (ESOPs) received 5 to 12 percent higher wages and had three times the assets in their retirement plans than employees of non-ESOP firms. *Fortune* magazine's listing of the "Top 100 Companies in America to Work For" found that 31 had broad-based employee ownership plans. This chapter and later chapters on civil privitization discuss the problem of combining worker ownership with worker participation.

4. In the 1960s, Delbert Miller and William Form began to study the changing patterns of employee participation as a long-range trend, starting at the beginning of the twentieth century. The change developed in the following pattern. 1. Management gives *orders* in an authoritative manner, and workers follow them with *obedience.* 2. Management gives *advice,* and labor accepts that advice. 3. Management *shares information* with labor and then *negotiates* with labor as an equal party. 4. Management asks for *joint participation with labor in governance* within the command system (*Industrial Sociology* [New York: Harper, 1964], 763ff). Michael Quarry, Joseph Blasi, and Corey Rosen, *Taking Stock* (Cambridge, Mass.: Ballinger, 1986), review the steady increase in worker ownership.

5. The government has begun to play a role in supporting self-managed companies. The Connecticut General Assembly created an $8 million fund to reduce interest rates for worker-owned firms. California authorized the state's Business Development Department and local development offices to give technical assistance to employee-owned firms. But governments at little or no cost can also do much more. A state governor can sign an executive order directing all state agencies to report on what they have done to encourage employee ownership. Agencies that lend money to firms, support research on the economy, regulate stock ownership, and hold conferences and workshops for business could focus their activities on this goal. The federal government could alter its employee stock ownership plan (ESOP) legislation so that *pass-through voting rights* and employee training would be mandated (Joseph Blasi and Douglas Kruse, *The New Owners* [New York: HarperCollins, 1991]).

6. The empirical evidence for making such assertions about the advantage of self-managed firms (such as saving jobs, etc.) is found in Severyn T. Bruyn, "The Labor Market," chap. 3 in *A Future for the American Economy* (Stanford, Calif.: Stanford University Press, 1991). "Self-managed firms" are less likely to locate abroad to lower labor costs in foreign nations and hence would not contribute to unemployment and subsequent welfare costs at home. These firms help maintain stability in neighborhoods that have become disorganized and drug ridden, reduce the need for police and drug squads, help keep capital in the locality because incomes circulate locally, and *tend* to be more responsible to the environment, reducing the need for environmental protection agencies.

7. Blair suggests two different arguments as to why the conventional system of shareholding does not perform well: (1) shareholders do not have enough power to control management and prevent misuse of corporate resources, and (2) pressures from the financial markets cause managerial myopia, which implies that shareholders *should* have even less influence than they do. A significant part of that influence should, instead, go to employee stakeholders (*Ownership and Control* [Washington, D.C.: Brookings Institution, 1995]).

8. Robert Ozaki, *Human Capitalism* (New York: Kodansha International, 1991), 7. Ozaki also speaks of a "mutual" consultation system between management and labor that goes beyond that of any U.S. firm (106, 191). During recessions, top salaries are cut first. Work hours are reduced in order to rotate work. Surplus employees who need to be let go in one department are shifted into other departments. "Generalist thinking" is encouraged among employees in the firm. Both superiors and their subordinates select new managers.

9. William Whyte and Kathleen Whyte, *Making Mondragon* (Ithaca, N.Y.: Cornell University Press, 1991). There is often a failure in U.S. co-ops to retain sufficient capital due to an annual distribution of the whole profit, a tendency not to hire skilled managers, and a tendency to be purchased by outsiders when they become successful. These self-destructive tendencies are overcome in Mondragon. In addition, Mondragon participants have established a systemwide coordination of firms in banking, retail, farming, housing, social security, and education, a system that is designed so that people can work together in the interest of the whole community.

10. A field study of the Mondragon systems reveals that male-oriented (paternal) norms persist within its democratic structures. Nevertheless, the democratic system is allowing women to fight the old norms. See Chris Clamp, "Managing Cooperation at Mondragon." Ph.D. diss., Boston College, 1986.

11. *Grassroots Economic Organizing Newsletter* 20 (January/February 1996), P.O. 5065, New Haven, Conn. 06525. Sharryn Kasmir spent time socializing with Mondragon workers, and her research suggests that some alienation exists in their lives. She notes how visitors to Mondragon are given special treatment by managers and are not shown the shadow side of the system. For example, cooperative workers do not make use of the participatory channels available to them. She is favorable to union representation in the system, a countervailing power to the line hierarchy of managers in these firms (*The Myth of Mondragon* [Albany: State University of New York Press, 1996]).

12. Researchers find it difficult to determine empirically how much worker councils have improved corporate performance. Some have examined the efficacy of "works councils" in Europe and suggest that councils improve competitiveness and

performance by promoting efficiency within firms. Councils also provide management with accurate information about the state of their company. Finally, they argue that works councils improve the quality of corporate decisions and facilitate their implementation (Joel Rogers and Wolfgang Streeck, *Works Councils* [Chicago, Ill.: University of Chicago Press, 1995]; see also Severyn Bruyn, "On Becoming a Self Managed Firm," *Social Report* (no. 2 [June, 1983]).

13. "United States: Lessons from Abroad and Home," in Rogers and Streeck, *Works Councils,* 404.

14. United Airlines made a promising start under employee ownership, gaining a larger share of the market and increased productivity and profitability more rapidly than its competitors. Its stock price tripled after the buyout, compared to increases of about 30 percent in shares of other airlines. For more on these issues, see David Levine, *Reinventing the Workplace* (Washington, D.C.: Brookings Institution, 1997); and James Lieber, *Friendly Takeover: How an Employee Buyout Saved a Steel Town* (New York: Penguin, 1997).

15. Joseph Blasi, a key analyst of ESOPs, argues that the current loophole that allows a company to set up a profit-sharing plan without giving employees voting rights should be eliminated where there is more than 15 percent employee ownership and that every 15 percent of employee equity in companies should entitle worker-owners to choose a member of the board of directors on a one person/one vote basis. Blasi argues that there should be pass-through voting rights on all stock in majority-employee-owned companies (*Employee Ownership* [Cambridge, Mass.: Ballinger, 1988], 239ff.).

16. Christopher Gunn, *Workers' Self-Management in the United States* (Ithaca, N.Y.: Cornell University Press, 1984); Robert Oakshott, *The Case for Workers' Co-ops* (London: Routledge and Kegan Paul, 1978).

17. For details on the history and variety of "community-based corporations," see Severyn Bruyn and James Meehan, *Beyond the Market and the State* (Philadelphia, Pa.: Temple University Press, 1987).

18. In 1989, there were 130,000 community associations in the United States, according to the Community Associations Institute, involving 30 million Americans. Some of these are just small condominium associations, but 80 percent of them own land as well and have an average of 543 dwelling units. This trend toward community associations has its positive and negative sides. These local associations can become ghettoized communities, like Leisure Hills in Laguna Beach, California, where guards stand at the gates to check the identity of all visitors. They could simulate the walled cities of medieval Italy and, like small states, end up fighting one another. Or, these associations could build cooperative ties with other communities outside themselves and create new modes of market self-governance through confederations.

19. Seeing the seriousness of the problem, leaders in both the Democratic and Republican parties united to create CDC legislation to be handled through the federal Office of Economic Opportunity (OEO). Although this office was dismantled by later administrations, local leaders continued to construct successful CDCs across the country. Today they have become a vital part of a communitarian model, the emergent economy of self-governing markets. Some states today award grants to community development corporations, which strengthen low-income communities by developing housing, creating jobs, and enhancing public safety.

20. Investing locally often invokes issues of diversity. On feminist issues, Dolores

Hayden sees the local housing market as undergoing a historical shift as the United States changes gears from the dream of owning a home to the aim of building whole communities that take into account the concerns of women. Hayden argues that Victorian gender stereotypes of development are no longer viable. New designs must include "work" related to home; that is, new spatial planning must connect employment patterns and household work. *Private life* in the home and the *public life* of work cannot be separated today (*Redesigning the American Dream: The Future of Housing, Work, and Family Life* [New York: W. W. Norton, 1984], 33–34). On race issues, see Andrew Hacker, *Two Nations* (New York: Charles Scribner's Sons, 1992). On ethnicity issues and community corporations, see Shelley Green and Paul Pryde, *Black Entrepreneurship in America* (New York: Transaction, 1990); Peggy V. Beck, Anna Lee Walters, and Nia Francisco, *The Sacred: Ways of Knowledge, Sources of Life* (Flagstaff, Ariz.: Navajo Community College Press, 1990).

21. The problem in such utility cases is that local shareholders are given votes per share rather than votes per person. There remains an imbalance in power; the more money one has, the more votes one gets on the board. These innovations of customer ownership are a step in the right direction but not the basis for establishing true equity and accountability—which requires respecting the power of each individual citizen regardless of his or her ability to buy stock ("Company and Performance Roundup," *Business and Society Review* 49 [spring 1984]: 68).

22. For a study of the relationship of "accountability systems" between mega-sized U.S. banks and community-based organizations (CBOs), see Steve Waddell, "The Rise of a New Form of Enterprise; Social Capital Enterprise" (doctoral dissertation, Department of Sociology, Boston College, 1996).

23. Ram Cnaan, "Neighborhood Representing Organizations: How Democratic Are They?" *Social Service Review* 65, no. 4 (December 1991): 614–34. See also Alan Twelvetrees, *Organizing for Neighborhood Development* (Vermont: Gower Publishing, 1989).

24. Because CDCs are relatively vulnerable enterprises, local leaders in Boston, Massachusetts, created friendly legislation. The state organized its support for CDCs into three distinct programs. The Community Development Finance Corporation provided debt and equity financing and special loan guarantees to business ventures and real estate development projects sponsored by CDCs. The Community Economic Development Assistance Corporation offered technical assistance services to CDCs. The Community Enterprise Development Program helped communities organize new CDCs (*Changing Work: A Magazine about Liberating Worklife* [spring 1986]: C3).

25. I review these cases in *The Social Economy: People Transforming Business* (New York: John Wiley, 1977), 176ff.

26. Steve Kelman, *Regulating America, Regulating Sweden: A Comparative Study of Occupational Safety and Health Policy* (Cambridge, Mass.: MIT Press, 1981).

27. See Victor Pestoff, *Between Markets and Politics: Co-operatives in Sweden* (New York: Campus Verlag and Westview Press, 1991).

28. The capacity of trade associations to be self-regulating, to establish codes of conduct for the common good and enforce them, has not yet been recognized as a basis for making public policy. Political leaders have yet to see how beneficial it has been to have product-safety agreements among firms in the toy industry or to have

agreements on nutritional standards among competitive firms in the food industry. An essential hypothesis may be posed here. If industrial codes were encouraged in public policy and close working relationships were established among the federal government's Consumer Product Safety Commission, Food and Drug Administration, Environmental Protection Agency, and other agencies to support them, government staffs could be reduced by the degree that market self-monitoring becomes fully operative. Trade associations can be encouraged to set public standards.

29. Details of these problems and their corrections can be found in my book *Future for the American Economy,* chaps. 3 and 8.

30. The tribunal was organized in 1938 to protect local dealers against unjust cancellations of contracts by middle management. This was first reported by Peter Drucker, *The Concept of the Corporation* (New York: John May, 1940). The system was studied later by H. Vollmer, *Employee Rights and the Employee Relationship* (Berkeley: University of California Press, 1960); and William Scott, *The Management of Conflict* (Homewood, Ill.: Irwin, 1965).

31. *Directory of American Firms with Operations Abroad* (New York: World Trade Academic Press, 1991).

32. The representatives in the Council of Churches in Puerto Rico and members of the island legislature discussed this plan. The exploratory actions of Kennecott and Amax were stopped, and a Swedish firm became interested in the plan, competing with the U.S. firms, but at that point the price of copper in world markets declined, holding the plan at bay. Now, the proposal has not been implemented, but it remains in the minds of local leaders as an alternative model. Local citizens in this case became informed and armed themselves with a plan to implement a contractual arrangement with a global firm that would protect the environment and local employees from exploitation. The details of this model are found in Bruyn, *Social Economy.* See "Appendix: The Social Economy of Copper Mining."

33. J. G. Craig, *Multinational Cooperatives: An Alternative for World Development* (Saskatoon, Saskatchewan: Western Producer Prairie Books, 1976).

34. The legal details for establishing international ESOPs are complex and can be found in the National Center for Employee Ownership, Veronica Mason, *International Employee Stock Ownership Plans (ESOPs) for Multinational Corporations* (2201 Broadway, Suite 807, Oakland, Calif. 94612, 1994).

35. In this prophecy, Weyl concluded:

Such a world corporation would be a financial aggregation immensely greater than any in the past. . . . In each country a board of directors would hold control over constituent companies, and at London, Paris or New York a high Federal Council would settle controversies and make arrangements for the business of the world. Each company would have two elements of protection against unfair treatment: a community of interest secured through an interchange of stock and a representative on the Federal Council (*American World Policies* [New York: Macmillan, 1917], 282; the second quote follows on 282–83).

36. Richard Barnet and Ronald Müller, *Global Reach* (New York: Simon and Schuster, 1974), 13.

37. Many examples could be cited on the trend toward decentralization among global firms. Aeroflot, once the world's largest airline, is now 80 different airlines. AT&T (American Telephone and Telegraph), perceived by many critics as a mo-

nopolistic hierarchy, is being reconfigured under the leadership of its chairman, Robert Allen. The company has been reorganized into 20 separate product areas. For the first time, each product area is responsible for its own pricing, marketing, product development, and profits. AT&T is shedding its monolithic structure and reorganizing intself into a network of independent organizations (John Naisbett, *The Global Paradox* [New York: Avon Books, 1994] 9, 10). For the IBM partnership with Co-operative Bank, see "Co-operative Bank Signs $100 Million Contract Expansion," <http://www.ibm.com/services/pressrel/PRESSREL_26517.html>.

38. Gilder also describes the decentralized structure of Cypress Semiconductor, an organization of six separate companies with a network of on-line workstations. Cypress combines the unity of computer networks with greater autonomy and personal freedom for its employees ("Into the Telecosm," *Harvard Business Review* [March/April 1991]; also quoted in Naisbett, *Global Paradox,* 11).

39. Mason, *International Employee Stock Ownership Plans,* 2.

40. Current academic thought in the field of management is moving along these lines. Business analyst Michael Porter at the Harvard Business School recommends a diversification and reduction of shareholders in corporations. Basing his opinion on a two-year research project on corporate investment, he suggests cultivating "long-term owners" with a more direct voice in governance. In effect, he suggests the nomination of "stakeholders": that is, owners, customers, employees, and community representatives on the board of directors ("Capital Choices," in Goodwin, ed., *As If the Future Mattered,* 35; this article is also available in the Global Development and Environment Institute [G-DAE], the first volume in the present series, Evolving Values for a Capitalist World; <http://www.tufts.edu/GDAE>).

41. In an age of technology transfer, nuclear weapons, and environmental destruction, solutions go beyond the capacity of any single nation. The destruction of forests in Brazil and the Philippines affects the air people breathe in the United States and China. The production of auto gases in Los Angeles affects the ozone layer and the health of people in Tel Aviv. The U.S. Congress appointed a commission to study the United Nations to determine what can strengthen it as "a steward of nations," working in the interest of peace and world order. The commission has not yet fulfilled the purpose its originators had once hoped for.

Proposals for building a system of political democracy at the world level have been advocated by the United World Federalists and members of the United Nations Association. One model follows the pattern of federalism in the United States, recommending a house of representatives and a senate of nations. It requires a "permanent peace force" to settle problems when one nation invades another nation. The plan sets up an international court backed by enforceable world law. Advocates argue for strengthening the United Nations so that it can function effectively in times of crisis and can help stabilize world markets in banking and commerce. See A. Leroy Bennett, *International Organizations* (Englewood Cliffs, N.J.: Prentice-Hall, 1988); Benjamin Ferencz and Ken Keyes, *Planethood* (Coos Bay, Oreg.: Vision Books, 1988).

Chapter 3

1. The dynamics of business competition favor "cost externalization," and the result is a race to the bottom, avoiding health/safety standards and public accounta-

bility. The sociological literature on the loss of community life in the United States is extensive, but recent studies show industrialization and the automobile destroying community life. See Jane Holtz Kay, *Asphalt Nation* (New York: Crown, 1997); Moshe Safdie with Wendy Kohn, *The City after the Automobile* (New York: Basic Books, 1997). Barry Castro, professor of economics and management, recently studied the substantial "civic and social costs" associated with declines in manufacturing employment ("Manufacturing Jobs, Local Ownership, and the Social Health of Cities—A Research Note," *Responsive Community* 8, no. 1 [winter 1997/98]: 63ff.). For a review of classic sociological studies, see Maurice Stein, *The Eclipse of Community* (Princeton, N.J.: Princeton University Press, 1960).

2. Critics of globalization go further, to argue that corporations deplete community capital by moving production to places where they can pay less than a living wage. They use the threat of moving jobs to break up labor unions and bargain down wages. They hire young women in places like the Mexican *maquiladoras* under conditions that lead to their physical burnout after three or four years. Once women workers experience eyesight problems, allergies, kidney problems, and repetitive stress injuries that deplete their efficiency, they are replaced by a fresh supply of younger women. We note in chapter 8 that corporations also deplete the earth's natural capital through local strip mining, destroying forests, fisheries, and mineral deposits, dumping wastes, and aggressively marketing toxic chemicals. The point is that globalization of markets is one cause for local civic movements around the world. See Samuel Bowles and Herbert Gintis, *Democracy and Capitalism: Property, Community, and the Contradictions of Modern Thought* (New York: Basic Books, 1986). For the positive side, see William E. Halal, *The New Capitalism* (New York: John Wiley, 1986).

3. Recently, the "gated community" has developed, which is highly controlled and privatized, typified by guardhouses, physical barriers, and hired security forces. Its governing body is a homeowners' association that augments services (like police protection) supplied by nearby governments. These are "prestige communities," or "lifestyle communities," built for leisure, around golf courses and Sun Belt marinas. Their residents are affluent and often retired. Studies of gated communities suggest that the residents fear the changing forces outside. The fear of crime and vandalism becomes an obsession; indeed, the primary values of people in such communities are "safety" and "security." Researchers suggest that they add to the fragmenting urban sprawl that is developing along the edge of cities in an apparently inevitable process (Edward Blakely and Mary Gail Snyder, *Fortress America* [Washington, D.C.: Brookings Institution, 1997]).

4. Iris Marion Young, "The Need for Regional Democracy," *Good Society* 7, no. 3 (fall 1997): 26.

5. Frederick Starr, "The Third Sector in the Second World," *World Development* 19 (1991): 65.

6. Paul Hirst, *Associative Democracy: New Forms of Economic and Social Governance* (Amherst: University of Massachusetts Press, 1994); John Mathews, *Age of Democracy: The Politics of Post-Fordism* (Melbourne: Oxford University Press Australia, 1989).

7. David Korten, *When Corporations Rule the World* (Hartford, Conn.: Kumarian Press, 1955), 295.

8. See articles in *YES!: A Journal of Positive Futures* (spring 1997); Thomas

Greco, Jr., *New Money for Health Communities* (Tucson, Ariz.: Thomas Greco, 1994).

9. Julie Fischer, *The Road from Rio: Sustainable Development and the Non-Governmental Movements in the Third World* (Westport, Conn.: Praeger, 1993), 91.

10. Jeremy Rifkin, *The End of Work* (New York: G. P. Putnam's Sons, 1995), 275–77. The former UN secretary general Boutros Boutros Ghali has given different figures. "In France, 54,000 new associations have been established since 1987. In Italy, 40 percent of all associations have been set up within the last 15 years. This phenomenon is also occurring in developing countries. Within a short space of time, 10,000 NGOs have been established in Bangladesh, 21,000 in the Philippines, and 27,000 in Chile. In Eastern Europe, since the fall of communism, non-governmental organizations have been playing an increasingly important role in people's lives" ("Foreword," in Thomas Weiss and Leon Gordenker, *NGOs, the UN, and Global Governance* [Boulder: Lynne Rienner, 1996], 7–8).

11. "World Volunteerism Group Forms," *New York Times*, December 21, 1993, p. A12.

12. Various writers speak dramatically of these movements. In India, Tasmania, Canada, Thailand, France, Hungary, and elsewhere, people say "no" to dam projects that threaten their homes, livelihoods, and wild places. The women of India's Chipko movement wrap themselves around threatened trees to save them from loggers; Penan tribal people of Srawak, Malaysia, blockade logging roads. The 1 million strong Future Forest Alliance has organized protest demonstrations and media campaigns in Canada. People mobilize to protect mangroves in the Ivory Coast, reef systems in Belize, and wildlife in Nambia. They are opposing toxic dumping in the United States and campaigning to protect Antarctica as a natural preserve. Japanese citizens are pressuring Japanese logging companies to change their practices abroad. Germans are calling for an end to foreign aid that destroys primary forests. Indigenous pocket miners, farmers, and fishers in the Philippines are mobilizing to challenge the right of a few powerful mining corporations to destroy the livelihoods of thousands of people. Many of the civic organizations resulting from such movements are described as a "community enterprise economy," melding market forces of capitalism with the community forces of the social economy (Bishan Singh, "A Social Economy: The Emerging Scenario for Change," in *Civil Society and Sustainable Livelihoods Workshop Report*, ed. Tina Liamzon [Rome: Society for International Development, 1994]; referenced in David Korten, *When Corporations Rule the World*, 312).

13. The following statement was adopted at the 1995 General Assembly of the International Cooperative Alliance (ICA) held in Manchester, England, on the Alliance's centenary. "Cooperatives are based on the values of self-help, self-responsibility, democracy, equality, equity, and solidarity." For an elaboration on their definition and a history of U.S. consumer co-ops, see Jerry Voorhis, *American Cooperatives* (New York: Harper, 1961).

14. Government support has helped co-op development in the United States just as government subsidies have helped big business. For example, in 1935 only 750 out of the 6.8 million farms in the United States had a central station electric service. At that point, President Roosevelt launched the Rural Electrification Administration (now called the Rural Utilities Service) to build electric co-ops. Now there are almost 1,000 rural electric cooperatives providing electric service to more than

30 million people in 46 states, covering 75 percent of the geographic area of the United States, operating more than half of the U.S. distribution lines, serving 2,300 of the United States' 3,200 counties. The Natural Rural Electric Cooperative Association represents them. Out of their success, they built a bank to meet financing needs, the National Rural Utilities Cooperative Finance Corporation, which now has $9 billion in assets and is interested in supporting cooperative utility development around the country. Now, the Northeast faces deregulation in the electric industry, and the fight is on to start consumer co-ops in competition with conventional firms. The choice for consumers began in January 1998 (Lynn Benander, "Energy Co-op Development in the Northeast," *GEO Newsletter* 26 [April/May 1997], RR 1, P.O. Box 124A, Stillwater, Pa. 17878). Co-ops often link their democratic businesses together into confederations. In Great Britain, retail (consumer) co-ops became prevalent and bought shares in wholesale co-ops, which then purchased goods from producer co-ops. British consumer co-ops were given voting rights in wholesale co-ops according to the number of purchases they made from them.

15. The Japanese Consumers Cooperatives Union was founded in 1951. By 1990, it had 674 member organizations with 14.4 million members and sales equal to 2.5 percent of the total Japanese domestic retail trade. Han-based buying clubs as opposed to 56 percent from retail stores generated 44 percent of co-op sales ("Seikatsu," *Grassroots Economic Organizing Newsletter* [March/April 1994]: 1–8).

16. "Cheticam Co-ops Development: Lessons from an Acadian Community, April 16, 1998, http://www.ccn.cs.dal.ca/Environment/SCN/CommLink/CCD238 EP.html.

17. This is my summary. Co-op Atlantic was originally part of the larger Antigonish Movement, started by Moses Coady in 1928 (David Bedford and Sidney Pobihushchy, "Towards a People's Economy: The Co-op Atlantic Experience," *Interculture* [summer 1993]). For historic origins, see Moses Coady, *Masters of Their Own Destiny: The Story of the Antigonish Movement of Adult Education through Economic Cooperation* (Antigonish, N.S.: Formac Publishing, 1967). For more sources and details on the Seikatsu and Atlantic models, see Roy Morrison, *Ecological Democracy* (Boston, Mass.: South End Press, 1995).

18. Today there is a move on the part of some CEOs of these mutual insurance firms to dismantle policyholder (customer) ownership. David D'Allesandro, president of John Hancock Mutual Life Insurance Co., sought to create a separate holding company, one that strips the rights of policyholders to any assets in the company. Hancock and other like-minded companies said they wanted to raise billions of dollars in new capital to be used in acquisitions. These CEOs have contended that a new "holding company" is needed to place the final power in the hands of a new set of trustees.

Critics argue that corporate centralization of power in these insurance firms—eliminating the decentralized cooperative structure—is part of today's globalizing reality. At the same time, a different approach to "demutualization" by other insurance companies includes paying policyholders the company's entire surplus—assets above those needed to support the policies it has written. The policyholders of State Mutual Life Insurance Co., for example, received a median payout of $2,500 in stock. Yet neither choice will restore the original purpose of the company based on the principle of mutuality ("Mutual Insurers Divided on How Best to Go Public," *Boston Globe*, January 28, 1998, p. C16).

19. Switzerland has about 80 percent of Swiss cheese and almost 100 percent of hard cheese manufactured in about 1,500 village dairies. The local cooperatives normally own the buildings and machinery of about 1,500 village dairies, about 80 percent of which are independent cheese makers, family enterprises often employing only a few people, while about 20 percent are run by the cooperatives themselves. Because of the wide and dispersed memberships of this co-op, the cheese manufacturer's association is divided into many regional subgroups and employs a full-time professional staff. Both the cheese manufacturers and the industrial dairies are democratically organized. For case studies on European cooperatives and trade associations, see Phillipe C. Schmitter, ed., *Private Interest Government* (Beverly Hills: Sage, 1985).

20. Civil-society proponents are suspicious of top-level corporate statements favoring decentralization; a business corporation is still a command system. Here are examples of mergers where "decentralization" was advertised, but the claim for more "people power" remains to be proven in practice. (1) When Bell Atlantic merged with TeleCommunications, Inc. (TCI), and announced a $33 billion merger, the media focused on its huge size, but the purpose of the merger was advertised as positioning the new (merger) organization to better serve localities and individuals. The coming together of Bell Atlantic and TCI was intended to enable people to talk back through new systems of communication. (2) IBM had conversations with Time Warner about collaborating on advanced digital cable-TV technology and with TeleCommunications about developing a two-way information system. CEOs argued that the potential for giving more power to local voices was now within the realm of possibility. (3) AT&T was scheduled to invest 3.8 billion for a stake in McCaw Cellular Communications, the United States' biggest cellular telephone operator, suggesting the possibility of wireless systems and putting AT&T back in the local telephone business. *Decentralization* was the declared intent.

These goals can be put down as the wiles of executives seeking more power and higher profits, but the technological future is still to be determined. This new "combine" of telecommunications firms is worldwide. Digital Equipment Corp. (DEC) increased its share in Italy's C. Olivetti & Co. BCE, Inc., a Canadian telecommunications firm situated in a small home market, announced a major alliance with Cable and Wireless PLC, a leading British telecommunications company, which, in turn, paid $4.3 billion for a 20 percent stake in MCI Communications Corp., the U.S. long-distance carrier. Merging continues as a new era in telecommunications approaches. No one can fully predict how fiber optics, cellular telephones, computers, pagers, and new computer software will combine to localize "voices" and decentralize authority. Many optimistic business analysts believe that these mergers will be in the direction of a more humane and decentralized system of communications. See Naisbett, *Global Paradox*.

21. Cases of recent decentralization that need further inquiry for their impact on people include the key supplier alliances at Digital Equipment Corp.; Pacific Telsis's union-management partnership; a pseudonymous high-tech joint venture; MCR's stakeholder's relations (suppliers and customers); and joint ventures at Banc One. For more on such changes, see Rosabeth Kanter, *The Change Masters* (New York: Simon and Schuster, 1983); *When Giants Learn to Dance* (New York: Simon and Schuster, 1989). On this research, see Rosabeth Kanter and Paul S.

Myers, "Interorganizational Bonds and Intraorganization Behavior," in *Socio-Economics*, ed. Amitai Etzioni and Paul Lawrence (New York: M. E. Sharpe, 1991).

22. This story is drawn from my conversation with personnel at the Milwaukee Journal. For details on company origins, see Will Conrad et al., *The Milwaukee Journal* (Madison: University of Wisconsin Press, 1964); the Journal company publishes *Partners in Ownership*.

23. Whyte and Whyte, *Making Mondragon*. The Governing Council of ULARCO originally consisted of three members from each member cooperative. The council is responsible for planning and coordination, for recommending annual and long-range plans for each co-op member, and for coordinating commercial policies (60ff.).

24. For more details on the Weirton case, write to ICA Group, 1127 Park Plaza, Boston, Mass.

25. Barry Bluestone and Irving Bluestone, *Negotiating the Future* (New York: Basic Books, 1992).

26. I have drawn this summary from Michael Shuman, *Going Local* (New York: Free Press, 1998), 3–5.

27. This summary is drawn from William E. Halal, *The New Management: Democracy and Enterprise Are Transforming Organizations* (San Francisco: Berett-Koehler, 1996), 118. His sources were "The Tough New Customer," *Fortune* (autumn/winter 1993); Rahul Jacob, "Why Some Customers Are More Equal Than Others," *Fortune* (September 19, 1994). More and more CEOs are thinking "creative decentralization." Dee Hock, "father of the bank card," has created a global organization called the Chaordic Alliance to develop new and equitable concepts of organization (Mary Hock, "Dee Hock," *Business Ethics* [May/June 1996]: 38ff.).

28. Michael Schrage, "To Reshape IBM, Gerstner Should Work from the Boardroom Down," *Washington Post*, April 2, 1993.

29. Makower, *Beyond the Bottom Line*, 130.

30. *The Jobs Connection: Energy Use and Local Economic Development*, Cities and Counties Project, U.S. Department of Energy, National Renewable Energy Lab, July 1994.

31. The first three cases in sustainable energy cases (model 4) are drawn from Alice Hubbard and Clay Fong, *Community Energy Workbook* (Rocky Mountain Institute, 1739 Snowmass Creek Road, Snowmass, Colo. 81654, 1995), 3. The fourth case (Davis) is from David Morris, *Self Reliant Cities*, (San Francisco: Sierra Club Books, 1982), 122–23.

32. James Coleman, *Foundations of Social Theory* (Cambridge, Mass.: Harvard University Press, 1990), 360–61. Political scientist Robert Putnam argues that civic organizations add social capital to the community, creating an order of mutual trust. See Robert Putnam, *Making Democracy Work* (Princeton: Princeton University Press, 1993); "Bowling Alone: America's Declining Social Capital," *Journal of Democracy* 6 (1995): 65–78. I would say that Ularco's confederation of companies added social capital when it was designed to create an order of mutual confidence among employees. An organization creates "social capital" when it reduces the costs of labor strife and government regulations.

Theoretically, a civil economy develops from democratic associations and civic organizations promoting social capital with the principles of democracy, freedom, and justice as well as profitability, efficiency, and productivity. The problem in cultivating a civil economy is dependent upon whether these different values can be linked effectively. The practice of civil economy articulates this integral process.

33. See the *Social Report,* Department of Sociology, Boston College, Chestnut Hill, Mass. 02167. This preamble to their "social constitution" was formulated in 1974.

34. Robert Monks, "Growing Corporate Governance: From George III to George Bush," in *The Legitimate Corporation,* ed. Brenda Sutton (Cambridge, Mass.: Blackwell, 1993), 171.

35. I discuss this model in more detail in *Social Economy,* 182–83.

Chapter 4

1. Patricia Annez, "Livable Cities for the Twenty-First Century," *Society* 35, no. 4 (May/June 1998): 49.

2. For these arguments, see Arthur Okun, *Equality and Efficiency* (Washington, D.C.: Brookings Institution, 1975). In his 1986 budget message to Congress, President Reagan expressed this view on privatization, saying that government should not compete with the private sector. Governments supply the type of services that would not be provided by the marketplace, but, he said, over the years, the federal government has acquired many commercial-type operations. Hence, he proposed the sale of unneeded assets, such as loan portfolios and surplus real estate, and advanced the practice of contracting out federal services.

3. E. V. Savas, *Privatization* (Chatham, N.J.: Chatham House, 1987), 13–14. Milton Friedman contends that freedom is eroded and prosperity undermined through government laws, regulations, agencies, and spending. He describes how good intentions produce deplorable results when government is the "middleman" (Milton Friedman and Rose Friedman, *Free to Choose* [New York: Harcourt Brace Jovanovich, 1980]; Friedman, *Capitalism and Freedom* [Chicago: University of Chicago Press, 1963]). Friedman is an example of "public choice" economists who argue that people should have the opportunity to pick between government and private alternatives. Government agencies often become inefficient and costly to taxpayers. This inefficiency becomes subsidized to keep prices low to customers, but it is actually a monopoly that keeps the market from entering to bring administrative costs and prices down further. People should have the "freedom to choose" between a government and a private firm. The subsidy should be eliminated to allow private firms to enter and test their capacity to serve customers better.

4. Robert Leone gives a thumbnail sketch of the government's influence over the steel industry's inputs, processes, output, and general environment.

> Its *inputs* are strictly regulated: labor costs are controlled by state and federal Occupational Safety and Health Administration (OSHA) agencies, the Employee Retirement Income Security Act (ERISA), and the Department of Health, Education, and Welfare (HEW); the cost and availability of raw materials are regulated by the Bureau of Mines, the Department of Energy, and the federal power authorities; and returns on capital are effectively regulated by the policies and practices of the Internal Revenue Services. . . . Outputs are even more closely controlled. The size of the market available to domestic producers of steel is regulated by foreign trade policies; price levels are controlled—albeit implicitly—by jaw-

boning. Even product characteristics are effectively dictated by the purchasing criteria of the nation's biggest consumer—the federal government ("The Real Costs of Regulation," *Harvard Business Review* [November/December, 1977]: 57).

5. Harry Johnson, "The Multinational Corporation as a Development Agent," *Columbia Journal of World Business,* no. 3 (May/June 1970). Political scientists who ally themselves with the neoclassical school of economics often express this fourth position.

6. Osborne and Gaebler, *Reinventing Government,* 285ff. The authors argue that governments originally focused on "prevention." They used to build sewer systems to prevent disease and enact building codes to prevent fire, but today they simply deliver service programs. As fire departments professionalized, they developed the art of "fire suppression," not prevention. As police departments professionalized, they chased down criminals instead of helping communities to prevent crime. Today, government has a command-and-control strategy with a number of drawbacks. Briefly: (1) It does not change the underlying economic incentives driving firms or individuals. (2) It relies on the threat of penalties, but in a political environment, many of these penalties cannot be assessed. (3) It is a very slow process. (4) It has a tendency to focus on symptoms rather than causes. (5) Regulatory controls that specify the exact technology that industry must use, for instance, to control pollution, discourage technological innovation. (6) Such a command-and-control system slaps the same requirements on industries all over the country, making it very expensive and ineffective. (7) Government agencies like the EPA focus too exclusively on large institutions, whether business or government. In sum, agencies create "turf problems," which means that officials defend their work at all costs, even when they no longer fulfill their original purpose. They are not self-correcting in the face of failure; rather, agencies are self-promoting to save their own jobs. They do not die even when they are no longer needed (300ff.).

7. Thus, the most effective way to be successful in privatization is by taking account of intricate exchange networks. Every firm should be seen as "socially embedded." See Mark Granovetter, "Economic Action and Social Structure," *American Journal of Sociology* 78, no. 6 (1985): 1360–80; Gernot Grabher, "Rediscovering the Social in the Economics of Interfirm Relations," in *The Embedded Firm,* ed. Gernot Grabher (London: Routledge, 1993), 1–32.

8. Stark compiled data on the ownership structure of the largest 200 Hungarian companies and found that the state was involved in the majority of these enterprises by means of shares held by the State Property Agency and the State Holding Corporation. Privatization had led back to state ownership. But he also found that interfirm ownership was prevalent. The pattern of co-ownership was different from wholly owned subsidiary systems. Mutual shareholding among firms was prominent. And this grouping of shared ownership among firms suggested, for him, a more effective approach to privatization.

9. In cases like Poland, it was more advantageous to develop small and medium-sized enterprises than to privatize state enterprises as a method for moving toward a free-market system (Dennis Rondinelli and Jay Yurkiewicz, "Privatization and Economic Restructuring in Poland: An Assessment of Transition Policies," *American Journal of Economics and Sociology* 55, no. 2 [April 1996]).

10. During the first wave of privatization, only 28.1 percent of investable points

were held by individual citizens, while 71.9 percent were held by 429 investment privatization funds (IPFs), or investment firms. The nine largest investment firms ended up with 48.5 percent of all available voucher points. The board seats of the privatized firms were typically distributed to the largest blocks of shareholders, and these large investment funds gained those seats and subsequent control over markets. In other words, privatization led *straight back to state control over the market* (David Stark and Laszlo Bruszt, "Restructuring Networks" [paper prepared for the Thematic Session of the Annual Meetings of the American Sociological Association, New York City, August 1996]).

11. Marshall Goldman, "The Pitfalls of Russian Privatization," *Challenge* (May/June 1997).

12. John Logue, Sergey Plekhanov, and John Simmons, *Transforming Russian Enterprises: From State Control to Employee Ownership* (London: Greenwood Press, 1995). This summary is drawn from pp. 259–61.

13. Despite the fact that the firms were incorporated as closed stock companies at the time of the study, practically all of them were eager to bring in outside investment capital, including foreign capital on the company's own terms. Finally, we should point out that the managers' motivation for privatization through employee ownership in most cases was driven by the fact that it was the only form of privatization then permitted, rather than a belief in employee ownership. Ibid., 261. For more on the complexity of the Russian case, see Joseph Blasi, Maya Kroumova, and Douglas Kruse, *Kremlin Capitalism* (Ithaca, N.Y.: Cornell University Press, 1997).

14. On the *keiretsu,* see Michael Gerlack and James Lincoln, "The Organization of Business Networks in the United States and Japan," in *Networks and Organizations,* ed. Nitin Nohria and Robert Eccles (Cambridge, Mass.: Harvard Business School Press, 1993), 491–520. On the Chaebol, see Eun Mee Kim, "The Industrial Organization and Growth of the Korean Chaebol," in *Business Networks and Economic Development in East and Southeast Asia,* ed. Gary Hamilton (Hong Kong: Centre of Asian Studies, occasional papers and monographs no. 99, University of Hong Kong, 1991). See also Gary Gereffi, "The Organization of Buyer-Driven Global Commodity Chains: How U.S. Retailers Shape Overseas Production Networks," in *Commodity Chains and Global Capitalism,* ed. G. Gereffi and M. Kornzeniewicz (Westport, Conn.: Praeger, 1994), 95–122. On "late stage capitalism," see Werner Sombart, "Capitalism," *Encyclopedia of the Social Sciences* (New York: Macmillan, 1930).

15. Allan H. Meltzer, "Asian Problems and the IMF," *Cato Journal* 17, no. 3 (May 30, 1998).

16. Hartcher describes Japan's attempt to disengage the close connection between big business and big government, but he does not yet see a serious process of reconstruction (*The Ministry: How Japan's Most Powerful Institution Endangers World Markets* [Boston: Harvard Business School Press, 1997]). My own interest in how MITI promoted success in global markets and my concern about collusion between government and big business are discussed in Bruyn, *Future for the American Economy.*

17. Many personal-social problems (suicides, divorces, disabilities, and diseases) have been shown to rise after mass layoffs and market failures. Governments generally pay for these social costs. They are not calculated as part of costs in the market system. See Sydney Cobb and Stanislav Kasl, *Termination: The Consequences of Job*

Loss (National Institution of Occupational Safety and Health Research Report, publication no. 77-224, June 1977).

18. The concentration of ownership went to a top management consortium. Many trade union leaders were unhappy with the transfer of power to executives—not true self-management they said—but economic analysts argued that the change was remarkably successful when compared with the state's "rigid system that subjected them [executives] to constant official interference . . . contrary to their commercial objectives" (John Naisbitt and Patricia Aburdene, *Megatrends* [New York: Wm. Morrow, 1990], 158).

19. David Pett, "From State Ownership to Employee Ownership: The Role of ESOP in the U.K. Privatization Program," *Journal of Employee Ownership Law and Finance* 7, no. 4 (fall 1995), The National Center for Employee Ownership, 1201 Martin Luther King Jr. Way, Oakland, Calif. 94612.

20. Corey Rosen, director of the National Center for Employee Ownership, Oakland, Calif., personal communication with author.

21. Alan Wolfe, *Whose Keeper? Social Science and Moral Obligation* (Berkeley, Calif.: University of California Press, 1989), 189.

22. Amitai Etzioni, *The New Golden Rule* (New York: Basic Books, 1996), 143. For moral issues in the business sector and the field of economics, see his book *The Moral Dimension: Towards a New Economics* (New York: The Free Press; Macmillan, 1988).

23. Secondary goals are consumption, sustainability, hope, enhancing activities, and economic justice. The field of traditional economics does not integrate welfare goals into its framework, but this interdisciplinary field adds critical information to the practice of civil privatization (Goodwin, *Social Economics: An Alternative Theory*, 26–27).

24. By reporting to government agencies, I mean those cases where government is organized variously to protect *customers* (e.g., the Consumer Product Safety Commission), *labor* (e.g., the Labor Department, Mine Safety and Health Administration, and OSHA), *competitors and consumers* (e.g., the FTC, FCC [Federal Communications Commission], FDA [Food and Drug Administration], Federal Regulatory Commission, Antitrust Division, Federal Energy Administration), *the poor and the unemployed* (e.g., the welfare system), *travelers and transportation* (e.g., the CAB [Civil Aeronautics Board], National Highway Traffic Safety Administration), *minorities* (e.g., Equal Employment Opportunity Commission), *citizen survival* (Environmental Protection Agency), *small business* (e.g., the SBA [Small Business Administration]), *overseas business* (e.g., Commerce Department), *buyers and sellers* (e.g., Commodity Futures Trading Commission, Securities and Exchange Commission), *retired people* (e.g., Pension Benefit Guarantee Corporation), and many other categories of citizens. *Civil* planners take account of these public functions and look for ways to substitute for them through a self-managed (cooperative) system of competitive markets.

25. The law states that trade and professional penalties (e.g., fines) can be heavy enough to curtail future violations but not so heavy that they put a competitor out of business. The details on business self-regulation are discussed more elaborately in Bruyn, *Future for the American Economy.*

26. Let us clarify this theoretical framework as it applies to civil privatization: The *individual* in the workplace is relatively self-governing in fact but can theoretically

increase that personal authority through mutually governed autonomous groups on the assembly line or in an office system. *Work groups* are also somewhat self-governing, and they are within a system of mutual governance of departments and divisions of the firm where their authority can be increased. All this time, a system of command governance is copresent in a hierarchy of offices, which runs back through the president to the board of directors. That system of command changes in *type* as responsibility is increased at lower levels. Next, the *firm* is relatively self-governing within a network of firms in the market, as well as being mutually governed along with other firms—through its trade association and its contractual relationship with suppliers and customers. Its trade association is designed intentionally to increase the power of its members in that market sector. A *whole industry*, in turn, is relatively self-governed as well as mutually governed through affiliated business associations and corporate networks. Next, the *entire economy* is relatively self-governed as it is distinct from the national government. It is governed through its vast networks of industries and peak associations (e.g., the National Association of Manufacturers), which themselves are part of the larger organization of different trade sectors. Finally, the *global economy* is subject to the same analysis as it evolves with its degree of self-governance, its own proportion of independence from nation-states, and its own systems of mutual governance and exchange that reduce the need for a big world government. This theory is discussed further in Bruyn, *Future for the American Economy*.

27. This is a theoretical point that cannot be explored here. The two sides of the apparent binary of *freedom* vs. *order* (or *private* vs. *public*) should not be seen as totally opposed as separate dichotomous values but rather as capable of being brought together in practical ways, thus becoming complementary through organizational inventions. We gave examples of organizational inventions in chapters 1 and 2, but this is a constant process. At one time in history, there was no Council of Better Business Bureaus to help make a bridge between *private* and *public* responsibilities in business. Today this organization is institutionalized, so to speak, a one-time invention that still promotes private interest and the public interest in some measure. The National Advertising Review Council (NARC), formed in 1971, is another example that seeks to integrate private and public interests. NARC was formed by the advertising industry and four leading trade associations to foster truth and accuracy in national advertising through voluntary self-regulation. NARC established the ground rules for the National Advertising Division (NAD), the Children's Advertising Review Unit (CARU), and the National Advertising Review Board. NAD and CARU are investigative arms of the advertising industry's self-regulation program. Their casework results from competitive challenges from other advertisers but also from self-monitoring traditional and new media, including the Internet. The National Advertising Review Board (NARB), the appeals body, is a peer group from which ad hoc panels are selected to adjudicate those cases that are not resolved at the NAD/CARU level. The members of the Council of Better Business Bureaus, Inc., funded these self-regulatory systems. Some examples of their work are as follows. On November 11, 1996, NAD and the bureaus announced that the Oreck Corporation had agreed to modify performance superiority claims in its advertising for Oreck XL hotel vacuum. The NAD determined that Oreck's demonstration was an inaccurate representation of cleaning superiority. The Hoover Company challenged the accuracy of Oreck's broadcast and print advertising and its product demonstration.

For more cases, see <http://www.bbb.org/advertising/html>. These "organizational inventions" can be improved by adding countervailing powers to their organizations, but they are essential steps in the movement toward a self-regulatory economy.

28. We do not have space to develop the details of dialectical theory that will be discussed in a forthcoming book. Here we note that "civil development" refers to the capacity of markets to optimize the value of each opposing side of a polarity as the problem presents itself to people in a market situation. Each value that has been isolated—or is viewed in contradiction with its opposite—is now connected by a so-cial invention. Civil planners aim to create more freedom for enterprise by advancing civil rules in a common field of competitive markets.

29. Emile Durkheim in the nineteenth century described this type of cooperative system as "socialism" without government controls (*Socialism and Saint-Simon,* ed. Alvin Gouldner, trans. Charlotte Sattler [Yellow Springs, Ohio: Antioch Press, 1958] 21–22).

30. Yvonne Daley, "Worldly Workers," *Boston Globe,* December 31, 1996, pp. 1, A10. See "Designing an ESOP at Carris Reels," *Employee Ownership Report* 16, no. 6 (November/December 1996): 5.

31. Joel Makower, *Beyond the Bottom Line,* 48, 174.

32. NCEO, "Employee Ownership in Egypt," *Employee Ownership Report* (September/October 1997): 10.

33. Ibid., 251–52.

34. We know the following about the position of unions in U.S. takeovers. First, unions have variably aided and resisted the creation of employee-owned firms. Second, unions have represented workers in big self-managed firms. Third, unions have supported pension plans in worker-owned firms. See Severyn T. Bruyn, *The Field of Social Investment* (Cambridge: Cambridge University Press, 1987), 85. The details on such issues are also discussed in Raymond Russell, *Sharing Ownership in the Workplace* (Albany: State University of New York Press, 1985); Charles Hecksher, *The New Unionism* (New York: Basic Books, 1988).

35. In chapter 5, we explore the differences between the costs of private and government programs. In this case, a number of studies compare the cost of electric power in private vs. governmental sectors, each of which requires careful scrutiny because they mix types of fuel and markets, limiting their validity. In one important study, Richard Hellman compared market service with government service and government-regulated franchises in the sector of electric power, finding that market arrangements produced lower prices among private firms than did regulation. However, prices of municipal power were still lower. Walter Primeaux also studied communities where households had a choice of electricity suppliers. He concluded that competitive arrangements were more efficient than monopolies or government franchise; the former had an average price 33 percent lower than the latter (Richard Hellman, *Government Competition in the Electric Utility Industry* [New York: Praeger, 1972]; Walter Primeaux, Jr., "Estimation of the Price Effects of Competition: The Case of Electricity," *Resources and Energy* 7 [1985]: 325–40). In the United States, 87 percent are served by about 2,200 municipal or state systems.

36. This is my brief summary drawn from Thomas Grillo, "Public Housing's New Private Life," *Boston Sunday Globe,* January 5, 1997, sect. G.1, p. 6. But, as in any organization, there is no guarantee that a good tenant management will continue to flourish with perfection forever. (For bad times, one can look into the history of a

church, business, or government.) For example, in 1968, a grant from the Office of Economic Opportunity was offered for a tenant management experiment; government officials in Boston began looking at a housing development called Bromley-Heath that was poorly maintained and had a high crime rate. In 1973, tenants took over complete operation and were instrumental in getting a health clinic and a drug treatment program. In April 1978, tenants set up a patrol force and began to negotiate a second five-year contract with the Boston Housing Authority (BHA). Subsequently, the tenant organization was praised nationally for the good work it had accomplished, negotiating rents, cleaning up graffiti, planting gardens. In late October 1998, however, the BHA took control of Bromley-Heath after the U.S. attorney's office indicted 38 people on charges of distributing cocaine.

37. Schuman, *Going Local,* 140.

38. Government control began as early as 1844 when Congress appropriated $30,000 for the first telegraph line, between Washington, D.C., and Baltimore. In 1918, Josephus Daniels, the secretary of the Navy, proposed to nationalize the radio industry and place it under military control. The idea of "public broadcasting" did not become a widespread idea under after World War II. In the 1960s, Fred Friendly and the Ford Foundation debated a plan that would have had the FCC launch a communications satellite, with the commercial networks paying to use it and the fees going to fund public television (James Ledbetter, *Made Possible by . . . The Death of Public Broadcasting in the United States* [New York: Verso, 1997]).

39. When television was introduced in West Germany during the early 1950s, it was evident that not every regional radio station would be able to produce its own independent television station. The radio stations then organized an Association of Public Broadcasting Corporation in 1952 to handle the financial and technical operations through a central facility. The association has maintained a system of decentralized authority in the regions. Management by its members operates on a rotating basis, the chair rotating every two years. I observed these conditions during my visit to West Germany in 1977. See also H. W. Conrad, "Radio and Television in the Federal Republic of Germany," *Sonderdienst, Inter Nationes* (Kennedyallee 91–103, D-53 Bonn Bad Godesberg 1, Bundesrepublik, Deutschland, So 7–77). For a discussion of "public journalism" in the United States see Jay Rosen et al., *Public Journalism: Theory and Practice,* occasional paper, Kettering Foundation, Dayton, Ohio, 1997.

40. Other speakers at this conference focused on one piece of legislation that they believed should be repealed: the Telecommunications Act of 1996. They called the act "the biggest corporate giveaway in the history of the world." I report on this conference from an article by Ronnie Dugger, "Democratizing the Media," *Nation,* November 24, 1997, pp. 6–7.

41. A review article of Hugh Hawkins, *Banding Together* (Baltimore: Johns Hopkins University Press, 1992), by Steven Diner, *Contemporary Sociology* 22, no. 4 (July 1993): 21.

42. There are broad theoretical propositions here. (1) People in firms, associations, and governments are transforming the meaning of isolated values inherited in the culture of capitalism. (2) Cultural values are written into philosophical binaries, such as freedom vs. order, individual vs. community, and private vs. public. (3) People are inventing practical new structures that remove the total opposition that has existed in these abstract ideas. (4) Civil (common) rules in markets have the potential to create greater market freedom at practical levels of exchange. Each side of a

popular polarity—private vs. public, individuality vs. community, planning vs. spontaneity, cooperation vs. competition, profitability vs. accountability, and freedom vs. justice—has its own value in market self-regulation. A theory of civil self-development evaluates the effectiveness of privatization as these values are enhanced by stages in their practical and partial expressions. In sum, civil privatization takes place at best when each side of a great opposition is recognized, valued, optimized, with no negation or diminishment of one side or the other. Philosophers would say that people are "concretizing universals," that is, producing practical (particular) solutions to universal polarities. Abstract ideas are important but become detailed (actualized) differently in each epoch. Today the details of opposing universals—like freedom and order—can be uniquely juxtaposed and connected in the marketplace. Self-accountable firms and markets with greater transparency are on the way to transforming the abstract idea of a *private* economy into a more *public* (transparent, accessible) economy with government assistance.

43. Joseph Stiglitz, "More Instruments and Broader Goals: Moving Toward a Post-Washington Consensus," Helsinki, January 7, 1998. This speech is in PDF format, suitable for printing offline: wider.pdf [140K], p. 9.

Chapter 5

1. One current case in this study is close to the idea of civil privatization. In Jersey City, Mayor Bret Schundler hired private firms instead of using municipal employees to remove graffiti, with an added twist: The firms were picked by neighborhood residents (John C. Weicher, "Making Cents: Better City Services for Less," *Society* 35, no. 4 [May/June 1998]: 42).

2. Not all studies are based on purely financial issues. One economic study revealed a civic benefit to the community. It compared municipal and private systems and concluded that trash collection was more equitable in terms of the "quality and fairness of service of buyers" when contracted out to private firms. This study noted that when a municipal agency cannot meet its daily collection schedule (because of vehicle breakdown or absenteeism), it tends to handle the problem by postponing collection in the less affluent sections of the city, sections with less political influence, often minority neighborhoods. The private contractors, however, tend to look at the city merely as a workload to be completed, rather than as a set of political districts to be placated differently. Furthermore, a city government may find it easier to insure that a contractor completes his or her daily collection route by imposing a penalty for not doing so than to order its own workforce to put in overtime. This study found that municipal agencies are 10 percent more likely to miss a collection than are contract firms ("Customers Rate Refuse Service," *Waste Age* [November 1981]: 82–88; based on Donald Sexton, "Effectiveness, Equity and Responsiveness of Solid Waste Collection Services," Center for Government Studies, Graduate School of Business, Columbia University, 1979). An issue not fully covered in this study concerns the possibility that private firms will not serve low-income neighborhoods where they find it difficult to obtain regular resident fees for their service.

3. Robert M. Spann, "Public versus Private Provision of Governmental Services," in *Budgets and Bureaucrats: The Sources of Government Growth*, ed. Thomas E. Borcherding (Durham, N.C.: Duke University Press, 1977), 71–89.

4. Harry M. Kitchen, "A Statistical Estimation of an Operating Cost Function for Municipal Refuse Collection," *Public Finance Quarterly* (January 1976): 56–57.

5. "Improving Municipal Productivity," (Washington, D.C.: National Commission on Productivity and Work Quality, 1976). The study found that New York City's Sanitation Department was so poorly managed that 36 percent of its trash collection trucks were in the shop during 1969.

6. Werner Hirsch, "Cost Functions of Government Service: Refuse Collection," *Review of Economics and Statistics* (February 1973): 85–93.

7. Peter Kemper and John M. Quigley, *The Economics of Refuse Collection* (Cambridge, Mass.: Ballinger, 1976). A Columbia University study found similar results when it looked at 340 different public and private refuse collection firms in an equal number of cities (Barbara J. Stevens, "Scale, Market Structure, and the Cost of Refuse Collection," *Review of Economics and Statistics* [August 1978]: 438–48).

8. Bennett and Johnson analyzed trash service charges for some Virginia suburbs of Washington, D.C., where 29 private firms serve almost the same geographical areas as the government enterprise, giving a good basis for comparison. They found that, even though the government enterprise was exempt from all taxes, license fees, and bonding requirements, it was still more expensive, about twice as costly as private refuse collection (James T. Bennett and Manuel H. Johnson, *Better Government* [Ottawa, Ill., and Ossining, N.Y.: Caroline House Publishers, 1981], 46). My thanks to these authors for referral to other studies on refuse collection.

9. E. S. Savas, "Policy Analysis for Local Government: Public versus Private Refuse Collection," *Policy Analysis* 3, no. 1 (winter 1977): 4974; see also Savas, *Privatization* (Chatham, N.J.: Chatham House, 1987). Professor Savas suggests, imaginatively, that a city can divide its political districts to encourage competition between the municipality and different firms in each district. He recommends competitive bidding. The city in this case competes for contracts along with business. The city of Indianapolis, for example, created 11 districts. The Department of Public Works won the contract in four, while the others went to four different private companies. All the winners must provide effective service or risk losing the contract when it comes up for renewal in three to five years.

10. The Madison Police District also took a revolutionary step: "*The employees elected their own captain and lieutenants. They developed their own staffing and work schedules. They designed and built their own district building*" (the author's own italics) (Osborne and Gaebler, *Reinventing Government*, 260–61).

11. The pattern of stockholding in these particular firms is complex in its details. It led to certain problems as well as new solutions in worker self-management. In this case, there was ethnic prejudice (the original owners were Italian, and some members opposed non-Italian owners) and legal problems (the city charter limited profits to no more than 5 percent profit). Yet, the system revealed a great deal about how labor problems can be solved in this market sector of waste management. See Stewart Perry, *San Francisco Scavengers: Dirty Work and Pride of Ownership* (Berkeley: University of California Press, 1978). A new introduction and epilogue by Perry and a foreword by Raymond Russell can be found in Stewart Perry, *Collecting Garbage* (New Brunswick, N.J.: Transaction, 1997).

12. Private water companies use two different arrangements in France. One is a franchise awarded to the low bidder (for prices to users) in which a private firm

finances, builds, owns, operates, and maintains all necessary facilities for the duration of the franchise (about 30 years) and then turns the system over to the public authority. The second system is similar except that the private firm simply builds, operates, and maintains the facilities while the government finances and owns them (Steve Hanke, *On Privatizing Water and Wastewater Services* [Baltimore: Johns Hopkins University Press, 1982]).

13. W. M. Crain and A. Zardkoohi, "A Test of the Property-Rights Theory of the Firm: Water Utilities in the United States," *Journal of Law and Economics* 21 (October, 1978): 395–408. The later study was by Susan Feignebaum and Ronald Teeples, *Public versus Private Water Delivery* (Claremont, Calif.: Claremont Graduate School, June, 1981).

14. Richard Grouard and David Phillips, "Construct Operations Save over 2 Million," *Public Works* 16, no. 4 (April 1985): 31.

15. See Local Initiative Support Corporation, Suite 1100, 1825 K St. N.W., Washington, D.C. 20006, Tel. 202-835-8931.

16. Edward Morlok and Philip Viton, "The Comparative Costs of Public and Private Providers of Mass Transit," in *Urban Transit,* ed. C. A. Lave (San Francisco: Pacific Institution, 1985), 233–54. The testimony of the general manager of a privatized regional bus line in West Germany speaks to the value of freedom and the potential for innovation in his case. As a manager on the private line, he could make faster decisions, and "didn't have to worry about politicians." He was able to supplement earnings by chartering buses for excursions and vacation groups and had more flexibility in a schedule of selling off used vehicles, as opposed to a fixed life-cycle policy for government vehicles. Reported in *Urban Transportation Abroad* 8, no. 2 (summer 1985).

17. Gabriel Roth and George Wynne, *Free Enterprise Urban Transportation* (New Brunswick, N.J.: Transaction, 1982), 14.

18. Pett thinks that the idea of employees acquiring a controlling interest in the sales of big public utilities and larger government-owned companies (such as British Airways, Rolls Royce, Associated British Ports, British Airports Authority, and Britoil) is "impractical" but still workable in other cases (Pett, "From State Ownership to Employee Ownership.")

19. Tom Peyton, "Standards for Public Building Maintenance, *APWA Reporter* 44, no. 10 (October 1977): 28–29; James Stewart, "Public Safety and Private Police," *Public Administration Review* 45 (November 1985): 758–65; William Cunningham and Todd Taylor, "The Hallcrest Report: Private Security and Police in America," in *Crime and Protection in America,* ed. Daniel Ford (Washington, D.C.: National Institute of Justice, 1985). Municipal police officers have been reporting in sick and then working lucrative detail assignments for private companies that supply them with money well above their own salary. In the past 2 1/2 years, Boston police officers reported being sick 1,326 days in which separately maintained detail assignment records show they were working for a private company. In many cases, officers were paid for both a sick day and their private work, doubling their pay (David Armstrong, "'Sick' Officers Working Details," *Boston Globe,* September 14, 1998, p. A1).

20. General surveys of U.S. cities indicate that residents believe that local police do not respond quickly when called. A survey of New York City residents revealed that 69 percent of the people in the neighborhoods either pay for private security or

say they would pay up to $120 a year for it. Fifty-nine percent believed that more police officers on foot patrol were needed (Robert McFadden, "Poll Indicates Half of New Yorkers See Crime as City's Chief Problem," *New York Times,* January 14, 1985).

21. There are problems to be overcome in this approach. It is difficult for police officers to be both "enforcer" and "helper." In difficult cases, social agencies are engaged to do this community work (James Q. Wilson and George Kelling, "Making Neighborhoods Safe," *Atlantic* [February 1989]).

22. Louise Bruyn, "Theater for a Living Revolution," in *Nonviolent Action and Social Change,* ed. Severyn Bruyn and Paula Rayman (New York: Irvington, 1979), 276.

23. Marshall Clinard, "The Group Approach to Social Reintegration," *American Sociological Review* 14 (April 1949): 255–62.

24. Such examples are described in Schuman, *Going Local,* 128.

25. The Scottsdale firm was studied on a cost comparison basis with paid, volunteer, and mixed fire departments in 49 cities, and the study concluded that the cost of contract fire protection in Scottsdale was only 53 percent of the estimated cost of supplying the service by a government agency (Roger S. Ahlbrandt, *Municipal Fire Protection Services: Comparison of Alternative Organizational Forms* [Beverly Hills, Calif.: Sage, 1973], 45).

26. Professional companies can be related to community corporations with options for companies to compete against one another and still be organized to support the common good. They can offer local people fire prevention training and educational programs that teach citizens how to inspect their buildings for safety. Firms can organize a volunteer fire prevention corps to protect public schools and can create fire prevention standards with support standards for energy conservation in public buildings.

27. Linda Punch, "Contract Management Companies Manage Growth Rate of 13.3 Percent," *Modern Healthcare* (August 15, 1984): 45–52.

28. *For-Profit Enterprise in Health Care* (Washington, D.C.: National Academy of Sciences, 1986).

29. Dolores Kong, "Doctors and Nurses Plan to Protest at Tea Party Ship," *Boston Globe,* December 1, 1997, p. A7.

30. Alex Pham, "An Infected Relationship," *Boston Sunday Globe,* May 31, 1998, p. F1.

31. This is my summary of an article by Alex Pham, "One Battleground in a Bigger War," *Boston Globe,* June 2, 1998, pp. C1, C7.

32. Today the fund is being undermined by rising prices. Originally, the uncompensated care pool costs were covered by employers who paid "a little extra" for insurance. Employers no longer want to pay the little extra. The number of uninsured people in Massachusetts has climbed steadily to about 680,000 people (Charles Stein, "Free Market Straining Health-Care Safety Net," *Boston Globe,* April 21, 1996, p. 30).

33. Some cities help solve this problem of competition, which neglects economically disadvantaged people, by providing a special fund for treating indigent patients; others make contributions into a common fund underwritten by the network of local private hospitals, often with some government support (Martin Tolchin, "As

Companies Buy Hospitals, Treatment of Poor Is Debated," *New York Times,* January 25, 1985). There are thousands of problems to solve here. The "uncompensated care pool" was mandated by state legislation, but in a civil market, the pool would need to be negotiated through the cooperation of competitors in local hospital associations. The sharing of costs would likely require public pressure (e.g., the threat of government legislation) to provide a common pool to take away the motives for competing hospitals to refuse uninsured patients. The extra cost is then picked up collectively by the local hospital association. Criteria are established to determine how the common funds are allocated, and professional overseers determine the fairness of the arrangement. To put this another way, making hospital services available to people who cannot pay their hospital bills and yet whose incomes are too high for them to be eligible for Medicaid can be assumed by the hospitals working cooperatively through trade and professional associations. The associations write a social constitution that contains public standards for their members.

34. This summary is based on interviews with a member of the CEO office and William Torbert, a former board member of the Harvard Pilgrim HMO.

35. The practice of contracting seems to be growing, but I have no current statistics. Over a decade ago, there were more than 800 private ambulance companies in the United States, with annual revenues of more than 1.5 billion (Pamela Hollie, "Ambulances Go Private," *New York Times,* May 25, 1986).

36. Report of the President's Commission on Privatization *Privatization,* March 1988, xvi.

37. James E. Wallace et al., *Participation and Benefits in the Urban Section Eight Program: New Construction and Existing Housing* (Cambridge, Mass.: Abt. Associates, January, 1981). See also Office of Management and Budget, Major Policy Initiatives. The subsidization of public housing is reportedly large enough so that if it were given in cash directly to the tenants, it would lift them out of poverty (John Weicher, *Housing: Federal Policies and Programs* [Washington, D.C.: American Enterprise Institute, 1980]).

38. Robert Woodson, *Tenant Control of Public Housing: An Economic Opportunity* (Washington, D.C.: National Forum Foundation, 1985).

39. Osborne and Gaebler, *Reinventing Government,* 60ff.

40. For more information contact *CoHousing: The Journal of CoHousing Network* at Tel. 510-526-6124 or Tel. 617-491-4392; *Co-Housing* (Sourcebook), Co-Housing Co., 1250 Addison St. #113, Berkeley, Calif. 94702.

41. The courts appear to be adjusting to the charter school idea. Wisconsin's highest court turned aside concerns over the separation of church and state and ruled that Milwaukee should extend its voucher program, which serves 1,500 low-income students, beyond nonsectarian private schools to religious ones (Mathew Brelis, "Recreating Our Schools," *Boston Sunday Globe,* June 21, 1998, pp. E1, E5).

42. Different governance structures have developed within charter schools. Schools generally have some type of representative charter council and collection of committees with different areas of responsibility. The degree of control vested in charter schools varies. Some charter councils have autonomy over certain areas, like the instructional program, but not others, such as school revenues and expenditures. Studies show that there are different distributions of power and authority and sometimes conflicting perceptions about who is in charge. There are varying degrees of

authority vested in charter directors, charter councils, and sponsoring agencies. Yet, overall, the formation of these schools is indicative of a desire to try a different system of education. Experiments with charter schools and public-private partnerships are discussed in Seymour Sarason and Elizabeth Lorentz, *Crossing Boundaries* (New York: Jossey-Bass, 1998); Tom Loveless and Claudia Jasin, "Starting from Scratch," *Educational Administration Quarterly* 34, no. 1 (February 1998): 9–30; Ted Kolderie, *Beyond Choice to New Public Schools: Withdrawing the Exclusive Franchise in Public Education* (Washington, D.C.: Progressive Policy Institute, November 1990).

43. Private universities have been losing ground to public (state) universities all over the world. In Germany and Italy, government control of universities has been extensive. In Latin America, formal university autonomy is an ideal, but informal ties to the state are the reality. In Great Britain, the government has been usurping faculty power as royal commissions have helped modernize Oxford and Cambridge and, in so doing, have appropriated greater authority. Everywhere, state control of higher education is replacing what began long ago as a community of independent masters and students. The educator A. H. Halsey said, "The state exercises a large measure of control over the educational system in all industrial countries." The political influence on university systems has been growing for many decades and is a worldwide phenomenon (A. H. Halsey, "Educational Organization," *International Encyclopedia of the Social Sciences,* ed. David Sills, vol. 4 [New York: Macmillan and Free Press, 1968], 529).

44. Clark Kerr, *The Great Transformation in Higher Education 1960–1980* (New York: State University of New York Press, 1991), xii–xiii.

45. Daniel S. Cheever, Jr., *Boston Sunday Globe,* April 26, 1992, p. 73. Cheever is president of the Massachusetts Higher Education Assistance Corporation, a guarantor for federal student loans.

46. Susanna Finnell, "Higher Education: Teaching and the Deliberative Process," in *Higher Education Exchange* (Kettering Foundation, 1998), 51.

47. Our point is that education transmits a culture related to the idea of civil society, hence our question about how U.S. education should be organized and financed. In a philosophical sense, a civil system of education can never remove the tension between great opposing ideas *(instrumental vs. substantive, public vs. private, individuality vs. community)*, but such ideas set the boundaries for concrete solutions. We discuss more on this subject of education in a book that will follow this one.

48. Some of these issues can be studied in Gabriel Almond and Sidney Verba, *The Civic Culture* (Princeton, N.J.: Princeton University Press, 1963); Burton Clark, *The Open College* (New York: McGraw-Hill, 1960); Logan Wilson, *The Academic Man* (New York: Octagon Books, 1964).

49. Daniel Breneman, ed., *Strategies for Promoting Excellence in a Time of Scarce Resources* (New York: Jossey-Bass, 1997). Talking about "higher unity" brings up the issues of religious values and other issues in education. Public (government) schools prohibit teaching religious creeds, due in part to the constitutional separation of church and state, but many educators argue that religious life cannot be ignored in public education. The beliefs and creeds of all major ways of life—business, government, religion—are important in civil education. Real learning includes understanding religious beliefs, as well as political beliefs, as part of society's spiri-

tual and cultural life. Hence, in a civil society, it seems logical that experiments in teaching about (and of) religious life are essential without proselytizing special beliefs.

Chapter 6

1. The public interest report is by Caroline Smith De Waal. See Stan Grossfeld, "New Dangers Make Way to US Tables," *Boston Sunday Globe,* September 20, 1998, pp. A1, A30. Reports from the U.S. Department of Agriculture's Economic Research Service indicate that medical cost and productivity losses for meat contamination have been extremely high each year.

2. This is my summary. For more, see *Rachel's Environment and Health Weekly,* no. 612 (August 20, 1998). In late 1997, the *New York Times* revealed that the EPA had been ignoring the new law. Environmentalists wondered whether the mountains of campaign contributions to the White House and Congress had any influence in the case. The 1996 law was a compromise by the environmentalists. These groups had given up the Delaney Clause that completely prohibited carcinogenic pesticides from appearing in certain processed foods, such as applesauce intended for children. The Delaney clause was scrapped in favor of numerical "risk assessments" of the cancer-causing potential of pesticides, a change allowing "wiggle room" for companies to work on their data.

Years of neglect have made communities affected by industrial pollution deeply skeptical of EPA's ability to help them. Grassroots groups have become more militant, forming literally thousands of organizations, including the Times Beach Action Group, which is contesting EPA incineration of dioxin-contaminated soil in Times Beach, Missouri; Mothers Organized to Stop Environmental Sins, fighting to close a hazardous-waste treatment facility in Winona, Texas; and more.

3. Russell Settle and Burton Weisbrod, "Occupational Safety and Health and the Public Interest," in *Public Interest Law,* ed. Burton Weisbrod (Berkeley: University of California Press, 1978), 285. The researchers were not optimists in terms of efficiency. They assessed both the allocative efficiency and distributional equity of safety and health problems and found a "market failure." When workers do not have a perfect understanding of the hazards inherent in jobs, and if job safety and health hazards impose external costs on nonworkers, and if society's well-being is dependent on the well-being of the workers, there is a cost-benefit problem. These authors included many variables, including workers' information about the law, the burden to workers of gathering sufficient evidence to protest a safety problem, the information available to workers on what constitutes a hazard, the job-risk loss in reporting a hazard, and union efficacy in providing information to 21 million members, as opposed to the 60 million workers covered by OSHA.

4. Gar Alperowitz et al., *Index of Environmental Trends* (Washington, D.C.: National Center for Economic and Security Alternatives, 2000 P Street, N.W., Suite 330, Washington, D.C. 20036).

5. Deva Lee Davis et al., "Reduced Ratio of Male to Female Births in Several Industrial Countries," *Journal of the American Medical Association* 279, no. 13 (April 1, 1998).

6. Henrik Moller, "Trends in Sex Ratio, Testicular Cancer and Male Repro-

ductive Hazards: Are They Connected?" *Acta Pathologica, Microbiologica et Immunological Scandinavice* 106 (1998). According to a recent study reported in the journal *Pediatrics,* many girls in the United States are entering puberty much earlier than normal, and there is some evidence that exposure to environmental chemicals may be contributing to this situation. Chemicals that mimic estrogens could be involved. One study suggests that PCBs (polychlorinated biphenyls) and DDE (a breakdown product of the pesticide DDT) may be associated with early sexual development in girls (Marcia Herman-Giddens et al., "Secondary Sexual Characteristics and Menses in Young Girls Seen in Office Practice," *Pediatrics* 99, no. 4 [April 1997]: 505–12).

7. Risk assessment involves estimating how many people will be injured or killed by a particular business practice. For example, the EPA could be satisfied if experts derived the concentration in water of each contaminant that would result in a risk level not greater than one in a million to humans consuming fish. They would then sanctify that number by an administrative rule, but this is a complex procedure when one is calculating all the varieties of fish. Experts in corporate industry are often involved in the calculations, but most states do not even regulate most of the 126 EPA priority pollutants anyway, let alone the 70,000 chemicals in use by the industry.

8. Peter Montague, "The Precautionary Principle," *Rachel's Environment and Health Weekly,* no. 596 (February 19, 1998): 1.

9. Ibid., 2.

10. Paul Anastas and Tracy Williamson, *Green Chemistry: Designing Chemistry for the Environment* (Washington, D.C.: American Chemical Society, 1996), xi. This is part of an ACS Symposium Series sponsored by the Division of Environmental Chemistry, Inc.

11. Chemical hygiene plans (CHPs) are often prepared for firms and universities by outside experts. For example, Boston College's CHP was prepared by Arthur D. Little, Inc., in January 1993.

12. The issue is whether the research is in a responsible public (and scientific) interest. Research in the laboratory is always open to commercial use. Around the year 1900, Herbert Dow, the founder of Dow Chemical, split common salt to make commercially valuable sodium hydroxide, releasing, as an unwanted by-product, the high-toxic green gas, free chlorine. Mr. Dow was a chemistry teacher and soon began combining chlorine with other elements, thus creating "chlorine chemistry," giving rise to solvents, pesticides, and all sorts of other toxic chlorinated compounds, of which there now about 15,000 in commercial use. We do not have space to discuss the role of educational associations, but something should be said about their close connection with business. A risk connection develops when corporations offer research grants to universities. Faculties risk "collusion" between business interests and university research. Professional chemists are involved in creating—and solving—this problem.

13. Governments can be very effective in specific cases. After the 1986 Congress required manufacturers to report the quantities of some 300 chemicals they release each year (The Toxic Release Inventory), emissions were cut dramatically. Shell Oil cut its releases by 98.7 percent; Kennecott-Utah Copper cut releases by 89.7 percent; Monsanto came down 68.8 percent. The Chemical Manufacturers Association said that the pressure of public disclosure reduced emissions by its members 50 percent during the period 1987 to 1993. Monsanto's vice chair, Nicolas Reding, said the

emission percentages went down because companies knew the public would not like the high count produced by the industry.

14. As steps in this voluntary civil development direction are taken, there are new dangers of market-sector dominance. "Individualism" can give way to "association-alism." Too much emphasis on the power of associations, without looking carefully at how they are organized to optimize the values of each member, could lead to a reduction in the power of the individual. This concern leads to an emphasis upon how people organize themselves, as well as upon keeping alive the opportunity for people not to belong to an association.

15. Murray Weidenbaum and Melinda Warren, *It's Time to Cut Government Regulations* (St. Louis: Center for the Study of American Business, Washington University, 1995).

16. Carroll, *Business and Society,* 242ff.

17. Melinda Warren, *Reforming the Federal Regulatory Process,* occasional paper 138, St. Louis, Washington University, Center for the Study of American Business, 1994. In the executive branch of the federal government, 6,000 high-ranking government executives run 14 departments, 61 independent commissions, and other types of government organizations.

18. Speaking of the EPA's Carol Browner, the *New York Times* said in an editorial, "As a practical matter, the task of issuing individual permits for thousands of companies nationwide is beyond her staff's capabilities" ("Environmental Defiance" [editorial], *New York Times,* December 20, 1996, p. A38).

19. James E. Post, William C. Frederick et al., *Business and Society* (New York: McGraw-Hill, 1996), 413.

20. Concerns over the unpredictable size of jury awards and the high cost of liability insurance are a motivation for business associations to write their own rules and issue their own penalties with professional arbiters and overseers. But self-regulation can be resolved only under the guidance of government agencies. After a spill of a wood preservative product made by Monsanto, a jury required the company to pay $16 million in damages. Because of high liability charges, business leaders want a uniform (federal) liability code. The code would set limits on awarding punitive damages. Consumer groups, of course, oppose such legislation.

Hence, any government effort to help associations create self-governing rules involves countervailing powers, like consumer groups. The negotiation is also adjusted to commercial law. Ordinary market transactions are subject to the Uniform Commercial Code, which has been adopted by all states except Louisiana.

21. Business scholar David Vogel describes civic activism along these lines as a public interest movement: "The central political mission of the public-interest movement is to enable those affected by corporate decisions in their roles as citizens, consumers, and taxpayers to have the same influence over public policy as business" ("Public-Interest Movement," *Fluctuating Fortunes* [New York: Basic Books, 1989], 622).

22. Rules are established by competitors at every level of the market. People are not fully conscious of the extent of this rule-making practice. I remember shopping in a Mexican market and finding that the shopkeepers had agreed that they would not try to sell their product to a customer standing in front of someone else's booth. The rule civilized their competition. The same thing happens in big U.S. markets as stakeholders (competitors, consumers, employees, communities, buyers, and sellers) become involved in civil agreements.

In my opinion, most people want to see corporations compete within a civil (public standard) framework. If associations do not set rules, civic leaders could argue that the government will continue to do so for them. Government courts regularly set rules. For example, U.S. constitutional principles are interpreted as applying to the business system. Courts have assumed in some cases that free speech is a human right for employees in business. The question is, under what conditions does the principle of free speech apply? When does it become acceptable within a corporation? Here is another example. The courts introduced "due process" into the market as a principle to follow in resolving conflicts between business associations (Ronald C. Moe, "Exploring the Limits of Privatization," *Public Administration Review* 47 [November/December 1987]: 453–60).

23. Gabriel Kolko, *The Triumph of Conservatism* (New York: Free Press, 1963).

24. Senate Majority Leader Trent Lott (R-Miss.) personally endorsed S. 866, which gives immunity to violators who self-report violations. Notably, S. 866 specifically prohibits the EPA from revoking enforcement authority of states that pass audit privilege laws. A companion bill was introduced into the House of Representatives as H.R. 1884. Some 80 citizen groups have formed a vigorous coalition to fight audit privilege laws. Contact the Network against Corporate Secrecy led by Sanford Lewis in Boston: Tel. 617-254-1030.

25. Ferdinand Tönnies, *Fundamental Concepts of Sociology* (New York: American Book, 1940). For Tönnies, social order is composed of the most general and complex of norms, based primarily on concord or convention. Law is the complex set of norms enforced by judicial decision, based on custom or intentional legislation.

26. When a paper mill pollutes a river with its toxic effluent, the cost of health care for those living downstream, the loss of fishing due to dying fish, the cost of cleaning the river are not borne by the paper mill but by others. In economics, the term *externalities* refers to the expense and output that occur outside of trade competition itself. For more details, see Goodwin, *Social Economics,* vol. 1, 47, 49, 55–59. In conventional markets, it is assumed that governments should pay for externalities. In the concept we propose here, trade and professional associations are encouraged to reduce/eliminate externalities. If trade associations do not solve a public problem, governments should encourage them to do it. In the case of externalities of pollution created in the auto industry, we can invoke an imaginary case.

In this imaginary case, the government would pressure associated industries to coordinate the changes that are needed to eliminate the externality of air pollution. Let us say that the government gives incentives to (or pressures) the auto industry to manufacture electric cars and the construction industry is encouraged to develop photovoltaic cells for rooftop housing. By means of a three-sector consultation, which includes professional associations of engineers, a plan is developed to recharge car batteries for electric cars without using conventional electricity. The auto industry assesses the second-car market, and it looks profitable. Trade and professional associations then begin developing a solution to the negative externalities of transportation. A new market is developed for electric cars with federal assistance, but the transportation industry remains free to manufacture gasoline engines and also to invent new solutions to the problem of air pollution in its own interest.

27. This is my summary report on TUR based on their publications. Companies that are at a certain "threshold" pay fees. They find they can save money by inventing safer (better) technologies. The Toxic Use Reduction Institute (TURI) staff has

demonstrated that companies in this program do save money in the long run. More information can be obtained from the Massachusetts Toxic Use Reduction Institute, University of Massachusetts Lowell, One University Ave., Lowell, Mass. 01854-2881. James Gomes, "A Report on the Implementation of the Toxic Use Reduction Act," Environmental League of Massachusetts, May, 1994.

28. For more information, call toll-free 1-800-ASK-SBA. Or, consult <www .y2k.gov>. Also, consult U.S. Small Business Administration—<www. sba.gov/ y2k>. This is an example of a government policy that respects the autonomy of business associations and energizes them to work for the common good.

29. Grover Starling, *The Changing Environment of Business* (Cincinnati, Ohio: South-Western College Publishing, 1996), 334.

30. The center also found that employee-owned firms with OBM outperformed conventional firms with OBM ("Open Book Management and Corporate Performance," *Employee Ownership Report* 28, no. 1 [January/February 1998]).

31. Kim Clarke, Robert Hayes, and Christopher Lorenz, *The Uneasy Alliance* (Cambridge, Mass.: The Harvard Business School, 1985), 103–4.

32. Social investors are laying a basis for uniform auditing in their experiments with *social screens*. Social screens are composed of ethical criteria that guide investors who also want to maximize economic returns through their use. University schools of management have been developing courses around social-financial audits as part of their curriculum. Some groundwork is being laid quietly for nationwide social auditing. See Kinder, Lydenberg, and Domini, *Social Investment Almanac*. For more on ethical codes and social auditing, see Makower, *Beyond the Bottom Line*, 74ff. For a collection of readings on codes of ethics in business associations, see Ivan Hill, ed., *The Ethical Basis of Economic Freedom* (Chapel Hill, N.C.: American Viewpoint, 1976).

33. Makower, *Beyond the Bottom Line*, 79.

34. "Securities and Exchange Commission," *Financial World*, October 26, 1993, pp. 49–50.

35. The Securities and Exchange Commission (SEC) was established in 1934 to protect stockholders' rights by making sure that financial markets were run more openly and fairly and that investment information is fully disclosed. The agency generates its own revenue to pay for its operations. A question has been raised about whether this agency might be privatized with a public board—very much as we indicated in the model on mass communications (chap. 4) with key associations of society represented on the board.

36. Marc J. Epstein, "Accounting for Product Take-Back," *Management Accounting* (August 1996): 30.

37. Marjorie Kelly, "Introduction," *Business Ethics*, Special Report no. 1, 1996, 2.

38. In order to gain tax-exempt status, nonprofit charitable organizations have to file an application, called Form 1023, with the Internal Revenue Service. Nonprofits must provide the names of founders, disclose information about their finances and bylaws, and describe their charitable purpose (Jean Field, "Public Interest, Private Records," *San Francisco Bay Guardian*, March 12, 1997, p. 16). Consumer watchdogs, like the National Charities Information Bureau and Interaction (a coalition of relief organizations), have adopted fiscal, ethical, and accountability standards that go beyond what the law requires.

39. Governments that decide to engage in civil-economy planning must take ac-

count of all the countervailing and competing interests *between* market sectors, as well as within them, as in the transportation industry (airline, auto, bus, train) or as between the fields of chemistry, plastics, silk, and textiles. Unless government planners are careful, the practice of increasing the civic responsibility of market sectors will also unduly increase their lobbying power. Trade sector monopolies must be avoided. If civil associations are decentralized and organized with countervailing powers, taking into account the adequacy of their democratic structures, they should not have undue power. This issue of market-sector organization will be treated separately in a forthcoming book.

40. Here are some arguments from civil-society advocates on why the term *public* should not be identified solely with government and why its usage is changing. First, governments often will not give critical information to the public because of broad ranging criteria for national security. Second, critics argue that the federal government is not accountable to sectors of the public, such as residents in local communities, partly due to their centralized bureaucracy. Third, employees in a government agency cannot be fully accountable to themselves, that is, self-managing and self-directing, because the administration is a command system whose chiefs are appointed by a governor or a president. For a more extensive discussion on the idea of the "public," see Benjamin Barber, *Strong Democracy* (Berkeley: University of California Press, 1984); Jeff Weintraub and Krishan Kumar, eds., *Public and Private in Thought and Practice: Perspectives on a Grand Dichotomy* (Chicago, Ill.: University of Chicago Press, 1997).

41. Jeff Weintraub, "Public/Private: The Limitations of a Grand Dichotomy," *Responsive Community* 7, no. 2 (spring 1997). We would say that the purpose of a public, civil market system is to enhance the autonomy of firms and the individuality of all people within it.

42. A corporation becomes a public entity when its shares are placed on the New York Stock Exchange. The Securities and Exchange Commission regulates the New York Stock Exchange, in turn. Yet, a business corporation itself is called private because it is separate from government, while remaining public because of these regulations. At the same time, when corporations create codes of conduct for the common good, they are saying, in effect, that they are part of a public domain.

43. The competitive environment was greatly altered through the abolition of interest rate ceilings and the breakdown of legal barriers distinguishing commercial banks from other financial institutions such as savings and loans. It ended in a near disaster. We noted earlier (in chap. 4) that this process had calamitous repercussions in every sector of society. We defined the problem as a lack of training in prudent investments and self-regulatory norms. The sudden change in government regulations was too much to handle in the private sector. The failure in the savings and loan industry so affected the public that it required immediate government action, instituting criminal charges, stabilizing the market, and repairing all the damages caused by the sudden deregulation. We learned how civil rules of order need to be established in the private economy. Yet, the nationwide lesson that followed the deregulation in the financial system can be applied to any institutional change in which people move rapidly from a protected environment to an unprotected one. Great problems developed with the deinstitutionalization of mental hospitals. Patients were released after having lived long under hospital rules, after having known the

security of hospital supervision and the certainty of a protected environment, and were transferred abruptly into complete freedom on the streets with no rules and little supervision. The result was harmful to many former patients. The best prisons engage in career and citizen training for inmates, preparing them to go on parole with careful supervision. That training will also involve some planning with communities where inmates will be going after parole.

44. The two prominent organizations in this period were the nonprofit CCC and the Federal Reserve System's Division of Consumer and Community Affairs (Randal Fitzgerald, *When Government Goes Private: Successful Alternatives to Public Service* [New York: Universe Books, 1988]). When H. J. Heinz (the Star-Kist brand), the Van Camp Seafood Company (Chicken of the Sea), and Bumble Bee Seafoods agree with environmentalists that it is wrong to kill an estimated 100,000 dolphins each year or when they pressure fishers in the eastern Pacific to stop catching yellowfin tuna in large circular nets that close around schools of fish to kill marine mammals, they are conscientiously integrating their corporate self-interests with the larger public interest. Public opinion has an influence within the business sector, but we are saying that this practice of corporate "goodwill" cannot be relied upon over time. Stakeholders need systems of trade sector accountability to assure environmental protection. As it happened, the "tuna accord," by itself, ran into trouble (Michael Straus, "Tuna Embargo Falls," *World Watch* 10, no. 6 [November/December 1997]: 7). In other words, we are not talking about conscientious practices by CEOs within individual corporations or establishing codes of conduct for separate companies—as important as they may be in their own right. Good companies and corporate codes help protect the public welfare, but we are talking about systems of marketwide accountability. These systems can function most effectively when neutral third parties are involved, as between countervailing powers and business organized in market sectors.

45. Critics say that private corporations are public because they get so much aid from the government. Michael Moore says sarcastically that the system needs a new name "ADC"—Aid to Dependent Corporations.

It's $1.6 million in federal funds for McDonald's, in part to help them market Chicken McNuggets in Singapore from 1986 to 1994.

It's Westinghouse getting to accelerate the depreciation on their machinery (something you and I can't do), saving them $215 million in taxes in 1993 while they eliminated 24,700 jobs.

It's giving $278 million in government technology subsidies to Amoco, AT&T, Citicorp, Du Pont, General Electric, General Motors, and IBM between 1990 and 1994 while together they cut 339,058 jobs and posted combined profits of $25.2 billion in 1994 alone.

It's Exxon being able to claim nearly $300 million in tax *deductions* on the settlement they paid when the *Exxon Valdez* spilled 11 million gallons of oil into Prince William Sound.

It's $11 million to Pillsbury to promote the Pillsbury DoughBoy in foreign countries.

It's forty-two Fortune 500 companies that paid no federal income taxes from 1981 through 1985 until a minimum tax was forced on them in 1986.

It's every city in every state in the country forced to clear land, build new roads, upgrade airports, waive local taxes, construct new sewer and water lines, and train thousands of new workers—all at the behest or threat of a corporation that is making record profits and could easily pay for these items themselves (Michael Moore, *Downsize This!* [New York: Crown, 1996], 44–45).

46. There were repeated campaigns for federal licensing of giant corporations at different stages in U.S. history. Presidents Theodore Roosevelt, William Taft, Woodrow Wilson, and Franklin Roosevelt all voiced support for a scheme of federal licensing that would use principles of accountability to guide the conduct of conglomerate corporations. Their campaigns were deferred repeatedly by legislative compromises in Congress, which included the creation of federal laws like the Sherman Antitrust Act and the security laws in the 1930s, and the addition of dozens of government agencies of enforcement such as the Federal Communications Commission and the Federal Trade Commission. Ralph Nader proposed a Federal Chartering Act in the 1970s that would cover major corporations responsible for many thousands of employees and who were listed on the securities exchange with more than 2,000 shareholders. Of the 1.8 million corporations at the time, about 700 would have been involved. Others have suggested limiting the number to essential corporations that invoke the public interest (Nader, Green, and Seligman, *Taming the Giant Corporation*).

47. Business competitors rely on government agencies to be their umpires. This constant lawmaking by legislatures and monitoring by government agencies cost the taxpayer too much. In my judgment, competitors should take more responsibility through associations. Competitors should internalize their social costs—not letting the government pay the costs for them. The members of a baseball league or the American Bar Association pay a fee to compete according to civil rules. They make a public contract with each other. Members then set standards within their associations and pay umpires, final arbiters.

48. When a basketball player engages in misconduct, such as threatening a coach, there is a penalty. If a football player is caught taking drugs—or any player breaks the jointly determined standards of competition—the league issues a fine or some form of punishment. If a priest or minister engages in unethical conduct, the church association appoints a court to issue judgments and penalties. Professional associations set up their own tribunals to deal with members who are accused of malfeasance, or cheating, or abusing a client/patient relationship. We have noted earlier that business has also moved in this very same direction, but it is not routine; indeed, the practice is minimal compared with that in other sectors of society.

49. Most people think about systems of exchange under an old capitalist ideology, which considers the marketplace to be a natural order. In the last century, social Darwinists held that a struggle for survival was the essence of evolution. Hence, in referring to free markets, this has meant "do not tamper with a good thing." In some cases, people still say, "There's nothing you can do about it. That's the way things are." Yet, we are saying that the market system is socially self-constructed. Corporations can remain competitive within civil associations.

Chapter 7

1. "Introduction," in *Understanding Global Issues,* ed. Richard Buckley (England, Cheltenham GL51PQ, 1997).

2. Peter Hall and Sidney Tarrow, "Globalization and Area Studies," *Chronicle of Higher Education,* January 23, 1998, p. B4. For a review of books that differ sharply on this subject, see Victor Roudometof, "Preparing for the Twenty-First Century," *Sociological Forum* 12, no. 4 (1997) 661ff.

3. Bennett Harrison, *Lean and Mean* (New York: Basic Books, 1994). For contrasting arguments that point toward a concept of civility, see Charles Sabel and Michael Piore, *The Second Industrial Divide* (New York: Basic Books, 1984); Charles Sabel, *Work and Politics* (Cambridge: Cambridge University Press, 1981); Michael Piore and Suzanne Berger, *Dualism and Discontinuity in Industrial Society* (Cambridge: Cambridge University Press, 1980).

4. Robert Reich, *The Work of Nations* (New York: Vintage Books, 1991), 3. In sheer size, the annual sales of the largest global firms exceed the gross national product of many nations.

5. Richard Barnet and John Cavanagh, *Global Dreams* (New York: Simon and Schuster, 1994). The largest number of corporate headquarters are in the United States, Japan, Germany, France, Switzerland, the Netherlands, and the United Kingdom.

6. Starling, *Changing Environment of Business,* 427.

7. In the past, the power of petroleum industry was the classic example of how global firms concentrate their power, but today it is the financial institutions and global manufacturing industries that are rivaling governments. Information technology has transformed global banking with major consequences for the future. Global finance operates "night and day" like a gambling casino with trillions of dollars flowing through major foreign-exchange markets at split second speed.

8. David Korten describes the problem as due to an expansion of the market economy. This expansion is "monetizing" human relationships, weakening the social fabric, and destroying livelihoods faster than jobs offering more than poverty-level compensation are being created. Economic globalization is shifting control over resources, markets, and technology from people, communities, and governments to transnational financial markets and corporations—placing these institutions beyond the reach of public accountability, making responsible local action to meet local needs increasingly difficult, and creating dangerous financial instability. Korten, formerly at the Harvard Business School, criticizes the concentration of economic and political power in a handful of global corporations and financial institutions, leaving the market with only its own short-term profit goals (*Globalizing Civil Society* [New York: Seven Stories Press, 1998], 12–13).

9. For many examples of runaway companies and the problems they produce in lowering standards and the details of this downward leveling, see Jeremy Brecher and Tim Costello, *Global Village or Global Pillage?* (Boston: South End Press, 1994).

10. The documentation on the loss of forests and related problems can be found in many sources. At the beginning of the 1990s, the *State of the World* pointed out that "Forests are shrinking, deserts expanding, and soils eroding" (Lester Brown et al., *State of the World, 1990* [New York: W. W. Norton, 1990], xv). Later annual edi-

tions of *State* continued to report on this condition. In 1998, Janet Abramovitz reports that the trend continues: "Between 1990 and 1995, at least 107 countries had a net loss of forest cover" ("Forest Decline Continues," in *Vital Signs, 1998,* ed. L. Brown, M. Brenner, and C. Flavin [New York: W. W. Norton, 1998], 124; also see Brown, *State of the World,* 15).

11. Lester Brown, project director, *State of the World, 1995* (New York: W. W. Norton, 1995), 9. On the declining situation in Puerto Rico, see "Appendix: The Social Economy of Copper Mining," in Bruyn, *Social Economy.* On the Philippines, see Robin Broad with John Cavanagh, *Plundering Paradise: The Struggle for the Environment in the Philippines* (Berkeley and Los Angeles: University of California Press, 1993), 31–32. In Indonesia, companies deliberately set fires that burned 2 million hectares of forest in 1997 to clear land for palm oil, pulp, and rice plantations or to cover the tracks of illegal logging. Haze shrouded much of Indonesia with hazardous air.

12. Janet Abramovitz, "Taking a Stand," Worldwatch paper 140, April 1998, 6–7.

13. The following items include what one writer says happens.

1949 Accident at Monsanto plant in Nitro, West Virginia, exposes workers to dioxin. 1953 Accident at BASF plant in West Germany releases dioxin into two nearby communities. 1962 to 1970 Agent Orange extensively sprayed in Southeast Asia during the Vietnam War. . . . Mid-1960s Outbreak of reproductive and developmental effects noted in fish-eating birds of the Great Lakes. 1971 Dioxin-laced waste oil first used to control dust on roads in Times Beach, Missouri; town evacuated in 1983 after flooding spreads dioxin throughout entire community. Dioxin found to cause birth defects in mice. 1974 Dioxin detected in breast milk of mothers in South Vietnam. 1976 Hoffman-LaRoche trichlorophenol plant explodes in Seveso, Italy, exposing 37,000 people to a toxic cloud that contains dioxin. 1977 Dioxin found to cause cancer in rats. . . . 1978 Dioxin discovered at Love Canal in Niagara Falls, New York. . . . 1979 EPA finds 40 parts per million dioxin in wastes at the Vertac plant in Jacksonville, Arkansas. . . . Yu-cheng rice oil contamination in Taiwan. . . . 1992 U.S.-Canadian Internal Joint Commission Sixth Biennial Report calls for a phase-out of chlorine (Lois Marie Gibbs and the Citizens Clearinghouse for Hazardous Waste, *Dying from Dioxin* [Boston, Mass.: South End Press], xxix–xxxii).

14. Ralph Ryder, "'Sustainable' Incineration and Death by Dioxin," *Ecologist* 27, no. 4 (July/August, 1997): 135.

15. Barnet and Cavanagh, *Global Dreams,* 289.

16. Brown, *State of the World, 1995,* 8.

17. Ann Platt McGinn, *Rocking the Boat* (Worldwatch Institute, 1998), 27, 43.

18. J. T. Houghton et al., eds. *Climate Change, 1995,* Contribution of Working Group I to the Second Assessment Report of the Intergovernmental Panel on Climate Change (IPCC); Robert Watson, Marufu Zinyowera, and Richard Moss, eds., *Climate Change, 1995,* Contribution of Working Group II to the Second Assessment Report of the IPCC (Cambridge, U.K.: Cambridge University Press, 1996).

19. Molly O'Meara, "Global Temperatures Reach Record High," in *State of the World, 1998* (New York: W. W. Norton, 1998).

20. The fuel industry associations have paid scientists to publish journals and advocate their position against global warming. They have been seeking to downplay a

consensus view held by 2,500 of the world's top climate scientists. The documentation for this extensive funding from trade associations is in Ross Gelbspan, "The Battle for Control of Reality," chap. 2 in *The Heat Is On* (Reading, Mass.: Addison-Wesley, 1997).

Government support for these industries should be considered in this battle. The U.S. federal government spends more than $20 billion a year subsidizing the oil, coals, and gas industries. This pattern of subsidies does little to promote cleaner energy technology or protect the environment (Doug Koplow, "Energy Subsidies and the Environment," in *Subsidies and Environment: Exploring Linkages* [Organization for Economic Cooperation and Development, 1996]).

21. Based on interviews by Gelbspan, *Heat Is On*, 153ff. For a study of the connections between violent conflict and environmental scarcity, see Thomas Homer-Dixon and Valerie Percival, *Environmental Scarcity and Violent Conflict: A Briefing Book* (Toronto, Canada: University College, AAAS, 1996).

22. Tourism is contributing to the complexity of this problem. In 1990, consumers in the world's industrial nations spent $232 billion on tourism. Tourists from Europe and Japan are traveling in ever-larger numbers. One result of increased tourism is the degradation of the natural environment. Congestion has virtually destroyed parts of Yosemite National Park. Wildlife preserves in Amboselli National Park in Kenya have been torn up by safari vehicles and by elephants trying to get out of their way. See Barnet and Cavanaugh, *Global Dreams*, 29–35.

23. *Wall Street Journal,* March 11, 1992. Reported in Barnet and Cavanaugh, *Global Dreams*, 336.

24. Jeremy Rifkin, "Should We Patent Life?" *Business Ethics* (March/April 1998).

25. Mae-Wan Ho, "The Inevitable Return to a Sane Agriculture," *Ecologist* 28, no. 5 (September/October 1998). See also chapter 9 of Mae-Wan Ho, *Genetic Engineering—Dream or Nightmare? The Brave New World or Bad Science and Big Business,* 2d ed. (Bath, U.K.: Gateway Books, 1998); Mae-Wan Ho, Hartmut Meyer, and Joe Cummins, "The Biotechnology Bubble," *Ecologist* 28, no. 3 (May/June 1998).

26. Peter Montague, "Is Regulation Possible?" *Ecologist* 28, no. 2 (March/April, 1998): 61.

27. Robert Kuttner, *Everything for Sale* (New York: A. A. Knopf, 1998), 164. Kuttner also describes how the outstanding, uncollectible third-world debt to money-center banks equaled more than twice the banks' capital. Regulators for the most part allowed banks to carry these nonperforming loans on their balance sheets at book value. If the regulators had chosen to crack down, or to let pure-market forces sort out the wreckage, the United States' largest banks were technically insolvent. Eventually, over a decade, the third-world debts were gradually written off, at about 66 cents on the dollar. The "putative gain to allocative efficiency achieved by the deregulation of banking was overwhelmed by loan losses" (23).

28. Geisst traces this history.

In 1825, the country experienced one of its frequent and severe economic slowdowns. State banks were issuing an excessive amount of notes, and the Bank of the United States was attempting to come to grips with the inflationary and liquidity problems that followed. The New York Bank failed, and the stock exchange in New York collapsed on its back (*Wall Street: A History* [New York: Oxford University Press, 1997], 30).

29. Financial analysts do not examine the "civil order" of economic life in their calculations. LTC placed much of its investments in crony capitalism overseas, in immature economies. The former Federal Reserve chairman, Paul Volcker, questioned the U.S. central bank's "official sponsorship" of the $3.5 billion rescue of Long-Term Capital Management. He doubted that the weight of the federal government should be used to bail out private investors who knew that they were taking big risks in emerging markets. Volcker said that the best way to restore stability would be for large industrial companies to make long-term investments in Asian nations. This sounds good, but Volcker does not assess how long-term investment increases absentee ownership of cheap land and the subsequent political effects in the loss of host-nation independence—for example, the possibility of riots in the streets against foreign ownership. The concept of self-governance for domestic economies is not an important part of the thinking of investors.

30. UN Human Development Program, *Human Development Report 1992*, 36ff. See also *Human Development Report 1994* and *Agenda for Development* (1994). The issues are complex. Students of global firms suggest that skilled workers in the Third World get rich while those in the First World get richer. See William Wolman and Anne Colamosca, *The Triumph of Capital and the Betrayal of Work* (Reading, Mass.: Addison-Wesley, 1997). In this era of global business, the inequality of wealth has grown enormously among people and nations. In the United States, the top 1 percent now controls 42 percent of the total wealth, up from 28 percent two decades ago.

31. David Landes, *The Wealth and Poverty of Nations* (New York: W. W. Norton, 1997).

32. Donald Barlett and James Steele, *America: Who Really Pays the Taxes?* (New York: Simon and Schuster, 1994), 196. They give an illustration of one advantage of being transnational. I summarize.

To see how it works, let us create a business—say, the Multinational Toy Company (MTC), a British company with headquarters in London that manufactures and sells a variety of toys and dolls. Suppose a subsidiary, MTC Indonesia, makes dolls in Indonesia. It sells the dolls to another subsidiary, MTC Turks, a trading company located on the Turks and Caicos Islands. MTC Turks sells the dolls to yet another subsidiary, MTC California, which in turn sells them to toy stores and department stores throughout that state. One other note: The dolls, along with other toys, are shipped in a vessel owned by another subsidiary, MTC Shipping. Let us assume further that it cost MTC Indonesia 75 cents to make the doll in Indonesia and that MTC California sells it to retail outlets for $15. Hence, the question: What is the profit on each doll subject to California income tax? Or for that matter, U.S. income taxes? You might guess that after subtracting the 75 cents, and a reasonable amount for shipping and handling and other miscellaneous expenses, the balance would be income subject to tax. Let us say $10. But you would guess wrong. That is because back in London, Multinational Toy Company, the parent company, has many options. MTC Indonesia could sell the dolls to MTC Turks for $1. MTC Turks, in turn, could sell them to MTC California for $14. Thus, after deducting its expenses, MTC California would show a profit of less than $1 on each doll. Meanwhile, back on the Turks and Caicos Islands, MTC Turks is sitting on a $13 profit. That is tax free, since the islands have no income tax.

33. The global stock and bond trading are now too complex for the SEC to monitor, much less regulate. For example, in the 1998 market downturn, investors who

for years had borrowed money in Japan at extremely low interest rates in order to invest in higher-paying dollar-denominated securities or hot European stocks quickly changed their position. The reversal of this popular arbitrage strategy put downward pressure on the dollar and other U.S. markets. Fearful that once-robust Asian markets were close to bankruptcy, investors pulled billions of dollars from East Asia, leaving companies without cash and people without jobs. It is clear that an unfettered global market exposes most countries to risks, pushing many into serious financial disruption. My thanks to Gerome Rothenberg for his clarification of the economic problems discussed here.

34. This note is drawn from a talk with José Ramos-Horta in Newton, Massachusetts, October 1998.

35. Saskia Sassen, "Economic Globalization: A New Geography, Composition, and Institutional Network," *Global Visions: Beyond the New World Order,* ed. Jeremy Brecher et al. (Boston: South End Press, 1993), 62–63.

36. *Benchmark Rating of TNCs,* Report of the 1995 Benchmark Survey of NGOs, commissioned by the Royal Ministry of Foreign Affairs, Oslo, Norway, 1995. Benchmark papers argue that GATT does not adhere to the standard of sustainability. It will override national legislation because such laws constitute trade barriers. GATT standards are "supersovereign," for they oblige national governments to apply them at local levels, even if the standards are lower. GATT makes no use of reporting procedures established by UNCTAD, OECD, FAO, WHO, UNEP, or Agenda 21. GATT cannot levy fines, and so enforcement reverts to trade retaliation by sovereign states. GATT's dispute settlement system is intergovernmental, and so the "public" has no standing, although victims of the new trade regulations will not be governments, but citizens, businesses, and the environment.

37. In chapter 1, we discussed the demand of nonprofit groups that U.S. oil refiners not use Ethyl Corporation's new manganese-based gasoline additive MMT. (It was marketed to refiners under the trade name HiTEC 3000.) The toxic effects on humans of high levels of airborne manganese, which include severe and progressive brain degeneration, were well documented. The EPA had failed to stop them, but nonprofit groups succeeded in their goal. This Canadian case focused on NAFTA rules and was settled financially out of court.

38. Gil Friend, "A Global Constitution?" *YES!* (fall 1997): 48.

39. The Multilateral Agreement on Investment (MAI) was an "economic pact" under discussion to establish *limits* on how governments can regulate investment in nations, states, and communities, basically an effort to reduce the power of nation-states to regulate business. The MAI negotiations began in 1995 at the Organization for Economic Cooperation and Development (OECD), a Paris-based international policy organization made up of 29 (well-to-do) countries. The Public Citizen, a public interest group started by Ralph Nader in the United States, joined with a coalition of other nongovernmental organizations to raise awareness about this effort to widen the powers of corporations in global markets. At this moment of writing, leaders in the European Community and the World Trade Organization are discussing the right to protect commercial patents of biological life, which many scientists believe to be unethical. For more information, contact Public Citizen, 215 Pennsylvania Ave. SE, Washington, D.C., Tel. 202-546-4996; Friends of the Earth, Tel. 202-783-7400; Preamble Collaborative, Tel. 202-265-3263.

40. Stiglitz concedes that temporary fixes may even have undermined pressures for further reform, that there was a well-defined set of market failures associated with

externalities. This list of market failures was subsequently expanded to include imperfect information and incomplete markets. Since the "fundamental problems were not addressed, some countries have required assistance again and again." The key issue is not "liberalization or deregulation but construction of the regulatory framework that ensures an effective financial system." He goes on to say that the government should serve as a complement to markets, undertaking actions that make markets work better and correcting market failures. In some cases the government has proved to be an effective catalyst—its actions have helped solve the problem of undersupply of (social) innovation, for example. "But once it has performed its catalytic role, the state needs to withdraw" ("More Instruments and Broader Goals." This speech is also available in PDF format, suitable for printing or reading offline: wider. Pdf [140K] p. 16).

41. Michael Best, *The New Competition: Institutions of Industrial Restructuring* (Cambridge, Mass.: Harvard University Press, 1990), 199. At the global level today, some economists say that to solve the global crisis, nations must be willing to cooperate and help one another, despite their losses. They must sacrifice because their own fate is deeply involved in the well-being of their neighbors.

42. See Ronnie Lipschutz with Judth Mayer, *Global Civil Society and Global International Governance* (New York: State University of New York Press, 1996).

43. Each national government cooperates of course, where possible, with other national governments (IGOs) to set international standards for global firms. The effort to create intergovernment regulations over global markets remains important—worthy of every effort, meriting every ounce of imagination—but, by itself, cannot deal with the problems we covered in chapter 7. To add to this problem, the UN Charter made no provision for ecological security; its framers never anticipated that environmental issues would one day constitute global threats (Patrische Mische, "Assuring Ecological Security for the Twenty-First Century: How Can the UN's Role Be Strengthened?" *Breakthrough News* [September/December 1997]: 1–7). See Christopher Flavin and Odil Tunali, "Climate of Hope: New Strategies for Stabilizing the World's Atmosphere," Worldwatch paper, June 1996. For more discussion on IGOs and NGOs, see A. Leroy Bennett, *International Organizations* (Englewood Cliffs, N.J.: Prentice-Hall, 1991), 2.

Chapter 8

1. The United Nations Conference on Trade and Development (UNCTAD), founded in 1964, helped organize a global negotiating forum when the proposed International Trade Organization (ITO) of 1948 was abandoned. UNCTAD has helped to negotiate a number of commodity price agreements. Yet, many important commodities like steel, oil, autos, and textiles have remained outside UNCTAD and also outside the General Agreement on Tariffs and Trade (GATT) (Sidney Dell, *The United Nations and International Business* [Durham, N.C.: Duke University Press for the UN Institute for Training and Research, 1990]).

2. Edgar Heermance, *Can Business Govern Itself?* (New York: Harper and Bros., 1933), 204.

3. Whyte and Whyte, *Making Mondragon;* Conrad et al., *Milwaukee Journal.* See chapter 3 of the current work.

4. For a review of CDCs, see Twelvetrees, *Organizing for Neighborhood Development.*

5. Conrad, "Radio and Television."

6. The American National Standards Institute (ANSI)—a privately funded federation of leaders representing both private and government sectors—played a large role in this effort to establish standards and hopes to coordinate the U.S. voluntary standards system. The National Institute of Standards and Technology (NIST) is a federal agency in the U.S. Department of Commerce that is responsible for helping to coordinate standards through the Commerce Department. It promotes economic growth by working with industry to apply technology, measurement, and standards by its focus on the nation's technology infrastructure. ANSI and the Global Environment and Technology Foundation (GETF) have created ISO 14000 Integrated Solutions, an analysis of the "ISO 14000 management scheme." It will accelerate the "environmental paradigm shift" required for corporations to compete in a global market. Chapter 8 examines in more detail the steps taken by this three-sector endeavor to establish civil markets.

7. Caroline Hemenway, ed., *What Is ISO 14000?* (CEEM Information Services, 10521 Braddock Road, Fairfax, Va. 22032-5900), 3. To learn more about ISO 14001, check the following Web site: http://194.177.160.201/standards/iso/14001/mtro/htm.

8. Ibid., 4.

9. This global movement toward the civil-market idea did not appear without precedent. Similar efforts had begun earlier in different countries. In England, the British Standards Institution developed a BS 7750, Environmental Management Systems. In the European Union, the European Commission adopted the Eco-Management and Audit Scheme (EMAS), which established specifications for environmental management systems of companies doing business in the European Union (EU). The United States was also moving in this direction. The American National Standards Institute is the U.S. representative to ISO. The ISO 14000 evolved through separate voluntary actions of governments, business, and NGOs.

10. Some of the dangers are discussed in a study by Benchmark Environmental Consulting (Benchmark Environmental Consulting, working papers *["The Benchmark Rating of TNCs"; "Working Papers on Toxic Chemical Control"; "The Social Benefits of Regulating International Business"; "Transnational Corporations' Strategic Responses to Sustainable Development"; "ISO 14001: An Uncommon Perspective; Exploring Regional Regulation of Transnational Corporations"; "Business Regulation and Competition Policy"]*, 49 Dartmouth St., Portland, Maine 04101).

11. See Agenda 21, chaps. 19.53 (d) and 20.30. Some commitments to sustainable development have come from banks such as the World Bank and the European Bank for Reconstruction and Development. I draw my information here from the European Environment Bureau, *ISO 14001: An Uncommon Perspective* (Benchmark Environmental Consulting, November 1995), 8.

12. Mary Saunders, assistant to the director of the Office of Standards and Services of the U.S. Commerce Department's National Institute of Standards and Technology, sees great value in the ISO effort. She said at a conference in June 1995 that although the ISO standards are written as voluntary consensus standards, some countries would adopt them as law or use them as a basis for contracting.

13. For example, there are the Franklin Research Corporation, CERES, the Sierra Club, Common Cause, the International Chamber of Commerce, UN affili-

ates such as the International Labor Organization and the World Health Organization—all with different mechanisms of influence and enforcement. But there is much more to be done through the organization of global workshops on civil partnerships.

14. First, institutional investors need more reliable data on social performance (environment, safety, health) so they can make better choices about investments. Just as accountants and auditors refined effective financial comparisons between companies, investor stakeholders can now work through groups like CERES to establish standardized indices of safety and sustainability. Companies have found that careful "analysis and transparency" improve management decisions and increase trust among various communities. Second, companies are abandoning the old view that environmental responsibility is in conflict with competitiveness in favor of the new view that a common ground can be set for competition. Third, companies are finding that interactions facilitated by NGOs (like CERES) can be helpful. All the participants, business, government, and NGO leaders, have found that willingness to talk honestly about differences can lead to unexpected consensus and change, making it unnecessary to disrupt the annual meetings of corporations. Today a delegation of executives from GM comes to every meeting of CERES and sits at the same table as some of their former adversaries. In turn, environmentalists are learning to appreciate the complexity of management.

15. The series of conferences cited in chapter 8 was discussed with former UN assistant secretary General Rosario Green, and basic ideas have been supported in conversations with various UN officials. Steps in this direction are important in the context of a UN budget crisis. We talked about the sponsorship of these forums as funded by all three sectors of society: business, NGOs, and governments.

16. Harris Gleckman with Riva Krut, "Transnational Corporations' Strategic Responses to 'Sustainable Development,'" paper for publication in *Green Globe 1995* (Oxford: Oxford University Press, forthcoming).

17. In chapter 6 we noted that as a response to such calls for phasing out chlorine as an industrial feedstock, the Chemical Manufacturers Association formed the Chlorine Chemistry Council (CCC) to defend the industry. The battle is still brewing, but in today's markets, it requires a global workshop to settle (*Rachel's Environment and Health Weekly,* no. 495 [May 23, 1996]).

18. On regional theories of global development and standards, see Michael Storper, *The Regional World* (New York: Guilford, 1997).

Appendix

1. Adam Smith, "The Theory of Moral Sentiments," in *The Essential Adam Smith,* ed. Robert Heilbroner (New York: W. W. Norton, 1986), 76. The reader can find Smith's complete work on the Web, but I refer to this book to encourage reading Heilbroner's interpretations.

2. Smith often used the word *justice* to mean substantially what Aristotle and the classicists meant by "commutative justice." For Smith, justice consisted of learning to refrain from injury to another person and from taking or withholding from another what belongs to that individual. It is distinct from benevolence, charity, or friendship, yet some order of justice was a necessary ingredient to a civil society. For

Smith, the law of justice was "informed Nature," so to speak. We think that there is more to the idea of justice than Smith understood, but in this moment, we are working through his framework. Smith speculates on anarchy, saying that Nature implanted the "seeds of an irregularity in the human breast, intending the happiness and perfection of the species. . . . If malevolence of affection were alone the causes which excited our resentment . . . every court of judicature would become a real inquisition." Smith said that sympathy is the "original passion." Today, others might call it empathy (*Essential Adam Smith*, 58).

3. A concept of moral development has remained in psychology but not in economics, sociology, or political science. One of the founders of psychology, William McDougall, said, "The fundamental problem of social psychology is the moralization of the individual by the society." The judgmental side of moral development for the individual continued in the work of Jean Piaget and Lawrence Kohlberg (William McDougall, *An Introduction to Social Psychology* [1908; reprint, New York: Barnes and Noble, 1960]).

4. German philosophers who were fascinated by this commercial sector in the eighteenth and early nineteenth century read Adam Smith's idea of civil society. In the early nineteenth century, philosopher G. W. F. Hegel argued that selfish energies unleashed by the market created "a system of complete interdependence, wherein the livelihood, happiness, and legal status of one man is interwoven with the livelihood, happiness, and rights of all." Hegel, however, saw a growing selfishness in the commercial system as a problem of moral society. He said that civil society was developing around individual *(particular)* self-interests and could not be reconciled with *universal* morality. This commercial sector was not a moral economy. Hence, he said, the state must be the final moral agency (Knox, *Hegel's Philosophy of Right*, 123). Karl Marx opposed Hegel's view, publishing a critique of bourgeoisie (civil) society in 1845, saying that social forces would replace both capitalism and the state. Once class conflict was resolved in the economy, the state would "wither away"; that is, the social forces of justice would finally overcome class conflict.

5. Philosophers like Karl Marx and Friedrich Engels contended that the ownership and control of the means of production—capital, land, or property— should be held by the whole community and administered in the interests of all. Friedrich Engels (*The Condition of the Working Class in England* [1845]) described the "brutal indifference" and the "unfeeling isolation of each in his private interest" (*Saint Simon, Selected Writings*, ed. Felix Markam [Oxford: Blackwell, 1952]).

6. Smith's original ideas have not disappeared. A debate about the meaning of Smith's morality is current in professional and business ethics. Some ethicists today refer to Smith's perspective in the context of market competition and a sense of justice in the field of medicine. Ethicists debate what an "ideal observer" is in its contemporary usage. Smith's advocates say that the impartial spectator is not a device for achieving distance but rather for achieving intimacy. The spectator is a way of appropriating a social relatedness, of admitting into account the common moral sentiments of a community. Smith never seems to have had in mind an omniscient vantage point, removed from social ties and personal loyalties. In fact, the impartial spectator is part of the move of imaginative sympathy so central to Smith's notion of moral judgment. Adam Smith did not imagine a "total perspective" of things.

7. Emile Durkheim, *Socialism and Saint Simon*, ed. Alvin Gouldner (Yellow Springs, Ohio: Antioch Press, 1958), 21–22.

8. See Kurt Wolff, *The Sociology of Georg Simmel* (Glencoe, Ill.: Free Press, 1950).

9. Simmel saw a task for outside observers to study the way society creates itself through *sociation. Sociation* is a difficult term to translate. But it is, let us say, the conscious association of human beings that results in societal forms, like families, clubs, churches, ethnic identity groups, and enterprises. The common basis for life originated in the assumptions and rules people make in their associations. For Simmel, sociation brings individuals into a double situation. Although people follow group rules, individuals are always in tension within their own group. In broad scope, society does not need an outside observer to find its "objective unity." By its nature, society becomes an objective unity created by its participants. Wolff translated *Vergesellschaftung* from German as "sociation," but it could be translated as "societalization." *Individual* existence is maintained through a process of consciousness that takes societal forms. A "societary connection" is realized directly through individuals who experience life together. From this standpoint, it is possible to observe how individuals work within a civil order of markets. People create civil order with the amount of spontaneity and the freedom allowed by the rules.

Sociability is the simplest (purest) kind of human interaction. Everyone acts as though the others in the group were equal. Yet, sociability is also artificial insofar as it is played within a corporation where members have different ranks or in a society separating rich from poor. Sociability cannot last between people in different occupational ranks. It becomes stressful and painful. Sociability happens only when people are divested of their formal roles and corporate intentions. The sociable play is a fabrication when the action and speech become an instrument of intention, as in a political or religious argument.

Simmel argued that the individual elements in any social organization always remain in their discreteness, yet undergo a unity in this higher synthesis in membership through associations. Simmel asked, "How is society possible?" in parallel with Immanuel Kant's question: How is Nature possible as an object of science?

10. In the field of medicine, we ask: Can "physicians" in the American Medical Association identify with a national association of "chiropractors"? In the field of religion, we ask: Can Protestants identify with Catholics in Northern Ireland? Self-identity is a social struggle to achieve and partly political. "Identity politics" could be seen as an expression of Smith's moral passions. People are in a process of social and political self-development in wider and more complex communities of identity. At every level of organized life, a multiplication of human identities has been actively constructing some partial association. Each association is organized differently, some very oppressive, some very dominating, others more democratic and informal, but this history of associated identities is constant, and it is changing. Today, mutual identities are related to race, gender, and class—for example, femininsts, gays/lesbians, African Americans, and Native Americans. See Patricia Hill Collins, *Black Feminist Thought: Knowledge, Consciousness, and the Politics of Empowerment* (London: HarperCollins, 1990); bell hooks, *Talking Back* (Boston: South End Press, 1989).

11. Many civil-society advocates find their values incompatible with those generated within a capitalist economy. We have argued that the economy is partly self-regulating. A more civil economy is cultivated by people who set public standards and rules that resolve their differences in the context of competition. The culture of

the market economy carries important values, such as *productivity, efficiency, competitiveness, self-interest, freedom, and profitability,* but to be adequately self-regulating, markets require systems that support a civil order of values, such as *social accountability, fairness, public interest, common good, cooperation, democracy, self-discipline, justice, welfare, civic responsibility, and self-development.*

12. In other words, the subject of political science logically includes *the market system itself. Political justice* can refer to the use of a judicial process to gain or limit power and influence. Max Weber postulated that the "political idea" should be applied to studies of power in commercial relations ("Class, Status, Party," in *Max Weber,* ed. and trans. H. Gerth and C. Wright Mills [1921; reprint, New York: Oxford University Press, 1946]). We propose that the notion of self government be applied to the organization of commerce, not just the state. The German jurist Otto von Gierke (1841–1921) saw some danger in the concept of the state as the exclusive source of power and law. He emphasized the similarities between the state and other social groups in an attempt to revive the German Genossenschaftsrecht (*Natural Law and the Theory of Society,* 2 vols., trans. Ernest Barker [1934; reprint, Boston: Beacon Press, 1957]). Gierke saw society constituted in human associations.

13. William Roy defined power as the capacity to shape the alternatives that others choose from (*Socializing Capital: The Rise of the Large Industrial Corporation in America* [Princeton, N.J.: Princeton University Press, 1997]).

14. Labor history is told better elsewhere. Charles Hecksher argues that there are two competing visions for the direction of unionism today: Should unions compete against management at the top (as in Europe) or as more decentralized associations? (*The New Unionism* [New York: Basic Books, 1988]). Some union leaders ask, "What is Right?" Others ask, "What is Left?"

15. Tina Cassidy, "AG Weighs Suit to Keep the Patriots," *Boston Globe,* December 4, 1998, p. A1. This sports market has many political ramifications. Missouri used antitrust claims against the NFL when it refused to allow the Los Angeles Rams to move to the smaller TV market of St. Louis. The team's move to St. Louis would have reduced revenues that are shared with all teams in the league. The state had built a $280 million government-financed Trans World Dome in St. Louis with the hopes of luring the team. The threat of a costly lawsuit, and the treble damages accompanying it, pressured NFL owners to change their vote and approve the move.

16. The system of power in markets changes rapidly, but there is also a civil order that is established that requires study as it goes into global markets. The following case is my summary of this rapid change in November 1998.

Some business leaders in the grocery sector were upset. Great corporations and trade associations were changing the political order of private systems of exchange. This battle for power among corporations in the grocery industry soon intensified. Discount giants like Wal-Mart jumped into a powerful position in the market by becoming big sellers of groceries as well as garden hoses. Then regional supermarket chains like the Kroger Company went into a frenzy of consolidation, merging to create national chains, seeking to compete directly with the big discount giants. As many corporations battled in their own self-interest, everyone became involved: associated manufacturers, wholesalers, distributors, and independent grocers. Many people risked being trampled upon, losing their businesses, and perhaps going bankrupt. In the same month, corporations took the struggle for power still higher in the global marketplace. The global corporation J. Sainsbury PLC of London, which owns Shaw's Supermarkets, Inc., in the United States, decided to buy Star Market Companies to provide more power for Shaw's, the second largest food operator behind Stop and Shop in New England. Stop and Shop was competing for power against Shaw's and needed protection on the global scene. Stop and Shop, of course, is located in the United States, but the stores are owned by Royal Ahold NV in the Netherlands, while Sainsbury is headquartered in Great Britain. James McCoy, president of the John Groub Company, ran a 30-store grocery chain in southern Indiana that was sold to Kroger. Then Wal-Mart's supercenters, selling food and general merchandise under one roof, moved in.

The story is elaborated in Dana Canedy, "Supersizing the Supermarkets," *New York Times,* November 13, 1998, p. C1.

Civil action in such cases means settling political differences in competing markets outside the government. It means finding the connection between market freedom and civil order, between public and private ways of life, all these things in the context of a capitalist market. Adam Smith in his day spoke of "self preservation" for the "species," meaning humanity, while today he might say that civil action occurs when people create social structures for the common good.

17. Mike Davis, *City of Quartz: Excavating the Future of Los Angeles* (New York: Vintage Books, 1990). Davis, a former meatcutter and truck driver, describes how great intellectuals (e.g., elite radicals like Theodore Adorno, Max Horkheimer, and Herbert Marcuse) became spectators of these destructive forces, that is, how they studied the artifice, superficiality, craziness, and malaise in this capitalist masquerade but were also part of it. Corporate forces were shaping the culture as intellectuals wrote about the maddening progression of capitalism. In the capitalist history of Los Angeles, Davis tells us how the finest artists were selling their wares in this monied scene. "[Igor] Stravinsky's big break was rearranging the "Rite of Spring" as a sound track for dancing brooms in Disney's *Fantasia*, while Schoenberg, otherwise invisible, tutored studio composers who made musical suspense for *noir* thrillers and monster movies." Davis saw Los Angeles grow into a lifeless city without public notice.

I was curious about Davis's reference to Igor Stravinsky in this book, so I rented the film *Fantasia* to see it again. Davis is not correct. The "Rite of Spring" is playing behind the cartoon imagery of "evolution"; it was not the music for dancing brooms in the "Sorcerer's Apprentice," which was composed by Paul Dukas. Dukas based his music on a story that goes back to ancient Egypt, a legend retold in Greek by a Syrian satirist who wrote a set of dialogues making a devastating attack on his contemporary philosophers, the Platonists, Pythagoreans, and Stoics. Looking at the film again, I could see satire upon satire, everything symbolized in ways not told by Davis. For those who see the film, look for the penises that hide within cathedrals, the innocent fish looking through webs, the depths of reality revealed, layer by layer, the foregrounds and backgrounds. The film should be seen by deconstructionists. Mickey Mouse chops the broom into a thousand pieces and then is overwhelmed by the flooding waters. I would argue that we have not yet understood the volcanic fires within the rites of society and ourselves. The economy is rooted in its own politics, yet not fully defined as a political idea.

18. In the twentieth century, it was important for the Mormon Church to own a newspaper, 11 television and two radio stations, a department store chain, an insurance company, and a controlling interest in the Utah-Idaho Sugar Company. It helped the church sustain its religious order. It was important for the Trinity Church to own 18 major business buildings in New York City, including the 17-story Standard and Poor's Building. That was part of its survival as a religious organization. It was reasonable for St. Paul's Episcopal Church to operate a 200-car commercial parking garage in Richmond, Virginia; it was understandable for the Southern Baptist Convention to own property in Firestone, Mack Truck, and the Borden Company. It was part of their sustainability. It was acceptable for the Jesuits to own stock in the steel industry, legitimate for the Baptist Church to own Yankee Stadium, and so on. This is not alarming for the twentieth century. We have spoken favorably of civil investment in the marketplace, but in the twenty-first century, the picture may change.

19. Pierre Bourdieu, *Outline of a Theory and Practice,* trans. Richard Niee (Cambridge: Cambridge University Press, 1977); *Language and Symbolic Power,* ed. John B. Thompson (Cambridge: Harvard University Press, 1991); (Craig Calhoun, Edward LiPuma, and Moishe Postone, eds., *Bourdieu: Critical Perspectives* (Chicago: University of Chicago Press, 1993).

20. Edward Tylor (1871) used the word *culture* to define the subject of anthropology. Culture referred to "that complex whole, which includes knowledge, belief, art, morals, law, custom, and any other capabilities and habits acquired by man as a member of society." Since Tylor, anthropologists have seen culture as also representing the material artifacts of human life and production. Many anthropologists write about the culture of a "society," not of societies in general. The relative word *culture* is often more utilized than the generalized *culture.* This different usage leads to questions of unity vs. plurality, an issue in cultural studies. If we see culture in a plural sense and keep our minds also on its more general sense, as compared with a civilization, we see a capitalist society with an overarching myth. The myth carries its premises as truth, yet, in the time of history, some part of culture continues beyond any single society. Indeed, some scholars see culture related to the primeval energies in humankind (Edward Tylor, *Primitive Culture,* 2 vols. [1871; reprint, New York: Harper, 1958]).

21. For Adam Smith, a deity authored nature and set all energy into motion. Nature, he said, carries an invisible hand, we might say metaphorically, playing a silent music through the universe. Smith might think about the universe as an opera or a symphony. A hidden orchestra plays an overture. The music moves quietly through the beginning of the big bang, sounding great disharmonies and harmonies, magnificent chords pulsating through the cosmos, creating stars in the universe. The symphony, if one could hear it, continues in the fires forming the earth. The music builds its majesty in the terrible struggle for survival on earth, finally reaching its climax in the construction of civilization. Yet, Smith might say, the silent sound remains; the great symphony is unfinished. At some point in Smith's mystery, civilization should go beyond itself into higher conditions of humanity. This is an imaginary scene, although important to remember.

On the other hand, for Karl Marx, an invisible hand is pure idealism. Evolution began with the material world of primitive life; then came the empire builders, next the feudal estates, and finally the capitalists. Marx concluded that any transformation that is "real" in the future should happen through social relations and within a material world, not a world of ideas.

22. Adam Smith, *Lectures on Jurisprudence* (Oxford: Clarendon Press, 1978), 208. Smith goes on:

> Power and riches appear then to be, what they are, enormous and operose machines contrived to produce a few trifling conveniences to the body, consisting of things the most nice and delicate, which must be kept in order with the most anxious attention, and which in spite of all our care are ready every moment to burst into pieces, and to crush in their ruins their unfortunate possessor. They are immense fabrics, which it requires the labour of a life to raise, which threaten every moment to overwhelm the person that dwells in them, and which while they stand, though they may save him from some smaller inconveniences, can protect him from none of the severer inclemencies of the season. They keep off the summer shower, not the winter storm, but lead him always as much, and sometimes more exposed than before, to anxiety, to fear, and to sorrow; to diseases, to danger, and to death ("The Theory of Moral Sentiments," in *Essential Adam Smith,* 121).

23. David McLellan, *Karl Marx: Selected Writings* (Oxford: Oxford University Press, 1978), 57. The brackets substitute for the word *man,* and the italics in the quotations are mine.

Index

DATE DUE MAR 0 6 2004

NOV 2 3 2004

HIGHSMITH #45230

Printed
in USA